The Complete Idiot's Reference Card

The Three Jewels

1. Buddha (The Awakened One)
2. Dharma (Buddha's teachings and what they pertain to)
3. Sangha (community of practice)

The Four Noble Truths

1. Life entails dissatisfaction (*duhkha*).
2. Dissatisfaction is a result of clinging, craving (*trishna*).
3. There's an end to all dissatisfaction (*nirvana*).
4. The way to the end of dissatisfaction is the path (*maggha*).

The Path

Wisdom	Morality	Meditation
1. Right view	3. Right speech	6. Right effort
2. Right thought	4. Right action	7. Right mindfulness
	5. Right livelihood	8. Right concentration

The Cardinal Precepts

1. Not killing	3. Not lying	5. No sexual abuse
2. Not stealing	4. No intoxicants	

ALPHA

tear here

The Three Marks of Existence (The Three Dharma Seals)

1. Impermanence   2. No abiding, separate self   3. Duhkha/nirvana

The Three Poisons

1. Greed   2. Hate   3. Delusion

The Four Brahmaviharas (Sublime States)

	Near Enemy	Far Enemy
Lovingkindness (*metta*)	Selfishness	Hatred
Compassion (*karuna*)	Pity	Contempt
Sympathetic joy (*mudita*)	Boredom	Jealousy
Equanimity (*upekkha*)	Indifference	Aversion

The Four Bodhisattva Vows

Beings are numberless; I vow to awaken them.

Delusions are inexhaustible; I vow to end them.

Dharma gates are boundless; I vow to enter them.

Buddha's way is unsurpassable; I vow to become it.

The Present Moment Is a Wonderful Moment

Smile.   Breathe.

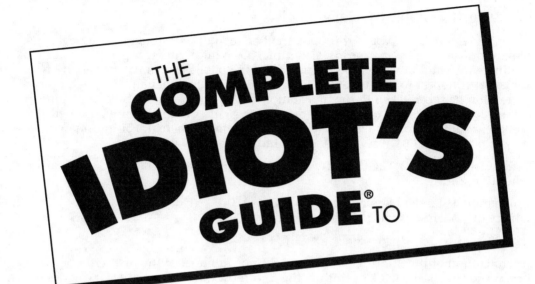

THE COMPLETE IDIOT'S GUIDE® TO

Understanding Buddhism

by Gary Gach

ALPHA

A Pearson Education Company

THE COMPLETE IDIOT'S GUIDE TO and Design are registered trademarks of Pearson Education, Inc.

International Standard Book Number: 0-02-864170-1
Library of Congress Catalog Card Number: 2001092311

04   03   02   8   7   6   5   4   3   2   1

Interpretation of the printing code: The rightmost number of the first series of numbers is the year of the book's printing; the rightmost number of the second series of numbers is the number of the book's printing. For example, a printing code of 02-1 shows that the first printing occurred in 2002.

Printed in the United States of America

Publisher
Marie Butler-Knight

Product Manager
Phil Kitchel

Managing Editor
Jennifer Chisholm

Acquisitions Editor
Randy Ladenheim-Gil

Development Editor
Michael Thomas

Senior Production Editor
Christy Wagner

Copy Editor
Michael Dietsch

Illustrator
Brian Moyer

Cover Designers
Mike Freeland
Kevin Spear

Book Designers
Scott Cook and Amy Adams of DesignLab

Indexer
Tonya Heard

Layout/Proofreading
Angela Calvert
John Etchison
Elizabeth Louden
Kimberly Tucker

Contents at a Glance

Contents

Appendix

Foreword

The complex and varied cultural and textural manifestations of Buddhism are bewildering to many modern Western readers. A living religion that has spanned half the globe over 2,500 years is not easy to encapsulate. You may feel like a complete idiot when confronted by the variety of forms and teachings of one of the world's great religions. All of the different strands of Buddhism are simultaneously being introduced to the West at this very moment. A trivial example is the color of Buddhist robes. In Southeast Asia, Saffron robes are worn; in the Tibetan traditions, red; Korean Buddhists wear gray; those from the Japanese tradition wear black.

The need for a guide through this vibrant thicket is clear. Gary Gach has taken up this difficult challenge in *The Complete Idiot's Guide to Understanding Buddhism*. Pointing out the similarities and differences in the complex weave of teachings of the cultures and practices called Buddhism, he puts them into a comprehensive context. It may be a guide for the complete idiot in that it assumes little, yet it avoids the traps of oversimplifying and dumbing down of the subject. The book explores and presents simply and creatively the practical and theoretical, the mundane and the sacred, of Buddhism.

I suggest that you keep in mind the following words of Eihei Dogan, the twelfth-century founder of Soto Zen in Japan, from his famous essay, *Genjo Koan,* when trying to come to grips with Buddhism:

> To study Buddhism is to study the self
> To study the self is to forget the self
> To forget the self is to be awakened by all things
> And this awakening continues endlessly

You can study Buddhism as an external object, but it is also an internal exploration. "To study Buddhism is to study the self." Not the study of old and antiquated artifacts, but of something alive and kicking. "To study the self is to forget the self." When you study the self, Buddhism as a separate object disappears. When you study and focus on yourself as a discrete object, the self loses its boundary. "To forget the self is to be awakened by all things." To let go of your habits and preconceptions is to experience things as they are, not as you have grown to expect them to be. "This awakening continues endlessly." By letting go of your conditioning, awakening is present in each moment. Thus, wisdom and compassion naturally arise.

I would like to close with an old Zen caution: "Don't mistake the finger for the moon." Buddhism, Zen, Christianity, Islam, Taoism, Judaism, Confucianism, and so on, are all useful fingers. Teachings that point the way to fully actualizing ourselves and benefiting others are pointers, but not the end itself. All religious teachings are about what is, but if we focus on the teachings as objects we miss the point. Enjoy this book, and allow your natural light to inform your reading.

Michael Wenger

Michael Wenger has practiced at the San Francisco Zen Center since 1972 where he is currently Dean of Buddhist Studies. A Soto Zen lineage holder, he is the author of *33 Fingers: A Collection of Modern American Koans* and editor, with Mel Weitsman, of *Branching Streams Flow in the Darkness.*

Introduction

It is a great honor, indeed, to present the message and practice of Buddhism to you. And it's a particular honor to do so in the format of the *Complete Idiot's Guides*. A few people may scoff that this is sacrilegious, or something. I don't know. I can think of no better reply than the words of British writer G. K. Chesterton, when he said, "Angels can fly because they take themselves lightly." Not that my feet are an inch off the ground, mind you.

Presenting the story and teachings of the Buddha in new ways, I only hope you find them no less stimulating and rewarding ... and sacred ... as they have continued to be for me, and hundreds of millions of others. But, please, don't expect to become enlightened by reading this book in one sitting. Instead, enjoy the journey, step by step, and I think you might find yourself thinking about things in ways you might not have before.

I think you'll find the merits of Buddhism penetrate beyond the intellect. People who practice Buddhism notice less stress in their lives, for one thing. Sharper concentration and focus is also a common feature of the path. Dealing with each encounter more fully is another by-product.

Buddhism also tends to allow people to accept and not cling, and so experience their life with greater calm and insight. Kindness is another common factor, kindness to others, but also to one's self. You might find twisted, negative emotional patterns resolving and clearing up. You might notice other people give you better vibes than before. If they remark that you have a halo, or a brighter aura, well, I don't know.

See for yourself.

How to Use This Book

If you were to learn only four essential things about Buddhism, they'd be ...

1. Buddha, the fully awakened.
2. Dharma, the teachings of the Buddha.
3. Sangha, the practitioners of the teachings.
4. The importance of putting Buddhism into practice.

The first three elements—called the Three Jewels—are the real nitty-gritty of Buddhism. So, along with the fourth idea, I've made them the blueprint for this book. Part 1, "The Buddha, Showing You the Way," looks at *the Buddha* and the spread of his teachings. Part 2, "Awakening: Basic Teachings," explores the essence of his teachings (*the Dharma*). Part 3, "Seeing Clearly and Deeply: Meditation and Its Paths," introduces the practice of Buddhism and surveys primary communities of practice (*the Sangha*). Part 4, "The Pedal Hits the Metal: Buddhism Applied to the World at Large," shows the importance of putting Buddhism into practice in further perspective.

Buddhism is amazing. It's composed of utterly simple pieces, like that. Put them together, they're a whole greater than the sum of their parts: equal to life itself. (And, in this case, equal to this book.)

In **Part 1, "The Buddha, Showing You the Way,"** we start out with a biographical short story: the life of the Buddha. Then I sketch the fascinating history of how the Buddha's teachings have spread and adapted to different lands. To sharpen the point on that, we'll zero in next on Buddhism in America. This may be the most interesting phase of Buddhism's history yet. (Since we're living inside of it, like a fish swimming through water, I indulge in some speculation as to directions this process seems headed.) To sum up, we'll compare and contrast Buddhism with major religions. It's compatible with them all, actually, including atheism. Next, having laid the scene, who Buddha was, and so on, we'll explore what he taught.

In **Part 2, "Awakening: Basic Teachings,"** you'll find the essence of what the Buddha taught in plain everyday language. (This might be a good time to tear out the stiff, perforated page at the front of the book, for a shorthand summary, if not a book-mark.) Here's the core essentials, beginning with the Three Jewels: Buddha, Dharma, Sangha. Next follows the Buddha's philosophy, the Four Noble Truths, four holy facts of life succinctly delineating the Buddha's unique approach. The last truth opens up a path, called the Eightfold Path, which we'll tour step by step.

Please don't skip the chapter on conscious conduct, even if its contents, the Precepts, might sound familiar at first glance. They're vital. As a capper, we'll delve into the concepts that really make Buddhism different from other ways of thinking and living. Along the way, I'll offer some simple exercises you can try for yourself. That paves the way for the next part, about putting all this into practice.

In **Part 3, "Seeing Clearly and Deeply: Meditation and Its Paths,"** I'll introduce you to the ABCs of Buddhist meditation. Plus, I'll spotlight each of the major schools of practice, which is another unique feature of this book. While I don't want to make Buddhism seem like a supermarket ("Attention, shoppers! Zen bread tasting in Aisle 4!"), one of the unprecedented aspects of Western Buddhism, particularly American, is the variety of schools coexisting side-by-side. And, as it transplants to Western culture, it's sending out roots that make several generations of teachers available, far and wide. This is a marvelous time.

So, after two chapters devoted to setting up a basic practice, we'll survey four major schools. There are other schools besides the four—Vipassana (Insight), Zen, Pure Land, and Vajrayana (Tibetan)—but these four are kind of like the basic food groups. And, as in a balanced meal, there's healthy interchange between them. From there, you might consider the book's concluding part a kind of buffet, with a wide selection of ways in which Buddhism can be tasted in the world at large.

In **Part 4, "The Pedal Hits the Metal: Buddhism Applied to the World at Large,"** we'll survey real-world interchanges with Buddhism, starting with our primary relations—from cradle to grave. Then, I've piggybacked Buddhist views on eating with its views on working, both earthy, everyday, essential facts of life. The next two chapters explore Buddhism and the arts, popular and fine, including movies, sports, music, your own writing, and life art. The chapter on science and Buddhism starts with revolutionary contemporary physics, and gradually develops into a look at psychology. These realms hold exciting possibilities for a renewed importance of Buddhism. Our next-to-last chapter spotlights crucial modern issues which Buddhism's addressing. And the final chapter features a kind of Buddhist travel section.

A Buddhist Bulletin Board

Part of the value and fun of any *Complete Idiot's Guide* are the boxed commentaries in the margin, called sidebars. (Until I wrote this book, I always thought they were called "little doohickeys.") For your reading pleasure, I'll incorporate four little doohickeys:

This Is

This sidebar highlights and defines key words and phrases. The picture illustrates a concept that's central to Buddhism, and the spiritual path in general: Don't mistake the finger pointing to the moon for the moon itself. Or, as semanticist W. I. Korczybyski put it, "The map is not the territory." Meaning: A word can leave you at the gates but can't take you through; it's up to you to make it real.

Hear and Now

This sidebar is for listening to notable folks who illuminate some gist or pith. A classic image of a Buddhist listener is the revered Buddhist of Tibet, Milarepa (1025–1135), usually depicted with his right hand behind his ear, listening to the planets twirling and the stars twinkling. (Hear them?)

Along the Path

This sidebar is reserved for various and sundry sayings and thoughts commenting on the text, like violets doodled in the margin. The picture isn't of any literal road, but suggests the forks and bends that life's path often takes, along which it's often nice to have road markers, such as "Elves Up Ahead: Pay Troll."

Leaves from the Bodhi Tree

A tree sheltered the Buddha during the meditation that led to his supreme enlightenment, and its descendant still grows today. This sidebar is for leaves from that tree, anecdotes illuminating aspects of the living organism that is Buddhism. Like, did you hear the one about the priest, the rabbi, and the guru ...?

Acknowledgements

I am humbly grateful to the following people who made my efforts come across as intended and sometimes even better than that: Randy Ladenheim-Gil, Michael Thomas, and Christy Wagner, the most superb editors one could ever dream of having; Brandon Hopkins; my agent, Jack Scovil, a most enlightened and enlightening gentleman; and all the artists and photographers, and our cartoonist Brian Moyers. Special thanks to Chungliang Al Huang for playing with Eastern and Western imagery in the 1980s in a book called *Quantum Soup,* and knowing I cannot help but light my candle from yours: I kertow. Gassho to Margery Cantor; Phil Catalfo, *Yoga Journal;* Judy Chen, San Francisco Public Library; Roberta Chin, Pine Tree; Russell Gonzaga; Wendy Johnson; Kimmer; Maxine Hong Kingston; Arnold Kotler and Therese Fitzgerald, Dharma Friends; Leza Lowitz; Travis Masch, Parallax Press; Susan Moon, Buddhist Peace Fellowship; National Japanese American Historical Society; Wes Nisker; Lena Nozizwe; Skip Press; Miriam Solon; Daishin Sunseri, Hartford Street Zen Center, and Stephen Toole. Also Wes Nisker, for his review of the chapter on vipassana; Reverend Don Castro, Buddhist Churches of America; Rev. Noriaki Fujimori; and Rev. Patti Nakai, Buddhist Temple of Chicago, for their comments on my section on Pure Land; Prof. Janis Willis and Peter Wood for their expertise on Vajrayana; and Prof. Lewis R. Lancaster and Michael Wenger, for their review of the manuscript as a whole. Any residual errors are my own. And, last but not least, my parents, family, sangha, and friends; and particularly Patricia and Ralph Hendricks for their true kindness, over many years now.

"Dream Deferred" by Langston Hughes, from *The Collected Poems of Langston Hughes,* copyright © 1994 by The Estate of Langston Hughes. Used by permission of Alfred A. Knopf, a division of Random House, Inc.

"The Red Wheelbarrow" by William Carlos Williams, from *Collected Poems* 1909–1939, Volume 1, copyright © 1938 by New Directions Publishing Corp. Reprinted by permission of New Directions Publishing Corp.

Best efforts have been made to locate all rights holders and clear necessary reprint permissions. If any acknowledgments have been omitted, or any rights overlooked, it is unintentional and forgiveness is requested. Any oversights will be rectified for future editions upon proper notice.

Special Thanks to the Technical Editor

The Complete Idiot's Guide to Understanding Buddhism was reviewed by an expert who not only checked the accuracy of what you'll learn in this book but also provided valuable insight to help ensure that it tells you everything you need to know about Buddhism. Our special thanks are extended to Professor Lewis R. Lancaster.

Prof. Lancaster was born in Virginia, and earned his B.A. from Roanake College, his M.Th. from USC-ST, and his Ph.D. from the University of Wisconsin. Since 1967, he has been affiliated with the University of California, Berkeley, in a number of key positions, notably as cofounder of its Buddhist Studies program, as well as serving on committees for numerous programs and departments, including the Program in

Religious Studies, the Center for Chinese Studies, the Center for Korean Studies, and the Department of East Asian Languages. He also serves on the adjunct faculty of the Graduate Theological Union and the Institute of Buddhist Studies (both also in Berkeley), and Hsi Lai University (Los Angeles). Advisor and consultant to a number of nonprofits, he's a renowned speaker at national and international panels, workshops, conferences, and symposia.

Editor of nine scholarly Buddhist books and of the Berkeley Buddhist Studies Series, his essays have been published in dozens of anthologies and journals. Most recently, he's been a pioneering contributor to the electronic publication of six CD-ROM collections of such definitive texts as 45 volumes of the Pali Canon, 11,000 pages of Sanskrit texts, 70 Chinese Zen texts with bibliography, 8,000 pages of archival materials on Korean Buddhist history, and an interactive database on Korean Buddhist thought. In addition to his research, lecturing, and writings, he currently devotes a considerable amount of his time to the Electronic Cultural Atlas Initiative (www.ias.berkeley.edu/ecai), an unprecedented international collaboration that will open new dimensions of scholarly research. That he's taken time from such endeavors to focus such considerable expertise and care to this book is an immeasurably great honor and aid.

Trademarks

All terms mentioned in this book that are known to be or are suspected of being trademarks or service marks have been appropriately capitalized. Alpha Books and Pearson Education, Inc. cannot attest to the accuracy of this information. Use of a term in this book should not be regarded as affecting the validity of any trademark or service mark.

Part 1

The Buddha, Showing You the Way

Let's start our tour by asking "Who?" Such is the beginning of various primary questions, as "Who wants to be a millionaire?" "Who's in charge here?" and "Who am I, really?" (And "So who wants to know?")

In this case, "who" is the Buddha. The Buddha made this occasion possible in the first place. So we start with him. The Original Teacher. The one who shows us the way in this world. I'm talking about the historical person, who embodied his teachings … and this is equally about the buddha within you. And within everyone.

No matter what your religion, your country, or your car, the Buddha has something to show you. So without further ado, I'd like to introduce the Supreme Physician … everyone's good old buddy … … … the Buddha …

Chapter 1

Why Is This Man Smiling?: The Buddha

In This Chapter

➤ Loving, if not falling in love with, the Buddha

➤ The life of the Buddha

➤ The Four Signs

➤ The Great Renunciation

➤ The Middle Way

➤ Supreme Enlightenment

➤ Then what?

We humans are curious. We're curious about ourselves and we're curious about other humans. Hence the existence of books and diaries, biographies and memoirs. Our own life is, of course, the world's greatest story, for sure; it's the one where we're most curious to find out what happens next. ("Tune in again tomorrow!") We're also inspired by others. Helen Keller, Babe Ruth, Spinoza, César Chávez, _____ (fill in the blank). Everybody has their favorites.

Some of these fellow human beans we designate as role models. We even set aside national holidays so we can contemplate their accomplishments. True, some teachings are independent of the life stories of its teachers, such as Taoism (see Chapter 2, "One Taste, Different Flavors: The Teachings Adapt to Different Lands." In other traditions, such as Christianity, Judaism, and Islam, the very lives of the teachers are, themselves, a teaching, as inseparable as an ember from a coal. This is certainly true of the man we're about to meet. Obviously, I think it's a story everyone should know. If you've never heard it before, just think: the life of the Buddha is known to one third of humanity. Join the club.

Are You Ready?: Waking Up to Yourself, Waking Up to Buddha

Once there was a man who discovered a realistic, commonsensical, priceless guide to happiness. *The Complete Idiot's Guide to Happiness,* if you will. The answer, he found, was available to every human being. Right in front of their face. But, as he would also discover, something so simple may not be for everyone. Why not? Well, for one thing, the Buddha only said he discovered something that worked for him, and invited others to try it and see for themselves. He was a guide but not a god, and some people prefer to wait for God or priests to tell them what they can find out for themselves or intuitively know already. (Might this be you?)

Moreover, some people prefer to imagine their happiness will last forever. (Could *this* be you?) Others have a hard time letting go of the accumulation of wounds and labels that have stuck to them throughout life, rather than appreciating the blue sky, solid earth, and tender green plants, always present for enjoyment. (Is *this* you?) And others tenaciously cling to sorrows, as if for ballast, rather than let go and sense the innate, ineffable lightness of the spirit. If you can see yourself in this portrait gallery (and who can't?), then join the club. It's sometimes called The Human Condition. Right there, in a nutshell, you have it. We spin around in our rat cage when all along the cage door is unlocked.

As long as there are people living their life as if sleepwalking through some kind of depressing bad dream, there'll always be someone or something called an awakener. That's what *Buddha* means, in essence. Thus it might be said that an alarm clock is a buddha, if it wakes you up spiritually, psychically, and physically. Really awakens. Or it could be the sound of a bird. Or the look of amazement on a baby's face. Stop, right now, be attentive, listen and look: a buddha voice or buddha sight will probably appear. Now, if all such things can be buddha, then we need to talk about the original Buddha.

The Buddha once said, "If you want to really see me, then look at my teachings." The reverse is equally true. That is, the life of the Buddha is itself a teaching, or series of teachings. Here one person utterly alone makes a difference. Alone meaning without divine

Hear and Now

"Don't believe a teaching just because you heard it from a man who's supposed to be holy, or because it's contained in a book supposed to be holy, or because all your friends and neighbors believe it. But whatever you've observed and analyzed yourself and found to be reasonable and good, then accept that and put it into practice."

—The Buddha

intervention or revelation. Utterly meaning that since he could do it, we can, too. After all, he did it all on his own, and we have him as a landmark, a trailblazer, our guide.

This Is

Buddha, derived from the Sanskrit root *budh*, to awaken, is a title, not a name; like King, or Christ. As such, it means Awakened One, Supremely Awakened. (There are degrees of awakening, culminating in supreme enlightenment.) The common Buddhist word for the daily round of sleep in which we seem bound is ***samsara,*** meaning faring on, a perpetual stream, a global flow of endless becoming—with the connotation of illusion, going around and around like a wheel.

The Buddha teaches that becoming intimate with life, becoming awake, is to awaken to ourselves, to our fullest potential as human beings, to the buddha within all of us. It's as important as life and death, and as easy as drinking a cup of tea.

Please note that, over the millennia, hard facts of biography have mingled with legend and even mythology to form one of the most multi-layered biographies of all time. Yet throughout it all, there remains the Buddha's ineffable smile, beyond words. You'll see. It starts like this …

The Birth of a Quest

One full-moon night in May, around 560 B.C.E., a woman on a journey gave birth. Her name was Mahamaya, and she'd been headed from her home to her father's house, about 50 miles away, to lay in waiting, as was the custom in India in those days. So she returned home to the foothills of the Himalayas, on the border between what's now India and Nepal, to present her husband his son. This would be no ordinary son. Mahamaya was a queen, married to King Suddhodana, the ruler of the Shakya people. Her son would be prince of their small but prosperous kingdom. They named him Siddhartha, meaning "a wish fulfilled" or "aim accomplishment."

According to the hereditary caste system of India at the time, the only class higher than Siddhartha's noble family were the Brahmins, the priests. So the king was quite concerned when a very wise Brahmin soothsayer predicted that Siddhartha would rule over all the land, but only if he were kept from the reality of decay and death. Otherwise, he'd be a great spiritual teacher. Either way, he was destined for greatness.

Along the Path

Sometimes it seems like this one guy had more names than a con artist has on a rap sheet. Here's the lowdown. Gautama (*go-tah-mah*) was his family clan name, and Siddhartha was his personal name. He's also sometimes called Shakyamuni, meaning the recluse or sage of the Shakya tribe.

The Life of a Prince

The king adored his son and wanted him to rule over his kingdom and so kept him cloistered within the strong, high palace walls—not unlike the way we cloister ourselves in our set ways and go about our lives unquestioningly. Moreover, some say the father went so far as to create an environment as artificial as a Hollywood soundstage, wherein sick people, the elderly, even dirt and withered leaves were all whisked from view. But, as the story reveals, the truth is always out there, where the persevering seeker will find it.

Anyway, the king brought the finest tutors to educate his son. The prince was a prodigy and excelled; he soon knew more than his teachers. Intellectually, he was unequalled in literature and math. Athletically, he surpassed everyone in swimming and running, archery and fencing. One legend has it that it was in a huge athletic competition that he won the hand of one of the most beautiful of maidens, Yashodhara (Keeper of Radiance), who became his bride.

Not only a whiz kid and a champ, he proved a compassionate and loving husband. The mark of success was upon him. Naturally, his father was delighted. He gave Siddhartha and his bride three different palaces, one for each of India's three seasons, hot, cool, and wet. There, the prince was lavished with beautiful attendants, endless fun and games, fabulous feasts, live concerts at the snap of his fingers, the whole bit. But Siddhartha started to champ at that bit.

Reality Bites: The Four Signs

Siddhartha wanted to know about the world outside the palace walls, the real world. So does anyone who wants to lead an authentic life. The king had to keep his son happy and granted his wish, yet made sure everything outside was as controlled as it had been inside.

Everywhere Siddhartha went, he saw prosperity and happiness until, somehow, a decrepit form passed through all the young, healthy people the king had arranged for him to see. Siddhartha asked his servant Channa, "What is this!?" The faithful servant told him that although he had white hair down to his knees, this was a man, an old man, using a staff to walk, and this is what happens to everyone eventually. All the way back to the castle, Siddhartha brooded, and when the king heard about this, he increased the budget for Siddhartha's pleasures until his son seemed again like the prince he wanted him to be.

A second time, however, on another trip to the country, Siddhartha chanced upon a maimed person with bloodshot eyes, groaning through a frothy mouth. "What is this!?" Siddhartha asked, and was told by his faithful servant that this was a person who'd become ill, but that Siddhartha needn't worry since the prince ate a good diet and exercised. Siddhartha returned home brooding, and so the king surrounded him with even more opulent pleasures.

A third time, reality broke through yet again. On another outing, Siddhartha chanced upon a funeral procession, mourners sobbing and waving their arms in all directions, while at the head of the procession a body was being carried, utterly still, as if sleeping. Siddhartha asked and faithful servant Channa explained what death is—that nothing could be done for it, and that it happens to everyone. No point in worrying, he said, just hope for a long life.

What a shock! Old age and sickness were bad enough. But now this, their final resolution! The ultimate, inevitable destination of us all. Is there anyone for whom the first encounter with death isn't one of the most unforgettable, difficult moments of their life?

Along the Path

Would that everyone with whom we come into contact in our lives would be as honest as Siddhartha's faithful servant! And would that we could always recognize and listen to our own faithful, internal, truth-telling servant. (The Four Signs are out there, in our own world, for us to see.)

Each of these encounters were but glimpses, but perhaps their having been withheld for so long made them even more of a revelation. In any event, Siddhartha saw they were a matter of his own life and death, and, by extension, of everyone he loved— and indeed, all mortals. Was there no way out!? Meanwhile, when the king saw his beloved prince brooding more darkly than ever before, and found out why, he despaired. He didn't want to lose his only beloved son and heir. But did he level with him? No, he pampered him all the more. Yet life as it really is broke through the walls again, a fourth and final time.

Journeying outside the palace walls, Siddhartha happened to see a man with shaven head, clad only in an orange sheet the color of liquid sunshine, walking slowly, holding only an empty bowl, his entire manner radiating majestic tranquility and serene joy. "What is this?" Siddhartha asked and was told that this was a monk, who'd renounced the world in search of spiritual truth. This silent monk seemed to be telling him, yes, there is an answer to the questions burning inside him since he'd encountered old age, illness, and death. An answer he'd never find as long as he glutted himself with physical pleasures, numbing his spirit. Well, when all this got back to the king, he was beside himself.

Just then, as fate would have it, Siddhartha's bride bore a child. Siddhartha probably was torn, as we can see from the name he gave his son, Rahula, which means "chain." The king took the occasion to stage a blowout celebration to keep Siddhartha close to hearth and home. But after the sumptuous feast, as Siddhartha was being entertained by the finest dancing girls in all the land, he yawned, laid down on his cushion, and closed his eyes. No point entertaining someone who isn't paying attention, so the dancing girls stopped, laid down, too, and napped. When Siddhartha opened his eyes again, he saw these women who just moments ago had been the quintessence of beauty, now sprawled in awkward positions, once lovely faces now drooling or gnashing their teeth in their sleep. So much for the pleasures of the material world! And what a cue for an exit!

Stealthily, he got up and tiptoed out. Passing by his wife's chambers, he took one last lingering look at his sleeping beloved ones, and then was gone—gone in search of an answer to the human riddles of disease, decay, and death, in search of the ultimate meaning of life.

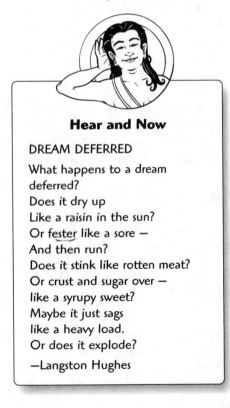

Hear and Now

DREAM DEFERRED

What happens to a dream
deferred?
Does it dry up
Like a raisin in the sun?
Or fester like a sore —
And then run?
Does it stink like rotten meat?
Or crust and sugar over —
like a syrupy sweet?
Maybe it just sags
like a heavy load.
Or does it explode?

—Langston Hughes

Setting Forth

Time out. Before we follow Siddhartha on his quest, we might pause for a moment to consider his break with his past, his renunciation. For one thing, it was extreme: a prince renouncing the wealth and power that was his birthright. In today's terms, he could have been a trillionaire. Actually, though, it was respectable for noblemen of India to go off in search of truth, but only in their retirement, *after* they'd fulfilled their family and social obligations. For Siddhartha, however, the truth couldn't wait.

Plus, Siddhartha would be walking away from his responsibilities as a father as well as a prince. Siddhartha was aware of the pain he'd cause others by leaving, but suffering seemed the ever-present essence of this ultimate riddle he intended to resolve, once and for all. Once he'd found the answer, Siddhartha intended to return, bringing it back home to his people and all the land.

We must acknowledge the courage of Siddhartha, the fearlessness necessary to stand up for his dream, his ideals, his quest, to seek sovereignty over his own life rather than over a kingdom. It's also interesting to notice that Siddhartha was casting aside inherited ideas, as well as inherited privilege. A message here, I think, for all of us is to look at life with our own two eyes, regardless of what Simon says, without asking "Mother, may I?"—seeing for ourselves, beyond the high, strong palace walls.

Into the Forest: Finding Out

So, Siddhartha gave his royal robes and jewelry to his faithful servant, shaved his head with his sword, leaving only a top-knot, and set out for the forests.

Now, in those days, India's wild forests and mountains were dotted with various seekers after truth. Siddhartha studied under one renowned forest teacher, then another. In relatively no time, Siddhartha learned all that his teachers knew and was offered a job carrying on their work, but that wasn't what he was looking for. True, he'd learned to transcend his senses and thoughts, his materiality and even his own consciousness, and to become one with space and infinity. But while these techniques transcended reality, they did not unlock it. They didn't resolve the problem of birth and death. They offered temporary bliss, but not permanent peace. They couldn't answer the pain still resounding in his heart.

Siddhartha had drawn to him a handful of companions. With them, he tried the ascetic path of self-denial and inaction to the point of self-mortification, as a means of attaining self-control and liberation. Soon, perfectionist and over-achiever that he was, he became so thin he could feel his spine when he rubbed his stomach. Indeed, even more so than his companions, he was on the brink of self-annihilation.

Just skin and bones. This astonishing sculpture depicts Buddha's extreme asceticism. His veins bulge over his ribs. His eyes stare out from sunken sockets. He remains steadfast in his quest. From Sikri, Pakistan (Gandhara). Second century C.E. 83.8 cm. Lahore Museum.

Along the Path

Ascetic, from Greek, originally meant "hermit," such as a person practicing austere self-discipline for religious purposes. Besides seclusion, common forms of **asceticism** are fasting, celibacy, and poverty. These self-disciplines are believed to sharpen the mind, heighten awareness, and free the practitioner from mundane attachments.

The Middle Way

At this point, a young girl from the village passed by with food her mother had given her as an offering to the forest gods. She saw Siddhartha, nearly unconscious, and put some rice-milk to his lips, and he drank. By so doing, he renounced not only asceticism but also extremism.

Many things are going on here. First, there's the wonderful recognition of the importance of our bodies and their relationship to our happiness! So many spiritual paths trod on the body as evil. Siddhartha realized he couldn't achieve his goal if his mind was in a trance and his body too weak to grasp and carry on the truth.

Moreover, he realized that self-denial didn't free him from attachments. Rather, self-denial was but another kind of attachment, another attachment to self. Of the many lessons which the life of the Buddha holds for us today, there is a supreme teaching, known as the *Middle Way*. We all meet with varying forms of extremism in ourselves and others. Siddhartha said to find a middle road. Don't tear the ground out from under your feet. Nihilism obviously gets you nowhere, as does chasing after disembodied essences. Interestingly, he had to experience extremism, that of both self-indulgence and self-denial, firsthand, in order to reject it.

Well, his eating solid food definitely blew his credibility with his five self-appointed disciples, for sure. They wandered off before he could explain his realization. And so he went at it alone. At some point, we all must. But the girl returned and offered him food every day. With the recovery of his health came fresh perceptions which led to new insights, which would ultimately lead to wisdom and compassion.

This Is

The **Middle Way** is a practical form of the Buddha's nondualistic thought. That is, Western philosophical and religious thought tends toward dualism: good vs. evil, self vs. other, mind vs. body, either/or, and so on. Buddhism, on the other hand, is more like fuzzy logic, which can see a door as both ajar and half-closed. (A whole school of Buddhism developed dedicated to studying the Middle Way, called *Madhyamika*.)

Enlightenment

Meditating in a healthy body allowed him to look at things around him with clarity. Whether looking at the food the girl offered before he ate it, or just sitting under a tree and looking at one of its leaves, he saw that each of these things was not independent. Food might come from a leaf. And the leaf? The leaf came from the sun in the sky, from the earth beneath him, and from the water in a cloud. And where did each of these come from? They were all interconnected. Interdependent. Interacting and inter-reacting. He saw now that self-denial would never liberate him from the intricate and vast web of life. Nor was the web of life at fault.

Looking further, he saw that nothing in life lasts. Nothing is permanent. The cloud passes away in the sun. The leaf falls to the earth. Similarly, he, too, was part of not only the interdependence but also the impermanence of all life. Meditating clearly now, these realizations made him appreciate each moment to the fullest. And why not? Why not live each moment to the fullest when each moment occurs only once, and when each instant potentially contains the whole of life?

Now he felt he was really getting somewhere. Now he was cooking! The meaning of suffering and death was becoming clear at last. Before sundown, looking at the evening star beside the full moon of May, he felt that tonight he'd make his final, ultimate breakthrough.

Sitting beneath the sheltering leaves of a fig tree (the Indian *banyan* variety), he endured thunderstorms, some say even demonic temptations, lead by Mara (embodiment of death). First Mara surrounded the Buddha with the most seductive women imaginable, but the Buddha remained composed. Then Mara unleashed the most bloodthirsty warrior demons upon him, but he had no fear. Lastly, Mara tried to tempt him away from his meditation by challenging his motives, saying, "Aren't you really doing this for selfish reasons? Even if you did attain enlightenment, who'd believe you? And what right have you to try, anyway?" Whereupon the Buddha looked at Mara and touched the ground with his hand, taking the earth as his witness, all of creation. Mara admitted defeat.

Buddha subduing Mara. Sukhothai school, fourteenth or early fifteenth century. Bronze; 101.6 cm. National Museum, Ayuthya.

Oblivious to all distractions, gazing deeper and deeper into his mind and the mind of creation, the heart of life. In the darkest night, he unlocked the enigma of life, that we are born to die, thus inevitably bound to suffer. Mortality leads to cravings which can never be fulfilled—and perpetuates false mindsets of self which only produce more suffering. He saw clearly now the jail in which we entrap ourselves and which we ourselves police.

Leaves from the Bodhi Tree

A tree is primal in the spiritual symbolism of many civilizations, often representing a medium and intermediary between the human world and the divine, a still point in the turning world. It's particularly interesting that Siddhartha would choose a fig tree, which is parthenogenic. That is, it doesn't need another to reproduce. Instead, it reroots its branches in the soil. Thus some believe this tree to be immortal. And thus, the tree seems to be saying: Renew! Every day, do it all over again anew, and yet again new!

He understood that what we call our life is but a wave, not the ocean. He became one with that ocean, and all the rivers and raindrops that feed it. He became enlightened. He saw the morning star in the sky, as if for the first time, and his heart, as wide now as the world, was overbrimming with understanding and love. The bright, keen, joyous starlight matched the smile on his lips. This was it. He had found out. Now he was fully awake.

Buddhaship attained.

After Enlightenment: Teach!

So imagine Siddhartha sitting there, at the culmination of a seven-year quest, now the most fully self-realized being ever in human history, so happy!, finally having found complete freedom from all mortal suffering. After some time, he stood up and took his first steps, just walking lovingly around the tree that had sheltered him. He felt the solid earth supporting his bare feet, the fresh wind caressing his cheek, as if he and the world had been born together just now. When the young girl brought food that day, she could feel his transformation in her own heart.

It's interesting to consider how he might have remained sitting beneath the tree in perfect nirvana for the rest of his days. Yet during his enlightenment he saw how the seeds of enlightenment are within the hearts of everyone, and so love for all beings and compassion for their needless suffering was bound up, part and parcel, with his ultimate insight. So he sought out his five former companions.

Along the Path

Siddhartha experienced a great awakening and attained supreme enlightenment. That means he directly perceived ultimate reality, free from the limits of the mind, his awareness and wisdom encompassing and one with all that is. To dwell in this state is called nirvana (meaning literally "extinguishment," extinguishing transient passions and illusory concepts). Living thus, he earned the title "Buddha." *Note: A logical mind might notice that these definitions refer to each other in a circular fashion: well, what goes around ...*

Now when they saw Siddhartha coming, they turned their backs. They remembered him as having copped out on the rigors of the ascetic path, but it just goes to show you that people change. As he drew nearer, they could recognize with their own two eyes that he was transformed. Supreme Enlightenment was evident just from his presence. They let their judgments and preconceptions fall away, and welcomed him.

This Is

Dharma, from Sanskrit (Dhamma, Pali), has a number of meanings, depending upon the context: the Buddha's teachings, doctrine, system, path, phenomena, reality, and truth (also virtue, law, standard, and cosmic order). One way to sum it up is to say it refers to the Buddha's teachings *and* that to which they pertain (which includes everything in life).

Sangha means "assembly, crowd, host." Generally, it refers to the Buddhist community; more specifically, to the Buddhist monastic order, which is the oldest monastic order in the world.

That night, he gave his first talk, known as "The Turning of the Wheel of Truth." Explaining his discovery, he introduced four premises, known as the *Four Noble Truths,* and a program for liberation, known as the *Eightfold Path* (see Chapters 5,

"The Handshake: Buddhism's Basic Beliefs," and 6, "Taking Steps: The Eightfold Path"). While the others were still mulling it over, one of his disciples got it immediately and became enlightened.

Buddha was a travelling teacher (peripatetic), on a perpetual pilgrimage. Thus did his teachings spread by foot. The traditional topknot of his hair is elongated to represent his enlightenment. His fingers are tapered to symbolize his ability to reach deep within. His gesture of one hand up means "Have no fear." The design displays an amazing balance of motion and rest. Sukhhothai, 3.53 cm × 2.35 cm.

And it was decided that these teachings would be called *"Dharma,"* the path. Those on that path would be called *"Sangha."* And Siddhartha would become known as *"The Buddha,"* the one who shows others the path in this world. Thus began the Buddha's course of teaching—to whomever would listen as he walked around the vast delta of the Ganges River, and to his growing band of disciples when they'd all go on retreat with him during the rainy season. All told, it was to be a journey lasting the next 45 years.

Aspects of the Buddha

The entire next part of this book is devoted to a survey of the Buddha's teachings, but here are a few more stories from this final phase of his life that shed light on his method and thought.

Buddha's persuasiveness can be judged not only for the truth of his message but also the simplicity, inclusiveness, realism, and care with which he would present it. For example, a woman named Kisa Gotami came to him, clutching in her arms the body of her only child, who'd just died. She'd heard he'd transcended the bonds of death and, weeping, implored him to restore her daughter to life. He could see the state of shock

15

she was in, clearly out of her mind with grief. Nothing he could say would get through to her. If you were the Buddha, what would you do?

The Buddha smiled. "Before I do anything," he told her, "go to the nearby village and bring me a handful of mustard seed. But, please, make sure the seed comes only from a home where death is unknown." And so Kisa Gotami hurried to the village, believing the Buddha would save her daughter, and knocked on the first door. When the owners of the house saw her, clutching her dead child, they invited her in and said they'd be glad to give her some mustard seed. But when she added the Buddha's stipulation, the woman of the house wiped away a tear as her husband told her of the death of his father. Second house, third house: same thing. Eventually, she'd knocked on the door of the entire village. Kisa Gotami returned to the Buddha's enclave in the forest, buried her child, and asked to learn the Dharma.

Amazing story. He hadn't told her to be happy. No, he showed her a way to reach deeper into her grief, a way that also enabled her to see something larger than her own loss, something in which she could take refuge—the universality of impermanence.

Leaves from the Bodhi Tree

Some people prefer to call Buddhism a way of life and thought. In Asia, "Buddhism" is often an alien term, because to them it merely refers to reality. Because the Buddha wouldn't deal with certain questions basic to metaphysics, there are reasons why his path isn't properly considered a philosophy. Likewise, because he never resolved questions about God or gods, or an afterlife, his teachings aren't precisely a religion. And since it teaches that the self is an illusory construction, it can be tricky to categorize it exactly as psychology.

The Buddha's Silence and Parables

Other times, the Buddha answered with silence. This was the case when asked questions not open to direct, personal experience, and so whose answer really did not matter. "It does not further," he might say, at best (meaning "time is too precious to go down that path"), when asked is space infinite, is the universe eternal, is the soul immortal, are body and mind identical. Had the Buddha heard of stand-up comedy, he might have replied with one-liners, like Woody Allen: "If man were immortal, just think of what his laundry bills would be!" Ba-dum!

Sometimes Buddha answered such imponderables with a parable. He'd say for example, that asking where the universe began was like a person who refused to leave a burning house unless he knew the origin of the fire. A variation is his story of the man struck by a poison dart, who won't allow himself to be taken to a doctor until he knows exactly who fired the dart, just what poison he used, precisely how the dart was made, and so on.

Parable is a favorite tool of the great spiritual masters, and the life of the Buddha is full of them. The most famous was yet another of his responses to questions that "do not further"—more particularly, the dogmatism that arises around them.

He'd been called to deal with some intellectuals debating some unprovable philosophical matter, who were now practically ready to come to blows. He told them the story of a king who'd entertained himself by assembling some local blind men in front of him and then leading an elephant into their midst. One man felt its leg and declared it was a pillar. One man touched the end of its tail and said it was a broom, whereas another who held the tail itself said it was a rope. One man touched the side and swore it was a wall, while another, feeling a leg, said, no, it is a pillar. Another touched its ear and called it a basket for winnowing grain. Yet another felt the tusk and yelled that he was touching a ploughshare. The king watched with amusement as they began arguing, each having seen only one aspect of the whole and then insisting that his was the only reality.

Another aspect of the Buddha was his egalitarianism, which contradicted the social order of India of his time, based on the hereditary caste system. If India were a body, the peasants were the feet; the merchants and craftsmen were the legs; the warrior and noble class, from which the Buddha hailed, were the arms; and the priestly Brahmins made up the head. As noted earlier, the Buddha and his disciples taught whomever they met, rich or poor, comparable to near heresy during the Renaissance in Europe, or radical income tax reform during twentieth-century America. But nirvana knows no boundaries, nor does spiritual liberation recognize social rank as an obstacle. The Buddha even touched the so-called untouchables, the outcasts

Along the Path

The parable of the blind men and the elephant is relevant to Buddhism itself, too. Some may call it a religion; others, a system of ethics, or a philosophy; still others, psychological therapy; and still others, spiritual devotion. When you see the whole elephant, you'll recognize how it has elements of each yet it's also really something unto itself.

Hear and Now

"It is the nature of all things that take form to return to what they once were. Be a lamp unto yourself. Don't look for the answer outside yourself. Hold on to the truth like a torch. Work out your own enlightenment with diligence."

—From the Buddha's last words

below the peasant class. And, during his sojourn back with his family, he accepted women into his order, first the stepmother who'd raised him, followed by his wife. He also taught that the prevalent customs of animal sacrifice were mere superstition, further alienating him from the Brahmin elite.

The Final Teaching

The end was sudden and unexpected. Some feed he'd been given as alms was bad. He lay down. Just as he had taught meditation while sitting, standing, and walking, now he taught while on his side. (See the first illustration in Chapter 19, "Happiness Is Not an Individual Matter: Engaging the World.") Naturally, many in the community feared they couldn't go on without him, but he reassured them it wasn't necessary for him to be there personally for them to practice his teachings for themselves. "The Dharma is the best teacher," he said.

"Even if I were to live for aeons," he told them, "I'd still have to leave you because every meeting implies a departure, one day." With his faithful disciples by his side, he died the way he'd lived for nearly 50 years, an exemplary spiritual teacher beyond compare. It is said that, as with his birth, and his enlightenment, his final nirvana (extinction) … was on the night of a full moon, in May.

And that's a quick sketch of the tapestry that is the Buddha's life: a life that is, itself, a teaching. From the very first, the Buddha, and each of us, was born with the capacity for a life of tranquility and joy. Harmony and love. Truth. This ability is a gift. And it is yours.

The Least You Need to Know

➤ We experience degrees of awakening. The ultimate aim of Buddhist awakening is enlightenment, and the supreme enlightenment is nirvana.

➤ The Buddha sought the answer to the human enigma of life and death, and found it. Because he attained enlightenment, we can, too.

➤ The Buddha realized the unity of all things and became one with all creation. In his wisdom and compassion, he recognized the cause of suffering and the way out of suffering.

➤ The Buddha was nondogmatic and nonauthoritarian—a guide, not a god. Pragmatic, he invites us to see for ourselves.

➤ Extensively, Buddha is whomever or whatever awakens us to greater intimacy with life.

Chapter 2

One Taste, Different Flavors: The Teachings Adapt to Different Lands

In This Chapter

➤ Life after Buddha's death

➤ Humble teachings plus a mighty king

➤ Adoption and adaptation in differing lands

➤ Evolution of schools and sects

➤ Modern times

Buddha never saw a light bulb, yet his teachings are as illuminating today as they were 2,600 years ago. Likewise, he never ate corn tortillas or drank a strawberry milkshake, but his message has proven universal. Food has different flavors, yet truth has but one taste. That's the underlying theme of this chapter. Now that Buddhism's developed over time and across space, it's interesting to look back and see how its truths have adapted to different lands while retaining their essence.

But changes are interesting, too. Consider a seed, how it transforms into a shoot, then to a young plant, then to a mature plant with blossoms spreading new seeds. In like manner, Buddha left guidelines intended to nourish the seeds of buddhahood within each of us. After his death, his path had taken on a life of its own. Here are some petals from the unfolding lotus of his teachings.

The First Disciples: India

Buddha spoke to rich and poor, rajah and outcast alike. The Buddhist community (*Sangha*) of monks (*bhikkhus*) and nuns (*bhikkhunis*) was a gathering of those who'd vowed to follow Buddha's teachings and their resonance in the world (the *Dharma*). In so doing, they pledged themselves to a life of simplicity, meditation, and teaching. Because their dwelling (*vihara*) was often close to the crowds of urban life, they were in that respect more like Christian priests than monks. They were usually celibate, but in some cases, as in Japan and Tibet, they might marry, again more like Christian priests than monks.

This Is

The Pali word **bhikku,** Buddhist monk, literally means "beggar," as monks beg their meals each day. A bhikku might initially be called *anagarika,* "homeless," just as the Buddha left home. A bhikku aspired to become an **arhat,** "one worthy," or "Worthy One" (in Chinese, *lohan;* Japanese, *arakan*). The ideal of arhatship means having nothing more to learn, free of cravings and desires, having attained nirvana (liberation, union with ultimate reality)—albeit a nirvana tempered with mundane conditions that would dissolve upon death.

The core sangha didn't have any day jobs other than meditation, teaching, and monastic upkeep. But the sangha was open to people who did work, the laity. So sympathetic merchants and noblemen who didn't become "full-timers" by joining the monastic order might instead donate money or land. Thus monasteries arose in such large cities as Rajagrija, Shravasti, and Viashala. And rulers of major principalities joined the sangha.

By the time of the Buddha's death, the Dharma had spread across some 50,000 square miles, cutting across some seven nations of central India. Considering that Buddha and his followers travelled on foot, this was no mean feat (no pun intended). And the Buddha designated no centralized religious structure, no Head Office, nor official disciples. He said, instead, "Listen up, everyone: Work out your *own* salvation with diligence."

After Buddha died, 500 arhats assembled and recited from memory all he'd said, to agree on his teachings and the codes of monastic discipline. (If such a prodigious feat of memory seems extreme today, bear in mind that oral culture and the art of memory were commonly highly developed in pre-modern civilizations.) This powwow became known as the First Council.

The Second Council was convened a century later, in 383 B.C.E., to clarify such monastic practices as the use of money. (Buddhist merchants were obligated to make change, even though change must come from within. Ba-dum!) Friendly interchange between monasteries took place regularly. Nevertheless, over time, differences evolved from one monastery to another, about interpretation of the teachings or monastic policy. A branching into two schools of thought would emerge. We'll see the result further on in this chapter, but first we must pay our respects to Buddhism's greatest sponsor.

King Ashoka—Instrument of the Dharma

One man was largely responsible for the emergence of Buddhism as a world force. Two centuries after the Buddha's death, the Buddhist community remained small and little-known. But within a mere 50 years more, thanks to a king named Ashoka, the Dharma took hold across the land. (We were taught about Alexander, when I was a boy, but why not King Ashoka!? Such a hero! What a role model!)

Reigning from 272 to 236 B.C.E., Ashoka held vast power in his hands, ruling the southern tip of the Indian subcontinent and part of Persia. Following the atrocities of his bloodiest of war triumphs, he hung up his sword and took up the Dharma.

Along the Path

You might think of Ashoka's conversion as like that of Constantine the Great (280–337 C.E.), the Roman emperor whose conversion to Christianity marked the decline of paganism and the rise of the Christian West. Yet Ashoka went to great lengths to define a universal moral dharma so that citizens could still follow other faiths and even offered material aid to other religions. Indeed, it could be said that Ashoka attempted to establish the world's first universal religion.

Ashoka replaced his former hunting expeditions with pilgrimages; military parades now became devotional processions. A tree-hugger, he ordered that forests be preserved. Out of compassion, he not only had hospitals built but saw to it that animals had medical care as well. Egalitarian, his citizenry could call on him anytime, day or night, whether he was in his carriage or on the throne, in the dining room or in the boudoir. It's interesting to note that under his peaceful reign nobody revolted and no outsiders invaded.

He also sent envoys to teach the Dharma all around the Indian subcontinent and beyond, to Syria, Egypt, Macedonia, and Ceylon. Following the Buddha's example, these ambassadors didn't try to convert anyone, only inform. No crusade or coercion, but rather spreading of the faith by truth and gentle example. Spreading Buddhist truth (Buddha-dharma) would be rather like telling someone that the sum of the angles of a triangle equals 180°. And if the speaker had a good vibe, people would likely to want to check out where he or she is coming from. That's Buddhist evangelism, at its best. Thanks to the enlightened patronage of Ashoka and his son Kanishka (78–123 C.E.), Buddhism flourished in India for a millennium, and the Buddha ultimately became a worldwide influence, not a mere footnote to history.

Another factor in the spread of Buddhism was education. The Buddhist university of Nalanda (average enrollment: 10,000) was so successful it survived from the seventh to the twelfth centuries. Courses included medicine, grammar, and logic, as well as various Buddhist studies, including an interpretation of Buddhism no less rigorous than Aristotle's logic, called Madhyamika, centered on the Middle Way.

In about 100 C.E., a final (fourth) Council was convened by King Ashoka's son, Kanishka. Kanishka tried to mend fences between the several schools that had evolved. But factionalism persisted. Only today, over distance and time, are we beginning to see the schisms as less of an irreconcilable difference than had been thought. Instead, we can see the schools as complementary.

Two Schools of Thought

Divergence is only natural. Polarity is a law of nature, and of human nature. So a separation within the sangha arose between what could be called conservative and liberal elements—a traditionalist, literalist camp and a more interprative, populist camp.

On the one hand, there were those emphasizing the Buddha's original teachings as central. On the other hand, there were those wanting to adapt and open the teachings out for the wider community. Rather than the ideal of the individuated *arhat*, seeking liberation for one's self, for example, they'd emphasize the ideal of the *bodhisattva*, someone who seeks enlightenment for the benefit of all beings, or who becomes awakened but, rather than dwell in nirvana, vows to help all beings become enlightened. Ultimately, the bodhisattva ideal is actually present in the seemingly more individualist tradition. And beyond the arhat and the bodhisattva, there's complete buddhahood.

Today, there's a tendency to think of the traditionalists as existing first, and the innovators as coming later. However, scholarship suggests that the two tendencies were present from the beginning.

This Is

...it, meaning awakened, wisdom, and way; "sattva" mean-
...erally an "enlightened being" or "essence of the Way." But
...whether attained or aspired to, is altruistic, for the benefit
...e vows to assist not just all people but all sentient beings;
...ent beings" to include all beings (period), since everything

...g the bodhisattva the Great Vehicle ("great" as in large
...us needs. The lay people, for example, who'd often
...ly wanted more representation. Fewer people aspired
...e traditional teachings seemed to call for further ex-
...called *sutras*) arose, for a period lasting four centuries.
...ually began, "Thus did I hear the Buddha say ..." so
...t and the letter of the Law.

...school evolved in Indian regions with the most for-
...e a Buddhism highly adaptable for export. Indeed,
...prevail in China,
...nd Nepal, Tibet, and
...er, more tradition-
..., tended to prevail
...e relatively iso-

...s often reflect the
..."elders" and the
...und like any po-
...tter became known
as *Mahayana* ("Great Way"), "yana" meaning
"way," "path," or "vehicle." And Mahayana called
the other camp *Hinayana*, "Narrow Way." But "narrow" had a decidedly pejorative spin; as in "lesser,"
"inferior," even "dirty." But "elders" implied the
others were newcomers, since *Theravada* means
"teachings of the elders" ("thera," elders; "vada,"
doctrine). The distinction gets even fuzzier when

This Is

The word **sutra**, from Sanskrit,
means "a thread," such as for
stringing jewels, or prayer beads,
perhaps. It also carries the connotation of "story," the way we hear
"tale" in the word "yarn." It comes
from the same root from which we
derive the word "suture," meaning
to sew, to connect.

considering such instances as Vietnamese Buddhism, where the two tended to blend, and Tibetan Buddhism, which describe three schools, Hinayana, Mahayana, and Vajrayana ("Indestructible Path").

Here in the West, boundaries are looser. You don't have to go from one country to another to learn a different brand of Buddhism. Maybe you'll hear about different practices instead of schools. The Theravada practice most common in the West is called *Vipassana* (pronounced *va-PAH-sa-na*, literally "insight") meditation. Leading Mahayana practices are *Pure Land* and *Zen*, and *Tibetan* either falling also under Mahayana or getting a category of its own, Vajrayana. But, whether dressed in robes or blue jeans, buddha is buddha.

Along the Path

Another factor which further dampens any rivalry between Buddhist branches comes from the Mongols. Though short-lived, the Mongol Empire had a deep impact on every land it touched. Following their encounter with the Mongols, Southeast Asian nations adopted a "new Theravada." This new Theravada not only had no nuns but no arhats, as well. So when Mahayana accuses Hinayana of only being interested in arhatship (individual attainment), it no longer pertains, since the latter hadn't produced any arhats for a thousand years.

Is India Mecca for Buddhists?

Today, King Ashoka's lion is part of the national emblem of India, and the Buddha's wheel of the Dharma is on the flag. But by the time this symbolism was instituted, there were hardly more than 180,000 Buddhists. It happened largely thanks to Dr. B. R. Ambedkar (1891–1956), who also urged low-caste Hindus ("untouchables") to reject the caste system and embrace India's ancient faith. Up until Dr. Ambedkar, Buddhism had all but died out in its country of origin.

For one thing, Buddhism slowly became subsumed into Hinduism. Today, Hindus say the Buddha was but one of the incarnations of the deity Vishnu. Moreover, it hadn't integrated itself into the daily life of the people, but remained centered in monasteries and monastic universities, easy targets for invaders. By the time the Turkic Muslims invaded India from the north, in the thirteenth century, Buddhism had already been in decline for six centuries. As these foreigners were on a holy war (a *jihad*), the sight of infidel statues of buddhas and bodhisattvas incited them to destroy the monasteries and burn down the libraries. Muslim Turkic rule over north India was established by 1192, by which time Buddhism had, as they say, left the building. But, then, the vanishing of Buddhism in its country of origin echoed the Buddha's last words: "Without exception, all forms in the world, motionless and moving, are subject to decay followed by extinction." The Dharma was proving to be Dharma, a living law.

This Is

Hinduism refers to the indigenous religion of the Indian people originating between 1700 and 500 B.C.E. Defined sects didn't appear until around the time of the Buddha. The word "Hinduism" itself is a modern, Western invention, though universally accepted. More correct might be the "Brahmanic traditions," referring to the common belief in *Brahman*, similar to God; or "Vedic traditions," referring to the primary scriptures (*Vedas*). Familiar in the West are some of its techniques for physical and mental discipline called **yoga.**

Wisdom of the Elders

What we now call Southeast Asia was once referred to as "Further India," by the Indians who'd colonized it. Commerce with India brought a flow of culture as well as goods.

Ceylon, now known as Sri Lanka, has enjoyed the oldest continuous Buddhist tradition in the world. In 250 B.C.E., the king of Ceylon invited Ashoka's prince and princess, Mahinda and Sanghamitta, to personally introduce Buddhism. A century and a half later, Buddhist scripture was committed to writing here, in a language called Pali, similar to Sanskrit. (In the Buddha's time, India had no single, common language.) The canon became known as the *Tripitaka* ("three baskets"), around a hundred volumes, each about 600 pages long. The three baskets are as follows:

➤ Buddha's talks (*sutras*)

➤ Ethical monastic conduct (*vinaya*)

➤ "Special dharma" (*abhidharma*)

Along the Path

The Buddha's first *sutra* was his explanation of the Dharma to his five ascetic companions at the deer park in Benares. Today, there are a couple of hundred sutras and several thousand volumes of commentaries in the *Tripitaka*. (Don't worry, you won't be quizzed. Buddhists aren't "people of the book." It's enough to know what the Four Noble Truths are.)

Ethical rules were established in the Buddha's Sangha on a case-by-case basis, as various situations arose. So the *vinaya* illustrates each rule with the story of its origin.

The *abhidharma* includes precise, in-depth cosmology, natural science, philosophy, and psychology, plus a thesaurus.

The Tripitaka would form the nucleus for the Theravada tradition to dominate in southeast Asia—notably Siam (Thailand) and Burma (Myanmar), besides Ceylon (Sri Lanka). In the fifth century C.E., a monk from India named Buddhaghosa arrived in Ceylon, collated commentaries on the Tripitaka, and wrote his own survey, *Visuddhimagga (Path of Purity)*, still widely read today. By the tenth century, the monastery conferred kingship, and up until the nineteenth century only a Buddhist could be king. Thus, in Ceylon, Buddhism adapted to social and political as well as religious duties.

Burma (Myanmar) originally had a mix of Buddhism and Hinduism. Mahayana and Theravada were both practiced. But when Anawratha became the first Burmese king, in 1044, he conquered the neighboring Mon country and brought back Theravadan monks and books as part of his booty, and Theravada became the dominant religion. He then had *thousands* of monasteries and temples built in Pagan, his capital.

Between the twelfth and fourteenth centuries, the people of southwestern China who populated Siam (Thailand) adopted Buddhism, which had first spread from Burma six centuries earlier. As a national kingdom evolved, Buddhism became the state religion. While there are thus temples in cities and towns, many serious practitioners are ordained in the forests.

Cambodia had received Theravada teachings as well as Mahayana by the second century C.E. Theravada became Cambodia's primary religion after the fourteenth century. During that century, the royal house in Laos also became Theravadan.

Before the Internet: The Spice and Silk Routes

Just as sheer information has become a hot item these days, along with the means of getting it (such as TV, wireless phone, Internet, and, oh yes, books), back in the Buddha's days it was silk, and the means to get it. And just as folks of late have developed a yen to have a pager, Chinese silk was the big status item of the day, as far West as Egypt and Rome. Even Cleopatra had to have it.

Because of silk, not too far from the Buddha's stomping grounds was a zone just north of India, south of Central Asia, and west of Tibet that was a hotbed of interchange. Present-day Afghanistan (then Greek Bactria) forms part of this fertile crossroads of the world, as well as Pakistan and China's Xinkiang region. In this relatively small niche, a mix of people settled: Tokharians, Kapisans, Soghdians, Bactrian Greeks who'd come with Alexander, and also Kushanas (Indo-Scythians). From this emerged a robust culture of international trade.

Thousands of years before FedEx and UPS, there evolved a 6,000-mile road now known as the Silk Route. Silk left China along this route, through Central Asia, passing from way station to way station. Meanwhile, from the other direction, caravans with gold, silver, and wools rode in. Always an exchange; roads go in two directions. And along for the ride came Nestorian Christians ... and Buddhist scholars and monks. Thus did Buddhism make its way across Central Asia and on to Russia, and east to Mongolia and China. And eventually there were Buddhist outposts at way stations, with monastic centers as well as hotels and hospitals.

Alternatively, one could be transported by the ocean between India and the Arabian peninsula, along what later became known as the Spice Route. Without borders, the Spice Route probably saw even more trade than the Silk Route, but traffic across watery ways leaves no traces.

The Silk Route also furnished another potent way for the Dharma to spread: Buddha images. Previously, the only devotional images were abstract, such as a wheel, footprints, or an empty throne ("the Buddha has left the building"). Now, Hellenism (devotion to Greek culture) had taken root in Northern India, following Alexander the Great's campaign there (fourth century B.C.E.). Under the influence of Greek art, Buddhist artists made bas-reliefs of Buddhist patrons and of the Buddha. One early example looked like Apollo in a toga accompanied by female lute players and floating cherubs. On the other hand, the Buddhist paintings in the caves of Dun Huang (a Silk Route terminal to outermost China) display a mix of styles—from graffiti to elegant visions. And so we come to China herself, for a confrontation of the two great civilizations of Asia, all because of our smiling friend, Buddha.

This Gandhara Buddha looks as Western as Eastern. Except for the amenities of toga, elongated ears (associated with his birth caste), topknot, dot on forehead, and halo—how could you ever pick him out in a crowd? (Well, there's the direct gaze ... a sense of complete presence ... and that smile ...)

(San Francisco Zen Center)

Leaving Home, Bound for the Center of the World

If the Silk Route gave Buddhism the horse (or camel) power from India to China—to get past blazing, barren deserts and perilous, precipitous peaks—Buddhism still had one last mighty obstacle to overcome: national identity and its dark flip side, xenophobia. China's venerable, highly developed civilization was rather allergic to imported beliefs. (Remember the Great Wall!) Indeed, you get the feeling that if Buddhism could make it here, it could make it anywhere.

It didn't help that the Chinese naturally looked askance at these Buddhists who didn't seem too patriotic, hadn't any sons to perpetuate the honor of their parents, and didn't work for a living—all contrary to Chinese values. But two lucky similarities played out in favor of the Buddhists. One, Buddhism seemed to answer questions that *Confucius* couldn't. Two, Buddhism clicked with a revival of *Taoism* that happened to be brewing.

This was a lucky break, since Tao and Confucianism composed the double helix of Chinese culture. Now, Buddhism and Taoism explored very similar themes, so monks took the opportunity to translate Sanskrit Buddhist terms into Chinese words already highlighted by Taoism. Since Taoism's chief proponent, Lao-tzu had, in his old age, headed west and never come back, the notion arose that Buddhism was the result of Lao-tzu's teachings abroad, his "conversion of the barbarians." That works! And that way China wouldn't be importing something foreign into the culture—merely welcoming back a native tradition they'd exported in the first place. (More on the Tao in Chapter 4, "Different Travel Agents, Same Destination?: Interfaith.")

This Is

The Tao (pronounced *dow*) means "the Way," and its chief writer was Lao-tzu (b. 604 B.C.E.). The philosophy-religion of **Taoism** holds that 1) what's really real is that which never changes, and 2) we're each a part of this reality, through our innate, individual character. **Confucianism,** on the other hand, follows Lao-tzu's contemporary, Confucius (551–479), China's "philosopher king" (his philosophy becoming imperial ideology). Where Lao-tzu was a carefree mystic, Confucius was a duty-conscious, humanist agnostic.

So China adapted Buddhism, making it theirs the kind of the way kids customize their cars. Emperor Ming (206 B.C.E.–220 C.E.) invited Buddhist envoys in 67 C.E. During the political chaos from 221 to 589 that came with the collapse of the Han Dynasty, Buddhism started to become a strong presence in China. Monasteries and temples were permitted and flourished across the land, and Buddhism integrated itself into daily life.

The Chinese often concocted their own blend of Confucianism, Taoism, Buddhism, ancestor worship, and folk cults, unlike India or Southeast Asia where people follow one religion at a time, or at least keep them separate. (Chinese religion thus often resembles a Chinese restaurant menu: "Pick one from *Column A* or two from *Column B*.") Chinese religion, in general, tends toward the practical over the philosophical. Whatever works.

Hitting the Heights

Buddhism peaked in China, roughly coinciding with China's Golden Age, the T'ang Dynasty (618–906). Women practitioners were particularly drawn to the embodiment of compassion, named Avalokiteshvara in India but now (cleverly) transformed into a woman in China, named *Kwan Yin*. Sometimes she's a delicate white-porcelain lady (as seen on the altar shown in Chapter 9, "Taking the Plunge: Beginning and Cultivating Your Practice," and another version in Chapter 12, "See? Words Cannot Express: Zen"). Other times she has a hundred faces and a thousand hands, with an eye in each hand (symbolizing her boundless compassion, ever-present, ever-ready). Kwan Yin became like the Virgin of Guadalupe of Buddhism.

By this time, five major schools were prominent. Widely known in the West is *Zen* ("*Ch'an*" in Chinese), which incubated and was refined in China. Indeed, it's been said that Zen is a quintessential synthesis of India and China. With its emphasis on meditation as direct perception of truth, applicable to all activities of life, and its spontaneity, immediacy, innovation, and dry wit, it's proven to be one of the most historically resilient schools of Buddhism. (Chapter 12 awaits with more on Zen.) No less popular is the *Pure Land* school (also known as *Amidism*, spotlighted in Chapter 13, "Paths of Devotion and Transformation: Pure Land and Vajrayana"). Both Pure Land and Zen became synthesized within the Chinese Buddhism that spread to Korea, Japan, and Vietnam.

Besides commissioning translators to render Sanskrit into Chinese, China also printed Buddhist books. Indeed, in 868, about 500 years before Gutenberg, monks assembled copies of *The Diamond Sutra* and disseminated it hither and yon, via the first printed book. The Chinese already knew how to fabricate paper. It's possible that the technique of woodblock printing was created in order to spread the Dharma and earn merit. (The first book printed with movable type was probably also Buddhist, crafted in Korea. It was then just a matter of time before the printing of *Complete Idiot's Guides*.)

This Is

Ch'an literally means "meditation." It can also imply the wisdom of enlightenment. It's derived from the Sanskrit synonym *dhyana*, pronounced *djana* in Pali. The Japanese, Korean, and Vietnamese equivalents are *zen*, *son*, and *thien*, respectively, with the Japanese being now the universal form in the West. Emphasizing faith in Buddha's compassion, the **Pure Land** school focuses on recitation of the name of Amida Buddha. This school of Buddhism in China and Japan has the most followers.

China became a hub of Buddhism. As some countries were learning Latin to learn of Jesus, others were learning Chinese to learn of Siddhartha.

What Goes Up Must Come Down

Problem: By the middle of the ninth century, China's Buddhist monasteries were richer than the Emperor's court. Indeed, the throne looked with alarm at the possible economic crash this could cause. Farmers were leaving the fields to help construct monasteries. (Who'd feed the country?) Buddhist monks didn't work and so produced no revenue. (Who supported them? Members of the royal court and wealthy aristocrats, who could've been underwriting Imperial Projects instead.) And what value had gold or silver now that those ores were being used to cast Buddhas and other accoutrements of this foreign craze? So the empire struck back.

Monasteries and temples were shut down or choked off under strict government supervision. State Confucianism was encouraged instead. Here, as elsewhere in Asia, Zen survived adversity. During the T'ang dynasty, Zen was still the most influential form of Buddhism in the land, and continued so through the subsequent Sung dynasty (960–1278).

Smaller Gardens

From India to China, Buddhism spread further east to Korea and Japan, and south to Vietnam. In each land, it mixed with various local practices—not unlike the Catholic church's accommodating indigenous pagan celebrations, as seen today with Halloween/All Soul's Day.

Korea

Many people are aware of China and Japan's Buddhist legacies but don't realize that Korea, in between the two countries, adopted Buddhism a century before it touched the shores of Japan. This began in the fourth century. Over time, Korean Buddhist masters arose to whom China would look for clarification and guidance.

Leaves from the Bodhi Tree

Korean monk Wonhyo set out for China to study Buddhism. On the road one night, he took shelter in a cave. He found a gourd of pure water which he drank, and he fell asleep, content. In the morning, he awoke startled to discover he'd spent the night in a tomb and that he'd drunk putrid water from an old skull. It came to him in a flash that "mind creates all things, all things are products of the mind alone." Realizing this, he turned around, as there was no longer any need to study in China. He studied his own mind instead and went on to become one of Korea's greatest Buddhist teachers and scholars.

Korean Buddhism blended with indigenous shamanism. (Still practiced in today, Korea and elsewhere, *shamanism* is a system of practices and beliefs, dating back to the Neolithic, centered upon a magical figure called a shaman who contacts and mediates with supernatural forces, thus combining duties of priest, doctor, psychologist, psychic, and weatherman.) Monasteries were often built on mountains patronized by an immortal old man no one ever saw, accompanied by a tiger deity from heaven. Korean Zen ("*Son*") emerged as Korea's three kingdoms were unified in the Koryo Dynasty (1140–1390), at a time when Buddhism in general became the state religion and then the national religion as well. *Son* is refined but earthier and less formal than Japanese-style, as typifies Korean culture in general. As with China, beginning in the thirteenth century, Confucianism took the upper hand in the royal court and the power of Buddhism waned, not due to any weakness on its own part. For two centuries, no monk or nun could so much as set foot in any major city. But following a vacuum in the nineteenth and twentieth centuries, Buddhism there is now stronger than Christianity.

Japan

A century after they first encountered it, Koreans brought Chinese Buddhism to Japan. Initially, the state looked to Buddhism for possible magical powers to protect it during the Heian period (794–1184). It mingled with or formed an alliance with local beliefs, such as the indigenous Shinto cults. Japan developed its own version of esoteric schools (intended only for initiates), such as *Shingon,* and philosophic schools such as *Tendai.* Japan also developed its own version of Pure Land called *Jodo Shin Shu* ("True Pure Land Religion," sometimes abbreviated to just *Shin*). Shin's chief patriarchs were named Honen (1133–1212) and his disciple Shinran (1173–1262).

This Is

In Japan, the indigenous religion is **Shinto,** centered on the spiritual essence *(kami)* present in gods, human beings, animals, and even inanimate objects. "Shinto" is an umbrella term for hundreds of different customs, and was coined in the sixth century when Japan felt it needed to distinguish its own, native beliefs and practices from new foreign concepts such as Confucianism and Buddhism.

Honen became one of the most knowledgeable priests of his day. Though he studied for 30 years at Mt. Hiei monastery, he was concerned about humanity outside the monastery walls. At age 42, he dedicated himself to chanting Amida Buddha's name (also known as the *nembutsu*), through which he'd attained awakening and which he felt was a sure path to salvation for the man in the street. Realizing Buddha cared for him personally, he had only to call Amida to be granted access to his Pure Land. Further repetition of his name wasn't necessary but would naturally result from deep entrusting in and continual gratitude for Amida's compassion.

It's interesting to note that three separate, radical developments of Japanese Buddhism were led by dropouts from the monastery of Mt. Hiei: Besides Honen and his student Shinran Shonan, there was Dogen (1200–1253) and Nichiren (1222–1282). If Honen's practice could be summed up as "Just do Nembutusu,"—Nicheren's would be "Just do Daimoku" (recitation of the title of the *Lotus Sutra,* "Namu myoho renge-kyo" in Japanese), representing the *Lotus Sutra school* named after Nicheren. And Dogen's motto would be "Just sit," a summation of his profoundly influential Zen practice.

Zen was a unique adaptation of Buddhism that emerged in Japan during the Kamakura Era (1185–1333). Seizing power from a decadent imperial aristocracy, the military elite (*samurai*) established a military government (the *Shogunate*), at Kamakura. Soldiers of fortune, the samurai loved the irreverence, intuition, spontaneity, and strict discipline of zen, and so they supported it. Embracing a wide spectrum of culture surpassing that of Chinese Buddhism, Japan has been the leading proponent of Mahayana Buddhist schools (Zen, Pure Land, and Lotus Sutra) throughout the twentieth century.

Vietnam

Vietnam is normally not grouped with China or Japan. Theravada was introduced in the south by the Indians, and by the Khmers along the border with Cambodia. But Mahayana monks from India arrived in the second century, and the Buddhism that Vietnam adopted was largely Chinese and thus Mahayanan. Between the sixth and thirteenth centuries, the common people practiced a blend of Confucianism, Taoism, and Pure Land Buddhism, while Zen ("*Thien*") prevailed in the monasteries.

At the Roof of the World

Let's look back a moment. Buddhist history can be conveniently divided into 500-year periods. Although Theravada and Mahayana existed simultaneously, the development of Theravada dominated for 500 years from the time of the Buddha, around 500 B.C.E., until 0 B.C.E. The next 500 years was marked by development of Mahayana schools. In the years 500 to 1000 C.E., two important trends were the rise of zen and *Vajrayana* (largely Tibetan) Buddhism. So, following the major dispersal of Buddhism throughout south, southeast, and east Asia, we come next to Tibet's turn at the wheel of the Dharma.

The delay in Buddhism's adoption here was due, in part, to Tibet's remoteness. Close to India, it's nevertheless separated by the Himalayas and different climates (India's subtropical, Tibet's 12,000 feet above sea-level). India's civilization is largely agricultural; Tibet's, pastoral. No wonder it took about 500 years before Buddhism took hold in Tibet after its introduction in 650. As elsewhere, it had to make terms with indigenous practices and beliefs, beliefs called *Bon,* marked by shamanism and animism (the belief that animals, objects, and places are sacred) and supported by the nobility. Interestingly, Tibet at this time was pre-literate but devised an alphabet in order to learn Buddhism. Like India at the time of the Buddha, Tibet was not a unified nation, and Buddhism helped unify this patchwork. Buddhism became more than a state religion, going the extra degree to becoming a theocracy (rule by divine sanction), or more properly a Buddhacracy, and, at one point, it became the first country in the world with a monk on the throne.

This Is

Tibetan Buddhism can also be classified as **Vajrayana** and **Tantrayana.** Vajra means "diamond." Lama Govinda notes that the diamond, "king of stones," is "capable of cutting asunder any other substance but which itself cannot be cut by anything." Thus Vajrayana means the Indestructible Path. It combines both Theravada and Mahayana elements with its adaptation of a school of Hindu yoga (*tantra*), plus a dash of pre-Buddhist elements (*Bon*). It's arguably the most complex branch of Buddhism.

Chapter 13 spotlights Tibetan Buddhism, but we can get some historical elements out of the way here. The Buddhism that made its way up to Tibet from India bore elements called *tantra* which were diffusing throughout both Hinduism and Buddhism in India at that time. (When China tried exporting Buddhism to Tibet, it clashed with tantra, and the Chinese were expelled from Tibet near the end of the eighth century.)

This Is

Tantra means "threads"; as in threading through the labyrinth of delusion to find liberation; also "continuity," such as manifest by innate buddha nature (like a silver lining within everything). It also has the meaning of weaving, continuum, or system. The word also refers to Vajrayana teachings of the Buddha, and so Vajrayana is sometimes called *Tantrayana*, almost interchangeably.

Basically, four major schools developed: *Nyingma, Kagyu, Gelup,* and *Sakya.* Nyingma (meaning "Ancient Ones") was first, originating with an Indian scholar-mystic named Padmasambhava ("Born-of-the-Lotus"), who arrived in Tibet in 747, converted Bon deities into Buddhism, and co-founded Tibet's first Buddhist monastery. It's from Nyingma that we get *The Book of the Dead,* and *Dzogchen,* a form of practice recently becoming known in the West.

After Nyingma became established, and following the pillaging of monasteries in India by the Huns, Indian Buddhist adepts brought texts to Tibet for preservation. Since Buddhism had developed further in India by then, Tibetan Buddhism amassed the world's largest collection of Buddhist scripture. Two more schools then arose in 1000. One new school was Sakya ("Grey Earth") a scholarly group which unified teachings of the sutras and tantras. Another school was called Kagyu, which counted among its ancestors such celebrated teachers as Naropa (1016–1100), Marpa (1012–1097), and Milarepa (1052–1135).

The final school, established in the fourteenth century, is called Gelug, "Way of Virtue." Gelug was a reformist movement combining elements of the other three schools, while returning to original Indian sources. The Gelug became the largest school and initiated the office of the *Dalai Lama.*

Modern Times

We Westerners like hard-edged numbers, such as statistics, pie graphs, and sports scores. But any census of practitioners of the Buddha's way can only be an approximation. Not only is the word "Buddhist" largely a Western invention, but Asians are often likely to play spiritual mix and match: Someone in Japan might follow Shinto as well as Buddha, plus maybe an ancestral family practice; a Vietnamese or Chinese might follow the way of the Tao as well as Buddha and/or Confucianism, and so on. Thus, most Asians might answer "Yes" to three or more religious categories.

This Is

Dalai Lama means "teacher whose wisdom is as great as the ocean." The title was bestowed upon the head of the Gelug school by Mongol ruler Altan Khan in the sixteenth century. Both a religious and a national ruler, Tibet has been ruled by Dalai Lamas since the fifth Dalai Lama in the sixteenth century.

Rough Estimate of Modern Buddhists

Country	Population	Buddhists as Percentage
Bhutan	1,750,000	75
Brunei	285,000	14
Cambodia	10,265,000	95
China	1,200,000,000	91 (Officially no religion.)
India	920,000,000	1
Japan	125,000,000	90
Malaysia	19,300,000	7
Myanmar (Burma)	44,300,000	89
Nepal	21,100,000	5
Singapore	2,900,000	29
Sri Lanka (Ceylon)	18,200,000	70
Thailand (Siam)	60,000,000	95
Vietnam	73,200,000	85

Census conducted around 1990.

Buddhism is the one common heritage uniting the peoples of Asia today. (What else? Rice!) And when each Asian country looks to its past, it often finds its greatest historical periods coinciding with times when Buddhism flourished. But Buddhism has had to adapt to modern times as well as to foreign lands—such upheavals as wars, invasions, revolutions, and exile. For example, many Asian lands have been spiritually developed but materially underdeveloped. (The phrase "underdeveloped nations" depends on your perspective.) Many took to socialism or communism to advance themselves materially, with the result that Buddhism was often repressed—Karl Marx (1818–1883) having branded religion "the opiate of the people." (An ex-communist friend of mine once laughed when he saw the graffiti, "Revolution is the opiate of the people," but that's all another story.)

Has the spread of Buddhism been worthwhile? It's enlightened masses of human beings and peacefully helped establish or unify nations and empires. It's provided a culture that's fostered the development of medicine and other sciences, furnished the basis for a world religion and a viable military conversion to peace, and sparked such agents of civilization as the printed book and movable type. And it's helped fuel literacy, national identity, and self-determination—as well as contemporary movements for the environment and social justice. The promise of all these gifts remains yet to be fulfilled, but then history is a golden book whose next chapter is always awaited with steadfast anticipation.

The Least You Need to Know

➤ Buddha's teachings (Dharma) have continued to flourish as a dynamic, living force through its growing community of disciples (Sangha).

➤ Buddhism often had to go along with new cultures it encountered in order to spread within new lands. In so doing, it evolved myriad aspects. But all its forms have a fundamental identity at heart.

➤ Two main branches, or collections of schools, developed: Theravada and Mahayana. In the West, Theravada's most popular manifestation is Vipassana ("Insight Meditation") and Mahayana's are Zen and Pure Land.

➤ Tibetans describe three branches of Buddhism: Theravada, Mahayana, and Vajrayana. The latter combines the teachings of the first two, plus tantric teachings.

➤ Tolerance is one of Buddhism's leading social characteristics.

Chapter 3

What Might an American Buddha Look Like?

In This Chapter

➤ Buddhism and modern thought

➤ Conditions conducive to American Buddhism

➤ American Buddhist teachers

➤ Issues and themes in American Buddhism

Rudyard Kipling echoed the popular sentiment of his day (1889), when he wrote, "Oh, East is East, and West is West, and never the twain shall meet." On first glance, the coming of Buddhism to the West was unprecedented—seemingly impossible. Yet eighth-century India and China were quite different from each other, and the transplant of Buddhism from India to China was a success (albeit something that took centuries to happen). As we'll see, the awakening of the West is proving no less remarkable. Twentieth-century historian Arnold Toynbee noted that of all the historical changes in the West, the most important, and the one whose effects have as yet been least understood, is the coming of Buddhism to the West. It looks like Buddhism will become a mainstream religion here.

How can Buddhism survive in a land where the greatest good is often equated with acquiring the greatest goods? Selflessness, in a culture that glorifies self? Or is it better suited here than we think? After all, the Buddha was quite a pragmatic, self-starting, can-do, no-limit kind of guy. He said, "Hey! I tried this: works for me. See for yourself." Who knows how long before American Buddhism really hits its stride, but why wait? See for yourself!

Preparing the Ground: Mulching the Cultural Soil

Dharma, truth, is a living process. Cultivate soil. Plant seeds. Water them. New life emerges. The transplant and transformation of Buddhism here in the West begins with conditions that have cultivated the soil.

Modernism: Einstein, Freud, Darwin, Marx, Buddha

As the twentieth century dawned, the work of four figures unglued conventional notions of the universe and self. Einstein spoke of the universe as a process; Freud, of the self as an interplay. Darwin contradicted the image of humans as a predetermined goal, for whom the rest of creation was like a toy. And Marx's global idealist vision further deconstructed both society and self, analyzing both as being determined by economic conditions.

So modernism shifted the focus away from divinity, fixity, and permanency (God and the Church), transferring attention, instead, to the worldliness, fluidity, and transience of reality and the many ways we can perceive and interpret it. So conditions were ripe for Buddha's teachings to take root and flower in the West.

Hear and Now

"Do not see the full realization in one teaching, one phenomena, one body, one land, or one sentient being. You should see the full realization everywhere, in all places."

—The Buddha

The Parliament

The turning point was the World Parliament of Religions, held in 1893, in conjunction with the Chicago World's Fair. Zen Master Soen Shaku was there, accompanied by D. T. Suzuki, Nyogen Senzaki, and Shaku Sokatsu, each to become important American Buddhist pioneers. Representatives of Jodo Shinshu, Nicheren, Tendai, and Shingon were also there. And Anagarika Dharmapala, founder of the Maha Bodhi Society, from Ceylon, delivered a key address.

The vast, placid mind of the Buddha had now come alive beneath the wide open skies of America. Like a stone cast in a lake, the ripples would ring outward, touching the farthest shores.

Seasons and Lunar Phases Conducive for Growth

National cultivation of Buddhism is like individual cultivation on a larger scale. Certain conditions need to be present. Peace is an important element, as is survival.

Hear and Now

"Possibly the impression gained in India from the reception of its representatives in Chicago may be correct, viz., that there is great religious unrest among us, and a growing dissatisfaction with Christianity, that people are longing for another more satisfying faith, and that the present is a most favorable time for the dissemination of Buddhistic views. ... It may be well to take a fresh and, if we can, impartial review of Buddhism ... and to inquire seriously—Shall we all become Buddhists?"

—Henry Melville King, Pastor, First Baptist Church of Providence

A Time for Peace, a Time for War

Peace is composed of nonpeace elements. The first Buddhist king, King Ashoka, is said to have come to Buddhism after his bloodiest battle. At the start of the twentieth century, World War I (1914–1918) put traditional values to the test. As disillusioned soldiers returned back home with dangerous, never-before-seen shell shock, intellectuals of the time were confronted with a call for a reevaluation of all values.

Then, as the second World War extended to Asia, many Asian women who happened to be Buddhist married Western soldiers and brought their traditions with them to their new homes. And many veterans who'd never seen chopsticks before studied Asian languages and such on their G.I. Bill.

The war was a particular tragedy for Japanese Americans. Following Pearl Harbor, Buddhist priests were the first Japanese Americans to be interned, and placed in prisoner-of-war camps. Of over 120,000 Japanese Americans interned in civilian camps during the war, half were Buddhists, mostly Jodo Shinsho (which renamed itself "Buddhist Churches of America" following the experience, reflecting their realization of the need for American assimilation). Some, forbidden to return to the west coast, established temples on the east coast.

Various foreign political upheavals have also played a role in American Buddhism. Some see American Buddhism as a phoenix arising out of ashes of foreign wars and genocides. Vipassana teacher S. N. Goenka, for instance, left Burma due to the 1960 socialist coup, which in turn gave him an unexpected audience of devoted students in the West. Living in political exile from his native Vietnam, Zen master, pacifist, and poet Thich Nhat Hanh never intended on becoming a spiritual teacher in the

West. Seeking religious freedom, numerous Tibetan teachers have come West where Tibetan Buddhism is developing a large lay following, unlike back home.

Kindred Rebels: Transcendentalists and Beats

Just as wars are cyclic occurrences, so do certain ideas keep cropping up over time. It's curious that in both the 1850s and 1950s, a relatively tiny group of writers would exert such a large influence on American culture. Each group was rebellious against the "Boston Brahmins" or "the Establishment" of their day. They were self-reliant, yet they looked to the ancient East for news.

Winter, 1846: A young American watches as the ice of Walden Pond is being broken up into huge blocks, for export to India. His name: Henry David Thoreau (1817–1862). Okay, if India would drink at his well, he figured, then he'll drink at theirs.

So he reads Hinduism and Buddhism under the New England trees, an influence very clearly expressed in his writings. And in the writings of Emerson, and of Walt Whitman. And of those who, in turn, read them.

Flash forward. Winter, 1953: An ex-collegiate football star named Jack Kerouac (1922–1969) reads Thoreau's *Walden,* which inspires him to go to the library to read more about Indian spirituality. As he begins to find his voice as a writer and as a spiritual seeker, he rewrites the life of the Buddha in his own words. His journals of this time flip-flop back and forth between Buddha and his own life saga.

Kerouac is in the audience when six poets hold a reading of their work in 1955 that would mark the beginning of the Beat Movement. Of those six, four were or would become Buddhists: Allen Ginsberg, Philip Whalen, Gary Snyder, and Michael McClure. In 1958, the year after Kerouac publishes *On the Road* and becomes a celebrity, he follows it with a novel entitled *The Dharma Bums.* On the cover: a drawing of a man seated cross-legged in meditation.

Hear and Now

"Perhaps indeed the efforts of the true poets, founders, religions, literatures, all ages, have been, and ever will be, our time and times to come, essentially the same—to bring people back from their persistent strayings and sickly abstractions to the costless average, divine, original concrete."

—Walt Whitman

Give Peace a Chance: The Sixties and Beyond

In the timeline I've posted online (bodhi.to/timeline.html), when you get to the 1960s things start clicking like a geiger counter near uranium. Alongside civil rights, Earth Day, holistic health, organic food, martial arts, popular psychology, feminism, and quarks—the East, including Buddhism, makes major appearances in the West. Yet the spiritual transformations of the sixties were eclipsed by more noticeable manifestations, neatly summed up by its three poster children: sex and drugs and rock 'n' roll. Upon reflection, these could be seen as outcroppings of a deeper seismic shift of worldview taking place. Women who could take control of their bodies with the availability of contraception (like the Pill) could also more viably undertake a quest for enlightenment, for example.

Rock 'n' roll and spirituality? For the first time, American youth was suddenly thrust in the role of consumer. Rock culture captured an audience as big as North America, because kids could buy their own music. So when George Harrison made a spiritual pilgrimage to India, then brought over the other three Beatles, suddenly anything Indian was in—yoga, incense, patchouli oil, sitar music, Transcendental Meditation, and ... on quiet feet, Buddha.

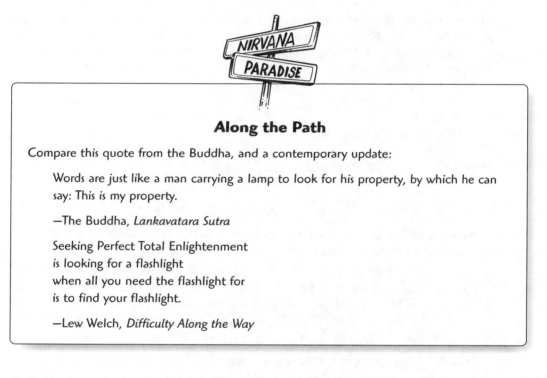

Along the Path

Compare this quote from the Buddha, and a contemporary update:

> Words are just like a man carrying a lamp to look for his property, by which he can say: This is my property.

—The Buddha, *Lankavatara Sutra*

> Seeking Perfect Total Enlightenment
> is looking for a flashlight
> when all you need the flashlight for
> is to find your flashlight.

—Lew Welch, *Difficulty Along the Way*

Drugs? Like rock, drugs were no longer confined to marginal subcultures, and they, too, reflected spiritual impulse. One survey found over half of white baby-boomer Buddhists had come to the path following chemical experimentation, now ready to discipline themselves to access their minds without psychedelics. (*Psychedelic* means "mind manifesting.")

But like I say, these events upstaged even deeper changes more quietly taking place. Consider how many Buddhist meditation temples opened during this period. Only two percent of the thousand or more flourishing today were in existence before 1964. In that decade, by 1975, the number had multiplied fivefold.

One more thing about the sixties. In 1965 the national quota system for immigrants was cast aside. This quietly signaled the beginning of what would become a steady inflow of Asian newcomers to America that continues today. In my home state of California, at the dawn of the twenty-first century, where whites count for only half the population, Asians and Pacific Islanders make up a healthy 12 percent. Of the three to four million Buddhists estimated in America at the dawn of the millennium, 800,000 were white, plus or minus. So let's examine American Buddhism next in terms of who brought what to the banquet.

Gardeners in the Fields of the Buddha

Just as a transplant needs a gardener, so does Buddhism depend on people for propagation. Following is a look at some footprints of American Buddhist pioneers: pilgrims from the East; pilgrims from the West; interpreters, translators, and scholars; and living teachers.

Leaves from the Bodhi Tree

Among numerous cases of "discovery" of North America before Christopher Columbus, we must consider Buddhist monk Hu Shen, who sailed here from China in ... 499 C.E.! He named our continent "Fusheng" after the Chinese name for the maguey plant (agave). It's likely he landed in Mexico. But he stayed 40 years, trekking through forests and across mountains and deserts and even seeing a huge canyon with bands of color along its sides and a river at the bottom (the Grand Canyon, perhaps?). Next question: Was he a fluke, or might there not have been other similar explorers from China, unrecorded?

Eastern Pilgrims Come to America

At the gates of that huge train station known as New York stands the Statue of Liberty, who proclaims "Welcome to Hotel California!" China had its own nickname for the United States, "Gold Mountain," after the Gold Rush of 1848. Many who undertook the long voyage wound up laying track for the transcontinental railroad, linking the east and west coasts. In 1853, they established America's first Chinese Buddhist temple, in San Francisco. Imagine: over in New England, Emerson and Thoreau were waxing rhapsodic about religious customs they'd never even seen first-hand (and sometimes mistaking Hindu with Buddhist), while literally hundreds of

Chinese temples were springing up in California like mushrooms after a good rain, some with Buddhist priests, others with Taoist masters or Confucian scholars. Then America passed the Chinese Immigration Exclusion Act in 1882, denying any further immigration of Chinese workers. In 1888, the Act was extended to include Chinese women except merchants' wives. Gold Mountain suddenly became steeper than Mt. Everest.

Entrance to Kuan-yin Temple, Spofford Street, Chinatown, San Francisco, on a summer day sometime between 1895 and 1906. (Note that one gentleman wears a traditional hat while the others in the scene sport various snazzy Western brims.)

(Photography: Arnold Genthe)

Along the Path

Democracy means America is a living tradition. So American Buddhism's not an isolated object of scrutiny but rather a process, a work in progress, bringing together various forces, themselves in a state of flux. When we say "American Buddhism," we mean Asian Americans who've carried Buddhist traditions across the Pacific, transplanted them to the New World, now beginning their second century of practice. When we say "American Buddhism," we also mean European Americans who've taken to Buddhism along with or in place of Christianity or Judaism. Each has a distinct culture. All are American.

In 1899, two Japanese priests came to support the 10,000 Japanese living in America, many resistant to conversion to Christianity. These two became America's first permanent resident Buddhist clergy, whose flock today (now called the Buddhist Churches of America) numbers roughly 20,000 members.

In 1924, a national immigration act limited the annual quota of immigrants from any country to 2 percent of the number of individuals born in that country and resident in the United States in 1890. The relaxation of immigration restrictions in 1965 resulted in a tide of Asians coming to North America. Rural North Americans, for example, are being surprised to discover acreage adjacent to their farms being bought and settled by monks in orange robes. The following table gives a sense of the rise of just Theravada Buddhists in America since 1965.

Theravada Buddhists in America

	1960	1971–1980	1981–1990
Immigrants in the United States from Thailand, Laos, and Kampuchea	6,313	105,770	613,887

Western Pilgrims

Early Western pilgrims to the East were like advance scouts returning to our campfires to tell us what they'd seen over the mountain ranges. Russian noblewoman Madame Helena Blavatsky (1831–1891) teamed up with Colonel Henry Steel Olcott (1832–1906) and founded the Theosophical Society in 1875. They travelled in south and southeast Asia from 1879 to 1884. In Ceylon, in 1880, she and Olcott became the first Europeans to formally take vows of Theravadan Buddhism. But it wasn't until 1966 that the Theravada tradition she'd discovered would have a home in America, with the establishment of the Washington Buddhist Vihara, in Washington, D.C. All good things all in good time.

In 1923, Alexandra David-Neel (1868–1969), well-versed in Sanskrit, became the first European woman to enter Tibet's forbidden city of Lhasa. She stayed in Tibet for 14 years. Her subsequent books helped somewhat to dispel the romantic myths spun by the fiction of James Hilton, Talbot Mundy, and H. Rider Haggard. One of her visitors there, Ernst Lothar Hoffmann, stayed in Tibet, India, Ceylon, Burma, and Sikkim, as Lama Anagarika Govinda, later becoming a venerated teacher in the West. It would take another half-century before Tibetan teachers would establish their own bases in the West.

In the late 1960s and early 1970s, veterans of the U.S. Peace Corps returned from South Asia, sharing their inspiration with their peers, and fueled a subsequent wanderlust for trekking to India, Burma, Thailand, and Ceylon. Stephen Batchelor, Daniel Goleman, Joseph Goldstein, Jack Kornfield, Ram Dass, Wes Nisker, Sharon Salzberg, and Lama Surya Das are among the more famous Western pilgrims who've since brought back home and taught what they learned over there.

Meanwhile, in Japan, following World War II, a few priests were surprised to discover a couple of white pilgrims coming to their temples requesting instruction in zen. The priests agreed to teach them, on the condition that no concessions be made for cultural differences. One of them was poet-ecologist-anthropologist Gary Snyder (fictionalized in *The Dharma Bums* as Japhy Ryder), who practiced zen in Kyoto from about 1956 to 1966. Philip Kapleau was a war crimes reporter in Japan in 1953 who returned and studied zen for 13 years. His book *Three Pillars of Zen* was the first doorway into living zen for thousands of Westerners.

Interpreters, Translators, and Scholars

Translation of teachings was always a key factor in the dissemination of Buddhism throughout Asia. It's equally essential for Westerners, who often can't read a foreign menu without a trained diplomatic interpreter (also known as a waiter). Thoreau officially published the first American translation of a Buddhist sutra in 1844, giving the wheel another turn West.

Hear and Now

"... looking deep, he saw ... / How lizard fed on ant, and snake on him, / And kite on both; and how the fish-hawk robbed / The fish-tiger of that which it had seized; / The shrike chasing the bulbul, which did chase / The jeweled butterflies: till everywhere / Each slew a slayer and in turn was slain, / Life living upon death. ... / The Prince Siddhartha sighed."

—*The Light of Asia*, Edwin Arnold (1892)

Sir Edwin Arnold (1832–1904) gave the wheel a big spin. No Eastern linguist, yet he penned a book-length retelling in Victorian verse of the life and teachings of the Buddha titled *The Light of Asia*. Published in 1879, it went through 80 editions, selling upward of a million copies, making Buddhism a household word. Arnold went on to mobilize like-minded souls to help restore such venerated sites as the Bodhi Tree, in Bodh Gaya, which had become a trash heap when Buddhism waned. In so doing, leading white Buddhists of the day came to know each other, forming more of a context for their individual Eastern endeavors. Along with Buddha and Dharma, the West was learning the virtues and values of Sangha.

It wouldn't be until after World War II that American universities would include serious programs for intensive study in Chinese and Sanskrit. Some compare that turning point to the impact of the rediscovery of Greek and Roman art upon the European Renaissance, a romantic notion perhaps, but one which bears at least a grain or two of truth.

We may be experiencing just the beginning of such a second renaissance. A 1995 survey of over 675 faculty members at over eleven academic institutions revealed 59 proficient in Sanskrit and 43 in its cousin Pali; 49 proficient in Japanese, 37 in Chinese; 33 know Tibetan, and 2 Korean. I remember, when I received my own baccalaureate degree, learning how it carried traditions that hailed from thirteenth-century monks. Buddhist teachers in academia today could thus be considered an American Buddhist monastic tradition of sorts. By 1997, at least 850 academic dissertations and theses were on file dealing with Buddhism.

And let's not forget Naropa Institute. Founded in 1974 by Chögyam Trungpa Rinpoche, Naropa now occupies four acres near the Rocky Mountains. Besides continuing education students, it has several hundred candidates studying for a range of BA, MA, and MFA degrees, from Buddhist Studies to Writing and Literature. More recent Buddhist or Eastern-oriented colleges in North America include California Institute of Integral Studies, Hsi Lai University, Institute for World Religions, and Soka University of America.

Hear and Now

"Sometimes we think it is impossible for us to understand something unfamiliar, but actually there is nothing that is unfamiliar to us. ... Of course Buddhism cannot be separated from its cultural background; this is true. But ... I am living in your cultural background .... I am communicating with you in your language. Even though you do not understand me completely, I want to understand you. And I may understand you better than anyone who can speak and understand English."

—Shunryu Suzuki

Living Teachers

By the dawn of the new millennium, Buddhism in the West had arrived at an interesting point in its evolution. At first, all anyone knew was theoretical, usually book learning, often in difficult translation. Then seekers journeyed East and found teachers who were living expressions of the Way. Next, Eastern teachers themselves came West, and many more people began to entertain sustained practice and see for themselves what the Buddha had meant. (I'd first read of zen and zen practice in 1958, but it was a dozen years before I met Dainin Katagiri Roshi, bless his heart, who first showed me correct sitting technique.) And now former Western students of such Eastern teachers on Western soil have gone on to become teachers themselves, to new generations of Western seekers, both now speaking the same language. Very interesting.

Founder of the San Francisco Zen Center and of the first Zen monastery in the West, and author of Zen Mind, Beginner's Mind, Shunryu Suzuki Roshi (1904–1971) has been arguably the single-most influential figure in the adoption of Zen practice in America. Maybe his smile will begin to tell you why.

(Photo: Robert S. Boni)

For the record, historically, Eastern teachers arrived in three waves to European Americans in the twentieth century. First, the 1920s marked the rise of insight (vipassana) meditation in the West. Then zen became popular, beginning in the early 1960s. Shunryu Suzuki Roshi headed the San Francisco Zen Center, and Hakuyu Taizan Maezumi Roshi helmed the Zen Center of Los Angeles. A decade later, Tibetan Buddhism came to the fore, with teachers Chögyam Trungpa and Tarthang Tulku a prominent part of the first wave.

Would you buy a used car from this man? I sure would! Only he's not selling anything. (Not anything!) His name's Robert Aitken Roshi (Roshi, meaning Zen Master), and he's arguably America's oldest living European American Buddhist teacher—and timeless.

(Photo: Tom Haar)

Buddhists and Buddhist Groups at the Dawn of the New Millennium

Country	Buddhists	European/ American Buddhists	Centers	Population	Percent Buddhists
USA	3–4M	800,000	500–800	261M	1.6
Australia	140,000	14,000	150	18M	0.8
South Africa	5,000	2,500	40	42M	0.01
Great Britain	180,000	50,000	300	58M	0.01
France	650,000	150,000	130	58M	1.15
Germany	150,000	40,000	400	81M	0.2
Italy	75,000	50,000	30	57M	0.1
Switzerland	20–25,000	?	80	7M	0.3
Netherlands	20,000	5,000	40	15M	0.1
Denmark	8,000	5,000	32	5M	0.16
Austria	13,000	5,000	25	8M	0.16
Hungary	6,000	6,000	12	10M	0.07
Czech Republic	2,000	2,000	15	10M	0.02
Poland	4,500	4,000	15	38M	0.01
Russia	1M	40,000	100	149M	0.7

Hot Buttons and Cool Breezes

Today, Buddha's roots are over two and a half millennia old, and continuing. Buddhism's like that fig tree beloved for sheltering the Buddha in the forest. It grows broad roots that support long branches. And it renews itself by planting those long branches in the soil and using them as new roots. Those branches now extend as far as the Mediterranean, Europe, and the Americas. Conditions for Buddhism's flowering in the West have proven very, very good: fertile soil, receptive environment, loving gardeners tending the shoots and sprouts of the new roots.

To survive, Buddhism has always had to adapt to native conditions. It's too soon to predict what the outcome might be. But in the dance between tradition and change, Western Buddhism has thus far manifested a number of distinguishing issues and themes: acculturation, feminism, egalitarianism, integration into daily life, ethnicity, and ecumenism (the movement for greater dialogue and cooperation between religious groups). As is customarily the case in Buddhism, each component intertwines with the others.

Along the Path

"Many Westerners have gotten involved in the chopsticks, tatami mats, flower arrangements, green tea, etc., thinking them to be Zen. This is a terrible shame. The Japanese made use of their own forms to express meditation, and there is just as much Zen in golf or car driving or jogging. ... We must let Zen permeate our daily lives, not graft on a foreign artificial lifestyle. Remember the Buddha did not eat with chopsticks and never in his whole life chanted in Japanese."

—Jitsudo Baran and Isan Sacco

Foreign vs. Domestic

Imagine an American Buddhist truck driver or barber—why not?! Defining a New World Dharma, many American Buddhists rightfully question whether they're attracted to exoticism, a pasture seemingly greener because it's on the other side of the fence. But Buddha shows there's no fence, no "other," no dualism. So why not a baseball cap?

And how much dogma and foreign ritual is necessary? A certain amount of ritual seems appropriate in any sustained spiritual path. American Buddhist monks and nuns at Shasta Abbey, for instance, eat on tables instead of on the floor, replace the Japanese tea ceremony with English tea, and chant Gregorian-style rather than in Japanese. Out in the world, they wear Christian ecclesiastical robes. Yet they maintain the Asian custom of bowing, and some reportedly have even bowed at almost anything, breaking down Me-Me self and learning to see everything as buddha. (Try it: It works. And once you get it, every act can be an act of bowing, too.)

Buddhism doesn't just adapt to host cultures. A host culture has often gone back and reinstated elements from the original teachings that they had once customized to fit native correspondences, as was the case of Chinese monks who went west on the Silk Route, to India to bring back original texts. But ultimately there's an interplay in America between dressing Buddha in blue jeans and recognizing the unchanging virtues of his teachings and practices. Could you pick out an American Buddhist in a crowd? One school of thought suggests that Buddha mind is everyday mind: no need to wear robes if you actualize the truth in your daily life, whoever you are.

Women Buddhas: Gender Equity

In the Buddha's time, it was forbidden for women (and slaves) to read Hindu scriptures, nor could women pray on their own. In defiance of the Brahmins, the Buddha ordained nuns, albeit after much hand-wringing, starting with his own stepmother and then his former wife. (Don't ask who wrung whose hand.) His order of nuns is one of the earliest women's associations in the world. Today, an international association exists called Sakyadhita, which networks women practitioners, supports their studies, and fosters ordination of women. (*Sakyadhita* means "daughters of the Buddha.")

Hear and Now

"Part of Buddhism's appeal is that it has this extraordinary flexibility and non-dogmatism. And so it doesn't contradict science. It doesn't come into opposition with other beliefs. And that's one of its great fortes, and one of the reasons we see it moving through cultures so easily and without violence. It draws heavily on self-reliance, on independence, on personal experience. These are all of the most cherished ideals of America."

—Helen Tworkov

There are now dozens of American women Buddhist priests and teachers. Women also seem to have a great eye for picking up on social imbalances, perhaps in part due to their historic exclusion from so many situations of power themselves. So it's no surprise that contemporary women have been critical of abuse of power in Buddhist sanghas and dealt with it appropriately. Women have often replaced hierarchical models with more communalist approaches, sharing power with a free flow of responsibilities and roles back and forth from periphery to center. Which brings us to democracy.

The Cherry Blossom Grafted onto the Hickory: Buddhist Democracy

Under the skies of America, the premise of democracy is that everyone can make their own choices about their lives. Buddhism is similarly predicated on the idea that every being can perfect itself. All beings are created equal. All beings are endowed with the right to life, liberty, and the pursuit of happiness. All beings carry the seeds of their own enlightenment.

Hear and Now

"As Buddhism comes to North America, a wonderful process is happening. All of us, as lay people, as householders, want what was mostly the special dispensation of monks in Asia: the real practice of the Buddha. American lay people are not content to go and hear a sermon once a week or to make merit by leaving gifts at a meditation center. We, too, want to *live* the realizations of the Buddha and bring them into our hearts, our lives, and our times."

—Jack Kornfield

Just as Buddhism appeals to the democratic spirit, Buddhism has strong appeal to the Yankee spirit of self-reliance and experiment. (When I think of self-reliance, not only Emerson's essay of the same name comes to mind, but also Frank Sinatra saying, "Don't tell me—suggest it to me!") If you want to do breathing meditation, fine; presumably, you know how to breathe. Not a problem! And Buddhism's adaptability is suited to the American workbench, seeing as we're a nation of tinkerers, continually inventing and reinventing ourselves as well as stuff.

Buddhism balances a dynamic between authority (the teachings) and egalitarianism (the community). How will Americans innovate our own forms of organization, apart from the "gentle authoritarianism" common in Asia? While some people may want to all face one master, others will prefer to all face in the same direction, teaching and learning from each other. We'll continue awakening, whether in formal temples or in a neighbor's living room, which brings us to the next element ...

Along the Path

A survey was conducted following an American Buddhist retreat. European Americans tended to say the retreat calmed them or made them feel better about themselves. Asian Americans tended to say that they came away humbled or with shame at not having done enough for their mother or father. The difference was interpreted to underscore a cultural difference: European Americans tend to be more self-oriented individualists, whereas Asians tend to be more collectively minded, subordinate to family and community.

Hear and Now

"In Europe, intellectualism takes precedence over tradition; in the East it is the reverse. In Dharma terms, the European has an excess of *panna* (intelligence) over *saddha* (faith), and he tends to reject what he cannot understand even if it is true; the [Asian] has an excess of *saddha* over *panna*, which leads him to accept anything ancient, even if it is false."

—Nanavira (1963)

Integration into Everyday Life

Another characteristic of American Buddhism is the blurring of traditional lines of lay and monastic life. Monastic practices can be integrated into everyday life that includes homes and families and jobs. And conversely, many American sanghas bypass monastic celibacy and allow a member to maintain a family life, plus hold an outside job, while still undergoing the full course of training of a monk or nun.

Emphasis on the laity could bear potential danger to the stability which a monastic tradition confers. And this might be one reason why many Buddhist centers pack up their tents and fold, lacking a strong succession of monastic teachers and administrators. There's a lesson to be shared between "convert" Buddhists (European Americans) and "ethnic" Buddhists (Asian Americans). Asian American Buddhist temples are now entering their second century in America. One reason for the stability of the latter is their emphasis on community and continuity, which European Americans are often still discovering. This brings us to two final issues to examine as American Buddhism makes a way for itself: ethnicity and ecumenism.

Ethnicity

Race matters. Race is, indeed, a koan in the American experience. Thus, concerned people of color have been forming study groups and sanghas to deal with racism, and white folks are taking workshops to explore their own mindsets toward racism. Buddhism seems to provide an appropriate lens with which to view and understand and heal the scars of racism. Not only the wounds of being conditioned to treat oneself as less than human, but also the wounds of internalizing that racism toward others.

It's also worth noting that for many Asian Americans, Buddhist liberation has had a unique connotation of freedom from racism. Conversely, born-again Buddhist European Americans need to recognize that they didn't exactly discover Buddha. So an evolving North American Buddhism will necessarily be nourished by the cultural traditions of Buddhists of any color and culture, red, white, yellow, and brown. And purple! (For more on this topic, as well as gender equity and other matters, see Chapter 19, "Happiness Is Not an Individual Matter: Engaging the World.")

As Buddhism develops into a mainstream religion in America, it draws forth a diversity of trailblazers. The first African-American Indo-Tibetan scholar, Jan Willis, has personal insight into Buddhism's answers to the koans of diversity and its potent medicine for healing the wounds of race. Like a Buddha, she offers her findings to all who need.

(Photo: Marlies Bosch)

Ecumenism

Americans are used to having seven brands of soap from which to choose. For better or worse, so too with spirituality. ("Attention, shoppers! Krishna's playing flute in Aisle 9!") But in Asia such religious pluralism can be as rare as an overweight postman. An average Buddhist in Burma might know relatively little about Lama Surya Das or Thich Nhat Hanh—that is, any Buddhism but their own. Only in the West do Theravada, Mahayana, and Vajrayana traditions co-exist side-by-side, not to mention mingle and even rub elbows with yoga and tai chi (Taoist yoga), Sufism and Kaballah … macrobiotics and Ayurveda (the 5,000-year-old science of healing originating in India). So long as technique isn't mistaken for committed practice, the occasion is historically unprecedented. And exciting.

Yet old habits die hard. Like tends to flock with like. New blind spots need to be filled in. Surveying Asian American Buddhist temples, one finds that Thai, Korean, Vietnamese, Burmese, Chinese, and Japanese Americans don't visit each other's temples all that much yet. Nor do whites and Asian Americans visit each other's temples in any appreciable way yet. It takes time, but also effort. We each have something to say to and learn from each other. An ethnic Middle Way awaits discovery. Buddha can show that way with consciousness and compassion.

So, following its spread across the eastern part of the planet, no new petals had blossomed from the Lotus for a thousand years. Yet when a plant makes a new flower, its other parts diminish their activities and contribute to the new creation. Now Buddha the Gardener has gotten his passport stamped and headed West, planting seeds, tending sprouts. This is a wonderful time.

Leaves from the Bodhi Tree

A Dharma teacher was leading her sangha one night when two newcomers entered the room. They'd probably heard about the group from a flyer. They were an Asian American couple, middle-aged. Whatever Buddhist upbringing they might have once had might possibly have lapsed with assimilation. Well, by the look on their faces they were clearly taken aback as they looked in and saw *a black woman in front of the sangha.* (Little did they know she herself hasd been raised in the south, without ever seeing white people, much less Asian Americans.) She glanced back with a look that said, 'So you've been away. Welcome back.'"

The Least You Need to Know

➤ The impact of the Buddha upon the West can be equated as of equal importance as that of Marx, Einstein, Darwin, and Freud.

➤ American Buddhism bears a unique, diverse history, unprecedented in Buddhism. It is destined to become a mainstream religion.

➤ American Buddhism includes Asian immigrants and European Americans, plus other ethnicities, all of whom have much to say to and learn from each other.

➤ American Buddhism brings a number of issues to the table, such as acculturation, feminism, integration into everyday life, ethnicity, and ecumenism.

Chapter 4

Different Travel Agents, Same Destination?: Interfaith

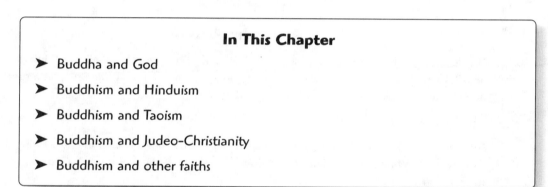

In This Chapter

➤ Buddha and God

➤ Buddhism and Hinduism

➤ Buddhism and Taoism

➤ Buddhism and Judeo-Christianity

➤ Buddhism and other faiths

King Ashoka's India was a model for spirit without borders. One reason Buddhism has been called "the gentlest religion" is that it has never forcibly converted anyone. Rather, it's very tolerant of different faiths and creeds. Such tolerance is crucial in our times, on all levels.

When I was a lad, "interfaith" meant maybe comparing Genesis 15 with Luke 1, Sarah and Mary, and, more practically, accommodating for marriages between Christians and Jews. Today, interfaith has come to mean a crucial dialogue—between societies, between ourselves and others, and within ourselves.

Beyond Ideology: Buddhism Isn't Exclusive

Earlier on, we stated how Buddhism isn't exactly a religion. Yet, because of its universal net effect spiritually, it does qualify as one. All religions maintain perennial values at their core. Neglect of these core values appears to be a direct cause of the illnesses now polluting families, cities, the world, the planet. Let's see how Buddhism figures in the religious mix.

We've looked at Buddhism as if it were an organism—not a fixed object but a living process. And so are all religions, in their way. Hang on to any fixed concept of them, you're left holding a shell without the juicy nutmeat. "Salvation" or "enlightenment," "prayer" or "Buddhism"—these are merely words. Husks. Shells. The Bible says, "O taste and see!" To appreciate difference, we must experience commonality. Otherwise, we're like the blind men confronting an elephant, each insistent that his point of view is the only one.

Along the Path

"By detachment from appearances, abide in real truth. I tell you, thus shall you think of all this fleeting world: a star at dawn, a bubble in a stream ... a flash of lightning in a summer cloud ... a flickering lamp, a phantom, a dream."

—Buddha, *Diamond Sutra 32*

"All flesh is grass, and all its beauty is like the flowers of the field. Grass withers, flowers fade, when the breath of the Lord blows upon them .... But the word of our God will stand forever."

—Isaiah 40:6–8

It's an exciting time to be alive. A diversity of healing and holy resources new and old is flourishing. Now, some religious leaders, even Buddhist, might tell you to shun all other paths. I think this is like a hospital asking your religion before surgery; kind of scary. (I like Joe Gould's answer: "In the summer, I'm a nudist; in the winter, I'm a Buddhist.") My question to myself is, instead, the very first thing when I wake up in the morning: "Who am I?" And the answer that invariably comes is that I don't know, but I'm awakening. (And the second thought? It's a good day. Be happy!)

Continuing a persistent medical metaphor, consider how many different *kinds* of remedies people turn to these days. It's not uncommon to find an herbal extract alongside a pharmaceutical in a medicine cabinet. What was once branded "alternative" is now just called "complementary medicine," as different modes complement each other, forming a whole, to heal the whole person. Both/and; not either/or. So it can be with the spiritual path. But whatever you practice, Buddhism, atheism, Islam, Christianity, Judaism, or just being a good person, practice it all the way.

Do Buddhists Believe in God?

Let's begin our survey by tackling the commonest stumbling block to Buddhism: God. But my answer's easy: The Buddha never said! So it's all up to you …

Is Metaphysics to Reality What Ornithology Is … for the Birds?

Buddhism has its metaphysics (abstract reasoning) but doesn't grasp after the First Cause of All Things, to settle once and for all such burning questions as "Do I have a soul?" "Is my soul immortal, or, if not, what kind of batteries does it take?" "Will my soul go to Heaven after I die?" and "If I do get to Heaven and dance for joy on the clouds, are you sure I won't fall through?" The Buddha simply remained mute to these kinds of questions. What did they further?

Hear and Now

"Aware of the suffering created by fanaticism and intolerance, we are determined not to be idolatrous about or bound to any doctrine, theory, or ideology, even Buddhist ones. Buddhist teachings are guiding means to help us learn to look deeply and to develop our understanding and compassion. They are not doctrines to fight, kill, or die for."

—*The Order of Interbeing.* First Mindfulness Training: Openness

Instead, the Buddha demonstrates a powerful way to pack up our sorrows. And he does so (as we'll see in detail in Part 2) independent of matters of eternity, infinity, and immortality. Those questions he felt don't really further anyone to ask; they're luxuries when more important matters are at hand.

In Chapter 1, "Why Is This Man Smiling?: The Buddha," I explained the Buddha's silence in terms of his parable of the man hit by a poisoned dart—he wastes precious time asking unanswerable questions when he could be removing the dart of suffering. A similar example I personally recall was when church attendance started dropping in the sixties, considerably, and theologians began what became known as The Death of God Debate. Graffiti neatly summed it up:

"Nietzsche said, 'God is dead.'"

"God said, 'Nietzsche is dead.'"

Ob-la-di, ob-la-da, life goes on.

The Buddha, on the other hand, explained his enlightenment in very scientific and pragmatic terms. To him, the existence or nonexistence of God has next to nothing to do with the fact that liberation from suffering is possible. Rather, the gold standard for judging his truth isn't theoretical but experiential, practical; what can be observed with your own two eyes and used in your own two hands.

If your experience in practicing Buddhism confirms your belief in something divinely sacred, then fine. (I remember how a rabbi with whom I once studied would call God "The Most High." At the time, I took this to mean the highest anyone can conceive of when on the highest peak of awareness. Worked for me.) And if you're an atheist, the Buddha doesn't ask you to believe in what to you may be like the tooth fairy. Buddhist meditation puts you in touch with the heart of creation; whether or not that's the same as the heart of your creator is up to you.

Deities and Heaven and Reincarnations

Someone once asked Ananda K. Coomaraswamy, curator of Indian art at the Boston Museum of Fine Arts, why God allowed for the existence of evil in the world, and he replied, "To complicate the plot!" So, just to complicate the plot, or anticipate any subsequent confusion, let me note that sooner or later along the Buddhist path, you're going to encounter what appear to be various deities, as well as heavens and reincarnations, and all that.

"Aha!" some wary skeptics might snicker from the back row. "Buddhists believe in angels in Heaven!" Well, yes and no. Buddhism picked up a good deal from Indian culture of the day, when a thought was frequently regarded as a spirit. (Indeed, sometimes I myself wonder where my thoughts come from, and so does my editor!) So, for example, after the Buddha became enlightened under the Bodhi Tree, some say that he was going to sit there forever until a deity appeared and debated with him whether he should stay put or get up and share. Some people treat Buddhist deities as anthropomorphic embodiments of real ideas or ideals.

Similarly, you can take Buddhist pictures of paradise, such as the "Western Realm" or "Pure Land," as an actual hereafter. Or you can see it, as I do, as also meaning paradise here and now; the Kingdom of Spirit within each of us; our own minds, purified of petty slaveries. And likewise for traditional Buddhist cycles of rebirths: actual reincarnations? or spiritual rebirth within the same lifetime? the progression from one unique moment to the next? Again, it's your call. Remember: Buddhism is the Middle Way. No divisiveness.

So—having seen how Buddhism operates on a plane apart from ideology and theology, let's look at the interaction, the Middle Way, between the Buddha and major faiths of East and West.

Leaves from the Bodhi Tree

Someone meeting the Buddha once asked, "Are you a god?"

He said, "No."

"Are you an angel?"

"No."

"Then what are you?"

"Awake."

Roots: Bringing It All Back Home

We've seen how "American Buddhism" doesn't mean one single thing. There are many Buddhisms, as there are many Americans. And Buddhism is being influenced by America, just as America is being influenced by the Buddha. Similarly, our appreciation of the Buddha deepens by exploring his Asian spiritual roots.

Buddha Came from India: Hinduism and Yoga

Buddha was from India. So naturally he had affinities with Hinduism and yoga, and Indian culture in general. Let's look at the culture, then the yoga.

Indian Culture

Indian culture is like being Jewish or Italian: as hard to change as a zebra its stripes. One Indian cultural component influencing the Buddha which we've already touched on is karma, a kind of moral cause and effect. Everything we think or do is bound up in a larger web of interactivity. You'll often hear karma referred to in terms of cycles of rebirths: You're the product of all the karma of your past, or past lives. (If you can't remember what you had for breakfast, then maybe that might as well have been a past life.)

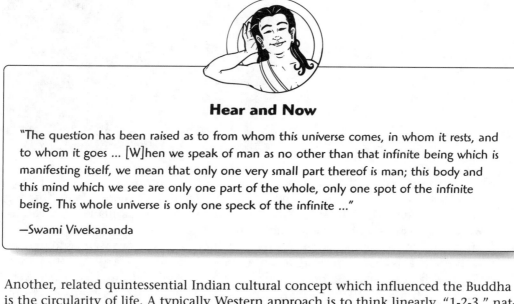

Hear and Now

"The question has been raised as to from whom this universe comes, in whom it rests, and to whom it goes ... [W]hen we speak of man as no other than that infinite being which is manifesting itself, we mean that only one very small part thereof is man; this body and this mind which we see are only one part of the whole, only one spot of the infinite being. This whole universe is only one speck of the infinite ..."

—Swami Vivekananda

Another, related quintessential Indian cultural concept which influenced the Buddha is the circularity of life. A typically Western approach is to think linearly, "1-2-3," naturally predisposed to mechanistic thinking, "insert big toe into Slot B and twist," therefore and thusly. Our primal symbols of life's unfolding include the procession, the chain, the ladder, and this month's credit card bill. In India, the wheel is an archetypal symbol of cyclic rather than linear thought. The seed which becomes a flower will decay into mulch in order to fertilize a new seed. Round and round we go, as with a merry-go-round or a spinning top. And it makes for playful thinking.

While Western traditions view the universe as a measurable thing—God's *creation*, signed in the lower right-hand corner—in Indian culture the universe is more of a play. A performance, a dance! Life's a ballroom, and we and everything around us are produced by a never-ending cosmic dance of the gods boogying with themselves and us, intermingled. So life is a big square dance, where dancers get mixed and reshuffled, do-si-do your partners. Hide-and-seek: peek-a-boo! In a sense, it's like the limitless, undifferentiated God of the Hebrews creating our universe and us humans so that He might know Himself in us. (And, now and then, a word from our sponsor ...)

The Hindu vision of the universe as a playful and fluid process is epitomized in the dance of the god Shiva. He dances on the back of ignorance, dances the world into existence, maintaining it in a ring of fire, transforming it, destroying its illusions only to create it all over again. Olé!

(Photo: Archaeological Survey of India)

Hindu shorthand for this principle is "thou art that." A mighty concept to contemplate. Since we're part of one cosmic dance or dream of the gods, everything we see is but foam and wave of the same vast ocean of which we're all made up. So although we identify with our masks and roles in the stirring pageant (or soap opera) we call life, we're also part of a greater, cosmic unfoldment—the universe playing peek-a-boo with itself. This theme crops up again with the idea that we're all buddhas, only we don't know it yet (such idiots we mortals be!), until we wake up to our place in the process of truth. A variant you'll also hear is that everyday reality mirrors cosmic reality. So when you're hungry, eat. When you're tired, sleep. Buddha nature is as ordinary as that. And, conversely, an ordinary radish is a messenger of the cosmos.

Against that background, however, we still find Buddha disagreeing with Brahmanism. The Buddha rejected the caste system, priestly power, animal sacrifice, and image worship. (There is no higher power than innate, fully realized buddha nature.) In a word, where Buddhism and Hinduism seem to fundamentally diverge is over "self." Hinduism seeks to realize the innate union between the inner self (*atman*), one's unique essence; and the Overself—the transpersonal, eternal Self (*brahman*), the source and essence of reality. But to Buddha the ultimate reality is "no self" ("*an-atman*," "*an*" in Sanskrit being like our prefix "un-"). Self is a fiction called ego, getting caught up in and identifying with our moment in the soap opera. Addicted to the drama. ("Don't touch that dial! We'll be back with scenes from next week's all-new episode—starring … you!")

More on this in Chapter 8, "The Fine Print: Touching Deeper." For now, frankly, I'd say the difference between higher self and un-self may be largely bureaucratic and semantic. You'll hear talk of "big mind" in Buddhism, and "selflessness" in Hinduism, so hey! Coca Cola, Classic Coke, and the Un-Cola are all soda pop. Different travel itineraries and connecting flights to the same place. The proof is in the pudding—the experiential, the practical. Now that the West provides a lab for Buddhism and *Yoga* to formally coexist side-by-side as equals, many report sliding from Buddha to yoga, yoga to Buddha, without having to check any sense of self or nonself at the door.

This Is

Yoga means yoking, much as "religion" means tying. (It's the same word as in Matthew 11:29–30: "Take my yoke upon you … my yoke is easy and my burden light.") Here the yoking is discipline, training. Yoga is one of the six schools of classical Hinduism. Paths of yoga include *jnana* yoga, the path of knowledge; *bhakti* yoga, the path of love; *karma* yoga, the path of deeds; and *raja* yoga, the path of meditation. Physical and breathing exercises are *hatha* yoga.

Yoga

Remember, too, Buddha was a yogi. Not just any yogi but a Grandmaster Level-Ten Yogi. When he went off into the forest, he studied yoga with two leading masters of his time and took their teachings to the limit. But still he wasn't satisfied, and went off in his own direction. Around two centuries after his death, a man named Patanjali first codified Hindu yoga teachings and techniques: His yoga system or schema was an eight-spoked wheel, curiously mirroring Buddha's eightfold path (discussed in Chapter 6, "Taking Steps: The Eightfold Path").

Indeed, Buddhism and yoga are parallel paths with various intersections. Both emphasize nonattachment and nondualism, taming the mind and seeking liberation. When we see the Buddha sitting in the *lotus position* (cross-legged, feet resting on the opposite thighs, soles upwards), it's a basic yoga position (*padmasana*). Just as yoga offers meditation on breathing (*pranayama*), so does the Buddha devote an entire sutra to breathing. And Buddhism has its own particular yogic techniques.

Remember, too, how the Middle Way opened up for the Buddha when he ended his fasting, realizing his body was the mothership without which he couldn't attain anything, much less enlightenment. (Except as some disembodied busybody, at best.) This acceptance of the body is quite a relief for those whose spirituality has urged them to abandon the body, as an evil vessel, in order to attain higher, purer realms. (Speaking of purer, let's not forget that America's Puritan roots include an ascetic heritage that denies the body.) The Buddha's Middle Way affords the splendid opportunity to engage life with body and soul, head and heart, as one.

In utterly practical terms, yoga makes a great warm-up for Buddhist meditation. At minimum, a series of four or five basic yoga postures (*asanas*) can do wonders to loosen muscles and tendons before sitting (as illustrated in Chapter 10, "Base Camp: Meditation Basics"). Sitting regularly for as little as a half-hour can be demanding of neck and knees, for example, two anatomic features that haven't changed a heck of lot since we redistributed our weight from four legs to two. And when withheld energy starts flowing during meditation, it's wise to be bodily grounded, lest (*yikes!*) blue sparks start flying out of the top of your head.

And Buddhism makes a great addition to yoga. While yoga includes meditation, many yogis are sliding across the hall to Buddhist meditation workshops, to open their wisdom eye (that is, to see deeply and understand). So, many yoga *ashrams* (the Hindu name for a gathering of disciples) and Buddhist centers offer courses in both practices. (Further yogic influences can be found in Tibetan Buddhist practices. See Chapter 13, "Paths of Devotion and Transformation: Pure Land and Vajrayana Buddhism.")

China's Version 1.0: Buddhism + Taoism

Of the four great civilizations of the ancient world—Egypt, Greece, India, and China—two are wedded ... by Buddha. As we noted in Chapter 2, "One Taste, Different Flavors: The Teachings Adapt to Different Lands," when Buddhism first came to China it found an initial toehold there due to its similarities with Taoism. Indeed, if you were to read just one non-Buddhist book for ecumenical, interfaith awareness, hands-down I'd say it would be the *Tao Te Ching* (pronounced *dow deh jing*), a mere 5,000 words in Chinese.

There's a clear, fundamental identity shared between Tao and Zen. It's as if zen is a child born of the marriage of Indian Buddhism and Chinese Taoism. Both Zen and Tao are imbued with the spontaneity and playfulness of a newborn kitten, the intuitive wisdom of finding the light switch in the dark, the commonplace simplicity of a glass of water, and the completeness of swallowing the whole world, in a single gulp.

Taoism holds that 1) what's ultimately real is that which never changes, the one thing beyond realms of contingency and form, and is called the Tao, the Way; and 2) we're each a part of this reality, through our innate, individual character. One way to realize our connection to the Tao would be through *tso wang*, sitting with blank mind, forgetting our transient self, and finding *hsin tsung*—the heart within the heart, the mind of the mind, the still point within the turning world, the ground of our consciousness in cosmic process. This idea of perfecting the self through selflessness is similar to the Hindu yoking (*yoga*) of *Atman* and *Brahman*, and the technique is very similar to the Buddhist practice of sitting meditation to reach innate "buddha nature," "buddha mind."

Like Zen, the Tao is beyond words, and any attempt to pigeonhole it is to miss the point. To speak of the Tao is not the Tao. Or, as Louis Armstrong said of jazz, "If you got to ask, you'll never get it." Yet it has a symbol which is very instructive, the *tai chi* symbol of yin-yang.

This Chinese symbol of the Ultimate Principle of All Things (often referred to as "yin-yang") seems to resemble two fish forever trying to catch the other's tail in its mouth. (Ain't life like that?!)

Interestingly, in depicting the origin of all polarities—male and female, light and dark, outer and inner, self and other, vanilla ice cream and pickles—this symbol also represents their unity. That is, it beautifully illustrates the grounding of the Middle Way in nondualism. Within the heart of the darkness there's a bright spot; and vice versa. But the most direct path between the two isn't a straight line. Try and walk across this map via any "straight narrow path" and you step in black and white equally. The contact or boundary between the two equal halves isn't fixed or static (like a fence, or words) but fluid and flowing (like a dance, or a river).

While the two are clearly distinguishable, they're clearly interdependent. One defines the other. There's no buying without selling, no selling without buying. There's no me without you, and this book is proof: no writers without readers. The more extreme my position is, the more it embraces my worst enemy's. The more I try to control and pin everything down with labels, the more everything turns to goo. And the more I let everything just flow, the more everything reflects an uncanny, inherent order—like the fractal formula for the pattern of a seashore which matches that for the outline of a cloud, if you've read up on Chaos Theory (illustrated in Chapter 18, "The World Within and Without: Buddhism and the Sciences").

The Middle Way isn't some statistical mean, but a very dynamic process. Buddha stopped fasting himself to death because there's no awakening when there's no one there to awaken. Here's a fundamental difference between Buddhist and Christian worldviews, between Eastern and Western mindsets. The Western mindset is *dualistic,* the self split asunder from the world (in order to, say, put up a parking lot), man split off from God, body from soul, life from death. The Eastern mindset, on the other hand, sees humanity and the cosmos as *interconnected,* intertwined (see the landscape reproduced in Chapter 12, "See? Words Cannot Express: Zen," for an example.)

And, last, if you say yin-yang is a symbol of two things, you're wrong, because it's one picture. If you say it's one picture, you're wrong again, because it clearly shows two different things. Buddhism recognizes heads and tails as two sides of the same coin—without attachment to either the one-ness of the coin, nor the two-ness of the sides. As zen says: "Not one, not two." (And keep the change!) Indeed, born from this profound view of nondualism, a direct by-product is nonattachment—equanimity— the most supreme of joys. (That's why Buddhists don't vacuum in corners: They don't have any attachments.)

Leaves from the Bodhi Tree

Who can judge good from bad? In a taoist story, a farmer's horse once ran off into foreign lands. The neighbors all said this was terrible, but the farmer shrugged, "Maybe, maybe not." Later, the horse returned with a foreign horse of fine breed. The neighbors all said this was wonderful, but the farmer shrugged, "Maybe, maybe not." The horses mated, and the farmer eventually became a wealthy horse trader. One day his only son was riding and fell and broke his hip. The neighbors all said how horrible, but the man shrugged, "Maybe, maybe not." Next year, foreigners invaded. All able-bodied young men were drafted. Almost all died in battle. The army had taken all the man's horses, but his son, because of the broken hip, was spared.

Conversions: Zen Judaists and Catholic Buddhists

In Chapter 3, "What Might an American Buddha Look Like?" I noted that the majority of American Buddhists are of Asian heritage. One step closer than the rest of us to being directly descended from the Buddha. And more likely to feel naturally at home in Buddhist culture since birth. European Americans who come to Buddhism come from a Jewish or Christian or even Islamic heritage.

Newcomers look to Buddhism for one of two things: new roots, because the spiritual tradition of their parents has become for them inaccessible or stale—or, they've been raised in an active, vibrant spiritual heritage, which Buddhism further vitalizes and strengthens. A good fit, either way.

Judaism

Let's look at Jews first, because of the disproportionate representation. That is, Jews comprise less then 3 percent of the American population, yet at least 30 percent of non-Asian Buddhists. What's behind that?

Historically, for a number of reasons, modern American Judaism seemed to lose spiritual juice for many Jews. Perhaps their parents had done too good a job assimilating ideals of the Protestant work ethic as they participated in an incredible postwar economic boom. Feminists have had a hard time dealing with patriarchal biases. Maybe, too, the bar for entry to Jewish meditative traditions was too high, a topic not even to be mentioned until after the age of 40. Not to mention the incomprehensibility of the systematic mass-murder of one third of all the Jews in the world. And of those destroyed, more than 80 percent were rabbis and teachers. So there are a number of reasons.

Some Jews fear that Buddhism will dilute an already weakened population. Yet as more and more Jews discover Buddhist meditation, they act as spiritual ambassadors, helping lead the way to a rediscovery of Jewish meditation traditions, coinciding with a worldwide movement known today as *Jewish renewal*, grounded in Judaism's prophetic and mystical traditions. Indeed, Jews have been practicing spirituality for about six millennia, with an evolved mystical tradition called kaballah and a more recent tradition known as Hasidism. (Like Zen, and Sufism within Islam, Hasidism represents an egalitarian rebellion against dogmatism and elitism, emphasizing every person's innate powers of directly accessing the sacred in everyday life.)

Certainly, Buddhism and Judaism share much in common. This-worldly rather than otherworldly, Judaism is based in the here and now. A path of unity, to be a Jew is to be one with the source of creation, and to see all of a day's various encounters as opportunities to realize that oneness. And once a week, Jews go on a spiritual retreat, called *shabbos* (Sabbath), equivalent to a Buddhist day of mindfulness. Indeed, Judaism has strong roots in the East, sometimes called the "Middle East," sometimes "Southwest Asia." (Quick: Can anyone say what's the boundary between East and West?)

In this new millennium, we might well consider Sylvia Boorstein, who proclaims "I am a prayerful, devout Jew because I am a Buddhist." It's interesting to note she's not saying she's a Jew by birth and a Buddhist by practice. Rather, the awakening that is the Buddha and Buddhist meditation makes her more awakened as a Jew. So it's only natural she keep the path that returned her to her cultural roots, the faith of her ancestors.

Or consider Alan Lew and Norman Fischer. Both were schoolmates together, both later sat zen together. Alan went on to become a rabbi. Norman became a Zen priest. Norman's been a guest dharma teacher at the meditation group that meets regularly at Alan's temple, Beth Shalom (House of Peace), and Alan periodically joins Norman at Tassajara Zen Center for an extended retreat on Buddhism and Judaism. Would that the world's spiritual leaders got to know and work with each other that closely!

Interchange is never one-sided. (The Silk Route traveled in two directions, remember?) In 1990, for example, the Dalai Lama invited eight Jewish scholars and rabbis for a Tibetan-Jewish dialogue. He became engrossed in a very lively dialogue with one rabbi about angels, but throughout the summit a key question was the "Jewish secret" of survival in exile. Tibetans, like the Jews, recently experienced the anguish of genocide, and with it a rupture in the oral transmission of wisdom traditions. As one guest later reflected, it was "… a reasonable question, even if it's the first time anybody ever asked us."

Rabbi Zalman Schachter-Shalomi responds to a question by the Dalai Lama about angels.

(Photo: Rodger Kamenetz)

Christianity

Of course, at the heart of any interfaith dialogue is Christianity. In the Judeo-Christian West, Jews represent but a small fraction. When I went to Hebrew school, a rhyme that went around one summer stated "Roses are reddish, violets are bluish, if it weren't for Jesus we'd all be Jewish." The field trip to a Catholic church our Hebrew school took proved, alas, mostly a lesson in deportment. Interestingly, for me, it was through Buddhism that I came to deeply understand Jesus.

That is, when I understood the Buddha's teaching on the inevitability of suffering and how to deal with suffering as instrumental in finding true happiness, I began to understand how Christians could worship an image of a human being suffering so horribly, on a cross; the ultimate sacrifice and redemption. Both Buddha and Christ come to us with a message of love having participated in the sorrows of the world out of compassion for the human condition. (Those who mark the difference between the physical agony of the crucifixion and the mental anguish of leaving one's own wife and child will miss my point.)

When asked to pick up Jesus' cross for myself, I'm touched to recognize my own sorrows, and transform them into fertilizer for my own flowers of peace, and to bear witness to the needless sorrows of others. In the bodhisattva ideal, pain is overcome by bearing it for others, with others. Vowing to save all beings. (Those who try to split the hair of difference between enlightenment and salvation will miss my point.)

When I'd touched "the peace that passeth understanding" for myself, through my Buddhist practice, and experienced how it's available at any time, all the time, then I understood the Kingdom of Heaven within reach of all us. The seeds of enlightenment are within all of us. The Quakers ask, "Where shalt thou turn if not to the light within?"

Along the Path

"Be still and know that I am God."

—Psalm 46

"'Be still' means to become peaceful and concentrated. The Buddhist term is *samatha* (stopping, calming). 'Know' means to acquire wisdom or understanding. The Buddhist term is *vipassana* (insight or looking deeply). When we are still, looking deeply, and touching the source of our true wisdom, we touch the living Buddha and the living Christ in ourselves and each person we meet."

—Thich Nhat Hanh

There are many books on Buddhist/Christian dialogue. It's interesting how one just tabulates the similarities between the sayings of Buddha and of Christ, in two columns. Seek and ye shall find; the Buddha said, "He who would may reach the utmost height—but he must be anxious to learn." "Judge not, lest ye be judged," a perfect example of Buddhist equanimity. The list of correspondences is lengthy, though the real places of convergence aren't in books but in practice.

Different paths can lead to a common destination. These images of Buddha and Christ seem to have been drawn by the same person, though one was made by a Tibetan artist, the other by a Russian. From 1981 to 1992, these images hung on the sign outside the School of Sacred Arts in New York City, the Buddha facing east, Christ facing west.

(Buddha by Tupten Norbu; Christ by Vladislav Andreyev)

Many Christians are rediscovering living contemplative traditions which had been replaced by "mental prayer" and ritual. Through meditation of mindful breathing, many Christians are rediscovering what St. Paul meant by praying without ceasing (1 Thessalonians 5:17).

Hear and Now

"Originally, the Christians weren't even called Christians .... they had simply been called 'followers of the Way.' The great challenge I see before us is to make followers of the Way out of 'Christians.' As long as we're 'on the way,' we're all followers of the Way .... We follow different paths in different garbs and different vehicles—that's the cultural part—but there's only one way of being on the way: to be on the move, *that's* the Way."

—Brother David Steindl-Rast

There's much in Buddhist practice a Christian can look to for nourishment. The Buddhist meditation called *tonglen,* for example, enables a practitioner to literally love one's enemy as oneself. And Buddhist recitation, be it a passage from the *Lotus Sutra* or the name of Amida Buddha or a few Sanskrit syllables, is reminiscent of early traditions of Christian prayer, such as recitation of *Kyrie Eleison,* and the Jesus Prayer (or *Hesychasm*) still practiced by Eastern Orthodox Christians. The similarity between Christian and Buddhist rosary beads is another reminder that spirit knows no boundary.

Had Jesus and Shakyamuni met, they'd be two good buddies. Some even say that Buddhists were present in the Galilee of Jesus' time. Be that as it may, Christ and Buddha are still meeting today, and the ongoing dialogue is making for many good hearts. Amen.

Leaves from the Bodhi Tree

As a young man, John Main (1926–1982) served in the British Foreign Service in Malaya. An Indian monk there introduced him to meditation. After he returned to London, he became a Benedictine monk in 1958. But he was eventually advised to stop practicing silent, nonconceptual prayer. Then, in 1969, he rediscovered a Christian tradition of meditation, or "pure prayer" as it was called: Practiced by the first Christian monks, the Desert Fathers, it had been taught to Saint Benedict in the fourth century by John Cassian. Main's dedication to teach this lost tradition, familiar to Buddhists, Hindus, Sufis, and Kaballists, is now carried on by a worldwide community for Christian meditation.

Make Room for Rumi: Other Creeds

Coming to the West, Buddha is encountering many faiths and creeds for whom his message is pertinent. Like Jews and Christians, Muslims also share the Abrahamic tradition. A kindred Buddhist spirit in Islam is the Sufi tradition, representing its mystic paths. An early Sufi proverb prescribes: "An hour of meditation is better than a year of ritual worship." The most famous Sufi in the West is the thirteenth century Sufi master and mystic poet Rumi, who viewed all religions with the same eye. Rumi wrote: "Though lamps will vary, the light's the same ... / To stare at any lamp is surely to get lost ... / disagreement between Muslim, Zoroastrian, and Jew / all comes down to point of view."

At the same time, as North Americans become more aware of the spiritual traditions of the continent's first peoples, Native Americans have incorporated Buddhist mindfulness meditation into their practices. One gal from Cuba who's led a sangha for people of color at San Francisco Zen Center said she'd have no problem envisioning Zen Santeria (Santeria being Cuban voudon, or voodoo).

But I've already said too much about Buddhism and too little about everything else. (Or is it vice versa?) Whenever you want to read up on more, please refer to our bibliography, online at awakening.to/bibliography.html. (But, like most Buddhists, I maintain that there's a limit to books and tapes. Buddhism is something to be lived.) So far, we've laid a firm foundation, introducing ourselves to the Buddha—his life, and the spread of his teachings, and their relationship to other teachings. But, wait! What exactly are his teachings? Well, when we continue (continue to begin), we'll apply what we've seen to finding out what the Buddha taught—and continues to teach, in fact, in every moment.

The Least You Need to Know

➤ Interfaith dialogue is one of the most crucial topics of our times, and Buddhism converses well with all other faiths.

➤ When asked about God, Heaven, and the immortality of the soul, the Buddha simply remained silent, because he didn't see these issues furthering release from suffering.

➤ Buddha was part of the culture of his time and place. So, Hindu practices such as yoga are a natural part of his heritage.

➤ When Buddhism came to China, the confrontation was made easier by the preexistence of the Taoist religion, which in turn influenced Zen.

➤ Indo-Europeans usually come to Buddhism with a Judeo-Christian background. Buddhism has a mutually rewarding dialogue with both.

➤ Interfaith interchange can be reciprocal. For example, Buddhism influences Judaism and Christianity, and Judaism and Christianity influence Buddhism.

Part 2
Awakening: Basic Teachings

You're awake. Your eyes are open. But how do you know you're truly awake? Have you ever had such vivid dreams or powerful fantasies you could swear they were real? Or haven't you felt at times that life is like a dream? Taoist sage Chuang-tzu confessed he didn't know if he was a man dreaming he was a butterfly, or a butterfly dreaming he was a man. (Don't swat that fly! It may be Napoleon.)

The Buddha stands us on solid ground and shows us our fantasies and dreams in the plain light of day. He shows us how to perceive ultimate reality directly, with our own eyes. Moreover, he shows us our innate capacity to be free of the bondage of delusions, and to live our lives to the utmost. It only takes waking up to it.

It's that basic. Here's the core, the essence of the Buddha's teachings about life. The Dharma. The ABCs of Buddhism …

Chapter 5

The Handshake: Buddhism's Basic Beliefs

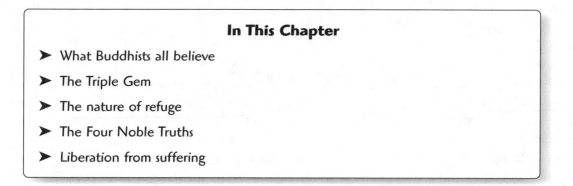

In This Chapter

➤ What Buddhists all believe

➤ The Triple Gem

➤ The nature of refuge

➤ The Four Noble Truths

➤ Liberation from suffering

What's important? In traditional times, people's lives harmonized with the course of nature. Our ancestors might have pictured the universe as a giant buffalo, if buffalo was the animal that provided them with hide for clothing and shelter, meat for food, bone for tools, and so on. Moreover, they knew not to take more than they needed; but now buffalo are nearly extinct. Gone too is a simple, common frame for the meaning of why we're alive. Contemporary life's typically out of balance, fragmented, and incoherent. (Press "5" for more options.) Sometimes it's hard to find any meaning except what we bring to the table.

So what, if anything, do all Buddhists believe? The Buddha left behind no central church, nor holy writ. He trusted the autonomy of each person to test, select, and self-actualize truth. Since this led to a diversity of schools of thought, and since Buddhism adapted to various cultures, we might ask: Is there any bedrock?

Is there any basic handshake the Buddha makes with us? Yes. Buddhists share core beliefs: the Three Jewels, the Four Noble Truths, and the Cardinal Precepts (five, sometimes ten). This chapter sets forth the first two basic elements. The precepts are the subject of Chapter 7, "The Art of Living: Cardinal Precepts."

The Three Jewels

While the Four Noble Truths present the Buddha's basic philosophy of life, as we'll soon see, the *Three Jewels* are more elemental. Also known as the Three Treasures, the Triple Gem, or the Three Refuges, they are:

➤ **The Buddha.** From the Sanskrit root *budh,* to awaken, this is the title given Siddhartha following his enlightenment. Lowercase, it could refer to any fully self-realized being.

➤ **The Dharma.** In Sanskrit, means virtue, law, discipline, reality, truth, phenomena. Capitalized, it refers to the teachings of the Buddha. Lowercase, it could refer to truth or cosmic process, as a falling leaf teaches impermanence.

➤ **The Sangha.** Means assembly. Uppercase, it refers to the monastic order established by the Buddha, plus lay followers. Lowercase, it could refer to various communities of dharma, even all living things.

Along the Path

A note on interpretation: The Triple Gem is open to interpretation, as is all Buddhism—so long as the interpretation isn't intended to fix meaning. Interpretation should give you a "for instance," but not a motto that limits it. Buddha's truth is a living law, not some artifact to be preserved beneath glass, or even corralled within a book. Rather, interpretation should open Buddha's applicability out into all aspects of life and make its vitality even more viable.

Why jewels? Jewels don't quite evoke the power they did 2,600 years ago. (Things change.) But we're not talking about synthetic diamonds nor healing crystals. The meaning also goes beyond a beautiful adornment (which these are) to include being rare … priceless … flawless. As gold once was, these jewels are—a touchstone, an index of value. Unlike the stock market, their worth never fluctuates. A slang for jewel is "rock." Here's the rock of Buddhism, like the lodestone of a compass … the diamond dormant in a lump of coal … the bedrock underlying everything. As being given a rare jewel might lift us out of material want, so can these jewels liberate us spiritually. Some think of a magic gem that fulfills their very deepest, profoundest wishes. Next we'll see how this is a threefold gem.

Flash back in time for a moment. The words "Buddha," "Dharma," and "Sangha" were first used together after Siddhartha left the Bodhi Tree when his five fellow monks found him again. Even before he spoke, they could see a certain lightness in his step, a radiance in his glance, a majesty in his presence. When he spoke, explaining why he'd left them and how he'd found the Middle Way, they saw he'd finally realized the truth they'd all been seeking. One of the five was reportedly enlightened on the spot—*Shazam!*

And we must imagine a certain loss for words at the scene. Siddhartha and the monks who joined him declared themselves to be Sangha, a community, a body of seekers and teachers along the path. "Dharma" became the word for the path itself—and "Buddha," the one who'd found and shows that path. Touch one aspect deeply, you touch all three. Next question: What relation could you or I have to the Triple Gem?

Hear and Now

"I've given Buddhism another name. I don't call it Buddhism. What do I call it? I call it People-ism (the religion of the people). Why? Because people become Buddhas. It isn't that the Buddha becomes a person, but the people can become Buddhas. So Buddhism can be called People-ism."

—Venerable Tripitaka Master Hsüan Hua

Safe Harbor: Taking Refuge

Along with precepts and vows, the Three Jewels are something in which *Buddhists take refuge*. That means they're solid as a rock. What's taking refuge? Using a medical analogy again, the Three Jewels are like a doctor's care. Your doctor will show you the way, but the mere existence of medicine or a doctor doesn't guarantee health. That is, if your doctor gives you a prescription but you haven't taken the medicine yet, then you still haven't taken refuge in his or her care. Taking refuge in the Three Jewels means you've evaluated them and decided they're good medicine. The Buddha's like a doctor; the Dharma, his medicine; and the Sangha, the hospital staff. You can put your life in their hands.

Drivers sometimes keep an image of St. Christopher or Jesus or a bodhisattva on their dashboard. That's another manifestation of taking refuge. If you were sailing a ship without a rudder, lost at sea in a high storm, the light from the Triple Gem is the North Star by which you'd steer. During the 1970s when people fled Vietnam on tiny boats,

This Is

The Tibetan language has no word for "**Buddhist**"—using instead *nangpha*, meaning, roughly, a person who looks within. Similarly, "Buddhism" isn't a word commonly used in Asia. The closest word is "*Buddha-Dharma*," meaning roughly "facts of an enlightened life," "awakened life-truth." "Isms" are a Western penchant. What's important is the nature of reality as Buddha pointed out. It's here and now.

those who made it across the ocean sometimes reported afterwards that what kept everyone from panicking was the presence of a single person meditating. Our mother's womb was our refuge when we were but tiny buds. Refuge is home. Calling home. Coming home.

Along the Path

Some Buddhist teachers encourage those who take refuge to maintain respect for other religions but demand that they not follow their teachings. That's their call. Taking refuge in the Three Jewels needn't preclude taking refuge in the Holy Trinity, or HaShem, or Allah, or anything else. After all, what religion is God? The Buddha isn't God and isn't asking for an exclusive contract nor being made into a one-course diet.

In Everyday Life

You can appreciate *Buddha* and *buddha nature* in your everyday life without having to formally take refuge. Meditation, for example, is a link to the Buddha deepening with practice. Meditation is the topic of the next section (Part 3, "Seeing Clearly and Deeply: Meditation and Its Paths"). Meanwhile, here's a meditation. Franz Metcalf came up with a wonderful mantra (a phrase to say to yourself to focus your mind on a certain energy) when he saw a book titled *What Would Jesus Do?* and decided to write a book titled *What Would the Buddha Do?* It's a question you can ask all the time, any time. In a crisis or at calm. "What would the Buddha do?" The more you think of Buddha, the deeper your understanding and bond will grow.

Similarly, you can appreciate the presence of *dharma* in your everyday life without formally taking refuge. I take refuge in it whenever I find it. It might not be capital "D" Dharma, something the Buddha said specifically, but—you never know. The Buddha never took a bus but his Great Vehicle carries us all. Just yesterday, in fact, while I was coming home from my writing studio, I was waiting at a bus stop during after-work rush hour. The bus was very late, and a large crowd had formed and was growing palpably anxious and tense. When the bus finally arrived, it was already crammed with people who'd accumulated in the long wait at previous bus stops.

At the front of this anxious crowd I saw a lady, of rather large girth, who'd undoubt-edly seen her share of trouble boarding crowded buses and, moreover, understood her part. The driver opened his doors and, completely out of patience, yelled at us all,

"Hurry up! C'mon, get on! C'mon, c'mon, move to the rear of the bus!" And the woman just stood firmly there and waited. So we all waited. Finally, when the driver realized what was happening outside his bus and made eye contact with her, she just said one thing to him which I'll always remember: "Please! Please don't make me get angry at you because then we'd be liable to say or do something for which we'd *both* be sorry!" The driver lifted his hands, sighed, bowed his head in apology, people made way for us, the drive was otherwise uneventful.

The dharma of the story?

➤ One, it takes two to fuel anger. Fighting anger with anger only generates more anger. If one person refrains then the other might, too.

➤ Two, dharma is where you find it. The voice of the Buddha is always clear, if you have ears to hear. A buddha waiting for a bus once taught this to the Rush-Hour Sangha of life.

Chapter 9, "Taking the Plunge: Beginning and Cultivating Your Practice," discusses forming or finding your *sangha*. Maybe you're still reaching for your relationship to the Buddha right now. That's fine. Or perhaps you're in between sanghas. Things change. Right now, you're a member of *The Complete Idiot's Sangha*—you and me and all fellow readers of this book past, present, and future; awakening.to/digitalsangha.html. Actually, we all embody a universal sangha of the four elements: the earth in our bones, the wind in our lungs, the ocean in our bloodstream and cells, and the fire in our metabolism. When I sit zazen, I do so with the whole universe. And the whole universe does so with me. We take refuge in each other.

Along the Path

"We take refuge in the Buddha because he is our teacher. We take refuge in the Dharma because it is good medicine. We take refuge in the Sangha because it is composed of excellent friends."

—Dogen (1200–1253)

"To realize the very heart of essential nature is to take refuge in the Buddha. To cultivate the garden of realization is to take refuge in the Dharma. To share the fruits of the garden is to take refuge in the Sangha."

—Robert Aitken

Theravada—Mahayana—Vajrayan

The major currents within Buddhism complement and reinforce each other in their focus and emphasis on the Three Jewels. Theravadans refer to Buddha as the historical Buddha; the Dharma, as the Pali canon, the Tripitaka, recording his teachings; the Sangha, as those who've attained enlightenment, and more generally the monastic community, plus the wider community of lay practitioners.

Along the Path

"The pure Mind is Buddha, the brilliant Mind is the Dharma, and the inexhaustibly pure, bright, and free-flowing Mind is the Sangha."

—Lin-chi (d. 866), Zen patriarch

"Where there is fire there is light, and where there is light there is fire. Think of the purity and clarity of the light as the fire, and the brilliance as the light itself. ... There is no light without fire, and no fire without light. They are inexhaustibly one and the same."

—Ven. Song-chol (contemporary Korean Buddhist teacher)

Mahayana perspectives are often interpretive and innovative. For example, if you prefer, the Buddha is realization, Dharma is truth, and Sangha is being harmony. Members of the Zen Peacemaker Order take refuge in:

➤ Buddha, the awakened nature of all beings

➤ Dharma, the ocean of wisdom and compassion

➤ Sangha, the community of those living in harmony with all Buddhas and Dharmas

With the Three Jewels, Mahayana Buddhists often take refuge in the path of the Bodhisattva, vowing to liberate all sentient beings from their needless suffering. With the Three Jewels, Tibetan Buddhists take refuge in an additional triplet (called "the refuge tree"), consisting of the *lama* (*guru*, teacher, living embodiment of the Buddha), *yidam* (personal deity, an enlightened being whose attainment we wish to emulate), and dharma protector (similar to guardian angel).

Whatever the spin, the Three Jewels are essential to the basic handshake we make with ourselves and the universe when we've begun to appreciate, understand, and live the path of the Buddha.

Along the Path

If you shine a pure, bright light in just one jewel, it would reflect that light to the other jewels. This is an example of another aspect of Buddhist interpretation: Looking really deeply, you find that each topic contains all the others. Call it *"interbeing."* Dharma being a living law, this fundamental Buddhist premise is applicable to aspects of Buddhist ways of life as well as to life itself.

From the Ultimate Dimension

I'd said, "the one thing Buddhists agree on is the Three Jewels"—even though this one thing appears to be three. No contradiction. Not unlike the Christian trinity, they form a unity. Indeed, early interpretations of the Three Jewels into English reflect missionary work. The Buddha was called the Saviour, the Dharma was called the Scripture, and the Sangha was called the Church. Even without any Christian overlay, the Three Jewels are so interconnected as to be one. And each contains all the others.

The Buddha is his teachings, the Dharma. After all, the Buddha's teachings are what enabled him to become Buddha. The Dharma is thus the essence of the Buddha. And Sangha depends on Buddha and Dharma to show people the way. Conversely, if the Buddha hadn't established the Sangha, then his teachings wouldn't ever have been preserved and kept alive. Buddha and Dharma depend on Sangha to be actualized. If there were no people, there'd be no Buddhism.

So Buddha, Dharma, and Sangha are ultimately one. One love.

The Four Noble Truths

The Three Jewels are at the core of being Buddhist. Now, of all of the Buddha's teachings, first and foremost are the *Four Noble Truths:*

1. Suffering (*Duhkha*)
2. Attachment (*trishna*)
3. Liberation (*nirvana*)
4. The path (*marga*)

In 25 words or less, 1) "There's suffering." 2) "There's a cause of suffering." 3) "There's an end to suffering." 4) "There's a way to end suffering."

You do the math. You don't have to be a rocket scientist to see that putting these four propositions at the forefront of your awareness, understanding what they mean, and testing them out could change your life—for the good. All the rest of the Buddha's teachings could be seen as elaboration—a great bonus, if you will. Just these four interlocking sayings can teach us to grasp the mystery of life and death ... recognize the origin of and cure for human anguish ... and awaken to life's perfections.

Four facts of life. "Truths" as in a proclamation: "We hold these truths to be self-evident." "Noble" because they can ennoble us. Revealing the nobility of what it means to be a human being. In Chinese, they're called the Four Holy Truths.

Leaves from the Bodhi Tree

Following his enlightenment, the Buddha adapted his teachings to the capacity of his listeners. Thus it is said that during his 50-some years of travelling and teaching, the Buddha taught dharma in 64,000 different ways. This led to the expression, "There are 64,000 dharma doors," meaning there are 64,000 different paths (or doors) to the truth. (This humble *Complete Idiot's Guide* is but one.)

Now imagine that rain could be counted, and came to 64,000 drops, and all drops fall equally, but big trees lap up more water, and dead trees can't absorb any at all. Thus we can see there are 64,000 different kinds of trees, all absorbing rain. And different kinds of people, all absorbing dharma. And different kinds of schools of Buddhism, adapted to different needs. And so we see how the *ultimate dimension* reflects the *relative dimension*, and vice versa.

In 75 words or less, 1) we inevitably reach the point where we'll say life sucks. Why? From 2) craving after things, or clinging to thoughts, which never truly satisfy ...

born from our unrealistic images of life … life being impermanent, and interconnected, yet we try to make out that it isn't. Nevertheless, 3) every human being can free themselves from such continual dissatisfaction. How? By 4) recognizing the truth we resist facing, and taking steps to actualize that truth. Okay, now let's look deeper.

The First Fact of Life: Recognizing Pain

It began with the young prince's stark confrontation with the facts of life: old age, sickness, and death, and the suffering (*duhkha*) they cause everyone. Not necessarily unique or unusual afflictions, they're unavoidable. Oh, maybe you're lucky: perhaps your body doesn't send you pain signals when something's wrong, your old age will be a bed of roses, and you'll die in your sleep when you least expect it. Even so, because life comes to an end, you'll never be able to have it all. (And even if you could have it all, where would you put it?!) And so you're bound to suffer, unless you wake up to reality. And that's a fact. Call it Fact Number One.

This Is

The Sanskrit word, **duhkha** (say *doo-kah*) is usually translated as suffering. It could also be sour, unpleasant, or unsatisfactory (with a rather British ring, eh what?). You might also call it difficulty, pain, frustration, disturbed emotions, stress, anxiety, anguish, angst. *Ick!* (The grimace is extra.)

The state of liberation from duhkha is **nirvana.**

Hear and Now

"Life is difficult. This is a great truth, one of the greatest truths. It is a great truth because once we truly see this truth, we transcend it. Once we truly know that life is difficult—once we truly understand and accept it—then life is no longer difficult."

—M. Scott Peck, *The Road Less Travelled*

The Second Fact of Life: Understanding Pain

Listen, do you want to know the secret of how to live forever? Bring me a grain of salt from a home that hasn't known death and I'll tell you.

The great myth is that you can avoid sickness and death … or, at least, for a very, very long time … or at least avoid old age and be young for a very long time. Shucks!

We're all mortal … prone to sickness and destined to age. Still, some of us assist the inevitable by poisoning ourselves in small doses (and there are all kinds of poison).

Or we try to hang on to life. Clinging, we crave something to stay with us, like the favorite cloth animal we had as a child. (Women understand this when they say, "The difference between men and boys is the price we pay to get them toys." Men may not throw a hissy fit if they can't get their boat, home entertainment system, or luxury car with all the extras, but they're just as attached to them as to a cloth doll when they were an infant.)

So we hatch schemes … spin elaborate fantasies and pretend they're real … in expectation of the future or reaching for something in the past … seldom ever living in the present, the only place where life ever is.

Recognition of this second fact clarifies the first. That is, we're bound to suffer *because* we try to run away from the truth of our life's invariable end. Sooner or later, the tide will come in and wipe out the sand castles and moats we've built to stave off the inescapable. Soon, and sooner than we may think, the sky will darken, and we won't be able to enjoy any more garden parties from our mansion on the hill. The ways we try to bargain with life's infirmities and impermanences are all bound to fail—and bring us further suffering. Instead of waking up, we seek alternative illusions, more of the same under different garb.

The second truth reveals that the cause of suffering is *trishna*, craving—craving the wrong things, or the right things in the wrong way, or what's beyond our grasp—a misplaced sense of values.

This Is

The Sanskrit word **trishna** is usually translated as desire. It's the root of our word for thirst. Like the thirst of a person all alone in a desert, it seems unquenchable. It can also be translated as attachment. Another good translation, in this context, would be clinging, grabbing. In modern, colloquial terms: being hung up, having a hang up.

This grotesque creature's called a "hungry ghost" (*Sanskrit*, preta; *Chinese*, li mei*), this one being of the Japanese variety called gaki. Its belly is immense, because of its ravenous hunger, but its throat's only as wide as a soda straw or sometimes only the eye of a needle. And so it's emaciated because it can't get enough food to nourish itself, let alone slake its enormous appetite. It symbolizes human craving for more than it can ever have. (When's the last time you were in a somewhat similar shape?)*

(Drawing: Gary Gach)

The Third Fact of Life: Realizing There Is an End to Pain

The third fact looks yet deeper. Like a compassionate surgeon, the Buddha looks beneath our craving and grasping and finds ignorance (ignorance of our symptoms, their diagnosis, and the medicine). But the *prognosis* is good because ignorance needn't be permanent. We can't end death, sickness, old age. But we can stop setting ourselves up for a fall. We can stop investing in an unrealistic outlook. We can face the fact we won't live forever. Accumulating more and more stuff won't prevent that final day when we'll have to give it all back. (And if we *were* immortal, just imagine what our Visa bill would be!)

We're like spiders caught in our own web. So what can we do? Break the continual self-perpetuating cycles (*samsara*)—our self-created rat cage, fueled by our greed, hate, and delusion (*the Three Poisons*)—recognize them and finally face facts. Then, step away. Freedom is just a step away.

Along the Path

"He who's no longer dependent on desire and views, realizing the emptiness of things, thus pastures in indescribable, limitless freedom—like the birds in the sky, his track cannot be traced."

—The Buddha

"He who binds himself to a joy does the wingèd life destroy. But he who kisses the joy as it flies lives in eternity's sunrise."

—William Blake

If Holy Fact Number One and Number Two amount to symptoms and diagnosis, respectively, then Holy Fact Number Three and Number Four are the prognosis and prescription. The prognosis is good because our poisons contain our medicine. Things can turn around, for the better: The reverse of our negative patterns, our samsara, is nirvana.

Recognizing our delusion that our happiness exists outside of ourselves, we're free to turn within and discover our innate capacity for unconditional happiness.

Recognizing how greed enslaves us to crave stuff endlessly without any permanent satisfaction, we're free to discover the true satisfaction of compassion and generosity. Recognizing how anger enslaves us, we're free to discover how to apply the power of truth to bring harmony and love.

We clutch our pain to our breast as if that's our identity, as deluded as poor Kisa Gotami, the grief-stricken woman who came to the Buddha clutching her dead child to her breast, thinking it could still live (see Chapter 1, "Why Is This Man Smiling?: The Buddha"). To use another Buddhist analogy, our delusion, our ignorance is like a small child, home alone, playing with toys while the house is burning down. Recognizing and understanding the delusions fueling our suffering, we can stop trying to put out the fire with gasoline and get to the source.

Rather than persist in playing with sandcastles or doll's houses, we can face our pain, duhkha, realize its needlessness, and forgive ourselves for having clung to it anyway. Then we have the rest of our lives to rediscover how precious each moment really is. To look at the world with the freshness and wonder of a child again, now with the maturity of a responsible adult—what a wonderful opportunity!

No, as adults we know our true happiness doesn't lie in our job title, nor our married name. Nor are we nothing, either. We're the unique crossroads of all the happenings within and outside us, of which we're unaware when we identify ourselves with our personal hang-ups. When we get all wound up and bound up in "self," we make a very small package. Shed that, and we find what we really are, way down deep. Our true nature. The inherent buddha nature all beings innately possess. Holy Fact Number Three: Enlightenment is *possible*. Holy Fact Number Four: There *is* a path (*marga*).

This Is

Nirvana represents the state of ultimate perfection. The Sanskrit word literally means "extinguishing": the extinction of duhkha, difficulties, pain; extinction of the causes that nourish suffering; liberation from **samsara,** the world of endless cycles. Samsara traditionally refers to a person's round of rebirths, but can mean repeating the same unsatisfactory patterns; the same illusions, duhkha, and bad karma, over and over. Nirvana also has the connotation of exhaling. (Try holding your breath long enough, clinging to life, and you'll see the impossibility.)

The Fourth Fact of Life: Stepping into Freedom

It's an unfortunate misconception that Buddhism is about suffering. The truth is, Buddhism looks unflinchingly at suffering, but as a wall in which a door can open out into freedom. (To be really clear about the fact that Buddhism is about happiness, take a good look at the face of the Buddha illustrated in this chapter.)

We have the ability to appreciate genuine happiness. It's in our very being. But somehow, somewhere along the way, we forget—unless someone comes and reminds us, as Buddha does. I live on a one-way street, and sometimes a car turns onto it, facing the wrong way. (Imagine it going the wrong way on a crowded freeway and you have a great image of duhkha.) Sometimes, even before another car comes, heading toward them, it dawns on the driver that all the cars on the sidewalk are pointed the other way, and he turns around. (Imagine a car going the wrong way on a freeway turning around and you have a great image of liberation.) This turning around, this *awakening of mind,* is like the beginning of the Path. (If there were a road sign for "Buddha" it might be "Change Your Mind.") The fourth and final Holy Truth is a roadmap to the way of harmony and love. The Path.

The Buddha's way—the Middle Way, the Eightfold Path—is designed to put our innate powers back into our hands, to reawaken our implicit unity and harmony with all of life. At times, it might seem like a tall order. Stepping out of suffering into freedom can seem like walking over the edge of a cliff. Only a complete idiot would do that, some might say. Yet the Buddha blazed a trail for us. We can't follow his exact footsteps, nor would he want us to. But once someone has invented matches, it's kind of silly to strike two rocks together to cook dinner for two. The Fourth Noble Truth is the recipe, the Eightfold Path.

We've noted how the first three holy facts are like the facts of life that initiated Siddhartha's quest:

This Is

The Sanskrit word **marga** means path. Like the wind, the sun, a tree—a road is a universal spiritual symbol. A path doesn't exist until it's trod. A path is also its steps— the steps taken to be on the path. In this case, the Buddha offers eight steps comprising one path, often known as the Eightfold Path. With the Middle Way, the Eightfold Path is the *way* of Buddhism.

Hear and Now

"It is the nature of life that all beings will face difficulties; through enlightened living one can transcend these difficulties, ultimately become fulfilled, liberated, and free. ... The way to realize this liberation and enlightenment is by leading a compassionate life of virtue, wisdom, and meditation. These three spiritual trainings comprise the teachings of the Eight-Fold Path to Enlightenment."

—Lama Surya Das

the elderly, the sick, and the corpse. The fourth holy fact is like the monk he saw. The monk said nothing to him. Yet to Siddhartha, it was as if the monk were telling him, "You're not alone. Join us." (Indeed, no one on a quest for awakening walks alone: The whole universe yearns for enlightenment, for nirvana.) And Siddhartha did try the ascetic path of the monk he saw, but overdid it. He tells us, "After trial and error, *this* is the path I've found. I say it's correct from start to finish. Please, try it and see for yourself."

You must take the path in order to really see it. Chapter 6, "Taking Steps: The Eightfold Path," presents the eight steps Buddha recommends for finding it yourself and keeping on it.

Theme and Variations

Four facts of life. Four truths to renew the nobility of our lives. They're like the very engine of the Buddhist vehicle. Here are some variations on ways of appreciating their meaning, so you can really understand and apply them to your daily life.

Objective, scientific, and compassionate, like a doctor, the Buddha made this compact list:

1. *Symptom:* duhkha, suffering
2. *Diagnosis:* trishna; ignorance; attachment
3. *Prognosis:* nirvana, liberation is possible
4. *Prescription:* marga, the Eightfold Path

Short and sweet. Like something jotted on those little prescription pads doctors use. Only it doesn't require anything external, like a drug. Rather, it's something to take home to study and use to cultivate our own natural curative powers.

Remember, *heal* has the same root as *whole* and *holy*. Remember, we compared the Sangha to a clinic, where Dr. Buddha prescribes medicine (Dharma). Here, the Fourth Holy Truth (the Eightfold Path) prescribes a whole plan of treatment, not unlike the way a doctor might recommend a balanced diet, enough exercise, and rest. Otherwise, a prescribed surgery or medication may not have any lasting effect.

Another way to embrace the Buddha in our lives is to consider the teachings in terms of active verbs rather than static nouns. (Actually, Sanskrit words work as verbs as much as nouns.) Buddha's a verb: to awaken; Dharma's being in harmony with what is; Sangha is gathering to follow the Way. As verbs, the Four Noble Truths proclaim:

1. Recognizing and understanding suffering
2. Letting go of self-centered craving
3. Realizing liberation
4. Cultivating the path

Yet another approach might be to phrase the four truths as questions. Once we've grown up, we forget how questions were such a reality to us as children. Some of that reality, we later learn, is unprofitable craving. "Can I have that red car?" "Can I eat just dessert?" They're like the metaphysical questions which the Buddha wouldn't answer because they didn't further. But other kid questions are really profound, like, "What is that?" And "Who says?" Questions are a wonderful way of finding what's overlooked, of amplifying what's really juicy, and of bringing forth answers already within us. Recently, Byron Katie has devised a method of inquiry and self-realization called The Work which can work miracles this way. (I've adapted the following questions from The Work, and you can see how they echo the Four Noble Truths; if you're interested in using Byron Katie's questions, see her Web site, www.thework.com.) Ask yourself:

Am I suffering? How so?

What am I attached to? Is it real? Is it here and now? Is it permanent?

What if I let go of my attachment? (To a situation that's not present, and the self-image I identify with that situation.)

How can I cultivate a better way of living that doesn't let me fall into the same trap I fell into all over again?

Indeed, the Buddha wanted us to try his teachings out for ourselves. So the four truths can be thought of as a Four-Step Program (even a computer program, perhaps, but certainly not a magic bullet). Are you happy? Set aside some time and write down one thing that makes you unhappy. A stressful situation, say, or a person. (Be like Buddha: Keep it simple.) Think, then write down, very simply, how a situation or person keeps you from being happy. Next, ask yourself if you'd be happy if the situation were only in your mind. Of course you would—but really think about this.

Have you identified yourself with your suffering? Or can you let it all go? Is the situation happening in the present moment? Or are you still hanging on to it, in your mind? Are you continuing to hate someone, for example, for something that happened to you long ago? If you can let it go, then allow yourself a big sigh of relief. You've moved on; been there, done that.

If you like, you might think about song lyrics echoing the four truths. Can't get no satisfaction? (*Duhkha* is often translated as "unsatisfactory.") You try and you try? (Unless you get to the root, dissatisfaction will keep cropping up.) You can't always get what you want (by craving for stuff), but if you try (observe the teachings) you can get what you need (nirvana). Whatever makes it real for you. As my grandmother would say: Get started and keep at it.

Why are these two people smiling? Maybe the Mona Lisa can't help but smile in the Buddha's presence. Each seems to have looked deeply into the heart of life and to invite us to do likewise. Each, in their own way, reminds us, "We've all known suffering. True happiness is the goal, the real accomplishment. Find it." (Leonardo da Vinci, Mona Lisa [c. 1505–14]. Paris, Musée du Louvre. Buddha in Meditation, Gongxian style. Grey limestone. Northern Wei Dynasty [386–535]. 95.3 cm. Honolulu Academy of Arts, Gift of Mrs. Charles M. Cooke, Sr. 1930 [3468].)

The Least You Need to Know

➤ Buddhists all agree on the importance of the Three Jewels and the Four Noble Truths.

➤ The first is the basic structure of Buddhism. The second is the basic belief of Buddhism.

➤ The Three Jewels are the Buddha, the Dharma, and the Sangha.

➤ The Three Jewels are so valuable and solid that we can take refuge in them.

➤ The Four Noble Truths deal with 1) the existence of suffering, 2) the origin of suffering, 3) the cessation of suffering, 4) the way to live without suffering.

Chapter 6

Taking Steps: The Eightfold Path

In This Chapter

➤ Putting theory into practice

➤ Including wisdom and conduct along with meditation

➤ Understanding the eight elements of the path

The whole wheel of the Buddha's teachings, the complete pizza, is summed up in two principles: the Four Noble Truths and the Eightfold Path. The Four Noble Truths (see Chapter 5, "The Handshake: Buddhism's Basic Beliefs") set forth his doctrine for you to understand. The Eightfold Path outlines his discipline for you to practice. And as your practice deepens your understanding, the two build on and feed each other.

Doctrine and discipline, theory and practice. Apparently, the Buddha intended both to go together hand-in-glove. He intertwined the last Noble Truth and the first step on the Path. Of the two, the Path is less commonly written about. Yet I cherish it, as I think you might, too. So we turn next to Buddha's thought in action—that we may put it into action for ourselves, and learn by doing.

The Path

Sometimes the journey of a thousand miles begins with a leaky tire or a broken fan belt. Sometimes it begins with an inheritance from a rich uncle you never knew you had. Sometimes it begins with just one step. The way of the Buddha has eight steps, factors, aspects, each an integral part of the path.

Hear and Now

"The spiritual journey does not consist of arriving at a new destination where a person gains what he did not have, or becomes what he is not. It consists in the dissipation of one's own ignorance concerning oneself and life, and the gradual growth of that understanding which begins the spiritual awakening."

—Aldous Huxley

The eight aspects of the Path are:

1. Right View
2. Right Thought
3. Right Speech
4. Right Action
5. Right Livelihood
6. Right Effort
7. Right Mindfulness
8. Right Concentration

Here "right" carries the notion of correct, proper. Righteous (but, please, not self-righteous.) If you like, think of "right" as an adverb: viewing rightly, thinking rightly, and so on. Or a verb, as in "to restore." Similarly, you could frame the eight steps as questions. "Am I viewing rightly? How would the Buddha view [such-and-such-a-situation] rightly?"

The Eightfold Path.

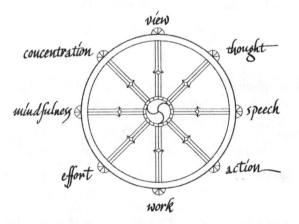

Likewise, you can write the steps down. *Exercise:* Take a blank sheet of paper and fold it in half. Now fold it in half again the other way. Then fold it in half yet again. Voilà!, you have eight little boxes, into which to write the name of each step of the path. Next, make some copies. Take one, fold it into eighths, and put it in your wallet or purse. Throughout the day, whenever you find yourself in a situation where one of the steps presents itself to you, write down a key word, a hindrance or an aid, a habit or a goal. For example, under "speech" you might write "gossip," or "KISS = Keep It Simple, Stupid." Soon you'll see all eight in your everyday life.

Connecting the Dots

Starting out, the path can be easily memorized as a series of eight links forming a step-by-step progression. First off, there's the introduction of this path already given in the Four Noble Truths. "A path is present." Like a doorway or hinge, the Fourth Noble Truth invokes the Eightfold Path. Reciprocally, the first step of the path, *view,* is a re-view of the Noble Truths—did we understand them?

Now, we could understand the Four Truths intellectually but without putting them into proper practice. So we must also have willingness to take the journey. More like good intentions, this link is called *thought*.

What's next? Well, to put right outlook and intent into practice, we need to conduct ourselves properly. It's counterproductive to proceed with all the best intentions and perspective, while still saying things that contradict the wisdom of our approach. Similarly, it's no good if we express our wisdom perfectly but don't practice what we preach. So *word* and *deed* are important steps. Plus, at the end of the day, it matters how we put a roof over our heads and bread on the table, in order to sustain our practice. That is, our job is to promote good for others as well as ourselves.

Along the Path

Being a circle, the wheel has no top, no bottom. All eight stages are needed in order to navigate the entire journey. A linear sequence is good for memorizing, but the path itself is multidimensional; no beginning, no end. We could also map it as a sphere. Or as a crystal, each facet reflecting all the others. Or as an eight-petalled flower.

Okay. But a road doesn't travel on its own. So it takes diligence to follow through. My grandmother used to call it "elbow grease." With such *effort,* we can access the Buddha's teachings deep within ourselves through our meditational practices, be they insight or zen, Pure Land or Tibetan, or a collage. So meditation means rolling up your sleeves and sticking to the task at hand. And meditation is a balance—between *mindfulness* and *concentration,* which are like a beam of light and a lens, respectively.

And so this linear view turns full circle again. Meditation furthers wisdom, which better informs our conduct—on and on, keeping the wheel turning round.

The Path can be simplified by grouping the eight factors under three general categories. Understanding and thought are traditionally grouped together as pertaining to *wisdom;* speech, action, and livelihood all pertain to *conduct* (ethics); effort, mindfulness, and concentration pertain to *meditation. Note:* Meditation alone is not the entirety of Buddhism if it lacks training in wisdom and ethics. And so on for each of these three major elements. Each amplifies and refines the others.

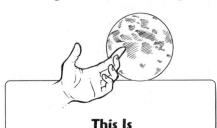

This Is

Holistic health treats the whole person—body, mind, and spirit. (You could say that ethics, meditation, and wisdom correspond to these three.) A holistic outlook focuses on patterns forming a whole, rather than breaking things down into parts and analyzing the pieces (the mechanistic outlook). The word "holistic" shares a common Old English root with "hale," "heal," "health," "holy," and "whole."

Tip: Take your time. Don't feel you have to dive in and put in an eight-hour day spending an hour on each element. If your doctor recommended eight ways to change your diet—for instance, no salt, less caffeine, no fried foods, less red meat, and so on—you'd modify your diet gradually, so as not to throw your metabolism into a state of shock. (Spiritual as well as physical crash-courses might result in a kind of adrenaline rush at first, but without sustained benefit.) Instead, by gradual adjustment and tweaking, they all eventually become integrated and second nature.

Remember, the Buddhist medical model is *holistic*. A pill or surgery might make a symptom vanish but may not necessarily eradicate the root cause. Stress reduction, exercise, diet, and medication, for example, all work together to get to the root.

Wisdom. (On the left, a block-style version; a more flowing, cursive version on the right.) One interpretation of the Chinese word sees the upper component as a broom, the middle as a hand, taking hold of the broom, sweeping the heart, below. In this view, wisdom isn't an accumulation of knowledge, but rather the shedding of ignorance. Another interpretation sees the three parallel lines with the vertical line through them as the centered connection of the heavenly, human, and earthly realms, directly pointing into the heart, making the meaning of wisdom.

(Calligraphy: Kazuaki Tanahashi)

Conversely, if, say, your kidneys aren't processing correctly, that could affect not only your stomach but your nervous system, and so on. The eight phases of the path each have their negative opposite (wrong view, wrong thought, wrong speech, and so on), and one weak link affects the whole chain.

Continuing an idea we proposed with the Three Jewels (see Chapter 5), you could consider the eight factors as jewels in a necklace, or, better, as facets of a crystal. Each would reflect a light shone into just one. In each, you could see the light reflected in all the others. Practicing just one single step well is to ultimately come to practice the others. Let's now look at each a bit deeper.

This is the character for "heart" in Chinese and Japanese. It depicts a human heart, with chambers and aorta. It's also the character for "mind." So here we see mind and body as one. (On the left, a block-style version; a more flowing, cursive version on the right.)

(Calligraphy: Kazuaki Tanahashi)

Viewing Rightly: You See!?

The French author Marcel Proust wrote, "The real voyage of discovery consists not in seeking new landscapes, but in having new eyes." Do we have the *right view?* Viewing rightly, having a proper outlook on life, means seeing things as they are. Not as we might wish, imposing our conditioning and projections, our grasping, but rather with no preconceptions, unconditionally. Starting out, at the gate, the Buddha shakes our hand, showing us the Four Noble Truths: but do we understand?

The Four Noble Truths cleanse our minds and perceptions of ignorance, conditioned to grasp at straws rather than accept what's in front of our nose. They enable us to experience things as they are. Just being, in the moment, attentive to what is. The noble truths open our eyes, and the eightfold path trains them—that we may see with the wonder of a child, the compassion of a beloved grandparent, and the wisdom of a sage. If only we understand, hold an appropriate outlook, a correct view.

Hear and Now

"Mind is forerunner of action, foremost of deeds. Everything's made up of mind. If your mind is polluted, sorrow will follow, as the wheel trails the heels of an ox .... if your mind is pure, happiness will ensue, the way your shadow trails along wherever you go."

—The Dhammapada (first-century B.C.E. sutra)

Thought: The Painter of the Backdrop

Thought, or thinking, here carries the sense of motive or intention, attitude, mindset. How we think about our path will color our journey. (Please check in your mental luggage before you embark upon the Path.)

Attitude helps determine reality. For example, consider the human brain as both a transmitter and a receiver. It sifts and interprets sense data about the world, and it coordinates your actions within that world, which in turn help to shape it. It creates a circular feedback loop. As computer programmers say, "Garbage in, garbage out." And, conversely, a positive outlook multiplies the good things in life.

People understand this who follow the stock market, which rests on people's perceptions. Events create perceptions. And perceptions, in turn, cause people to react and create new events. For a real dark example, consider paranoia. Like a self-fulfilling prophecy, if I walk around with a look of suspicion, sure enough, folks will lift their eyebrows, looking at me askance, and so I'll start muttering to myself, which behavior causes people to talk about me behind my back, and so it goes, on and on. True, we're all interconnected; paranoia looks at that fact through the wrong side of the telescope. And so it goes for fear, anger, jealousy, and the whole nine yards.

We suffer because we *think* we'll be happy by possessing things we lust after, but which only create more dissatisfaction, because they never change our misdirected thought patterns. Traditional thoughts to be avoided are greed, ill-will, and fear. Pure poison. Similarly, if we think Buddhism will provide an escape from commitment, or an easy answer, or a means of getting back at our parents, then forget about it. Yet we all come to the path with our residue of pain, so it takes continual self-examination to put out the fires and embers of suffering. To free ourselves, we personally check and reevaluate our motives continually.

Here's a cool tip: Cultivate each of the eight steps as an end unto itself, not as a means to anything else.

Indeed, do everything this way. Chopping wood, just chop wood. Ursula Le Guin put it very well when she said, "It is good to have an end to journey toward; but it is the journey that matters, in the end." When I was in college, an important thing I learned was "the grade is not the work." That is, what's important is what you get out of it. Moreover, unless we're really doing each thing fully, we're never really doing anything.

Thought as attitude. You can almost hear the cogitation in the Rodin sculpture, thinking with every muscle and fiber right on down to his very toes. The Buddha or bodhisattva sits straight, enjoying his breathing. Whatever thought comes is welcomed, like hearing the chirp of a happy bird. [tsw] Auguste Rodin, The Thinker *(1880). 79" × 51¼" × 55¼". The Rodin Museum, Philadelphia: Gift of Jules E. Mastbaum.* Bodhisattva Maitreya in Pensive Pose. *Korean National Museum, Seoul. Silla Period. Early seventh century. Gilt bronze. 90.8 cm.*

Attitude is all. An initial detour many people invariably encounter in starting out with Buddhism is searching for enlightenment. While my ultimate goal is enlightenment, I attain it by stripping away my conditionings and cravings, so enlightenment can happen of itself. I can't enlighten myself any more than I can surprise myself. Rather, through the discipline of the path I can make conditions right for enlightenment to occur, laying a strong foundation, and a space for that chance to take place.

Right Action: Good Karma

Think of this: scientists have zeroed in on the physics of thought so finely that they can rig up a prosthetic limb that can be operated by mere thought. So thought equals *action.*

The traditional definition of right action is a series of road signs, advising abstention from:

➤ Killing

➤ Stealing

➤ Wrong speech

➤ Sexual misconduct

➤ Unhealthy foods and intoxicants

These are collectively known as the Five Cardinal Precepts, and constitute the sole focus of Chapter 7, "The Art of Living: Cardinal Precepts." Chapter 8, "The Fine Print: Touching Deeper," explains in more depth the Buddhist notion of moral cause and effect, *karma*. For now, it's enough to say that what was done yesterday affects today and what you do today affects tomorrow.

Another lesson to be learned about action is that we're free to act, but we're not entitled to the fruit of our action. That is, if we're really present to ourselves and what's in front of our nose, in the moment, devoting our selves to that and that alone, we do each thing fully, without clinging to any. Hit each nail on the head, then move on.

Say the Word and It Will Happen

The Buddha asks us to monitor ourselves and listen as we speak. Traditional *speech* to refrain from includes the following:

➤ Lies

➤ Slander

➤ Harsh words

➤ Frivolous speech

How often do we put people down, or put people off, or put people on hold through our speech? How often do we speak of things about which we don't have any first-hand evidence? I believe words can create thunderstorms and earthquakes, and cool breezes and clear summer days. Interestingly, speech is considered an action, and included in the five precepts, so we'll explore it in more depth in Chapter 7.

Work Like You Don't Need the Money

To speak a bit righteously, we put our money where our mouth is by our *work*. That is, unless we're monks or nuns, we have a range of choices as to how we earn our daily bread. Traditional professions deemed unsuitable for Buddhists include trading in the following:

➤ Arms

➤ Human beings (slavery, prostitution)

➤ Flesh (breeding animals for slaughter)

➤ Intoxicants and poison

In modern times, the choices don't get any easier. Human transactions have advanced to an astonishing degree of complexity, to the point where job descriptions can't keep up, often putting classical morality to the test. For example, is it breeding an animal for slaughter when animals are used for medical experimentation which might save lives? (More on work follows in Chapters 7 and 15.)

Hear and Now

"The traditional Buddhist analogy for right effort is the walk of an elephant or tortoise. The elephant moves along surely, unstoppably, with great dignity. Like the worm, it is not excitable, but unlike the worm, it has a panoramic view of the ground it is treading on. Though it is serious and slow, because of the elephant's ability to survey the ground there is a sense of playfulness and intelligence in its movement."

—Chögyam Trungpa Rinpoche

Right Effort: Just Do It

When laid out on the wheel, *effort* is directly opposite from thought (motive, intent, attitude). In that context, intent's where we're coming from, effort's where we're going. It's our direction, our pole star, and keeping at it. As we see further in Chapter 9, "Taking the Plunge: Beginning and Cultivating Your Practice," a good teacher and sangha are important in this regard.

Many people move through their lives without direction. They never even think of it. We all know the third dimension is extension in space (think cube, instead of square). Now, the fourth dimension, in human terms, can be thought of as *direction*. A moving car instead of a motionless block. We may only be able to see as far as our headlights illuminate, as in the fog: Perseverance, plus a light touch at the wheel, will stay the course.

Like people who win the lottery, Buddhism has stories of people who become totally enlightened *Shazam!* at the drop of a coconut. It usually takes preparation. The Buddha sat for six years in the wilderness. The elimination of asceticism, self-torture, from the Middle Way isn't a cue for spiritual laziness. Remember, among the Buddha's last words were, "Be a lamp unto yourself. Seek your enlightenment *with diligence*." (Meaning: "You can do it, too—so get busy!") And if the Buddha were alive, he'd be that guy sitting way over in the back and to one side of the meditation hall … still practicing …

Mindfulness: Intelligent Alertness

Awareness is a primary characteristic distinguishing us from animals; we're warm and aware we're warm, cold and aware of it, hungry and aware of it. In the evolution from slime to worm to ape, you could imagine awareness as an extra fillip, a little doodling or filigree that nature added to human makeup. A jazzy extra resonance, like singing in the shower to hear our voice echo off the wet tiles, it serves no utilitarian purpose but fun to do anyway. But being aware of our awareness is a major evolutionary leap—as author and meditation teacher Wes Nisker spryly puts it, "mindfulness is the opposable thumb of consciousness." This enlightened self-awareness is part of what Buddha called *mindfulness*.

We're aware of life to varying degrees. As I write, I'm aware of my posture, the clothes I'm wearing, sounds outside the window, my breathing, thoughts coming and going, and so on. (I only imagine my editor's eagle eye over my shoulder, or what my readers might look like.) If I stop for a moment and just focus my awareness on one thing, like sounds, for example, I feel my innate awareness grow. I become aware of the phenomenal, rhythmic, continuous symphony of life's natural, unnoticed soundtrack, moment to moment. I might notice, too, how my mind might be drawn toward some sounds and repelled by others. "Birds, good! Garbage men, bad!" By noticing my desires and aversions, I can get a handle on them, get distance from them, and eventually let them go. We'll come back to this technique in more detail in Chapter 11, "Look Within and Know: Insight Meditation *(Vipassana).*" Indeed, the whole third part of our book is about meditation, but here's more.

This Is

The Sanskrit word for **mindfulness,** *smriti,* means "to remember." Our lives are genuine when we remember ourselves, when we remember to be present in the here and now. Mindfulness is a means of awakening our awareness, attentive to things as they are, in and of themselves.

Buddha taught a method of building a strong practice of meditation, in his *Satipatthana Sutra,* called the Four Establishments of Mindfulness. He asks us to shine the light of mindfulness in the following four directions:

➤ Body

➤ Feelings

➤ Mind

➤ Phenomena

At any given time, whatever we're doing, *without judging,* we can be mindful of our body (comfort or discomfort, being in motion or at rest, quality of in-breath, out-breath), grounding our practice, making it solid. We can be mindful of sense impressions and feelings (pleasant, unpleasant, happy, sad, angry, joyous), and thus no longer be swept away by their tide but, rather, sit on their banks, watching them flow out to sea. And we can make our mind both the focus of our mindfulness (noticing if we are peaceful, self-respecting, humble, faithful, caring, or greedy, angry, proud, ignorant, opinionated) as well as the phenomena to which our mind relates (such as the object of our care or faith, or anger or greed).

Leaves from the Bodhi Tree

A passing stranger encountered some Buddhist monks in a forest. He asked what they were doing. A monk stopped to explain that they were Buddhists and that he and his fellow monks were cutting wood. "Wait. I cut wood, too, for my fire," said the man. "I don't see anything extraordinary about that." Well, sir," the monk replied, "when we cut wood, we know we're cutting wood. We don't cut wood in order to build a fire. We cut wood in order to cut wood." The monk smiled, and added, "If we can't cut wood, how then can we build a fire?" Then he resumed his work, and the man went on his way.

Right Concentration: Hitting the Nail on the Head

To Westerners, *concentration* normally implies Rodin's thinker: furrowing your brow, making beads of sweat run off the bridge of your nose, and so on. The Buddhist meaning of right concentration is, rather, no thought, no thinking, no thinker. Only pure focused awareness. Focused awareness threads the needle, puts the ball in the hoop. The practitioner might begin by concentrating his or her mind on an object, but both object and mind become fused at a common center, a single point. Like a hammer hitting the nail on the head, this one-pointed attention is fixed on neither hammer nor nail but the concentrated *thwack!*

Meditation is a balance between concentration and mindfulness working in tandem. Concentration is like a lens; mindfulness places an object beneath the lens and looks through.

Mindfulness and concentration aren't the end of the path. They're spokes of a wheel, along the way. True, right mindfulness and concentration could proceed straight on linearly to right understanding, renewing the cycle. But at the same time they right thought, speech, direction, livelihood, and so on. Don't get too fixed upon any one spoke. (Life is full of endless cycles, wheels within wheels.) Stay centered. Remember: The center is the still point of the turning wheel. Enjoy the journey. You *are* the path.

Set one foot on the path and you'll see it everywhere.

Hear and Now

"Concentration and mindfulness go hand in hand in the job of meditation. Mindfulness directs the power of concentration .... Concentration furnishes the power by which mindfulness can penetrate into the deepest level of mind .... Too much awareness without calm to balance it will result in a wildly over-sensitized state similar to abusing LSD. Too much concentration without a balancing ratio of awareness will result in the 'Stone Buddha' syndrome."

—Venerable Henepola Gunaratana

The Least You Need to Know

➤ Buddhist practice (the eightfold path) and Buddhist theory (the four noble truths) mutually support each other.

➤ It's good to memorize the eight steps (and it's okay to change a word if it gets at the meaning better for you): (*wisdom*) view, thought; (*conduct*) speech, action, livelihood; (*meditation*) effort, mindfulness, concentration.

➤ Meditation is only one part of Buddhist practice, along with wisdom and conduct.

➤ You needn't practice the steps in any order, nor all at once. Develop each element gradually but steadily.

➤ Practice each training as an end unto itself. Indeed, everything you do, just do that—fully aware you're doing that, and nothing else.

Chapter 7

The Art of Living: Cardinal Precepts

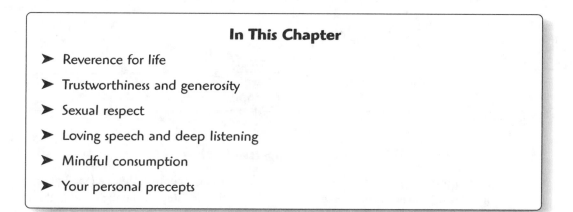

In This Chapter

➤ Reverence for life

➤ Trustworthiness and generosity

➤ Sexual respect

➤ Loving speech and deep listening

➤ Mindful consumption

➤ Your personal precepts

We've just seen how the Buddhist path is based on wisdom, meditation, and conscious conduct (ethics). To be wise, to lead a contemplative life, calls for guidelines called *precepts*. Since the time of the Buddha, the precepts have preserved the continuity and vitality of the sangha. Indeed, initiation into many Buddhist sanghas, the beginning of formal practice, is done through transmission of the precepts. You take refuge in them, in a ceremony in which you also take refuge in the Three Jewels. (Taking refuge means affirming one's appreciation of and trust in them.)

Actually, for monks there are 254 precepts. Some schools have 58, for everyone; others, 16. So there are different ways to cut up the ethical pie. You could boil them all down to one, the Golden Rule: Do unto others as you'd have others do unto you. These precepts are cast from that same gold.

The five we'll study are the real nitty gritty: no killing, stealing, lying, sexual misconduct, or intoxicants. You'll find the basic principles underlying them resonate with those of any religion, yet with some different emphases which you can apply to your own root tradition. Learn them. Practice them. Meditate on them. And see for yourself. They're the foundation of a path with heart.

To Not Kill: Reverence for Life

Consider how widespread murder actually is: in America it's the #10 cause of death. And that's not counting death occurring (daily) on other levels—international (war), intellectual (censorship), spiritual (walking zombies and human beasts), and so on.

In a recent survey of the murder rate for American males age 15 to 24, per 100,000 people, the figure was 24.4; the next-highest country was Canada with only 2.6. America carries a rugged legacy, it's true. It's our heritage. You can hear the violence of our culture in daily speech. In my own profession, I always pause before I say the word "deadline," hearing its military origins (Civil War) still echoing today, feeling its adrenaline. Nor do I wish for my writing to knock my audiences dead. (I'd prefer my readers might just levitate an inch or two off the ground now and then.) Others speak of making a killing in the stock market. And so on.

Along the Path

Central to Buddhist, Hindu, and Jain spirituality is the concept of **ahimsa** (Sanskrit, meaning "to do no harm; reverence for life"). It's the first step of the eightfold path of yoga. Ahimsa led to India's adoption of vegetarianism and abandonment of animal sacrifice (although animal sacrifice persists in certain places). Jain followers take great lengths to observe ahimsa: Monks filter water so as not to consume microbes. Priests wear white gauze masks so as not to breathe an insect in and don't walk at night so as not to step on a worm.

Whether or not you've served in the military, I'd say you're a veteran, given the profound impact of war upon all our lives. For example, who hasn't met a veteran with scars others bear?

But, unlike Judaism or Christianity, this Buddhist precept applies not-killing to not only other human beings but all beings. That's a very genuine recognition. Animals and trees can't write the congresspeople who represent their district, but this Buddhist precept speaks on their behalf. Such reverence for life, for all life forms, isn't unique to Buddhism. It's essential, for example, to Native American spirituality, exemplified by its wealth of marvelous tall tales starring coyotes, otters, eagles, spiders, salmon, and bears, as well as humans. By broadening the horizon to embrace all of creation, the negative tense of "not-killing" subtly flips to positive: what a missionary physician stationed in Africa named Albert Schweitzer termed "reverence for life." And life manifests in many forms.

Look: A lion with a lamb, a leopard and a cow, living together so peaceably! This is the first of many paintings of the peaceable kingdom prophesied by Isaiah (11:6–9). It was rendered by a gifted Quaker minister and visionary named Edward Hicks. In this, his first of many versions, its creatures are the most playful, its sky the most luminous. Edward Hicks, American (1780–1849), The Peaceable Kingdom. *Oil on canvas, 47.6 × 59.7 cm. © The Cleveland Museum of Art, 2001, Gift of the Hanna Fund, 1945.38.*

Vegetarianism

Whether you eat fish or fowl, greens or grain, if you eat mindfully, you cannot help but be aware of the life you're taking inside of you. Communion. The beet or carrot, for example, telling you what it means to live inside the earth, so moist, dark, and sweet. Or the lamb, being led to slaughter, sensing its fate, adrenaline of fright flooding its bloodstream.

I won't go into the valid health or environmental rationales for vegetarianism, which can be a totally viable diet if one has the option. Buddhists in certain terrains and economies don't have the option, and so eat meat. That's also an example of how it's up to each person to make terms with the precepts—how little or how much; how slowly or how soon.

Along the Path

Some famous vegetarians: Pythagoras, Lao-tzu, Plato, Virgil, Ovid, Plutarch, Jesus Christ, Leonardo da Vinci, Michel de Montaigne, John Milton, Percy Bysshe Shelley, Leo Tolstoy, Susan B. Anthony, Horace Greeley, Ralph Waldo Emerson, Louisa May Alcott, Hans Christian Anderson, H. G. Wells, Charles Darwin, Albert Einstein, Mahatma Gandhi, George Bernard Shaw, Dick Gregory, Isaac Bashevis Singer, Bill Cosby, Michael J. Fox, Paula Abdul, Drew Barrymore, Kim Basinger, Merv Griffin, and Scott (*Dilbert*) Adams.

I had a head start. As a little boy, my grandmother took me by the hand to visit a butcher. A kosher butcher, of course. That is, he exercised as much compassion as the act of slaughtering permits. I remember an animal hung from a hook, skinned. And intense eyes of chickens in cages. Feathers on the floor. Calmly, a man chopped up meat with a butcher knife, bones and all, *thwack thwack thwack!* How many people have even that much of an idea where the meat on their table comes from?

Eventually, I came to vegetarianism out of my practice of Judaism and its resonance with my own sense of things. But it wasn't easy and was, moreover, a gradual process of elimination and substitution, taking years. With it came dozens of adjustments, from how I moved (lighter, calmer, slower) to its social etiquette. Today, I'm challenged to not be attached to vegetarianism the way I was to meat. Stay open. Unless you have a medical issue, don't refuse food that's offered to you.

Abortion

Sooner or later, abortion comes up in any extensive discussion of the first precept. Dharma can compassionately see the suffering of both the fetus and the mother. Japanese Buddhists have evolved a very interesting and unique practice. Many Japanese Buddhist temples will conduct a funeral service for an aborted or stillborn fetus (in Japanese "water baby"). Zen master and teacher Robert Aitken notes, "It's given a posthumous Buddhist name, and thus identified as an individual, however incomplete, to whom we can say farewell. With this ceremony, the woman is in touch with life and death as they pass through her existence, and she finds that such basic changes are relative waves on the great ocean of true nature which is not born and does not pass away."

These stone Jizo images in Chichibu, Japan, are accompanied by umbrellas, shawls, and toys to express compassion for deceased children and the unborn, as well as prayers for their well-being in the world beyond. Jizo is the bodhisattva who protects children and travelers—here children in transit to either rebirth or the Pure Land.

(Photo: William R. LaFleur, from Liquid Life: Abortion and Buddhism in Japan *[Princeton University Press, 1992])*

Every "Shalt-Not" Has Its "Shall"

The precepts offer both a negative and a positive response to the human condition. Do's and don'ts. One reason they're phrased restrictively is because humanity has already developed bad habits. Yet, though they may sound like confinements, they promote freedom. A positive outcome results: if I eliminate harmful behavior, everyone will be much happier, myself included.

Reverence for life is a natural, positive outcome of not-killing, for example. But all too often we cling to the negative definition. For instance, we define peace in terms of the absence of war, perpetuating dualistic thought. (My hero, Jewish philosopher Spinoza, says, "Peace is not absence of war. It's a virtue, a state of mind, a disposition for benevolence, confidence, virtue.")

It's important to be clear about how we define our terms. A nonviolent demonstration might be so only because its members lacked weapons, for example. Pacifism, on the other hand, sees violence as only begetting more violence and, moreover, requires commitment to social change through the power of truth and truth alone.

Historical examples of pacifism aren't rare, but are rarely discussed. Examples of real peace deserve careful attention. King Ashoka hung up his sword and converted his military to peaceful uses, yet was never attacked and never faced internal revolt.

More recently, Mahatma Gandhi lead India to independence through pacifist demonstrations. (It's interesting that an African American minister, Howard Thurman, recounted his meetings with Gandhi to a young visiting minister named Martin Luther King Jr. And so the Dharma wheel came full-circle yet again—Gandhi having been profoundly influenced by Henry David Thoreau who, in turn, was influenced by Indian *ahimsa*, nonharm.)

Hear and Now

"In Buddhism the first precept of not killing, or harmlessness to living beings ... has a religious rather than a moral or metaphysical basis. By this I mean that it is grounded in our Buddha-nature—the matrix of all phenomena .... It is in Buddha-nature that all existences, animate and inanimate, are unified and harmonized .... To willfully take life ... means to disrupt and destroy this inherent wholeness and to blunt feelings of reverence and compassion arising from our Buddha-mind."

—Roshi Philip Kapleau

While every "Shalt Not" has its "Shall," there are no detailed maps. Each is up to you to determine. Thus, for example, there's no magic formula for peace. As Quaker minister A. J. Muste (1885–1967) put it so well, "There is no path to peace; peace is the path." The path begins with awareness, mindfulness. Every day, don't we kill our finest impulses ... slaughter our higher instincts ... through our casual, willful ignorance ... investing in a culture of cynicism and violence? In defense, it's argued that aggression is a natural response. If so, that doesn't mean humanity can't evolve. As Shunryu Suzuki Roshi used to say, "Everyone is perfect, but could stand a little improvement."

Eliminate those negatives. Accentuate the positives. And embrace the fuzzy in-betweens of the Middle Way.

To Not Steal: Trustworthiness and Generosity

You don't have to be a criminal to consider the precepts in your own life. Imagine you're at an airport to see your best friend off. All flights are running late. The area where you've been waiting has filled with people, then emptied out, then filled up again. You notice that aluminum suitcase someone's parked in the seat next to you is still there, and the owner's never come back. Okay, your friend is curious—and the brass tabs don't seem to be locked.

Imagine your surprise as you open it up and see the suitcase is packed with neat stacks of $100 bills. You close it, quickly, and look around to see if anyone else saw. Sure, it's a perfect setup for a nail-biter suspense thriller—but what would *you* do? Give it all away at the airport, on the spot? Give it to Lost and Found, leaving the temptation to them?

Or would you split it with your friend? Say you found out it wasn't counterfeit. Would you still wonder about its karma? Maybe it was payment for some black-market transaction. Or blackmail ... or a ransom ... or a bribe ... What if you and your friend decide to split it in thirds, giving a third to a charity? Which charity? Do either of you have a charitable cause? Have you examined charities to find one where your donation will be put to good use, without it greasing bureaucratic wheels or lining somebody else's pockets? And so the uncertainty widens even further, and the money still sits there, like radioactive plutonium. (Would a lawyer be the solution?)

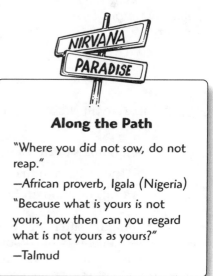

Along the Path

"Where you did not sow, do not reap."

—African proverb, Igala (Nigeria)

"Because what is yours is not yours, how then can you regard what is not yours as yours?"

—Talmud

Fiction; make-believe. Yet don't we encounter similar situations every day, implicated in the invisible nexus of property and poverty, credit and cash, without even thinking? To drive the point home, here's a very simple example. As I write, there's an apple on my desk. Because I have this apple, you don't. It's true!

But maybe you do happen to have an apple right now. What then? Well, there must be other people who don't have the apples that you and I do—the whole world, in fact. So, like I say, if you have an apple, I don't. Suddenly, world hunger stares us straight in the face. We have apples; they don't. The problem is simple: The poor don't have enough—and the rich have too much. It's interesting how money and property makes interbeing become more vivid to our imagination. Given the awareness, the challenge is to learn to live simpler to consume less needless stuff, and to cherish what one has.

I know, all this might imply that everyone should immediately donate all their possessions to the poor. The funny thing is, deep down, most of us know it's true. But then the poor would have things that everyone else would no longer have, and the cycle of poverty wouldn't be broken. That would violate the Middle Way of harmony and balance. So we learn to not take more than we need, and not to take what's not ours, and to share what we have with those who don't, without going in want ourselves.

This means "recycling station" or "recycled product." The three arrows represent Recycle, Reuse, and Reduce waste. Public domain (fittingly, for a Buddhist discussion of property).

These are timeless truths, but our society seems to be presently suffering from amnesia. What's Buddhist, here, is emphasis on …

➤ Compassionate awareness of property's potential for suffering or happiness.

➤ The realization that all property (things) is interconnected (as are deeds).

➤ Consideration of the karma created by the use to which things are put.

I realize that after you've considered the political correctness of your purchases in terms of country or corporation of origin, it seems hard to do anything except to stay at home and count your fingers. But, as we've seen, thoughts are deeds. And with consciousness can come consciousness raising, the next step in any tipping of the scales of justice. When I use a computer, for instance, I'm aware of how its miraculous silicon chips are often manufactured under very harsh conditions, often by immigrant women. And that a byproduct is toxic waste. What can I do? I don't condone suffering or potential environmental degradation, yet I am mindful of the suffering that is still part of my landscape. And now you know, too.

Sexual Respect: Respect, Intimacy, Trust, and Responsibility

Pardon my French, but in the common parlance of today the Thou Shalt Not here means to not screw around. That is, don't mess with the sexual urge that shaped us and throbs within us still. It's an elemental force, comparable to the intertwining of yin and yang. Daily, we interact with energy fields and physical reality in ways which are sexual, although we don't usually call them such. This precept, then, acknowledges the fundamental yin-yang dance of male and female and calls us to focus our mindfulness upon it, to let that energy flow for the good.

These ethics address adultery, incest, and rape—things which threaten the fabric of family, woven of sexuality. Sexuality's a social issue, because our society is woven of families. (Chapter 19, "Happiness Is Not an Individual Matter: Engaging the World," discusses Dharma, family values, and relationships.)

Our society's obsessed with sexuality, as you'll see from glancing at the tabloids at supermarket checkout stands. Look, too, at the ads. In our consumer culture, sex sells—everything from face cream to cars to violence. Since advertisers aren't known for hiring models that look like my Aunt Ida in Jersey, American women have starved themselves silly to emulate shadow-thin models, while men indulge in boyish fantasies. When a husband and wife look at each other in bed and don't see dream models, they roll over and lick their wounds of suffering self—and, presumably, go out the next day and buy more products to fill the void. Superficial social conventions can't fully answer the complexities of life, and so the pain continues.

Hear and Now

"... our social conception has managed to supply shelters of every sort, for, as it was disposed to take love-life as a pleasure, it had also to give it an easy form, cheap, safe and sure, as public pleasures are. ... For one human being to love another: that's perhaps the most difficult of all our tasks, the ultimate, the last test and proof, the work for which all other work is but preparation."

—Rainer Maria Rilke

Respect is essential; respecting Self and Other as really no different. With that foundation comes intimacy. This is a core experience in Buddhism. Respecting life, all life forms, we enter into the heart of creation, gaining a greater intimacy with life. When two people have a long-term commitment to each other, then sexual intimacy can be one of life's most profound human experiences.

Maybe, alas, that's not been your experience. At the dawn of this century, for instance, for every 100,000 women in America, 84 have been raped. (The next highest-ranking country, Sweden, had 15 instances.) Then factor in the people touched by that suffering. But numbers can never express the trauma caused by rape, abuse, incest; nor can words.

The practice of mindfulness helps heal the wounds of abused sexuality; the sangha can act as support group. As part of the path of healing, veterans of sex abuse can vow to keep others from experiencing rape, abuse, or incest. Being responsible for ourselves, we're responsible for others. Healing others, we heal ourselves.

Sanghas, themselves, are vulnerable. Given the power of priesthood, the trust of taking refuge, the intimacy of meditation, and the fallibility of human nature, a sexual scandal in a Buddhist community isn't totally surprising, though no less unconscionable when it occurs. Love is not a toy.

To Not Lie: Deep Listening and Loving Speech

The Ten Commandments don't directly address lying, per se, but rather false witness. Yet it's there. The Talmud (Hebrew books of biblical commentary) say that no one should talk one way with his or her lips and think another way in his or her heart. This is so universal it hardly sounds any different in, say, Taoism: "Do not assert with your mouth what your heart denies."

To lie is to automatically be dishonest about everything—to be indifferent to the truth. The Buddha is very clear about this. (Ready?) He says, "A person is born with an axe in his mouth. He whose speech is unwholesome cuts himself with an axe." So when we say, "love" in all sincerity, we actually bring love into the world.

True, Buddhism is aware of the inability of words to express spiritual truth. Yet, from a nondualistic approach we can find our Middle Way between speech and silence. I've expressed this third precept in terms of both listening and speaking. If some people say silly things, they've forgotten how to listen—to themselves and others. Listen …

The four components of this Chinese word for the verb "to listen" are: ear, eyes, undivided attention, and heart.

(Calligraphy: Chungliang Al Huang)

Bearing Witness

There's no secret to my craft of writing: it's writing and reading. Half of what I do is writing, and the other half is reading what I've written, then rewriting what doesn't read right to me. Then I show it to other readers for feedback, then editors, and so on. So words always imply two activities: writing and reading; speaking and hearing.

As a person who uses words yourself, you're probably aware of your Inner Judge, right? You know, the one who says, "Who *is* this guy?! What's he asking *me* for? Sheesh! Let's get on with the show!" This voice judges everything, makes lists of likes and dislikes, and never forgets.

Meanwhile, every moment awaits us silently, unconditionally. To turn down the volume on your internal Judge Jim or Judge Judy, you only need to become aware of that inner soundtrack in the first place. You're constantly sifting through your experience (we all do), commenting on it like a movie reviewer talking to his- or herself in a theater ("Liked that: two thumbs up!" "Now why'd that happen? That was all wrong!" and "Uh-oh! Boring part coming up!"). And it's always past or future, reviewing or rehearsing, never present tense.

One way to be in the present is to just *bear witness* to it. Right now, I pause to look out my window, and bear witness to how the buildings look more vivid in the misty morning fog. I bear witness to the unseen bird in the tree outside my window, its song mimicking the morning's mood and my mind. I bear witness to life. Try it yourself, anytime. Stop and listen to the life where you're living, as all of life, right now. What keeps us from being aware 360° all around is our inner narrator, who fades down only when we shift attention from everything being our story to the more expansive reality of what is—things as they are, in and of themselves—seemingly without limit.

Sometimes when I overhear two people talking, I get the impression they're playing verbal tennis. The rules are: Person A speaks for three minutes, then person B gets to speak for three minutes, then it's A's turn again. Talking *at* each other, they're listening with their mouth, not their heart. I once participated in a workshop in which Joan Halifax Roshi introduced an exercise in bearing witness which provided a healthy, potent alternative. We broke up into twos and sat facing each other. My job was to make myself as transparent as I possibly could, dropping all my masks and just manifesting my deepest, truest nature to my partner. As I did so, my partner did the same for me. In silence, looking into each other's open face, we gave our undivided attention to the Buddha nature we sensed. Then we each took turns telling the other what we experienced, with the same awareness. Then we took turns telling the group, and listening to everyone else. There was a common feeling of compassion and mutuality.

This Is

"When you go to **bear witness,** it means that you go with no preconceived notions about what you'll see and what will happen. ... Bearing witness means to have a relationship. ... Out of bearing witness, out of that relationship, a healing arises. In what form, through what activity or event, through what person, I have no idea."

—Bernie Glassman, *Bearing Witness: A Zen Master's Lessons in Making Peace*

It is said that Avalokiteshvara, bodhisattva of compassion, particularly in the form of Kuan Yin, can *see* the sounds of human suffering. Kuan Yin's Chinese name has two components: "gaze" (regard) and "sound." It is said she became enlightened through hearing.

If you believe in God, you might imagine you're a spy from heaven, acting as God's eyes and ears. Some Christian sects have maintained that life as we know it is what the Creator sees when looking into us. If the beginning was the Word, rather than argue over the wording, we might begin to hear It—whatever it happens to be, right now, clear as a bell.

Leaves from the Bodhi Tree

Roshi Tetsugen Bernard Glassman has been leading people on Buddhist retreats on the streets of New York City's Bowery since 1991. They live for five days on the streets without money or a change of clothes, learning from the unknown and the unexpected. And he's held retreats at the empty concentration camps at Auschwitz. Jews, Germans, and Arabs all come. At the outset, members of every group might criticize: "It shouldn't be done like this, but *this* way!" Meanwhile, he leads them all in on-site mindfulness meditation. By around Day Two, he's said people often wake up to the magnitude of the suffering still present, of those who worked as well as those who died there. When they access that, then healing energy can also arise.

Loving Speech

Speech goes with listening. They both create karma. I think of Claude Anshin Thomas, a helicopter crew chief during the American war in Vietnam, and his karma, for example. Now a zen priest, in 1998 he embarked on a peace pilgrimage across America. By foot. In some cities, he and his companions were about to be run out of town until a dialogue began, and then they were invited to dinner instead. Midway in his journey, a media photographer approached him and asked, "If you don't mind, I'd like you to stand beside that tree so I can shoot you." Without a word, Claude just walked away. I hope the photographer eventually heard within himself why. (The prize word was "shoot.")

Gossip's a common red flag indicating that loving speech is absent. My dictionary defines gossip as trivial *rumor*. Gossip can be good or bad, but it's about some one or thing not present. Loving speech is about the present moment. It isn't as if we don't have opportunities to practice it. But a recent survey found, alas, that working couples spend four minutes a day talking to each other with concentrated attention; a typical parent and child engage in meaningful conversation for only 20 minutes a week. Speech can be a great meditation. Listening to … and saying … each … word … with … love.

Mindful Consumption

In a strict Theravadan sense, this precept means no alcohol. Period. Alcohol can not only interfere with the practice of a monk or priest. By clouding the mind and releasing inhibitions, it could lead a practitioner to then proceed to break all the other precepts—killing, committing adultery, and so on.

Where's the Middle Way here? Recognition, perhaps, that abstinence forgoes pleasures on the one hand but harmful possibilities on the other. And awareness of the karmic implications. If I drink just a drop at dinner, then I'm acting as a role model for others, some of whom might not be able to have just a drop, or "hold their liquor."

It's like the opposite of the minimal amount of food the Buddha first ate following his asceticism: Just a few drops do not nourish but can destroy.

In a broader, Mahayanan interpretation, alcohol can be read as addictions. Here's the Second Noble Truth, *trishna,* craving: gotta gotta gotta have it. Following the Middle Way thus includes being addicted neither to righteousness nor to licentiousness, to neither good nor bad addictions. A few sanghas define the precept as "no intoxicants" and point out that the word means toxic substances, leaving the door open for interpretation as to drugs. In most sanghas, this precept extends beyond alcohol to all drugs (including pot and LSD) and cigarettes, and, for some, even the gamut of junk foods, plus such poisons as *toxic media.* And it embraces *mindful recovery.*

The Eightfold Path Meets the Twelve-Step Program

Whatever story of ruined lives it tells, alcoholism's but the manifestation of deeper causes, of which it's just a symptom. To frame it in primary colors, the United States spent nearly $150 billion at the dawn of the century on illnesses, premature deaths, car crashes, and crimes all caused by alcohol.

The recovery movement covers addiction in general, drugs as well as alcohol. But we live in a society of addictions. You can divide any roomful of people into two groups: those in denial and those in recovery. Food binges, the Internet, sleep—name your addiction.

The recognition of an addiction is just the beginning of a lifelong process. For people who have a hard time with emphases on God, higher powers (the eleventh step of Alcohol Anonymous), and judgmental, patriarchal mindsets in some recovery programs, Buddhism can provide a welcome relief, for forgiving one's self with compassion, rather than the Blame Game of shame or guilt. Mindfulness is synonymous with *sobriety* and health.

Hear and Now

"Zen is the ultimate and original recovery program. It exposes our denial of true self and shows us how we've suffered because of our diseases of attachment, judgment, and division. It suggests a program for recovering our original nature and teaches steps we can take immediately. It shows us how all our other diseases and discontents flow from our fundamental denial of unity with each other and the universe."

—Mel Ash

Media Toxins

I confess. I'm an accredited member of the media (in recovery). Today's papers tell you the date, crimes du jour, weather, and so on. "The news" seldom reports the three million other stories happening today—the good news. Mainstream media perpetuates a culture of cynicism. The Golden Rule of mainstream media is "He who owns the gold rules." And so, to spike circulation up and make stockholders happy, newsroom mottoes are "Sex sells," and "If it bleeds, it leads" (leads, as the Number-One Story). That rule, unfortunately, defines the media's role as mediating advertisers to readers, rather than readers to community, or furnishing us with news we can use. This is true too for TV ratings and movie box offices. And so, we're stuck with this Frankenstein monster of media on steroids.

For example, when the Dalai Lama was in America once, he'd been in a room where a TV was on. Glancing over at the screen, he'd see a pretty image, such as children dancing in a field of flowers. He'd smile, and look away, but when he'd look back again just a moment later, he'd see a terrible image, such as a man threatening another man with a chainsaw. Positive image, then negative image. And so it went, alternating light and dark in rapid succession. He concluded TV must make Americans really exhausted!

Of course, we don't notice how we're being manipulated—that's part of the agreement. We grow numb to the enormous strain our pumped-up media exerts upon our spiritual, psychic, and moral fiber. Think: At the dawn of the new century, an 18-year-old American will have seen 16,000 simulated murders, plus 200,000 other acts of violence. (Ever have to remind yourself, or your kids, "It's only a movie!"?) Is this reverence for life?

I'm not proposing a ban on violent movies or games. No one but we ourselves turn the TV on. And it can be an addicting consumption, a plug-in drug. (By the way, have you ever noticed how television even talks to you? "We'll be right back! Don't go away!" Check it out!)

Toxins are all around. *Caveat emptor:* Buyer beware. Be aware: Are you consuming something toxic to your well-being? Mindfulness can break the dragon's grip of addictions, change our consumption habits, support others in recovery, and, eventually, transform our toxic culture of addiction.

Practicing the Precepts

As Venerable Master Hsing Yun points out, we might consider three aspects to practicing the precepts: *form, practice,* and *spirit.* Form means grasping the idea. This whole chapter has been about the precepts' form. But once you understand the words, you must put them into practice. Then you'll see the inner spirit of the precepts, and can internalize them for yourself.

Hear and Now

"The Precepts are so fundamentally and eternally pure and spotless that you could not fully transmit their greatness if you painted them across the endless sky. They are so perfect that if the entire universe crumbled into powder, these supreme Precepts would remain indestructible."

—Venerable Song-Chol

People often take refuge in only those precepts with which they're comfortable, on a one-by-one basis. This is in accord with the Buddhist tenet of weighing everything against your own life experience. Use your intuition. Listen within. And, anyway, to observe just one precept deeply is to ultimately observe all the others, anyway. They're deeply intertwined: lying to one's self (denial) and addiction, addiction and sexual abuse, sexual abuse and violence, violence and greed, and so on.

To practice *all* the precepts might seem to require monasticism. Yet you can follow them and still carry on with regular, rent-paying daily life. That seeming impossibility, however, is important to note. It's an aspect of another Buddhist tenet in which we're constantly asked us to consider the seemingly impossible ... a snowball of purity in a blazing furnace ... or the sound of one hand. As we'll see in Chapter 12, "See? Words Cannot Express: Zen," a school of Buddhism really familiar with the seeming paradoxes and illogic inherent in the Buddha's way is Zen. ("Illogical" to our dualistic mindset, that is.)

A zen approach recognizes three levels to the precepts. The first level is *straightforward:* Don't do harmful things, such as killing, for example. The second level asks us to recognize that we're killing *all the time* (crushing microbes, quenching flames, eating vegetables, and so on). (Being aware of this keeps us from being too *self*-righteous.)

The third level asks us to recognize the *impossibility* of killing. Matter is never created nor destroyed. Destroy something here, and it pops up in another form elsewhere. This threefold approach applies for all the precepts.

The Precepts as a Mindfulness Meditation

In my own experience, the precepts reinforce my mindfulness, and my mindfulness illuminates my understanding of the precepts. They coexist beautifully. Within your ordinary mind is buddha mind, as you discover when you do one thing at a time, mindfully. This takes discipline. The precepts cultivate conditions to further your goal. It's not an imposition from the outside but rather a means of realizing that no one owns your mind but you, an opportunity of learning how to live that freedom.

Building upon an insight meditation exercise taught by American vipassana teacher Jack Kornfield, I'd like to invite you to make this Precept Mindfulness Month. (Actually, at least five weeks, one for each precept.) For one week, just notice the influence of the first precept in your life. Vow to bring *no harm* to any living creature through word, deed, or thought. Yourself included. Notice all the living beings in your world you might normally ignore. Weeds poking up through pavement. Bugs. Birds. Cultivate a sense of care and reverence for them. Houseplants and weeds are buddhas, too. Stones are, too.

Hear and Now

"To live by the precepts is to travel the Way of unity and harmony in which the road is smooth, the obstructions few, and the scenery strikingly beautiful. To transgress the precepts is to take a side road that appears interesting but which soon turns bumpy, becomes monotonous, and ends in the dead-end of regret and apprehension."

—Philip Kapleau Roshi

Next week, observe the *material things* in your daily life, including money. How do you handle the objects that cross your path—yours and others? Do you recycle? Do you waste water in the shower? Are you energy efficient? Are you tempted by what's not yours? And you might make this week one in which to practice random acts of spontaneous kindness. Act on your friendly, benevolent impulses. At the end of the week, measure your wealth in nonmaterial terms. How many sunsets or dawns did you watch? How many times did you play with kids?

During Week Three, notice how often *sex* arises in your consciousness. Each time, ask yourself what it's associated with. Power? Loneliness? Compassion? Stress? Self-esteem? Pressure? Pleasure? You might be surprised. You can extend this into an additional week of observing your sensuality, sensing your senses, and seeing what pulls you in. Yet another week could be devoted to relationships. Do you view others as objects? Where do you withhold, where do you yield? Where do you respond as an equal?

Hear and Now

"Establishing a virtuous and harmonious relationship to the world brings ease and lightness to the heart and steadfast clarity to the mind. A foundation of virtue brings great happiness and liberation in itself and is the precondition for wise meditation. With it we can be conscious and not waste the extraordinary opportunity of a human birth, the opportunity to grow in compassion and true understanding in our life."

—Jack Kornfield

Next, devote a week to *deep listening* and *loving speech.* Listening, see if you can completely give yourself over to it. Do you listen with an open mind, an open heart? Are you judging? … rehearsing what you'll say? … trying to show what a good listener you are? Speaking, listen to yourself. Do you see and mean each word? Try envisioning every noun, verb, and adjective in your mind's eye. Note how often you make frivolous, cynical and negative comments. And how often do you speak of things about which you really don't know first-hand?

Last, spend one week observing what you *consume.* Do you consume only things which promote health? When you have an urge to consume a little dose of poison, see what motivates your impulse. Refrain from smoking, drinking, or using any drugs, including caffeine. Notice your addictions and observe what beliefs they satisfy. Remember: Habits are habit-forming.

Personalizing the Precepts

If you're already practicing with a sangha, then you already have its set of precepts to live by. You can also adapt and personalize the precepts. The extended sangha of Thich Nhat Hanh, for example, call the precepts "mindfulness trainings," a means of keeping "our appointment with life." Here's a set created by author Celeste West:

> It is my sincere intention to align and harmonize myself with the Blessing Way via these Five Cardinal Precepts:
>
> I.   As a lover of the Way, I do not harm, but cherish all life.
>
> II. As a lover of the Way, I do not take what is not given or waste resources. I create abundance and fearless generosity.

117

III.   As a lover of the Way, touching the world, I do not misuse sensuality. I consecrate my senses in wonder and honesty and joy.

IV.   As a lover of the Way, I do not use false or harsh language. I choose clear and respectful words—or maintain deep-listening silence.

V.   As a lover of the Way, I neither cloud this precious consciousness nor poison this precious body. I nurture my body with wholesome food, exercise, and rest. I cultivate my mind/heart/spirit in lucid relaxation time and in wisdom/kindness action.

The Least You Need to Know

➤ Along with wisdom and meditation, the precepts are an essential aspect of the Buddha's way. Precepts are ethical guidelines for conscious conduct along the Path. A skillful means of correcting behavior, they aren't constraints but rather a structure for living in harmony.

➤ To not harm implies reverence for life, all forms of life.

➤ To not steal implies generosity and trustworthiness.

➤ Sexual restraint implies respect, intimacy, trust, and responsibility.

➤ Abstinence from alcohol implies sobriety and health as well as freedom from addictions of any kind.

➤ Practicing the precepts is an essential aspect of Buddha's way, integral to meditation and wisdom.

➤ The precepts are purely personal. Listen to how they resonate within you.

➤ Practice of just one precept will lead to practice of all of the others.

Chapter 8

The Fine Print: Touching Deeper

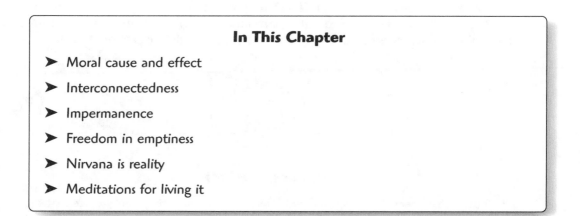

In This Chapter

➤ Moral cause and effect

➤ Interconnectedness

➤ Impermanence

➤ Freedom in emptiness

➤ Nirvana is reality

➤ Meditations for living it

Here's the capper to our tour of the Buddha's way. Now that you have a sense of the steering wheel, so as to steer clear of Old Man Sorrow and live well, here's what you might call a combination diagram of the stuff under the hood and a survey of the general lay of the land. (Part 3, "Seeing Clearly and Deeply: Meditation and Its Paths," is like driver's training, and Part 4, "The Pedal Hits the Metal: Buddhism Applied to the World at Large," offers some key sites.) You won't find the following concepts in a jar or on a shelf. And most of them are very uniquely Eastern. So get ready to see the world in a whole new way.

You'll find that the Buddha wasn't irrational or vague at all. Rather, the Dharma is a totally coherent, impeccably accurate system, as well as an amazingly perfect program for enlightenment. It can also be intricately multidimensional, more complex than you can imagine. So, as they say of a contract when you sign on the blank line, here's a recital of the key terms.

What Goes Around, Comes Around: Karma

Karma's a good place to begin our survey of essential concepts. (We've already touched on karma, only briefly, in Chapter 2, "One Taste, Different Flavors: The Teachings Adapt to Different Lands.")

Karma's as simple as pie. Whatever you think or say or do has its effect. Period. Just look at someone who's angry all the time, bickering, loud, abrasive, and you'll see how angry thoughts and words and deeds create a person people avoid. Same for people with intense fear, greed, conceit, and so on. (Utterly no sense of humor doesn't count.) Look at someone who's generous, kind, wise, and you'll see someone who attracts good friends. Poison creates more poison. Beauty generates beauty. It's that simple.

But I want to also give you a sense of how vast a web karma weaves, the long moral arc of the universe of which Dr. Martin Luther King Jr. spoke—which will, in turn, also give you a feel for the scope and genius of the Dharma in general.

Karma's a science—of cause and effect. Thoughts and words, as well as deeds. You can't undo a thought. Trying to only compounds the initial karma. Bad intentions and guilty consciences certainly affect us, enough to influence action.

Along the Path

"Though their merits for giving alms and offerings are infinite, they don't realize that the ultimate source of sin lies in the three poisons within their own mind [greed, hatred, ignorance]."

—Hui Neng (638–713)

"Suffering is a consequence of one's own action, not a retribution inflicted by an external power. ... We are the authors of our own destiny; and being the authors, we are ultimately, perhaps frighteningly, free."

—Shantideva (eighth century)

I think karma's often dismissed as some kind of misty woo-woo. Anyone who thinks Buddhism's vague hasn't yet encountered the systematic philosophy of the Middle Way (*Madhyamika*), or the ramifications of the notion of karma. Like I say, it casts a vast web, and has led to a rigorous science. So let's take a quick tour of four major categories of karma, as follows:

➤ Common and personal

➤ Primary and secondary

➤ Fixed and mutable

➤ Simultaneous

Personal karma is the typical idea of karma. Imagine, say, I've volunteered to be a soldier and then kill or maim innocent people in a war, no matter how just or unjust the cause. That's my own, personal karma. *Common* karma is collective, such as shared by a family or citizens of a nation. Say I was opposed to an unjust war but enjoyed the economic benefits it brought my country. That's common karma.

Then there's *primary* and *secondary* karma. To use a gardening analogy, primary karma is like a seed. Secondary karma encompasses attendant conditions, such as sun, soil, moisture, fertilizer, singing to the plants. Conditions are quite important. If I choose not to water seeds that are nevertheless ripe for sprouting, I can alter their course by affecting their conditions. Thus, Karma's not predestination.

Karma can be *mutable*. If I cultivate virtue and do good deeds, this might help reduce my karmic debts from previous bad deeds, as from an unpremeditated act of passion, or an unthinking whim. Fixed karma results from acts engaging body, speech, and mind, as in premeditated murder; fixed results are such things as the species and family I'm born into.

And karma can be *simultaneous*. Fantastic as it might seem, effect can be cause, and cause can be effect. When I plant an apple from a seed, I normally think of the apple as the result of the seed, the cause. Yet my apple (result) will produce seeds (cause). Similarly, Siddhartha was a person (cause) who became the Buddha (result) who then influenced other people (causes).

There are yet other categories of karma, but you get the idea. The web of karma is vast and deep, and its science (the Dharma) is very thoroughgoing. Going onward from that web, we'll look next at *interbeing*. Interbeing is the blank page upon which karma is writ. It goes something like this …

This Is, Because That Is: Interbeing

When I was a boy, I had a vision. I was in the first grade when it happened. Our teacher was giving us "busy work" before the lunch bell, asking us to raise our right hand, then our left hand, now our right, and so on. I could see this was going nowhere, so I stopped following her instructions, which I'd duly noted as insipid, odious, and demeaning. (That's how I thought in those days.)

Anyway, I looked out the window. Across the street, a house was under construction. A crew was hammering at a wood frame that would one day be a two-story house. This particular day was one of those for which Los Angeles is famous. Bright, gorgeous, sunny weather (particularly if you happen to be an orange). Listening to the rhythm of the hammers, and looking at the sun dappling down through the tree-lined street, my mind suddenly went on a riff.

It came to me all in an instant. Narratively, it went something like this. A house was going up … out of wood … as from the trees lining this very street. Trees are nourished by sunshine, just like today's … which also helped make the cereal which the workers had eaten that morning for breakfast before coming to work at the site. I could see the foreman had blueprints, made of paper, which was, in turn, made of wood … the blueprints drafted by some man, who'd eaten cereal … *all* nourished by the sun, the man, his ideas, the blueprints, the wood. (*Hammer, hammer.*) Wow, see the pattern to it all!? (*Hammer, hammer, hammer.*) And … since there were blueprints, a pattern, and patterns within patterns … … … then there must be a grand pattern to all the patterns. A master blueprint!

Aha! Seeing that with my own two eyes was an awakening. An illumination. Like seeing the face of God. (Or at least the veil.) I think everyone's had this recognition, some time or other … seeing one's self as part of the stream of life … sensing from whence it comes, and where it's going.

Hear and Now

"I have been a leader in battle … I have been a sword in the hand … I have been a bridge that crossed sixty rivers … I was bewitched into sea foam … I've been a star … I've been a light … I've been a tree … I've been a word in a book … I've been a book in the beginning."

—Taliesin (tenth century, Wales)

It's a feeling as of being part of something greater. A wave aware that it's part of something greater called "ocean." It's often a fact of life of our global village, even if for just a flash, a glimpse. That is, it's commonplace now to speak of the wings of a butterfly in a rainforest in the Amazon as affecting the weather in our own backyard. Or how the global economy can hit us where we live.

We don't always think of such things … like the 84 separate steps that food takes to get from a farm to our fork … or the split-second relays of modems and satellites to conduct a foreign currency transaction. Still, many of us recycle daily. We're learning to think, as this land's first peoples have, in terms of the impact of our actions upon the next seven generations.

This way of seeing partakes of the continual interactions we've glimpsed in simultaneous karma. A flower will wither, to become mulch for future flowers. The drifting cloud will dissolve only to become radiant, a rainbow, ahh!, only to dissolve again into rain … nourishing trees that might become a page in a book … with one important message for you. Life is happening all at once, right now, everywhere. Look deeply and you can see the rain in the texture of this page, and the tree which the rain nourished. And in this page is the cloud, and the sun.

This Is

Indra was a Hindu deity. Of various legends about him, one is that in order to give his daughter something to play with he created an infinite, galactic net, which we call our universe. At the intersection of each node on Indra's net, there's a jewel, glittering like a star. If you look at just one jewel, you'll see all the others reflected. And within each jewel reflected within this one jewel is the reflection of all the other jewels, *ad infinitum*.

Changing Mindsets, Different Worldviews

This is unlike the way we've been taught to see the world. We usually picture things in our mind's eye in terms of our desires, not the greater scheme of things. This is another source of duhkha—not realizing our happiness is interrelated to everything. Our schools compartmentalize reality into categories: we're taught science, sports, history, business, and we graduate with a degree in one of those subjects, but we're seldom taught the interrelatedness of all we've learned.

When you stop your hurried way of seeing and bring mindful awareness to a flower, you can see a messenger from the whole cosmos, equipped with everything there is: the *water* cycle … *fire* sparking its seed and the *sun* nourishing leaves … exhaling fresh *oxygen* … and *earth* grounding its growth. And so pretty!

So a flower is another example of how each aspect of the Dharma (life) contains the whole, and leads to all the other aspects. It's true about reality as well as Buddhism.

But it's conspicuously absent in our civilization's Aristotelian categories ... everything parceled out like ice cubes ... neatly packaged in vacuum-sealed units ... each unit wrapped with red ribbon tied off in a bow. So we don't commonly see in the Buddhist way. The Buddha's way views everything as interrelated. So the Dharma has this huge multidimensional aspect (thus taking a couple of chapters to lay out), in which any part reflects all the other parts and the whole.

There's a school of Buddhism just for this interconnectedness of reality. It's called *Hua Yen* (Chinese, pronounced *hwa yen*; Japanese, *Kegon*), the Flower Garland School. Its major sutra's the *Avatamsaka Sutra* (*Flower Garland Sutra*), which takes up three big volumes in English. Its motto is "One in all, all in one," encompassing unity and universal interdependence. It's often summed up with the image of *Indra's net*, a metaphor for the infinitely repeated interrelationship of beings and events in the universe—each sharing mutual intercausality and mutual identity.

Don't Sweat the Terminology

As we've just glimpsed in karma, the Buddha and his disciples studied and described the interconnected processes of the universe with thorough-going, scientific precision, particularly as they pertain to life and the mind. So don't be put off if you encounter Buddhist tech talk. (For example, the "chain of dependent origination" [?!] is merely a 12-spoked wheel—a wheel, again—showing the stages by which ignorance [of the reality that everything's impermanent, interdependent, and infinite] trips into motion a cause-and-effect wheel of duhkha. By walking the cat backward, as it were, following the links in the chain in reverse order, one can stop the wheel and be free.)

Hear and Now

"When there's This,
then That comes to be;
with the arising of This,
That arises.
When there isn't This,
That doesn't come to be;
with the cessation of This,
That ceases."

—The Buddha

Another gnarly sounding phrase is "codependent arising." It means the instant there's yin, there's yang, too. Everything interpenetrates. Thich Nhat Hanh calls it: "*interbeing.*" (Have you heard the word?) It refers to i.n.t.e.r.c.o.n.n.e.c.t.e.d.n.e.s.s. It's already being taught in some American public schools and might wind up in the dictionary. (*Karma* is already in my *American Heritage Dictionary. Guru*'s there, too.)

When we see that sun and cloud are present in this page, interbeing's the word for that state of affairs, that condition. It's the general category for when one thing's interdependent with another (this page depends on a tree which depends on a cloud which depends on the sun). Page and tree and cloud and sun inter-are. In my boyhood vision, I *saw* interbeing, but didn't know what to call it. As Dr. Martin Luther King Jr. phrased it, "We are all caught up in an inescapable network of mutuality."

A very basic implication of this is the oneness of all things, all of a piece. Trappist monk Thomas Merton said, "There is in all visible things … a hidden wholeness." It's not hidden from us by God, but by our inability to see it, by our identification with our "skin encapsulated egos" as author Alan Watts used to say. You and the universe are one. You inter-are.

Now interbeing unlocks some interesting doors. For instance, consider karma and interbeing. Karma is to interbeing as cooking is to food. If karma interlinks us all, interbeing's the web of all those links—and more. Interbeing helps us better understand not only karma, but also guides us still further into The Way Things Really Are (which is Buddha's Way). Interbeing can help us to appreciate the eternal workings of change, and to grasp the ultimately boundless, transparent nature of identity. First, let's look at change.

It Was, but It Isn't Anymore: Impermanence

The cherry trees have been blossoming, and here in Chinatown, I, like my neighbors, have a couple of branches in a large vase in the center of my living room table. I keep them even as the flowers start to lose their freshness, and now there are just a few pink clumps where not long ago there were dozens. Of all flowers, the cherry and the plum teach us most about the floating, fragrant fragility of life.

So why do they have to die? But that's part of their teaching, too!

All beings share the same nature, and so we all have the same potential for suffering and the same potential for enlightenment. The bended knee and praying hands of a fly about to be swatted are no different than mine, who'll also die.

Hear and Now

"Everyone knows that change is inevitable. From the second law of thermodynamics to Darwinian evolution, from Buddha's insistence that nothing is permanent and all suffering results from our delusions of permanence to the third chapter of Ecclesiastes ('To everything there is a season …'), change is part of life, of existence, of the common wisdom. But I don't believe we're dealing with all that means. We haven't even begun to deal with it."

—Octavia Butler, *Parable of the Sower*

Recall the Noble Truths (see Chapter 5, "The Handshake: Buddhism's Basic Beliefs"). The Buddha said if you really understand *duhkha*, fully see and penetrate its meaning, then you'll have understood all four of his Noble Truths at once: *duhkha*'s existence, its cause, its cessation, and the means of being free from it harming you. We've defined it as suffering and various shades thereof. A more essential (abstract) definition is *impermanence.*

Nothing lasts. When we try to ignore that fact, kerblam!, we stub our toe on it. We don't understand transience, or don't want to. So, in our ignorance or fear of all things passing, or our greed to try to have it all, we seek happiness in things that are also transient, like fortune or fame. It's like trying to put out a fire with kerosene. But when we accept things as they are, let go and go with the flow, *Ahh!* Suffering goes, too. Simple. You can't step into the same river twice!

Trying to push the river is the Second Noble Truth. Grasping at mythical solutions to the essential impermanence of life sets karmic duhkha spinning at our heels, like the wheel of a wagon yoked to an ox. Change is essential to life, and adapting to change is essential to survival.

Physician-poet Dr. William Carlos Williams reminds us, "What does not change is the will to change." Eastern gurus have gone one step further and rejoiced. Thich Nhat Hanh exclaims, "Long live impermanence!" Chögyam Trungpa Rinpoche declares impermanence is indestructible. Why? Without impermanence, a flower wouldn't blossom. Waves wouldn't break upon the rocks. This week's issue of *Star* wouldn't be replaced by next week's all-new sensational never-before-revealed issue. Our hearts wouldn't beat. Our lungs wouldn't pump. We'd be like statues. Now *that's* scary!

Where are the leaves of yesteryear?

(Photograph: Inke Schwab)

Of course, impermanence can be hard to accept. Personally. (Think of your first encounter with death in your own life.) This is what Siddhartha's father tried to keep his son from seeing. As they say, denial is more than a river in Egypt. We're like that caterpillar when the big butterfly fluttered by, who nudged another caterpillar and whispered, "You'll never get *me* up in one of those things." But the Buddha gives us tools—ethics, meditation, and wisdom—so we can look clearly at impermanence. Cope with it. Conquer the problems we have with its inescapability.

So we've now seen three essential ingredients of What Is: karma (moral cause and effect), interbeing (mutuality), and impermanence (one thing leads to another). Now, if impermanence represents time, we'll proceed next to space, for a supreme Buddhist concept. In all its glory, it takes up most of the rest of this chapter. And it's not anything. Now that's interesting.

Along the Path

Leaves falling
on one another ...
the rain beats on the rain.

—Gyodai

Among the grasses
of the passing autumn ...
the stream hides itself.

—Shirao

This dewdrop world ...
it may be a dewdrop,
and yet ... and yet ...

—Issa (on the death of his child)

It Is and Isn't: *Sunyata* (Openness)

Consider a rainbow. When conditions are favorable, it just appears. With sun and no rain, no rainbow. Rain but no sun, no rainbow. But put the two together, and ... *Ahh!* Or, if you happen to be a night person, there's moon-in-the-water. On a clear full-moon night, it's rippling, dancing, doing somersaults in a pond, a teacup, or even a dewdrop.

Merely creased by ripples, the ocean extends way past the horizon, and deeper than the eye can tell. Unperturbed by clouds, the sky above is even more boundless. Both are ripe with endless possibility; both are apt images of sunyata.

(Photo by Barbara Traub)

Now both rainbow and moon-in-a-dewdrop are devoid of any independent identity. So they're good metaphors for what Buddhists call *"sunyata"* (void; emptiness). Empty of any separate existence of their own, much less permanence, they represent Buddhist *emptiness*. Don't be put off by the words. When a Buddhist says "empty," it's shorthand for "empty-of-any-independent-existence."

This Is

Sunya (Sanksrit) "void, empty"; **sunyata,** "voidness, emptiness." It refers to reality's empty of separate, independent identity. In Theravada, it applies to the person; Mahayana extends it to all things; Vajrayana equates it to the feminine principle, unborn, unceasing, like space. Emptiness exemplifies the Middle Way between existence and nonexistence, wherein things inter–are, and are themselves impermanent. The profound manifestation of this is **tathata,** suchness: the wondrous, unconditioned nature of things, ever thus.

Buddhism's gotten a bad rap, I think, because Western critics mistake all the terminology phrased in the negative. Nonpermanence. *Duhkha* is often misconstrued to mean that Buddhism's pessimistic and believes in eternal suffering. That's like mistaking a closed door for the wall that enables it to be. So, too, emptiness isn't nihilism ("nothing matters"). Nor does the void mean falling off the edge of the earth and being swallowed up by a black hole. And none of this denies individual uniqueness by one hair.

Emptiness is not *nothing*. Like impermanence, emptiness is actually a positive idea, only 1) *verbally* expressed in the negative, plus 2) being shorthand, requiring explanation as to what emptiness is empty *of* (separate, lasting existence). If "no boundary" seems better than "empty," try that. Boundless. Without limit, infinite. Openness, too. Transparent, spacious. Fertile void.

Because everything's continuously interacting, interreacting, interrelated with everything else, if just one thing had its own separate, air-tight, permanent identity, 100 percent pure of any outside ingredients or conditioning, 100 percent permanent, then … nothing would ever come to be.

Just as we can say "Long live impermanence!" so, too, can we give thanks to emptiness. Impermanence allows events to keep happening. Emptiness permits being to inter-be and create existence. The spokes of a wheel depend upon and revolve around the emptiness at the hub. A potter sculpts a bowl by centering it around emptiness.

Things wouldn't exist without this fertile void. (Think of it as a cosmic cornucopia.) Right now, there's this book you're reading, and everything-that-is-not-this-book. That everything-else, radiating from the edge of this book out as far as the furthest stretches of the universe, is the fertile void out of which this book came and whence it eventually returns.

Hear and Now

"Emptiness is not a theory, but a ladder that reaches out into the infinite. A ladder is not there to be discussed, but to be climbed .... It is a practical concept, and it embodies an aspiration, not a view. Its only use is to help us to get rid of this world and of the ignorance which binds us to it. It has not only one meaning, but several, which can unfold themselves on the successive stages of the actual process of transcending the world through wisdom."

—Edward Conze

Take my pencil, for instance (wait a sec, lemme finish this sentence; okay, now, take my pencil). I've been using a #2 Maspero pencil. Now this #2 is but one of a billion or so made in the USA yearly. But where does a pencil actually come from? (It doesn't grow on a pencil tree.) Its graphite lead comes from Sri Lanka (Ceylon), its wood from a cedar forest in Northern California, its label from carbon black, its lacquer from a castor bean product, dyed yellow ... the metal ring at the end is made of brass, itself copper and zinc ... and, the crowning touch, the eraser, is rapeseed oil, from the Dutch East Indies, mixed with sulfur chloride and Italian pumice, bound together with rubber and pigmented with cadmium sulfide. Think, too, where each of *those* elements came from, in turn, and how *they* came together, and under what conditions: where the ropes came from, the workmen's coffee, etc.

Along the Path

I haven't conducted a survey, but I think women might have an advantage for understanding sunyata. That is, whether they've had children, or are keenly aware of that potential, they've personally sensed not having a separate existence and thereby become more open to presence. (Sorry, guys; no extra X chromosome. You'll have to make up for it in other ways.)

Along the Path

Its measure is longer than the earth, and broader than the sea.

—Book of Job

You look at it, but it's not to be seen; its name is Formless.

—*Tao Te Ching*

God made everything out of nothing, but the nothingness shows through.

—Paul Valèry

Of course its label says it's a pencil, but what *is* identity? Where is there any perma-nent, separate identity? Nowhere, says the Buddha, and says a pencil. (As my manu-script grows, my pencil vanishes.) My pencil's empty, not-separate, not-permanent, because if I returned all its elements to their sources—sorry, no pencil. The same is true of a car, a flower, a human being, and our thoughts and desires. All *conditional*. If this, then that.

Now all this is a metaphor, but it's actually experiential in meditation. Your average, daily stream of consciousness, your inner monologue, is like the interdependent ele-ments of a pencil, none having any innate reason for coming together, in and of it-self. By focusing awareness on breathing, and nothing else, we choose to set aside verbal conditioning—the "traffic jam of discursive thought," as Chögyam Trungpa Rinpoche puts it—and experience things as they are; open, transparent, bright, all there is. Thoughts continue to flicker, but we become conscious, too, of the space in between, the spaciousness in which they take place.

So now that we've opened out Buddha's way into a number of dimensions, let's ex-plore sunyata further (it's infinite!): what's the flip side; what are some essential char-acteristics; and does this mean you don't have to pay your grocer anymore?

Emptiness, Unique and Full: Suchness

Imagine: What would the flip side of Buddhist emptiness be? Not "separate identity" because sunyata shows how there ain't no such animal. We're looking not for the opposite, but the flip side of emptiness, the twin. "Somethingness" would be closer.

What fits emptiness like yang to its yin would be "suchness" (Sanskrit *tathata*; also translated as is-ness, thus-ness); its a positive, perceptible manifestation.

We've all experienced suchness. Just think of a moment that was ... well, indescribable. "You had to be there," is all you can say. The way the cat jumped off the refrigerator onto the kitchen counter and got a paw stuck in the empty jam jar. Or that moment in early winter when you feel a new chill in the air and, then, suddenly, there are raindrops. Consider, too, a new, unopened ball of twine, fresh out of the box. Or think of a pizza cut up into slices, each slice having its own slightly different personality.

Like a nonstop Ferris wheel, the fertile void is continually in motion, giving birth to unrepeatable interpenetration of impermanences (say that eight times fast), each time just "this way": pizza slices, kitty-cat dances, clouds about to rain, white chickens beside a red wheelbarrow. Each thing is empty of separate, lasting identity so each thing is *just so*, like the patterns of a mobile.

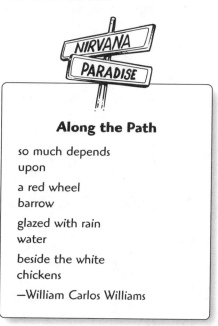

Along the Path

so much depends
upon

a red wheel
barrow

glazed with rain
water

beside the white
chickens

—William Carlos Williams

This Is

Scholar Christmas Humphreys defines **tathata (suchness)**, equivalent to Buddha nature, as "... the ultimate and unconditioned nature of all things. ... It cannot be called the One as distinct from the Many, for it is not distinct from anything. Nothing can be denied or affirmed concerning it, for these are modes of expression which exclude and thereby create opposition. It can only be understood by realizing that one can neither find it by searching nor lose it by trying to separate oneself from it. Yet it has to be found."

Just as you can see impermanence, interbeing, and sunyata in everything, so, too, with suchness. You can see it in unrepeatable calligraphy throughout the book, and the crisp clarity, the quality of light, in the two photos in this chapter. (Just *so*. Like *this*.) For further visual examples, look at the images in Chapter 17, "New Ways of

Seeing and Being: Buddhism and Fine Arts," particularly the persimmons and the hot-dogs. The hotdogs sit in their buns in different postures. The persimmons each have a distinct personality, as different as the first sip of tea is from the second sip, and the third.

I've said emptiness and suchness dance with each other like the interplay of yin and yang. There's a variant Buddhist motto for it: *"Form is emptiness; emptiness is form."* Form, here, is the word for matter but also means the way matter takes unique form, suchness. Think of form as a *wave*, exquisite as it swells, curls, rises to its majestic height and then spills down. Think of emptiness as the *ocean,* limitless, vital, the womb of life, with no fixed center. Waves = ocean; ocean = waves. The vast ocean of being; and (quoting American poet Charles Reznikoff) its "ceaseless weaving of the uneven waters." Or as Einstein put it, $E = MC^2$; energy becomes matter, matter becomes energy.

No Thing: Even Emptiness Is Empty

Besides suchness, some landmarks or road markers, for the experience of elusive but essential sunyata, are the following:

- ➤ Spaciousness
- ➤ Cycles
- ➤ Combinations
- ➤ Consecutiveness
- ➤ Relativity

When we meditate and strip away the partitions with which we compartmentalize our lives, it's common to experience *spaciousness,* physically and mentally. Instead of living in a cubicle, it's like living large, on the whole block. It's a great relief, but not the same thing as being spaced out. Many have described sunyata as our true home, like finally coming home.

Along the Path

Emptiness reflects varying approaches to the Buddha's way. Theravada compares things to empty vessels. Mahayana says there are no vessels, really. Contrasting Zen and Tibetan Buddhism (Vajrayana), Zen seems to prefer saying that form is empty, emphasizing the emptiness, while vajra seems to emphasize that emptiness has form, realizing enlightenment through the path of appearances. Zennists thus prefer the blank wall; Tibetans, ornament. Zen, the simple tea cup; Tibetan, human skull as bowl (reminder of impermanence). Each has its suchness.

We've already seen examples of *cycles* in simultaneous karma. Effect can become cause, a seed becoming a flower that bears new seeds, and so neither having any lasting, individual essence. Examples of *combinations* are the composite pencil, the rainbow, and the moon in water. Or consider how in the calligraphy for "wisdom," and for "listen" in Chapter 7, "The Art of Living: The Cardinal Precepts," separate pictures of things combine to express something else, an intangible. The real meaning (the sunyata) exists in between the things. In between the words.

Consecutiveness is like a movie, made up of short strips of film, themselves made up of consecutive frames. We think a movie's real, but is it? It is and it isn't. Breathing is consecutive, too. In between an in-breath and out-breath, there's sunyata.

Relativity was described by the Buddha way in advance of Einstein's Theory of Relativity ($E = MC^2$). But thanks to Dr. Einstein we're accustomed to thinking in Buddha's terms. When we say, "One man's meat is another man's poison," that's relativity and it's also an example of sunyata. Another example is words. Words vary according to context. Think of Groucho Marx's line, "Time flies like an arrow, fruit flies like a banana." A nun's habit isn't the same as an alcoholic's. *The Oxford English Dictionary* has seven pages of definitions for just the word "light," each depending on context. The word "emptiness" itself depends on context, and so is itself empty (of any lasting, unique, single identity), which brings us to one last aspect worth noting … … …

… … … *nothing.* (Or, better, no-thing … not anything … since the idea of nothing conjures up a vacuum, whereas no-thing is just blank. Like a movie screen. Or a blank piece of paper.) Since emptiness is a concept (you can't pin it to a bulletin board) and thus empty, the point here's to not get attached to any concept of it. Even saying it's ineffable or indescribable puts a label on it. The ultimate is uncategorizable. Better to remain open. Personally, I find the word emptiness or sunyata is a reminder that I *don't know.* A reminder to keep watching. Mindfully observing. Being attentive. Here and now.

So I'll say nothing more about that which can't be said, except to recount that when some priests and monks from Westminster Abbey were visiting a Japanese Zen temple for the first time, they paused at a large, framed piece of beautiful calligraphy of the word "no-thing" and asked what that was. Rather than explain the whole nine yards, as you've just seen here, the zen guide just said, "God," and they moved on.

The Chinese pictogram to the left shows a clearing, as made by a natural forest fire. To the right, the fire is burning. Together, they present the situation of no-thing (wu, Chinese; mu, Japanese).

(Calligraphy: Chungliang Al Huang)

133

Leaves from the Bodhi Tree

Another example of continuous succession of phenomena as manifesting Buddhist empti-ness, or openness, is the waves on a shore. Sir Kenneth Clark writes in *Civilisation* of the moment when eighteenth-century philosopher Jean-Jacques Rousseau, who was to influ-ence the French and American revolutions, listened to the sound of waves from his dwelling on an island in a Swiss lake where he took refuge. Clark writes, "Listening to the flux and reflux of the waves, he tells us, he became completely at one with nature, lost all consciousness of an independent self, all painful memories of the past or anxieties about the future, everything except the sense of being. 'I realized,' he said, 'that our existence is nothing but a succession of moments perceived through the senses.'"

You're You and You Aren't: Self and Nonself

Another word often synonymous with supreme emptiness is nirvana. But, before we reach nirvana, so to speak, there's one more line of fine print to note. If things don't have any permanent, separate identity, then neither do we. We're just a part of the ocean, called a "wave," that thinks it's permanent and separate. (Ha ha ha. *Ker-splash!*)

This was where the Buddha's enlightenment differed so from the accepted notion of spirituality of his day. The Buddha himself tried freeing "inner self from the bondage of the flesh and reuniting it with the OverSelf," but discovered, hey, the body isn't necessarily the slave-driver. The real culprit is one's own mind, ignorant of How It Really Is, and desiring the impossible ("Say it ain't so, Joe") … building a fortress around an illusion.

Having located both the cause of suffering and its cessation, the Buddha had no time to debate whether the soul is immortal or to map the body-mind connection. These things didn't *further*. What mattered was weaning attention from the illusion of a per-manent self with independent, separate existence, and waking up to What Is.

You might ask, "But if I have no self, then who becomes enlightened?" Don't worry: *"not-self,"* like "emptiness," is merely a word, a shorthand for a vast concept. You could say transparent self. Transpersonal self. Boundless self. Quantum self.

Hear and Now

"What is this story that many of us tell ourselves and hold on to almost all the time? It goes something like this—I'm here and you are over there, my life is separate from yours, the objects of my awareness are external to me. This story is almost instinctive. Once it arises, it is almost impossible not to grasp it as real. Attaching to it as real is the origin of our suffering. With this story we are well equipped with anxiety but not well equipped to face it, so we embark on a career of trying to avoid anxiety and blaming it on others instead."

—Tenshin Reb Anderson

It also comes suddenly, in a flash: Who are you when you drink the first mouthful of a pot of some fresh tea? Unless you're squandering the moment, you're communing with tea. Tea moment. Just *Ahh,* ever thus. The self you're so familiar with won't necessarily quit its day job and vanish overnight; it's an aspect of suchness. You'll always be the unique person you are.

Maybe a handwriting analyst can tell if you've experienced sunyata and nonself. In my own experience, after over 30 years along the path, I still have most of the neuroses I had when I started. Except, instead of being these big, scary dinosaurs, they're becoming more like little imps that sometimes scamper in and try to hide under my table. I know they're there and that they'll trip me up if I invest in them. As I cease nourishing the conditions that give rise to them, they diminish, and calmer, more contented aspects of my personality grow stronger, returning me more and more to my true nature, the wise, joyous suchness of the source.

So don't worry. And what is this self, anyway, you're afraid if you think you'd lose it? Emptiness of self is really no different than impermanence. It's like this: Once you were a child and could only imagine adulthood. A beginner at Buddhist practice (like the rest of us), you're only imagining enlightenment. Better to commence by saying "I don't know, let's see" than try to attain what you're only imagining. (You'll find there's *nothing* to attain: By merely being, you're already part of the ocean, only you didn't fully realize it before.)

As ever, it's experiential, not verbal, which is where meditation comes in. (This chapter ends with more meditation suggestions.) Meditation enables us to fully appreciate the present moment, unadorned, without attachment to past or future, self or nonself, suchness or sunyata. Mindful breathing shows us how impermanent even one breath is, yet how complete.

Sunyata doesn't mean that we become zombies, or hyped-up speed-freak fanatics, either. It's just a simple, scientific recognition. Like my pencil, I'm a tube of diverse elements all compacted together. The label "Gary Gach" pertains to I.D. cards and Internet passwords and, ah yes, that reminder of the relative amid the transcendental, my bills. Like the pencil, or the rainbow, "Gary Gach" is a series of moments, states, events, cycles—a composite, and all composite things decompose. (That's what happens to musicians when they die, you know—they decompose. Ba-dum!) The Irish poet W. B. Yeats expressed nonself eloquently when he wrote, "Ah, body swayed to music, ah, brightening glance, / how can we know the dancer from the dance?"

So the Buddha went into detail about nonself (*annatta*), which you can explore, too. Basically, he said what we call self is a knot of five clumps (also called "aggregates," or *skandhas,* in Sanskrit):

➤ Form

➤ Feelings

➤ Perceptions

➤ Thought processes

➤ Consciousness

They're each causal-and-effectual results of other things, without any lasting, independent identity of their own. Or as one Burmese teacher once summed it up, "No self, no problem."

Along the Path

Buddha never discussed an afterlife because it didn't further the recognition of and liberation from *duhkha*. His disciples elaborated, however. Since there's no self, there's no ectoplasm yearning for a new body. If at the moment of death, you're fully aware of the experience of death, without clinging, you'll be free of the cycle of birth and death, like flame with no more fuel. Otherwise, your karmic residue will continue in another cycle. Wrong? Come back and tell me in 300 years.

Hear and Now

"Nirvana is everywhere. It dwells in no particular place. It is in the mind. It can only be found in the present moment. ... It is empty and void of concept. Nothing can comprise nirvana. Nirvana is beyond cause and effect. Nirvana is the highest happiness. It is absolute peace. Peace in the world depends on conditions, but peace in nirvana is unchanging .... Suffering leads the way to nirvana. When we truly understand nirvana, we become free."

—Maha Ghosananda

You're IT: Nirvana NOW

Nirvana is the peace that passeth understanding. The highest bliss. It's the Third Noble Truth; the end of mortal anguish. The ultimate recognition that self and the world aren't separate. At one with the all.

When life's no longer filtered through the lens of self, the dualism of self/not-self falls away. There's no "I" that attains this enlightenment. There's unfiltered, direct aware-ness of what limitlessly is. (And all without a second phone line!)

Here are a few more landmarks along the path:

➤ The word "nirvana" refers to extinction of fire, but, without comparing ancient physics to today's, it could just as well mean "release." (Release from duhkha, re-lease from karma.) A common metaphor's "the Other Shore."

➤ The path to nirvana begins with taking refuge in the Three Jewels, realization of the Four Noble Truths, and practice of the Eightfold Path.

➤ Once nirvana's attained, the worthy one can continue living in a state of being *in* this world but not *of* it, until it comes time for death and total nirvana (*paranirvana*). When the Buddha is depicted on his side, it's at the end of his life, when he's ready for paranirvana.

➤ Mahayanan practitioners take the Bodhisattva Vow. They may taste nirvana but postpone it until all other beings have attained it, too. Theravadan practitioners recognize bodhisattvahood as a stage following nirvana, rather than before, but are never less than compassionate about helping others.

➤ The Mahayana school states that nirvana is attainable within this world, right here where we are standing. The motto is: "Samsara [this world of illusions] is nirvana; nirvana is samsara." What other shore?!

➤ For practitioners of the Pure Land school, a pure land is a stage right before or next to nirvana (see Chapter 13, "Paths of Devotion and Transformation: Pure Land and Vajrayana Buddhism," for more information on the Pure Land school).

Living It: Meditations in a Floating World

If you only understand the Buddha's philosophy intellectually but don't practice his teachings, then Buddhism's just books and tapes. A carpentry manual's not a guide to living in a house. Here are a few hints for actively seeking interbeing, impermanence, emptiness, suchness, and nirvana in your daily life.

Devote a few days to noticing *karma,* yours and others. Notice who seems to attract material things; observe whether they seem truly happy. Observe this potential in yourself. When you notice anger, in yourself and others, see how it creates more anger or confusion. When you notice calm, see how it attracts more calm.

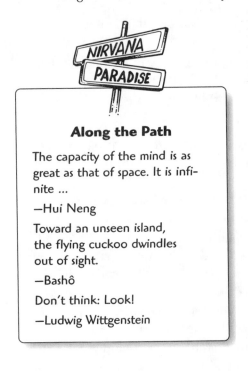

Along the Path

The capacity of the mind is as great as that of space. It is infinite ...

—Hui Neng

Toward an unseen island, the flying cuckoo dwindles out of sight.

—Bashô

Don't think: Look!

—Ludwig Wittgenstein

Devote a few days to noticing examples of *interbeing.* Play with prepositions. If you notice a pen on the table, remind yourself that the table is under the pen. See how they inter-are. Consider how many ingredients and steps went into making each thing you encounter, then look at that thing up close in a new light, the light of its interbeing.

Devote a few days to just noticing examples of *impermanence,* without comment or judgment. Seasonal changes. The end of a project. Notice how beginnings seem easier than endings. Examine your feelings about each. Extend your awareness further. Like the Buddha, going beyond the castle walls of security, be on the lookout for what you haven't seen before. If you sense attachment or surging feelings, make a note of those, too.

Devote a few days to noticing examples of *sunyata* and *suchness.* Take a blank piece of paper. Pin it up where you can look at it for a few days. Notice its texture, color, how it catches light and casts a shadow (its suchness), and how you could write anything on it (its sunyata). Also see the tree it came from, and the rain and cloud that nourished it (its *interbeing*). See the interrelations of all these things we've been discussing, and make them real for yourself, not philosophical concepts.

Just as we need a mirror to see our face, so can we use the heavens to see our mind. Weather permitting, go out and look up at a clear sky from a comfortable position. Look at the variations in light and color, and how far the sky extends. Imagine to yourself, "I am that." Let your mind slowly grow as blank, bright, and vast as the sky you're looking into. If thoughts come, think of them as passing birds, and let them pass uninterrupted. When you're ready to end the meditation, notice how the sky seems both endless and without any particular location anywhere. Then stay with the presence of "big sky mind" (sunyata) for a few minutes and let your "busy daily routine mind" (samsara) find its way back on its own. Notice if it's clearer. Calmer.

Devote a few days to observing how you define your *self*. What are your limits? Where do you begin and end? Set aside some quiet time to look at your hand. As you look, try to remember how your hand looked when you were little. Then see if you can see your parents' hand within the patterns of your hand ... the shape of the pads of your fingers, the finger prints, the pattern of pores on the back of your hand. When you're done, put your two palms together and notice your breath.

Devote a few days to considering *no-thing*. Notice how automatically you label and categorize things. Look at things as if you've never seen them before. Practice saying "I don't know" to yourself and others.

Think of song lyrics that illustrate any of these concepts. "I Got Plenty of Nothing" by the Gershwin brothers and DuBoce Hayward, for example, or "Tomorrow Never Knows," by The Beatles; songs of suchness, like "The Way You Look Tonight," and "My Favorite Things," and romantic farewell songs about impermanence. Celebrate these ideas: Sing these songs to yourself or with others. Feel free to make up new lyrics.

Devote a few days to just thinking about the Buddha and all he did. Consider your mind as part of Buddha's mind. Human beings are all related to common ancestors; concentrate on just him alone. Thinking of his name, consider that you're invoking his presence in your life. See if this makes you feel happier, if your surroundings seem more pleasant. Set aside a space in your thoughts for nirvana. A blank file folder for mental notes or observations. Check into it from time to time.

Once begun, all of these practices can be ongoing—and life-changing. So enjoy!

The Least You Need to Know

➤ Karma doesn't mean predestination or fate. Karma's the effects caused by our thoughts, words, and deeds, as well as the scientific study of those interrelationships.

➤ All things are interdependent, interacting, interreacting, interpenetrating.

➤ Things change. Impermanence is a primary cause of sorrow (duhkha) but without it life wouldn't be possible, and so it's also a cause for happiness.

➤ Sunyata (void, emptiness) is the boundless, open, transparent nature of all things. Like impermanence, it's not negative (nothingness), but creative, enabling things to come into being, each thing just so.

➤ Along with the things having no permanent separate identity, we include what's called self. Self is as much a product of transient conditions as a pencil or a rainbow.

Part 3

Seeing Clearly and Deeply: Meditation and Its Paths

Moving the spotlight from the Buddha and his teachings (the Dharma), we delve next into the practice (the Sangha). In this part, I'll fill in the supreme missing ingredient: you. And I do mean you. The Dharma, teaching about life, is meant to be lived, regularly. (You do breathe, don't you? See, that's a start!)

Fortunately, Buddhism's not like learning to use a parachute while skydiving. If at first you don't succeed, just keep on practicing. They say that if the Buddha were alive, he'd still be practicing. So now we'll see how to put theory into practice.

Besides the basics of Buddhist meditation, we'll survey the major schools. But don't sweat the -isms. It's how you practice Buddhism that's the important -ism. (Maybe they should have called it Youism. …)

Chapter 9

Taking the Plunge: Beginning and Cultivating Your Practice

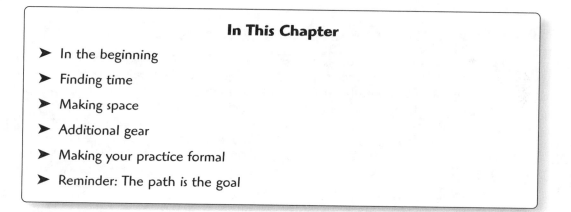

In This Chapter

➤ In the beginning

➤ Finding time

➤ Making space

➤ Additional gear

➤ Making your practice formal

➤ Reminder: The path *is* the goal

Most of what's been covered thus far may make perfect sense to you, in your head and in your heart. The missing ingredient is to make it real for yourself. Integrating the Dharma (the way things really are) into your life, internalizing and actualizing it, is done through *practice*—finding and staying on your path.

Calling Buddha's way a *practice* is a bit of a misnomer. The word usually implies something to repeat to be performed or enacted in the future, like athletics or music. Yes, it is repetitive, but there's no future destination here. No, practice here's all about the present. True, you're already present. But you're missing it when assessing the past or anticipating the future. Like the sign says at a casino in Las Vegas, "You Must Be Present to Win."

Practice is being present to your life. Which is a present, the greatest there is. Here's an introduction to appreciating life, the Buddhist way.

Leaves from the Bodhi Tree

Sharon Salzberg had been following the Way of the Buddha for 14 years when she became a student of U Pandita. She'd practice six days a week, and, when she'd describe her meditation experiences to him, he'd just say, "Well, in the beginning it can be like that." No matter what, he'd say the same thing. After weeks of this, it finally dawned on her that he was saying it's good to be a beginner, not burdened by expectations or preconceptions based on past experiences. When she understood this, he stopped saying that and went on to something else.

Getting Started—and Keeping at It

I'd like to let you in on a big, open secret. Maybe you've seen various books with titles like *Buddhism for Beginners*. Well, guess what!? Buddhists *are* beginners. The Dalai Lama calls himself a humble monk. It's a common trait of the wise, actually. Socrates was declared wise because he knew that he did not know. Fourteenth-century Christian mystic Meister Eckhart called it "learned ignorance." In Zen, it's sometimes called a "don't-know mind"; or *wu,* no-thing. Zen Master Shunryu Suzuki Roshi introduced the concept in the West as "beginner's mind."

Keep an eye peeled, you'll find examples of beginner's mind in daily life: such as someone saying, "I don't know, I'm new here." In my life, pounding the pavement, looking for work, has taught me how no prior experience can be a plus. You're not set in your ways; you're not going to say, "But that's not the way we did it where I used to work"; and odds are you might come up with winning ideas that way. Similarly, beginner's mind doesn't have any preconceptions of what nirvana should look like. Beginner's mind will know when it gets there.

The word *amateur* has a slightly disparaging ring today, but listening to the Latin root (*amare,* to love) reminds us it originally meant having a fondness for everything. Beginners' minds are willing to scale the highest peak,

Along the Path

"To understand truth one must have a very sharp, precise, clear mind; not a cunning mind, but a mind that is capable of looking without any distortion, a mind innocent and vulnerable."

—Krishnamurti

"How old would you be if you didn't know how old you was?"

—Satchel Paige

or to settle for peanut butter and jelly sandwiches. "Willing," meaning not passively waiting, without will; but not trying to will anything into being, either. Willingness implies flexibly working with what's already present.

Experts, specialists, professionals, and the like have a reputation at stake, and so grow timid, learning to like wearing blinders. As Suzuki Roshi put it so well, "If your mind is empty, it is always ready for anything; it is open to everything. *In the beginner's mind there are many possibilities; in the expert's mind there are few.*"

Beginner's mind. (A block-style version on the left; a more flowing, cursive version on the right.)

(Calligraphy: Kazuaki Tanahashi)

Leaves from the Bodhi Tree

A learned professor knocked on the door of the local zen temple, wanting to know about zen. The resident zen teacher bowed and invited him in to sit down, on a mat on the floor, and share a pot of freshly picked tea. The tea steeped, and when it was ready, the zen host poured tea into his learned guest's cup first. He poured, and he poured and poured, until the professor shouted, "What?! Stop!! It's overflowing! There's no more room!" The zen master put the tea pot down and replied, "Exactly. Like this cup, you're full of your opinions and preconceptions. How can I show you zen unless you first empty your cup?"

So keep an eye peeled, and an open mind. (Have you seen the bumper strip?: "Minds, Like Parachutes, Must Be Open to Function.") Here are three more examples of beginner's mind. 1) Many people have experienced beginner's luck in sports or games, such as with a perfect, first golf swing, or an initial lucky bet. 2) Being on vacation and playing tourist, everything's new. And 3), one reason I think we enjoy spending time with children is they have all of life ahead of them. They're absolute beginners.

All these examples reflect how the mind given us at birth, our beginner's mind, is still there beneath all the labels and decals and passwords laden over it, still impeccable, bright, fond of everything. Returning to that mind, is like coming home ... reclaiming our Buddha nature ... the boundless clarity of the mind at rest ... our *mu,* our not-knowing ... no-thing ... and all the freedom that affords.

Start with where you are. And don't just get started—keep at it.

There's No Time Like the Right Time

You've come this far. Why not put this book down for just a minute to enjoy a moment of meditation? Please try this exercise. Here's all you'll do: 1) Check that you're comfortable and seated solidly. 2) Close your eyes. 3) Listen to your breath. 4) Don't change anything. 5) Just take a mental snapshot of yourself, at this point in time. Okay? Now, try it.

Please keep that mental snapshot as a benchmark as you progress along your own way. Keep it in your mental wallet and take it out and look at it from time to time. And remember, stopping and taking time for your practice is essentially as easy as *that.*

The Time Has Come Today

How long you should practice is purely a personal matter. Just one mindful breath amid the hip-hop of daily life is practicing the Buddha's way. One-breath meditation throughout the day is never a bad idea.

Best is to go with what feels comfortable, and build on that. Ten minutes will get your feet wet. You want to familiarize yourself with what's worth doing regularly. (The sun comes up just as regularly.) When you feel that's comfortable to do, try 10 to 15 minutes a day. Eventually, you'll find, even in the busiest of schedules, 45 minutes is always there.

More important than how long you practice is doing it regularly, making it a foundation. See if you can practice once if not twice a day. Favored times are morning and evening: morning, first thing, and evening, either an hour or so before or after dinner, or before going to bed. Meditating right after a meal can be challenging as your blood sugar changes and the digestive plumbing and transportation systems see peak traffic. Minimize distractions.

A Retreat Isn't Always a Step Backward

These days, it's not uncommon for people to pack up and head for a *retreat*. It might be a work-related productivity booster, a get-together of any interest group, or a religious retreat. Actually, the Buddha was one of the first to initiate the practice. During the muddy, three-month rainy season in India, the Buddha used to go off with his disciples to one of their monasteries and practice together until the monsoons stopped howling. Thus began a tradition practiced in Buddhist life ever since.

Retreats are held anywhere: in a temple or church, rustic monastery or campgrounds, on a campus or in a hotel. A retreat doesn't have to be three months; it might be three nights, or a weekend. So retreat doesn't always mean defeat. Rather, a step back can be a treat.

And you don't have to sign up to enjoy a solo retreat. Set aside your own full day for mindfulness. Unplug the phone. Clean house and do any necessary shopping the day before. Vow that everything you do will be done mindfully. (Jews enjoy a one-day retreat weekly, on Saturdays. It's called *shabbos,* or Sabbath, a day of rest.) Besides devoting time for sitting meditation, dedicate yourself to conscious breathing while eating, walking, washing, and so on. (Chapter 10, "Base Camp: Meditation Basics," will tell you more about practicing such meditations.)

A retreat is an excellent opportunity for solidifying and deepening your practice. A retreat can give you a good taste of what practice is all about, and encourages you to fit what you find there into daily life. Which brings up the question of finding time.

Dharma Has All the Time in the World for You

For those who think they don't *have* time, let me respectfully relay my dear teacher Lew Welch's pronouncement about that: "That's not a valid excuse. Time is all we have, really." The Buddha tells us that no one owns our mind but we ourselves. The same is true for time. If it's absolutely necessary, there's time for it. I've heard that Alice Walker wrote *The Color Purple* in whatever pockets of time she found, such as doing the laundry.

If you think you don't have the time, then look twice at your life: what is it you allow yourself to have time for? Who tells you how to invest your time like that? And what is time for, anyway? It also made me think of the classical Japanese haiku: "The little birds / making fun of human beings / who have no time to sing."

Hear and Now

"Tomorrow's life is too late. Live today."

—Martial

"Time is but the stream I go a-fishing in."

—Henry David Thoreau

"To realize the unimportance of time is the gate of wisdom."

—Bertrand Russell

147

In terms of nirvana, there is no time. Time's like a river, everywhere at once: at the waterfall and at the docks, in the mountains, and flowing out to sea; always present tense. Again, the Middle Way pertains, basic yin and yang: motion and rest, there's no activity without stillness. Nevertheless, our society glorifies doing over being: Time is money, money is time, and business is equated with busyness. The Buddha, on the other hand, found the highest attainment in the mind at rest.

Buddha's in the House

Practice in community, sangha, isn't confined to meeting good friends. This morning, just before dawn, I practiced with the eucalyptus tree out back and the finches dwelling thereabouts. There are always signs of life, sangha, in the place where you are living. So now it's time to talk about place.

Breathing Room

With time comes space. Like a comfortable sofa, everyone can use a physical space in their lives where meditation (not to mention enlightenment) can take place. Breathing room.

It needn't be a room all its own, just a place where you won't be disturbed. It could be an area just large enough to lay a mat upon the floor. Preferably, near an open window, so the air's fresh. Shaded, so bright light won't distract you, and relatively quiet. Nothing more elaborate than that. If it's all you have, you could fold up your blanket and sit on it on your bed.

Hear and Now

"... a butsudan ... is a beautiful little cabinet. Inside you put things that represent the necessities of life: little candles for light, incense for smell, water, fruit, and so on. And you hang your gohonzon in there, too—a scripture, rolled up on a scroll. The butsudan looks like a little altar; but the idea is not that you're *worshipping* this piece of paper or anything. These things allow you to focus, to be in the right frame of mind to receive, and they are a form of respect."

—Tina Turner

Just knowing I have that space where I can go gives me a tremendously buoyant and warm feeling. I take refuge there, renew my vows, and meditate. Even thinking about it gladdens my heart and calms my mind quite a bit. So, every now and again, I celebrate my growing buddhahood and place a flower, from the park near my house, in a simple glass of water, beside my mat, near the window. A little living buddha, sharing the light and air with me and my practice.

Altars: The Buddha Within and Without

As we've noted previously, there isn't really a thing we can call "Buddhism" so much as numerous people practicing the way of the Buddha. Another open secret is this: There really aren't Buddhists, either. There are only buddhas, working on their buddha nature. (Was Jesus a Christian?)

For growing buddhas who've found the few minutes of time regularly, this is cause for celebration, no? By celebrating, we're not getting attached to these facts, but making them come alive for us through personal ritual. It's for this reason the statuette of the Buddha I have in my home is small. (If you haven't noticed yet, when you bow at something, it bows back. So my small Buddha gives me a small bow in return, every day; more than that I might have trouble with.)

Of her home altar, Jean McMann writes: "Kuan Yin, the spirit of compassion, is in her meditation pose, sitting in front of a page from last year's Life of the Buddha calendar. I fill these two old inkbottles with flowers like jasmine, because the fragrance is soothing. When I meditate I sit in a chair facing Kuan Yin's peaceful figure. The stones in front of her are from Muir Beach, where I like to walk. Thirty years ago, when my daughter Beth was in first grade, she made the small clay pot I use for incense.

(Photo: Jean McMann)

You might nurture your own buddhahood, your growing link with the historical Buddha, with an altar ... receptive to the right frame of mind, as a sign of respect ... a re-presentation of the Buddha's wisdom and compassion ... a reminder of Awakening ... a mirror of your own heart and mind ... an opportunity to let your buddha light shine. It could be a windowsill or shelf, an image or statue. You might add a flower, a candle, incense. Altars can have precise symbolic details, depending on the practice and the practitioner.

149

Vietnamese Buddhist monk Thich Tanh Thien explains, "You stand in front of Buddha, not to a statue, but to buddha inside yourself. It's important to know that, otherwise you're bowing to a piece of wood or metal. When you look inward to the Buddha nature, you feel peace in your heart. You give thanks to Buddha because without his teachings, you would not have found this way of understanding and loving."

Some altars include pictures of relatives and teachers and close friends, a place where a practitioner goes to share personal news with them. Some home shrines of enlightenment include cherished seekers, be it Thomas Jefferson or Sister Mother Theresa.

Along the Path

Seen against a Judeo-Christian background, an altar can smack of graven images, idolatry, paganism (*avoda zara* in Hebrew). Yet within Buddhism itself there's a parallel, almost identical warning: "If you see a Buddha along the road, kill him." One interpretation: Don't bind yourself to an image or concept but, rather, seek the light within.

Our Lady of Guadalupe next to Ramana Maharshi. For many, an altar's a way of deepening the meaning of home, making the divine personal.

The meaning of an altar or shrine grows over time. A devotional image or artifact is like that snapshot of a loved one which someone keeps in their wallet or on their desk. To us, it's just another face, but to the one who knows that person and looks at the picture at various times of the day, the image is a doorway to love.

Sometimes people invoke outside assistance in order to better realize how they are that which they seek. Remember, "Thou art *that*." Venerate the buddha within you, not a piece of metal or wood.

Before we leave the topics of time and space, remember that meditation's available *wherever* and *whenever* you are. You don't need to be sitting on a cushion in a temple. The real practice is continuous, immeasurable, precious, and flowing as the present moment, and your own mind.

Clean Socks and What Else?: Optional Gear

Like your body, clothes in general are important. You should feel comfortable when you meditate. No need for tight watches or collars, glasses or belts that constrict circulation, or starchy or scratchy clothes. Just as the best clothes for meditation don't make you aware of your body, preferred apparel colors in some temples are blacks or grays, so as not to distract anyone.

Some people sit with a blanket over their knees because circulation slows down during meditation, and it's important not to catch cold. Clean socks? Many temples ask that shoes be removed.

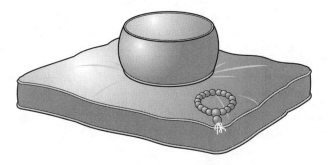

A zafu (cushion) *and a* mala *(string of beads).*

When sitting in meditation, your posture may call for elevating your fanny slightly higher than your knees and feet. A rolled up blanket can do. A more formal amenity would be a pillow. There's one specially designed for sitting meditation called *zafu*, in Japanese. The mat placed under a pillow is called *zabuton* in Japanese. Even in non-Japanese practices, zafus and zabutons are familiar fixtures.

Bells are a wonderful meditation tool. Listening to and just staying with the sound waves of a bell can return the mind to the fullness of the present moment, as for beginning a meditation session. A higher-sounding bell's often used to signal the end of sitting meditation, time to str-r-r-etch! Some people carry two small brass disks around with them, called a *tsingsha,* that make a very clear sound, a portable bell of mindfulness.

The Sanskrit name for a Buddhist string of beads literally means rosary (*mala,* a garland, rose). They could be no bigger than a bracelet, or as large as a necklace, with 108 beads, for the 108 impurities (in Buddhism, there's a numbered list for everything). The beads are used to count repetitions of a mantra or of the Buddha's name, or to keep attention focused on the breath. Beads can also be relaxing and fun to play with. Moved through the fingers, bead by bead, one for each breath (such as out-and-in as one bead), a string of beads quiets the mind.

You might also use beads to learn about the tendency of breath to naturally slow down during meditation. For example, counting in-and-out as one bead, halfway around 108 beads can take me 40 minutes, but then I'm way slow. See for yourself. An alternate use is for counting out-and-in as one bead.

Some people time their meditation to the length of one stick of good incense. (Bad incense, on the other hand, smelling like sweet perfume, might only give you a headache.) There's Japanese, Tibetan, powder, rope incense, and so on. Sandalwood was used by Buddha's disciples to help them

Hear and Now

Standing outside my pointed-
        roof hut,
Who'd guess how spacious it is
        inside?
A galaxy of worlds is there,
With room to spare for a zafu.

—Shih-wu (1272–1352)

151

concentrate during the heat waves. When the Buddhist monks from India took to the Silk Route, they brought along their incense. Like the fragrance of the Dharma, suffusing its ineffable fragrance everywhere, incense burns away impurities and refreshes body and mind. I find good incense stimulates a feeling of alertness and calm, like a cup or two of fresh green tea.

And nothing warms the heart like candlelight. But—just as Buddhism isn't books and tapes, it isn't just burning incense and lighting candles either. Don't mistake all the various lamps along the way for the real journey.

What's Missing?: Formal Practice

Having the time and making the space where practice can take place, plus keeping a beginner's mind, are all essential. Besides accessories, what else? Now, can't you just dig in? That is, why not practice the way of the Buddha on your own? Take refuge in Buddha and Dharma, but not Sangha?

True, it all begins with you. So you can certainly try and see if you can reach enlightenment solo. But, like trying to fill the Grand Canyon with marbles, you might have to practice 24 hours a day. But even then how would you know you're not just building yourself up … trying another way of making a sandcastle at the water's edge … a lonely enlightenment of delusion?

Along the Path

A practitioner without sangha is comparable to the tiger in Vietnam that leaves his mountain for the lowlands, unaware he'll be caught and killed by hunters. In America, an image that comes to mind is of homeless people scrounging for survival at the outskirts of malls. In Tibet, they say, "Only the snow lion among us can go into solitude in the wilderness and achieve enlightenment on its own."

To appreciate the value of sangha, a community of practice, consider these words which begin the *Visuddhimagga* ("Path of Purity"). We've noted in Chapter 2, "One Taste, Different Flavors: The Teachings Adapt to Different Lands," how the *Visuddhimagga* represents part of an oral tradition memorized by monks for centuries after the Buddha. It begins by asking: *There's inner tangle and outer tangle. This generation's all tangled up. Who can untangle this tangle?* Two millennia or so later, are things any less tangled? (As President Lyndon B. Johnson once put it, "The whole schmear is one big ball of wax.") Who can untangle this tangle?

As Michael Wenger, Dean of the Buddhist Studies Program at San Francisco Zen Center, explains, "When you take responsibility for the enormity of all that transforming yourself to Buddha is about, you realize that you can use all the help you can get." I'd add that if you don't yet grasp that enormity, a sangha helps you realize it.

True, the Buddha attained enlightenment sitting beneath a tree, after seven years, but he had a head start, being a prodigy who was given a kingly training in all things, including meditation. And, on the night in question, the Buddha called all of creation as his witness, the sangha of all beings. So your path isn't solitary. There's a community of beings, human and otherwise, life writ large, with whom your practice pertains.

Now, maybe your Buddhist practice will enrich an already grounded religious practice, such as Christianity, Judaism, Islam, Hinduism, in which case you already have the sangha of your fellow congregants. But you might still need a teacher. Whether for community or teacher, there's a range of options as to style or focus of practice.

Leaves from the Bodhi Tree

Contemporary Cambodian Buddhist patriarch Maha Ghosananda tells of a young monk who studied diligently, every day. But he grew upset that he couldn't learn everything, and soon couldn't either eat or sleep. Finally, he came to the Buddha and asked to leave the order. "Please," he said, "there are many teachings and I can't master them all. I'm not fit to be a monk." The Buddha told him, "Don't worry. To be free you must master only one thing." The monk begged, "Please teach me. If you give me just one practice, I will do it wholeheartedly, and I'm sure I can succeed." So the Buddha told him, "Master the mind. When you've mastered the mind, you'll know everything."

How Many Medicines Are in Your Cabinet?: Picking and Choosing

What'll it be? Insight? Zen? Pure Land? Tibetan? ... Zen Pure Land? ... Native American Tibetan? ... Taoist Zen Islam? There's no One-Size-Fits-All practice. As R. H. Blyth, scholar of Buddhism and haiku, once said, "For every person there's a religion. And for every religion there's a person." Amen. This holds true for the Buddha's way, as well. It's said that there are 64,000 Dharma doors (entrances to the Way) because there are at least 64,000 different basic kinds of suffering. (Here, too, there's probably a numbered list in some monastery.) But, remember: the Dharma has but one taste, the taste of freedom.

I think it's good to realize that the stuff awaiting you will always be there, ultimately the same no matter how many different teachers or styles you try. By all means, be aware of options. If you pick and stick with one teacher, then that bond will grow as you open up to each other more and more over time. It's also good to visit other sanghas, from time to time. If different teachers have a particular healing or message or precious gift for you, make room for it in your practice.

Leaves from the Bodhi Tree

The master of a monastery interviewed a new monk. "Who'd you study with before?" he asked. After the monk answered "So-and-So," the master asked what he'd learned. "Well, I'd asked him what's the meaning of Buddhism, and he said, 'The Fire God comes for fire.'" The master said, "Good answer! I guess you didn't understand it." The monk replied, "But I did understand! If the Fire God asks for fire, that would be like my asking about Buddhism, because I'm really a buddha already." The master shook his head, and said, "I knew it. You missed the point completely." "Well, how do you handle it?" The master said, "You ask me." So the monk asked him, "What's the meaning of Buddhism?" "The Fire God comes for fire," replied the master, and the monk got it.

Don't Sweat the Isms

The more experience you have of the variety of the Buddha's way, the more you'll appreciate *your* way. As you move through Buddhaland, don't be afraid to listen to and learn from Pure Land, Insight Meditation, and Zen ... Hinayana, Mahayana, Vajrayana ... and even Swami Beyondananda.

Understanding the essentials is always a good critical tool ("criticism" coming from Greek *kroinos,* to choose). And so the major branches are introduced in the following chapters. But they're only doors. The true Way is underneath your feet.

Hear and Now

"Any path is only a path and there is no affront, to oneself or to others, in dropping it if that is what your heart tells you. ... Look at every path closely and deliberately. Try it as many times as you think necessary. Then ask yourself and yourself alone one question: Does this path have a heart? If the path does, it is good. If not, it is of no use. Do they have a sense of humor? Do you feel better after you leave them?"

—Carlos Castaneda

When the Student Is Ready, the Master Appears

American author Erma Bombeck once said something very appropriate here: Never go to a doctor whose houseplants have died. That is, you could really like a *teacher*, but look around and look within. If, deep down, you don't feel comfortable with a teacher, then they're not right for you. Don't worry. Another will turn up.

Just like you, each teacher's a unique human being. Some might have thick black lines around themselves, clearly marking off where they stand. Others might be eclectic. Stephen Batchelor, for example, is an Englishman who studied Zen in Korea for many years. Then he studied Vajrayana for many years. In retrospect, he's said his Zen experience enabled him to drill straight down within himself, vertically, as it were, while the Tibetan experience filled out a missing horizontal expanse with a variety of trainings. Out of that, he teaches a lucid version of Buddhism he calls agnostic, or "Buddhism without beliefs." (True enough, Buddhism's not a religion about dogma or beliefs, but about what's in front of your face, right now. Thus, we might believe in Christianity or Judaism as a religion, whereas the Buddha asks us, rather, to practice his findings.)

Along the Path

Each practice emphasizes the teacher-student relationship differently. In Tibetan practice, the teacher, called a *guru,* must be worthy of unconditional trust, obedience, and love, and the relationship will often be lifelong. In Korea, monks might study under more than one teacher, rotating so as to not fix on any one master's version of the Dharma as definitive.

And just as each teacher's different, so will each student take what they need, differently. Whatever their background, a good teacher will optimize the conditions for your own practice. How you respond and what you make of it all goes to make up the wonderful mystery that's you.

Ultimately, choosing a teacher means learning to listen to your intuition. Once a cousin of mine was visiting a foreign city. She was in a store, trying on a coat. A saleslady walked by and my cousin snagged her attention by saying, "Excuse me. My husband's taking a nap at the hotel, so I'll ask you. Do you think this coat is right for me?" The saleslady looked, nodded okay, and replied, "Well, if you could choose a husband, I think you could certainly choose a coat." Teachers of all kinds are everywhere, including the Coat Department.

This Is

In a Japanese Zen context, a teacher is called **Roshi** (Japanese for "old master"), layperson or monk. In Thailand, a Buddhist teacher is called Ajahn. Tibetan practice is closely involved with a guru (Sanskrit for teacher) who acts as a mentor and guide; **Lama** and Rinpoche (*RIHN-poe-shay*) are Tibetan synonyms. They're all reflections of the inner teacher.

Besides your deep-down gut feeling, here are a few objective road signs to check out in choosing a teacher:

➤ Does the teacher communicate in a way you can readily understand?

➤ Is the teacher cold? Light's important, but so is warmth. In fact, compassion is numero uno.

➤ Do the teacher and the sangha seem harmonious and happy? Do they follow the precepts?

➤ Check credentials. What was this teacher's relationship to their teacher? What do you hear from others you know? Avoid gossip, but listen to wise counsel and experience.

➤ Has a cult evolved around the teacher? Do other students copy his or her dress or speech patterns?

➤ Do they claim to be enlightened or promise enlightenment? If so, personally, I'd pass. ("If you see a Buddha along the road, move on.") Likewise, remember, too, that teachers are only human and have their foibles.

Whenever You're Ready, We Are: Finding a Sangha

Pick a sangha first, or first pick a teacher. Same, either way. A sangha usually comes with a teacher, but you might pick a sangha first. If there isn't any sangha meeting where you live, maybe there's a group of Quakers with whom you can sit in silent meditation. And you can always start your own sangha, inviting a few friends to come over to join you. At this book's Web site (awakening.to), I've added a link to an online directory of sanghas around the world, called Dharmanet. I've also listed a book in the online bibliography, called *Guide to Buddhist America,* which is the leading directory for sanghas.

Whatever the variety, most sanghas meet regularly, such as once a week, to practice. Meeting with a group reinforces the good habit of practice. And, I think, on some mundane level, sitting and meditating with a group is more powerful than doing it alone. I don't mean to imply anything psychic or occult. Yet when I've read my writing to a few thousand people I've felt the difference in the hall that wasn't there when I'd read to groups of tens or a hundred. Consciousness is aware of other consciousness. I think we're all part of one big organism. My personal sense or awareness of this is magnified in sangha.

Sangha's like an ocean. I know I can set my boat on its waters, and it will hold me up. My practice is upheld by the sangha, as I uphold it by my practice. Sangha's also a community resource center. Sangha members are there for each other. Sangha is refuge. A dear member of my sangha once told us, following meditation one rainy afternoon, of his fatal cancer. He'd tried and given up on the painkillers. *"This,"* he said, "is the only thing that helps."

One last thing. Ending where we began, with beginner's mind (not knowing), let's dot an "i" and cross a "t" in our *attitude.*

Big Flashing Road Sign: Right View

Why meditate? Because it's good medicine. Now, for the medicine to be really effective, it needs to be practiced together with the Eightfold Path, which begins with Right View.

Right View begins our conduct, leading to meditation, culminating in wisdom which, in turn, further informs our conduct, making it conscious. What this means is that as we approach meditation our attitude, our mindset, our expectations and preconceptions, are like baggage to be checked at the door, like the shoes people slip off before entering a zen temple. Go barefoot, with sure steps.

Hear and Now

"Simply practice meditation in order to live a better life, or even just to live a good life, whatever meaning that holds for you. Or, meditate as a means of learning how not to be afraid—of death, or of all the insignificant concerns that paralyze your innate ability to live fully. Meditate to activate creativity. Meditate to recognize the value of the truly good things in life: friendship, honor, respect, compassion, and love."

—Ajahn Sumano Bhikkhu

Ask yourself, before you proceed, "Why meditate? What's my *inmost urgency?*" Think of the mental snapshot you took of yourself at the beginning of this chapter. Review it from time to time. You might well find the reason you take up practice might be different from why you were drawn to it in the first place. And you might stay with it for yet another reason.

Along the Path

Our inventive, do-it-yourself American society has evolved a culture for self-help and self-improvement. Our *Complete Idiot's Guide* series is a positive manifestation of all that. But a flashing road sign's necessary here. Buddhism isn't self-*development*. The heart-awakening way of the Buddha is *mind*-development and self-*effacement:* losing one's self in order to find one's true nature.

Many good intentions are prey to linguistic traps which result in confusions which could be avoided in advance. For instance, many people say "I want to calm my mind." Where is your mind? It's like asking to scoop up a rainbow into a pail. And you'll find that *trying* to calm your mind down makes your mind only more restless, like a wild horse at the sight of a harness. (Chapter 10 is about how the mind gets calm.)

So it's good to have a sense of where you are and where you want to go. But to get there, the best view is no viewpoint, complete acceptance of what's in front of your nose. Striving after enlightenment, on the other hand, is a setup. It's a vicious cycle. The self defined by opinion is an illusion. The true nature of mind is transparent, boundless. So when that limited, illusory self seeks selflessness by saying, "*I want* [grasping] to *calm myself* [believing there's a self to calm, and that it can be switched on and off]," that only reinforces the illusory self that perpetuates the pain in the first place. It's like trying to bite your teeth. (Don't go there.)

Enlightenment *is* the ultimate goal. But it can't be reached through grasping, only by letting go. Meditation reveals the delusions that have crusted over our true nature, shows us how to gently scrub, polish, and appreciate its innate radiance.

In terms of work, health, family, creativity, and your community, meditation can clear your thinking, sharpen your concentration, empower your intuition, deepen your compassion, elevate your wisdom, improve your tennis score, and on and on. But think of these more as possible bonuses, rather than goals.

And because the Buddha's way uses the mind to study the mind, and because the human mind is so powerful, it's not without potential peril, from headaches to insanity. So, Right View is eminently important (as is Sangha).

Grounded in the Buddha's basic teachings, the Sangha will help keep you on the path. Let the Middle Way also guide you. That is, don't use meditation to build up your sense of self. ("I can sit full lotus, nyah-nyah.") Nor try to annihilate your self through meditation. ("Out, out, damned spot!") Start with where you are. Work with what you have. Be compassionate towards yourself and others. Make friends with yourself and the universe. Take time. Why do you think they call it "practice"!?

So practice involves space and time, a teacher and community, and right attitude, such as beginner's mind. And one last reminder. Practice is continual. Whether sitting on a cushion or driving a car. It's all practice. *Enjoy!*

Along the Path

What about people who seek the Buddha's way in order to acquire material goods? If the Buddha's way is practiced sincerely, the good medicine can affect them. It's not the Buddha's way to seek an outcome contrary to karma. So if someone chants for a new sports car, their not getting it should make them look deeper within, become better persons worthy of their wish, and wish for things worthy of their true nature.

The Least You Need to Know

➤ Practice means finding and staying on your path. It's not like music you practice to perform at some later date, but, rather, an act to put you in touch with the present moment. It's more like musical scales, which musicians practice daily, no matter their level of achievement.

➤ The best approach is to take a beginner's mind, a "don't know" mind, with no preconceptions or judgments. Always.

➤ Everyone can find a place in their home for practice. It's more important to practice daily than for any particular length of time.

➤ Altars are an option. If you bow to an image of the Buddha, it's to acknowledge and nurture the buddha within you. Incense, beads, and a bell are also optional aids.

➤ Formal practice begins when you take refuge in the Three Jewels. When choosing a sangha, do some homework and listen to your heart.

➤ Understanding the basics of meditation will help clarify your attitude—and the results.

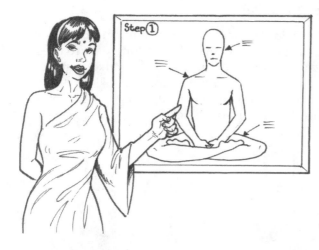

Chapter 10

Base Camp: Meditation Basics

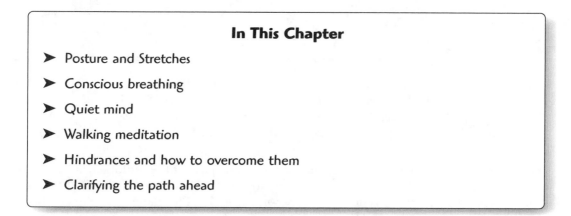

In This Chapter

➤ Posture and Stretches

➤ Conscious breathing

➤ Quiet mind

➤ Walking meditation

➤ Hindrances and how to overcome them

➤ Clarifying the path ahead

There are many paths up and down the mountain. Meditation's like the base camp. Meditation can also be like an oasis, where you can recharge your batteries while on your pilgrimage called life.

When we're tranquil, our minds are like a clear lake. If I were to toss a small stone into such a lake, we'd see it fall all the way to the bottom. With such clarity, we could discover a lost pearl of great price, slipped down to the bottom of this lake. That lake's like our mind, whose muddy waters can become clear and whose ripples flatten out, all on their own. That pearl represents our mind's natural luminosity, solidity, and pricelessness.

This chapter surveys these meditation fundamentals. Square One. Welcome to Base Camp!

Here's Where It Sat: Posture

Archeologists in the Indus Valley have dug up small figurines of men in the posture of yogic meditation dating back at least five millennia. That's a long time to be sitting. Sure, the sculptor might've been commemorating a sit-down strike or something. We don't know for sure; they didn't come with descriptive booklets. But just looking at them you sense a reverence. It seems almost as if the very posture of sitting cross-legged in the lotus position can mean so much.

In the full lotus, the classic meditation position, each leg's on the opposite thigh. In a half lotus, only one foot rests on the opposite thigh, the other rests on the floor or on the calf, and often with a pillow to support that knee. In a quarter lotus, the feet rest on the calves. And in the Burmese position, both feet are folded in front of your body, not crossed over each other.

In the accompanying drawing you see the classic pose of the Buddha. Have you tried it? Seated, cross-legged, you aren't going anywhere. The alarm bells of fright-or-flight, hard-wired into our physiology, always on the lookout for dangers in the environment, get dimmed way down. Your hands aren't manipulating any tools. There's nothing to say, nothing to do but sit and breathe, in the here and in the now.

With knees apart slightly, you can meditate while kneeling. You can sit on your heels or a small bench or your zafu on end. If you sit in a chair, don't rely on the back of your chair for support: Rely on yourself, and in good posture.

Just smiling slightly while taking a few breaths can actually make you happier. (Go ahead and try it, right now!) Stopping and taking a few, slow, fully conscious breaths can calm and sharpen awareness. Peace can be as simple and bold as that.

Ears over Shoulders: Basic Postures

The basics of meditation have remained the same for millennia. Ideally, you sit on a cushion on the floor, but a chair works, too. I've heard of someone experiencing initial enlightenment while sitting in a high school auditorium chair.

On the ground, your legs might take one of three positions: full lotus, half lotus, or Burmese. In full lotus, each foot is on the opposite calf or thigh. In half lotus, only one foot is on the opposite thigh or calf; the other rests on the ground (in which case it's often advisable to put a small, thin pillow underneath it, so both knees are equally level and balanced). Burmese-style, both knees are on the floor. Your contact with the ground should feel like a stable tripod, of knees and sit-space. Feel yourself sink down into this contact, like a mountain upon the earth. Your tailbone makes contact with the ground, and your anus tilts up, along with your hips.

Along the Path

At a café, when I see people hunched like Rodin's *The Thinker* over a sandwich, or a book, or their laptops, I wonder, "Are they getting enough oxygen to their brains, their hearts, their minds?" Bent over, it's hard to breathe fully and so writing, reading, or eating lacks full enrichment. Try it for yourself: *Sit hunched over and notice your breathing—then notice the difference in your breathing when sitting straight.*

Your back needs to be straight so breathing and energy can flow freely. Imagine there's a small ring at the top of your head, where your hair meets your scalp, and a hook comes down from the sky, engages that ring, and gently lifts you *up*, as far as your waist. Everything above your waist stretches straight upwards. Your lower back naturally curves in and your upper back naturally curves out. Overall, your spine is erect and stretched. Jon Kabat-Zinn, founder and director of the Stress Reduction Clinic at the University of Massachusetts Medical Center, points out another way you can imagine this: Sit in a way that embodies dignity. He's noted that whenever he tells his students this, everybody knows that feeling and how to embody it. It's a good practice for throughout the day: Remember "dignity"; remember "sky hook."

Hear and Now

"The state of mind that exists when you sit in the right posture is, itself, enlightenment. If you cannot be satisfied with the state of mind you have in zazen, it means your mind is still wandering about. Our body and mind should not be wobbling or wandering about. In this posture there is no need to talk about the right state of mind. You already have it. This is the conclusion of Buddhism."

—Shunryu Suzuki Roshi

Your shoulders are back so your chest can comfortably expand. Your ears are over shoulders. Your shoulders are over your hips. Your nose is aligned with your navel. Your eyes are horizontal with the ground, but you tuck your chin in, which lowers your head just a fraction. (You don't want to squish the back of your brain.) You might imagine your head supports the sky.

Your hands can rest on your knees, palms down or up. (More on hands in a second.) Now, test your position. Sway front and back, then left and right. Get centered.

Doing That Cool Hand Jive: Mudras

As the motionless posture of our legs and feet sends a message to our brain (that we're not going anywhere), so, too, does the placement of our hands hold meaning. An etiquette book, for example, may tell you not to put your little finger out at a 45-degree angle when you hold your fork, so as not to appear "backstairs refined." Two important gestures (called *mudras*) are those of greeting and meditation.

Palms together for bowing.

Joining palms is a universal gesture of spirit. There's a famous etching by Albrecht Dürer of two disembodied hands praying in and of themselves. In the East, putting palms and fingers fully together is a gesture of greeting (*namaskar/namastey*, Hindu; *añjali*, Sanskrit; *wai*, Thai; *gassho*, Japanese). In India and Thailand, you put your hands together at your chest and raise them to your forehead, often followed by a bow, still in that position—eyes and joined hands going outward and down to a spot on the ground equidistant between the greeter and the greeted. It says, "The sacred within me salutes the sacred within you." And "Have a nice day."

Cosmic meditation mudra.

More than a salutation, then, it can be an expression of devotion or gratitude, as well as supplication. As the action joins venerator and venerated, it's also an expression of unity, and an appreciation of suchness (see Chapter 8, "The Fine Print: Touching Deeper," for more on suchness). It's often used at the beginning and end of meditation. For example, you might gassho to fellow sangha members, and then to your cushion, before being seated. You might also gassho to a statue of the Buddha. (Buddhists also use the word *gassho* as a salutation in a letter, instead of "Yours truly.")

This Is

Hand gestures hold significance. The two-fingered V-sign is almost universal. Buddhism has a catalogue of gestures called **mudras** (Sanskrit for "sign, seal"). When the Buddha or a deity holds one hand up, palm out, that means protection, "don't fear." Fingers outstretched except the tip of thumb and index finger meeting in a circle is the mudra of teaching. By imitating certain gestures outwardly, it's thought that we can cultivate the inner state associated with them.

When seated, you can place your palms on your knees. Or you might try the earth-touching mudra, seen in Chapter 1, "Why Is This Man Smiling?: The Buddha." But the best is the standard pose, sometimes called the *cosmic mudra*. Put the back of your right hand on top of your left palm. Adjust how close or far apart your hands are so your thumbs make contact ever so lightly, at about the height of your navel. From the front, the space between your hands resembles an egg (hold it without dropping it), and behind it is a point below your navel called *dan tien* in Chinese, *hara* in Japanese, considered your true center—physically in posture, and spiritually as central repository of life-force, also known as *prana* and *chi*. When you've got the gesture, give yourself two big hands!

Facing Your Meditation

There are about 300 muscles in your face alone. Letting them all relax takes a little time. As you do so, you might ask, "What do I do with my tongue?" Answer: Rest tongue on roof of mouth. Tip to inside upper lip.

And why not smile!? Thich Nhat Hanh has coined the nifty phrase "mouth yoga"—lifting one corner of your mouth, slightly, like Mona Lisa or the Buddha. He remarks, "Why wait until you are completely transformed, completely awakened? You can start being a part-time Buddha right now!"

To see or not to see!? I like to close my eyes to rest. Seeing is really a very intricate, complex process when you think about it. It uses more than half the space our brain allots for the five senses. Shutting my eyes frees me from all that information, frees me from domination by objects, and directs my sight, instead, inward. Do I need to be aware of the rectilinear borders partitioning space? Eyes closed, I feel rounder and more boundless. Pitfalls to eyes-closed are possibly hallucinating or falling asleep.

Some zen teachers suggest keeping your eyes open, keeping this-worldly. (After I've checked in at Base Camp and feel calm, I usually do open my eyes for the duration of my meditation.) For that route, try focusing your gaze on a spot on the floor about a yard away. If you're in a group, the back of the person in front of you would do.

What If I Froze Like This?: Warm-Up Stretches

It can be hard enough just sitting for 45 minutes without composing a stunning speech to your lover or manager. But, as Oscar Wilde exclaimed, "Spare me *physical* pain!" That is, part of your job is to note the arising and passing of physical distractions as well as the mindwaves, without judgment, and to let them go. On a retreat, people often notice both physical and mental pain falling away at or after the third day. But, on the other hand, you're not inviting pain. So, as with any athletic physical culture, warm-ups are a sound investment in a healthy, happy practice.

Check out *The Complete Idiot's Guide to Yoga* for information on such poses as the Bound Angle, the Butterfly, the Cat, the Cobbler, the Cobra, the Cradle, the Downward Dog, the Hero, the Locust, the Lunge, the Supported Bridge, and the Triangle, and *The Complete Idiot's Guide to Tai Chi and QiGong* for tai chi warm-up exercises, all of which make excellent stretches for meditation.

Yoga instruction in such poses as the downward-facing dog (left) and butterfly (right) help keep the pain demons away from meditation sessions, and make you more feel human afterward.

Why Not Breathe? You're Alive!

As mentioned in the previous chapter, meditation can be one breath long … an impromptu mini-meditation … a pause that releases. One conscious breath. Breathing in, just being aware you're breathing in. Breathing out, just being aware you're breathing out.

Along the Path

From cradle to grave, we're breathing—but we're seldom aware of it. So why not check in for a moment? When you're ready, set this book aside, and just notice your breathing. Like a mental snapshot, a breath impression. Just pay some attention to how you're breathing. Don't judge. Don't try to change anything. Three or four breaths later, notice if you feel any more centered, grounded, for having checked in. That's all it takes. Try it.

No matter the spiritual tradition, breath's an essential ingredient. What could be more impermanent and insubstantial, yet vital and universal? In the biblical creation story, human beings were fashioned out of red clay and infused with the divine breath of life. It's interesting that the word used in the New Testament for spirit literally means *breath*. Thus in John 20:22, "Receive thou the Holy Spirit," the original is literally, "Receive holy breath."

I don't know if Jesus taught his disciples conscious breathing, but it's an interesting notion. (Consider Acts 2:4, for example, "And they were all filled with the Holy

167

Spirit"—filled with holy breath; perhaps also filled with the awareness of the holiness of breath?) Christians who practice Buddhist conscious breathing sometimes call it "resting in the Spirit." Meditating on breath brought Siddhartha to Grand Enlightenment. And so he specifically addressed conscious breathing from the very start. His *Sutra on Full Awareness of Breathing* is one of his most essential teachings.

This Is

The Sanskrit word for breath, **prana,** also means universal energy, life-force. The origin of the Chinese word for this, **chi** (pronounced *chee*, also spelled *qi*), is believed to be steam, vapor. The word **spirit** comes from Latin, *spiritus, spirare,* meaning breath; to breathe. (Inspiration means breathing in.) The Old Testament Hebrew and Greek words for spirit, **ruach** and **pneuma,** mean breath but also wind (merging within and without).

Breathing's universal and ever-present. Everybody breathes, and all the time. And it's integral to our state of being. Thus, it's a perfect vehicle for practice.

One-breath meditation can be a base upon which to expand. See what feels right. Add 5 minutes ... then try 10. It's kind of awesome to be aware of breath, and nothing else. Interesting, at least. You already have all you need for conscious breathing. So play with incorporating it as part of your practice.

Some people slide right into it, while others need a little hand-holding. So a few pages follow with some techniques to help center or guide your awareness. Read through and see if just one might sound interesting. Trying them all right now might be overkill. They're all designed to focus awareness on breathing and set aside anything else. For example, you might loop a string of beads around your hand and move one bead down with your thumb each time you've breathed in. (Works for me!)

Three more such mindful breathing techniques are as follows:

➤ Body

➤ Counting

➤ Mantras and gathas

Having a Gut Feeling That the Nose Knows

Two areas of your *body* can help center your mind on your breathing—and then help your breathing center your mind. You can focus awareness on either your *nostrils* or your *navel*.

With your mouth closed, your breath comes and goes through your nostrils. Rediscover this for yourself. Sitting still for a moment, right now, be conscious of that fact. When you're ready, put this book aside. You might direct your attention to the very *tips* of your nostrils. Breathing in, feel how cool breath can feel at your nostrils— maybe even how fragrant. Breathing out, feel how warm the breath feels at your nostrils—warm and fuzzy, perhaps.

Along the Path

You might think of these techniques or tools as bicycle training wheels to get you started. After a certain point, you might feel your breath slow, deepen, and calm, accompanied by an often pleasant feeling, like release. Still noticing how your breath flows, you can gently let go of your focusing technique, and just stay with your breath in the present, and nothing else.

That's meditation bedrock, for many; all that's needed. But your mind might naturally expand and want to explore. If so, you might direct your attention to your breath coming and going *through* your inner nostrils. And stay with that. When you can do that, and just that, for five minutes, congratulations!—you've established your meditation base camp.

Consider conscious breathing your base—from which to set forth, and explore, and to which you can come home. It's that center or "centering" you might hear about in spiritual circles. Maintain it with regular practice. Build upon it if you like by adding five minutes, until you're up to 30 to 45 minutes a day.

Alternatively, you can concentrate on your navel. Maybe you've heard the stereotype of Eastern meditations as being "navel-gazing." Actually, it's not the navel, but the *hara* or *dan tien* that you focus on. It's about the size of a dime, three or four fingers down from the navel. If our nostrils are the doorway, then this might be thought of as the palace basement, the storehouse, the secret treasury.

Focusing on belly breathing may run counter to the way you've been brought up. I know I was taught to keep my abdomen hard, military-style. "Hold it in," the expression went, and, since body and mind are one, this applied to emotions as well; aren't they often called "gut feelings"? So it's not uncommon to see people trying to breathe deeply by expanding their chest rather than their bellies. When frightened, babies breathe in their chests, as if scared of contracting something overwhelming in their belly. Some people often carry this trait over into adulthood as a basic policy toward life. ("Uh-oh, this makes me breathe deeply: Houston, we have a problem.") Notice how far down your body moves with your own breath. Don't try to change or judge it. Just observe.

Concentrating on your lower tummy instead of your nose, be aware of how your belly fills when you inhale, and falls when you exhale. As you do so, feel any hardness in your belly gradually soften, breath by breath. Breathe *into* any tightness in your belly. *Exhale* any tensions this might release. *(Ahh!)*

After a few sessions of conscious belly breathing, you might find your breathing fills your belly more than before, automatically. If so, just notice it. If not, no sweat. Breath eventually deepens of its own. Belly awareness creates conditions that can assist the process. This is the Buddha's way—providing the nourishment for seeds to become flowers.

Note: This isn't yoga. That is, you aren't trying to control your breath, nor make it any different than it already is. Your job is to just watch it. It may seem like a paradox: controlling the breath to control the mind, without controlling anything, just observing. But that's the name of the game. Try and control the mind, and it becomes even harder to tame, like a wild horse, or a child throwing a tantrum.

And these are just training wheels. Your meditation's not about nose or tummy (not to mention the parameningeal epigastrum). Basic meditation is about letting body, mind, and breath get reacquainted, and watching these old friends work together.

Making Each Breath Count

Counting's another way to focus awareness on breath, and keep your mind from wandering. Try this: *Calmly breathe out, say to yourself "one," then breathe in that "one," and breathe out, and begin "two."* Don't think of anything else but your breath. Just your breathing in, your breathing out, and then a very quick, light count. And nothing else. At "four," return to "one," again. If your mind wanders, as it does, begin all over again, at "one."

Here are two open secrets about counting. 1) You're not an idiot if you can't make it all the way to four. But if you can do four sets of "four," simple as 1-2-3, then just observe your breath without counting. 2) You don't have to feel like an idiot to return to such simplicity as 1-2-3-4; these are basics of life. Buddhism means back to basics.

Remember, keep your attention on your breathing, not the count.

Words to Meditate by: **Mantras** *and* **Gathas**

Besides body awareness and counting, two more options for focusing awareness on breathing and quieting the mind are verbal:

➤ Mantra

➤ Gatha

One mantra many people use when beginning conscious breathing meditation, is mentally saying to themselves "IN" while breathing in, and "OUT" while breathing out. Concentrating on each word focuses the mind on breathing. In. Out. One single word for one single breath. Some people mentally recite them "in-in-in" and "out-out-out."

This Is

A **mantra** (*mohn-trah*) can be a word or phrase repeated to aid our memory. Thus, when we repeat the Buddha's name, we're remembering him. They can also symbolize and communicate a certain energy or deity, as well as erase bad habit energy by substituting positive consciousness. Mantras can be recited aloud or mentally. Hindus might chant, "Om." Christians, "Amen" or "Alleluia." Muslims, "Allah." Jews, "Shalom." (However, Jimmy the Greek says you should take firm control of your spiritual destiny: Don't leave anything to chants.)

A Buddhist *gatha* (*gah-thah*) is a stanza or verse from a sutra, or an individual's expression of spiritual insight. Some can be recited mentally—you might think of them as prayers, but not exactly so because they're not expressed to any supreme deity. For example, a stanza in the Buddha's *Sutra on Full Awareness of Breathing* says:

> *Breathing in, I know that I am breathing in*
> *Breathing out, I know that I am breathing out.*

Using that gatha as a conscious breathing tool, say the first line to yourself when breathing in, the second when breathing out. It's very suitable for a 20- to 30-minute meditation. If you find that during meditation it's shortened to just the words "in" and "out," that's alright. Just keep your awareness on the breathing not the words.

Thich Nhat Hanh has written this lovely gatha, which I highly recommend for conscious breathing:

> *Breathing in, I'm aware of the present moment.*
> *Breathing out, I'm aware it's a wonderful moment.*
> *Breathing in, I calm my body.*
> *Breathing out, I smile.*

Think the first line to yourself, breathing in; the second, exhaling; the third, inhaling; the last, exhaling. Then return to the beginning. After you get the hang, you can use a kind of mental shorthand:

[In] think *"Present moment"*
[Out] think *"Wonderful moment"*
[In] think *"Calm"*
[Out] think *"Smile"*

Slowing, Deepening, and Release: A Distinct Pleasure

The preceding tools (skillful means) help spotlight breathing with a mindful ray of awareness. At first, you might not have even been aware you were breathing. Half the time, who is?! Gradually, you'll become more familiar with it and its landscape. If a breath's long, take notice of that fact. Just make a mental note. If another breath's short, just take notice of that.

Become aware too of the beginning, the middle, and the end of each in-breath and out-breath. Also pay attention to how breath begins: after an out-breath, and without your willing it, a new breath will appear. All by itself. ("Ta-DAH!") Notice, too, how breath flows. Is it powerful or soft; shallow or deep? And if there's a space in between breaths, notice that, too. Train yourself to notice each of these qualities. Emily Dickinson once called herself "inebriate of air," but connoisseur of air will do just fine.

As you learn to become more and more immersed in awareness of your breathing, one very interesting thing you'll eventually notice is that your breathing—and your body, and your emotions, and your mind—will calm. Slowing down. Deepening.

You might experience a feeling of at-oneness … a sense of release … and pleasure. A new kind of pleasure, maybe. If so, go with it. You deserve it. You've earned it. By simply being. Remember the picture of the smiling Buddha in Chapter 2? Meditation can bring not only peace but also great joy.

Returning to the idea of our nostrils as doorways, Suzuki Roshi gives a marvelous teaching when he calls breathing a *hinge*. We breathe in, he says, and air comes into the inner world; exhale, air goes to the outer world. Inner world / outer world—both endless. Actually, there's but one world, the whole world. Breath passes through us like someone going through a swinging door. "When your mind is pure and calm enough to follow this movement," Suzuki continues, "there is nothing: no 'I,' no world, no mind nor body; just a swinging door."

Hear and Now

"'I am breathing in and making my whole body calm and at peace.' It is like drinking a cool glass of lemonade on a hot day and feeling your body become cool inside. When you breathe in, the air enters your body and calms all the cells of your body. At the same time each 'cell' of your mind also becomes more peaceful. The three are one, and each one is all three. This is the key to meditation. Breathing brings the sweet joy of meditation to you. You become joyful, fresh, and tolerant, and everyone around you will benefit."

—Thich Nhat Hanh

Turning Off the Radio: Quieting the Mind

"Turning off the radio" is Robert Aitken Roshi's phrase, and I love it. Don't you just immediately know what he means?! Of course, since he coined it, it's become only more apt. That is, we've become a soundtracked nation, with music to study by, cassettes to drive by, CDs to walk by, and less and less opportunity for us to have big ears for the utterly unique and even amazing all-natural sounds all around, within and without. And the silence with which they're interwoven. Artificial stimuli usually don't quiet the *mind* but preempt it, with somebody else's agenda and doings. Quieting the mind is very basic. It's shushing the mind's verbal activity the way an audience quiets down when a concert or movie is about to begin. Stop, look, listen ... and hear. Here!

Radio noise can fade into the background. The drunken monkey can stop twirling the dial. Does it ever go entirely off, much less stay off? For now, don't worry about that. That is, don't *expect* your mind to go blank, and if it does, don't worry, it'll come back. Here are three tips for optimal *mind-watching:*

➤ Just notice what you notice.

➤ Appreciate sounds as well as silence.

➤ Be mindful and compassionate toward yourself.

173

This Is

A common Buddhist image of the **mind** is of a monkey swinging from branch to branch, from a smell to a sight, from mental remorse to emotional rehearsal, etc. More vividly, they say an untrained mind's like a drunken monkey stung by a bee. Not someone you'd like to invite home to meet your parents. Another comparison's to an elephant in heat; well, you can imagine. Basic meditation, then, is the opposite of all that: stopping and being still.

Notice What You Notice

Quieting your mind is like calming your breath. You're not trying to make anything happen. Your job's just to breathe and observe. Observe your breath, and all its qualities. And if thoughts come, observe them, too—but don't invite them to sit down with you for tea. Unattended, they'll go off on their own merry way. ("All conditioned things have their arising, and their passing away.")

Be like a mirror, or mountain lake, that reflects whatever passes before it. Tibetan Buddhists suggest just watching your thoughts the way an old person on a park bench watches children at play. Don't even pay attention to which kids are yours or not. Your thoughts aren't necessarily you.

Appreciate Sounds (Ker-Plunk!) *as Well as Silence*

The concept of silencing the mind is a stereotype. Meditation's not a sensory deprivation tank, though in a real sensory deprivation tank you'll still hear your heart, and your nervous system. So don't be surprised to find meditation accompanied by the gentle drums of your pulse, the lilting flute of your breath, and the hummmmm of body-mind. They're just part of the furnishings, along for the ride.

Treat your senses the same as your thoughts. You might hear the jagged yawp of a bird, the corkscrewing siren of a passing fire truck, the rumble of a window shaken by the wind. Just hear what you hear. Without reacting. Passing cars might be more soothing than you'd expect, more like ocean waves. (Let go of your prejudices and preconceptions, and listen.) And notice how sounds overlap in curious, unrepeatable rhythms! All they mean is that you're here, and now. Let whatever comes to your senses during meditation awaken you to that fact. And continue to enjoy your breathing.

Along the Path

Sound meditation. Sit where you won't be disturbed. Close your eyes. Relax. Take a few, slow, full conscious breaths. Listen to whatever sounds come to your ears. Be only ears. Big ears. Let sounds grow more vivid. Don't label, other than all being "The Sound of the Universe," or "Life." As if it's all music, a special symphony, and you've been given the best seat in the house. When done, take some time to reacquaint yourself with your surroundings. Listen for any encores.

Be Mindful and Compassionate Toward Yourself

Meditation can have its ups and downs. Remember to smile. Why not treat your mind as a mother would her own child. Have compassion for yourself. Smile at your habitual schemes and scenarios. By just letting them be, and being compassionately aware of them, you can let them go. Remember, there wouldn't be doors without walls, so don't bang your head on them! Be kind to yourself.

This also applies for dealing with other people's baggage. As you learn compassion for your own baggage—you'll have it for others'. Compassion for all beings includes yourself. If you can't be kind to yourself, who else can you be kind to?

Each Step You Take on This Green Earth Brings Peace

Walking meditation's my favorite. (The Japanese name for it is *kinhin.*) It's often used as an opportunity to stretch after sitting. But in and of itself it can be a marvelous and very powerful practice.

Indoors or outdoors, find some place where you can walk without obstruction or interruption. A backyard will do, a quiet street, a big emptyish room, or a long, clear hallway. Your hands can be at your side. Or you can form a cosmic mudra (which is

175

what I do). Some people join their palms in a gassho. Others make a fist and cover it with the other hand and hold them both to their navel or hara. Still others join their hands behind their back, like a bird with folded wings.

Let that sky hook pull your upper body up, and let your lower body just hang naturally. Your feet are apart about the width of your hips, and maybe bare, terrain permitting. Center yourself in your breathing for a moment. Then begin. Step forward with your left foot as you inhale. Exhale as you step forward with your right foot. One breath per step (yup! *that* slow). And when you come to a corner or the end of your allotted space, you just make a turn, 180 degrees or 90 degrees—two steps will do the trick—without breaking the pace.

Along the Path

It's thought that when primates first stood, that freed their forelimbs (wow! a whole new world). So brains expanded to meet that challenge. (Note which followed which.) Thus dawned the human species, the only species comfortable on two legs. In the mere act of walking, of being bipedal, we can reclaim an ancient wisdom hidden just beneath the whirl-a-gig surface of our ever faster-paced world: Walking literally creates the world, *our* world. Step by step.

Your assignment's to be aware of your breath *and* your motion, allowing them to co-ordinate comfortably, and see, too, how your mind interplays as you do so. At first, let the pace be slowwwwww. Thich Nhat Hanh has a few suggestions for you to get the hang. Visualize you're a king or queen, making a decree with each step. Or visualize yourself a lion or lioness, walking so slowly. Or visualize a flower blossoming from every step. Once you get the hang, and work up to 20 minutes of it, notice if there's anything different about how you feel.

It is said that, upon Enlightenment, the first thing the Buddha did was walking meditation, around the bodhi tree. Maybe that's one reason I like it so. What to do after the proverbially Hard Act to Follow; meditation-in-action, engaged in the world; arriving at choiceless awareness and animating it. For me, each step becomes a pilgrimage ... arriving at the only destination there ever is: the present moment, our true home ... a journey, stepping out, into the universe, the unknown ... feeling the earth coming up in response, meeting my foot ... grateful for that literal solid support, otherwise taken for granted ... and finding stillness, peace, and joy. And it's a fantastic body massage too! But that's just my attempt to verbalize my own experience of it. Everyone has their own. Try it, and see.

Some tips:

➤ Meditation is like dancing: You're not trying to reach any particular spot. There's no destination; you've already arrived: in the here and in the now.

➤ Notice what you notice, but don't be attached. (Dawn sunlight tingeing cloudtips rose-peach is no less lovely than the orange green iridescence of the wings of flies buzzing around some dung on the mosaic of the ground.)

➤ If you're distracted, look at the ground a yard or so ahead, or the back of the person ahead of you if you're in a group.

➤ Remember to practice mouth yoga.

➤ Coordinate your breathing and your walking, and stay with just that.

Hear and Now

"People say that walking on water is a miracle, but to me, walking peacefully on the Earth is the real miracle. The Earth is a miracle. Each step is a miracle. Taking steps on our beautiful planet can bring real happiness."

—Thich Nhat Hanh

Once you've accomplished 20 minutes of walking one-breath-per-step, I think you'll notice the difference. Then you can try three steps per breath. You might say "in, in, in" as you step left-right-left, and "out, out, out," with the next three. Or you can try the four-line gatha, in the preceding section, one line for each breath. You might discover your own gatha for walking meditation. As Dharma teacher and gardener Wendy Johnson was doing kinhin one day she found herself mentally saying to herself "Walking on the green earth" (*breathing in*), "each step is peace" (*breathing out*). (She says the words came up to her through the soles of her feet.) Try it out.

By taking just one peaceful step, you're affirming that peace in the world is possible. Don't just imagine it: Be it. Remember, "There is no path to peace. Peace is the path."

First-Aid Kit for Beginners' Problems

Meditation's like that center often referred to when people speak of being centered. Bull's eye. Accessible all the time. Your teacher and sangha are the best medicine for hindrances you may encounter along the path. Here are a few Standard Operating Procedure (S.O.P.) remedies:

➤ Mind-wandering is natural. Don't beat yourself up over it. Just start over again. And again.

➤ Allow your breath, don't force it. Sometimes people feel a little dizzy when meditating. In that case, intervene for a moment and add a few extra beats to your exhalation. Exhaling more than you inhale rids the body of excess CO_2. Then you can resume. (You might have been forcing.)

➤ If you're going around in circles, try this. Take a slow deep breath, filling your lungs then your belly. Then slowly let it all out, belly then lungs. Repeat twice. Now return to your practice.

➤ If you can't find 15 minutes a day, try 5. (If you can't find five, re-examine your life!) Establish a comfort zone, then extend the perimeter.

➤ Don't look for results. Subtle and gradual changes are just as good as dramatic and sudden. If a friend should remark that you seem calmer or happier lately, you're on the right track.

➤ You can't step into the same river twice. Don't expect today's meditation to be like yesterday's.

➤ "Take a friendly attitude toward your thoughts." —Chögyam Trungpa. Be kind to yourself.

All the little tips and tricks in the world are just that. Counting to 4 or 10, mantra or beads. They can be very useful. Cherish them when you use them, but don't grow attached to them. They're like a raft. Once you reach the other shore, you don't go walking around wearing your raft on your head like a hat; you leave it behind, and move on.

The Least You Need to Know

➤ Meditation's like that center referred to when people speak of being centered.

➤ Find the posture with which you're most comfortable.

➤ Breath is a primary gateway to the mind. Conscious or mindful breathing means being aware of your breathing. Nothing else.

➤ You're not trying to control your breath, or your mind. Just be aware of your breath. Just stopping and being aware can calm your breath—and your mind.

➤ Quieting the mind doesn't mean turning into a stone statue. Trying to banish thoughts and control your mind only creates more thoughts and restless mind. Simple awareness can clear mental clutter and sharpen your mind.

➤ Walking meditation can be a powerful part of your practice.

➤ Everyone encounters difficulties. Learn from others' wisdom about common hurdles in meditation. Take a friendly attitude toward your mind.

Chapter 11

Look Within and Know: Insight Meditation (Vipassana)

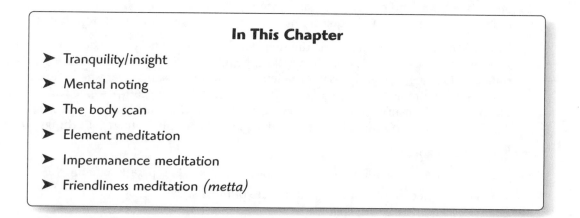

In This Chapter

➤ Tranquility/insight

➤ Mental noting

➤ The body scan

➤ Element meditation

➤ Impermanence meditation

➤ Friendliness meditation *(metta)*

When's the last time you experienced an *"Aha!"*? An *aha!* could be finding your keys and realizing why you hadn't been able to remember where they were; *aha!* You might be at a park and, suddenly, watching the behavior of some dogs, *aha!* you realize the answer to a puzzle that's been on your mind at work; *aha!* We all experience *aha!*'s. And, like realizing that by putting two building blocks next to each other you can put a third on top of them, *aha!* the accumulation of many little *aha!*'s lead to bigger *aha*'s: Awareness can lead to insight which can lead to wisdom. *Ahhh!!*

That's the gist of this chapter. In Hebrew, there's a word for this aha!-experience: *"Shazam!"* The bolt out of the blue striking precisely between the brows. It can also come from within. Insight/outlook; within/without—don't worry about seeming dualities, life intercommunicates itself. Learn the power of deep seeing. Look past outer walls and masks to Buddha's unerring teacher, your own living heart.

Stopping and Seeing

Now that you know how to establish your Buddhist base camp, I'd like to clarify the concepts of samatha (stopping) and vipassana (insight). Previously, we've just seen the basics of calming and sharpening the mind. In Sanskrit, it's called *samatha,* meaning cessation. Cessation can mean stopping whatever you're doing and checking in. ("Call home.") Samatha puts the chill on distractions and peripheral noise, and lets you relax into one-pointed concentration in the here and now.

Stopping is a very good practice, anytime. When you see something such as a hummingbird that awakens your heart, when you hear something such as a bell that resonates in your mind, you might consider them as opportunities to practice, on the fly: Stop, sense your breath, check in with the Here and Now. (Bowing is optional; an extra.) Stopping is synonymous with establishing and maintaining your Buddhist Meditation Base Camp. So, from time to time, take an opportunity to stop a bad habit, or stop trying to get anywhere, or stop trying to make sense to anybody. Just take a breath, in and of itself. Or take a step, just to feel the earth. And sitting and following your breath, for a quarter or half hour, makes for splendid stopping.

Now, while stopping (samatha) is the first step of meditation, it also goes hand-in-glove with what's called *insight*. In Sanskrit, insight's called *vipassana* (meaning penetrative vision, seeing clearly). Samatha lets your mind be calm, clear, sharp, and free; vipassana penetrates to the essential nature of things, so you can perceive reality directly. What's reality? As the Buddha expressed it in the Four Noble Truths: Attachment to phenomena leads to anguish, because all phenomena, all things are …

1. Impermanent
2. Open, interdependent, and so without any abiding, separate self, and yet
3. Perfect, free, beyond duality (in a state of *nirvana*)

This essential-reality-of-all-things is classically referred to as the *Three Marks of Existence* or *Three Dharma Seals*. (Some schools stress duhkha, suffering, instead of nirvana, release from suffering, which are like mirror images of each other.)

Surveying more examples of samatha and vipassana, we might consider some delineations made by the early, popular Chinese Buddhist commentary *The Completion of Truth* (*Chengshilun*, or *Satyasiddhi Shastra*). This commentary says that if samatha is like a calm meadow, then vipassana is like planting seeds there. With samatha, you can get a grip on weeds; with vipassana, you can cut those weeds away. And if samatha is like soaking beans in water, vipassana is like cooking them.

I've sketched out my own table of correspondences:

Stopping and Seeing

	Samatha	Vipassana
Meaning:	cessation tranquility	contemplation insight
Similar to:	meditation concentration	wisdom
Example:	washing	polishing
Example:	gripping	cutting

What color is your practice? The separation of stopping/calming and insightful inquiry is a definite Theravada trait found in vipassana meditation, whereas Mayahana practices tend to deal with them simultaneously, inseparably, different emphases of the same thing. (Tranquility generates insight; insight generates tranquility.)

But these are just various verbal expressions. Road maps. Your goal is to experience for *yourself*, to see things as they are, through direct perception, insight (vipassana). Having clarified some of the terminology, the rest of this chapter's devoted to five individual vipassana meditations: mental noting, the body scan, element meditation, impermanence meditation, and friendliness (*metta*) meditation.

Take Note!

The Buddha studied life by using his own life, particularly the four shocks that so moved him to renounce his castle—namely, old age, sickness, death, and the path of the seeker. Indeed, in so doing he unlocked these great mysteries of life. Having discovered that the human mind shapes our world and how we respond to life, he used his own mind as the key to fathom the nature of mind itself.

That's the Buddha's way. But it's up to you to see if it works for you. And, if so, how. For it to be your way, use your own mind to delve into the nature of mind—and your own life to understand the meaning of life. As Burmese Vipassana teacher S. N. Goenka says, "The whole process is one of total realization, the process of self-realization, truth pertaining to oneself, by oneself, within oneself."

Start where you are, with what you have. Your life this very moment is ample opportunity. With samatha (cessation, tranquility, calm, stillness) as meditation base camp, you can use vipassana techniques for gaining insight into the nature of reality. Now, the first of the five we'll see is the process of

Along the Path

Vipassana represents one of hundreds of resources available in Theravadan practice, which embraces the entire Pali canon of sutras and commentaries. Relatively free of metaphor, and translated into Western idiom, it's become the most popular Theravada "import" in the West. *The Sutra on the Four Establishments of Mindfulness* is the most popular sutra in Vipassana.

noting, first popularized in the West largely through Burmese teacher Mahasi Sayadaw (1904–1982). We touched on it already, briefly, in Chapter 10, "Base Camp: Meditation Basics," noticing what we notice as a means of quieting the mind. Here's a scientific version of that process, for insight.

The first step is basic meditation, stopping and sitting, however many minutes and weeks and months it takes for old drunken-monkey mind to sober up, given the chance. Once there, the dramatic parade of trials and tribulations is behind you. The storm's gone. You're at home in the here and in the now. Now, during meditation, when your mind wanders again, just make a mental note of it. Just say to yourself, "mind wandering, mind wandering." And return with your next breath to the present. If your mind doesn't wander, then fine. Just enjoy your breathing.

How you time this depends. Some people sit samatha for 15 minutes, then do vipassana for 30 or 45. Others might sit an hour a week for a couple of years and leave discontented. There's no telling, no guarantee. A weekend or 10-day retreat can be very effective. It's all up to you.

Tips and Practices

Here are some tips and practices from along the vipassana trail.

Mind-wandering can be tricky to track. At first, you might not even have been aware of your mind at all. Sometimes these mind-wanderings can go on and on before you even notice them, I know. In that case, you might note, "mind wandering, mind wandering; eight minutes" (guesstimate), and return to the here and now. Don't get embroiled in any running commentary, like a sports announcer. That is, don't comment on your noting, much less comment on such commentaries. So, instead of saying to yourself, "I'm remembering the last time I noted my mind wandered like this, and feel as ashamed of myself as I did then," just note "remembering, remembering." And move on. No need to narrate a whole chain of associations, which can never be reconstructed anyway.

Such mental notes are best expressed as verbs. And see if you can phrase your notes without putting "I" into them; not "I am aware my fingers are tingling," but "fingers tingling." As you progress in your practice, you might abbreviate even further to just "tingling." (Some practitioners repeat the note, such as "tingling, tingling," like a little bell.)

Three more generic mental Post-it labels at your disposal are the following:

➤ "... attracting, attracting ..."

➤ "... repulsing, repulsing ..."

➤ "... accepting, accepting ..."

Stopping, stillness, is a state of letting be as is. The little dances of monkey-mind are chitterings of "I like" and "I dislike," and the more neutral "okay." You might be surprised to discover how much mental activity's dedicated to this dance of thumbs up, thumbs down, and shrugs.

You'll also be surprised to discover just how powerful noting can be. It's as if each tiny note contains a drop of a secret-formula cleansing agent which melts dirt and grime, and polishes pristine, shining Buddha nature. Thus, use it with a light touch.

As with basic meditation, nothing's a gentle process. Go with the flow. Don't force the river. Don't be someone who staples posters to lamp-posts with your notes. Just tap the moment lightly, gently with your mental Post-it note, and move on. The idea's to note but not react. Your reactions to pain only create more suffering; your acceptance of your pain is the door to letting it go like a leaf falling from a branch.

Noting amplifies awareness: awareness of stimulus-sensations and responses, with glimpses of awareness (pure awareness). Insights gained during the process of noting are your own realizations of the Three Dharma Seals, the marks of existence: the impermanence of your thoughts and feelings, the lack of any lasting, separate self-identity, and how the door of suffering can swing the other way to nirvana.

Along the Path

Noting is a time-honored strategy for dealing with physical discomfort during meditation (tickle in throat, "tickling, tickling"; an aching knee, "soreness, soreness"). Don't react, just note. Stay open to being aware of everything. A throbbing toe can become quite small in relation to fragrance in nostrils, calm, and feelings of spaciousness (when they, too, are noted). See if a pain can be broken down into subcomponents, until there's nothing there. A wave eventually flattens.

You don't want to break your basic meditation, just incorporate noting into it. As you get the hang of it, you can go into greater detail of noting. For instance, as part of conscious breathing, be aware of and note the phases of your breath: "air fragrant at nostrils … air filling nostrils … belly expanding …" and so on, directly perceiving breath, as it is, insubstantial, limitless, and free; or however it seems to you.

Internalizing the Practice

With practice, you can engage in noting meditation all the time, 24/7, not just on your meditation cushion. In walking meditation, for example, note your movements as a continuous series of separate sensations. Be comfortable, go real slowwww, maybe one-in-breath-per-step / one-out-breath-per-step, and note: "left heel reaching out," "left heel touching down," "ball of left foot touching down," "right ankle rotating up-ward," "toes of left foot touching down," "right knee bending," "left foot and ground in full contact," "right heel lifting up," … and so on. Directly perceiving walking, can you see how impermanent it is, and without any separate identity apart from the ground? Where is your walk but in each step? And if any feelings accompany any of the phases, such as fear of falling or gratitude for solidity, note them. As they reoccur, direct your *mindfulness* there and inquire what else is associated with them.

Case in point: Last night, as I was taking my evening walk over Russian Hill, I was ex-periencing intense nausea and stomach ache, probably a flu. I was saying to myself, "Aargh! I'm in pain! Ouch! I can't make it go away! Can't concentrate! I'm not going to make it! Doomed!" and so on. I was practically ready to cry for my mommy, when I realized I hadn't noted any of it yet. So I shut up, got out of my own way, noted the sensation, "belly aching, belly aching." And *bing!* the problem collapsed and vanished the way a TV screen does when it's shut off. In its place returned awareness of my stomach rising and falling with my breathing of the beautiful early spring night air, and I was able to concentrate on each footstep again. As I walked, I inquired a little and felt that my tummy ache was an accumulation of stress I hadn't faced (couldn't stomach), and I was literally belly-aching about it, rather than facing and accepting it and moving on.

So it's important to *note* feelings that come up, as well as to experience them. Bud-dhism doesn't ask that we ignore the fear or anger or frustration of our emotional realms, but rather suggests that if they're experienced mindfully, they're no longer such threats. They no longer run us. We can let them go, let them be. And noting also furnishes the essential distance necessary to smile at unwanted habit energy, and let it cease and go away. The little Post-its of noting are like brackets placed around some-thing, [like this], which enable it be dislodged and separated, removed, and dropped. "Dropped" or "let go" are the correct words: no need to throw anything away. Throwing is too forceful, creating further karma to deal with.

Through noting, you can get a good handhold on bad habits, break them down, and let them crumble away as you relax into greater freedom. The precepts will guide your determining what's a good or bad habit. Let noting follow a sensation, not dictate it. Otherwise, you'll become attached to noting. Keep it natural. Once you become adept at noting, you may want to let it go, like training wheels, and move on.

(*Question:* How many Vipassana Buddhists does it take to screw in a light bulb? *Answer:* Two—one to screw it in, and one to note it.)

The Chinese word for mindfulness. "Now," above; "mind," underneath. Mindfulness brings our mind back to the present moment. Just one breath can bring body and mind together as one, in the now. (A block version of the word, on the left, cursive in the middle, and an even more flowing version on the right.)

(Calligraphy: Kazuaki Tanahashi)

Material Meditations

Common Misconception #7,462: "Meditation is all mental." *Au contraire!* Rather, Buddhism's an opportunity to integrate word and deed; body, heart, and mind.

Here follow two meditations centered in the body's innate wisdom, with powerful emotional and spiritual resonance, the Body Scan and Element Meditation. (These two will be followed by two more meditations, on impermanence and metta, friendliness.) These all have variations, and, again, they're best accomplished with a living, breathing guide. Meanwhile, here's the roadmap.

The Body Scan

First time out, start slowly. Give yourself 45 minutes to an hour for this exercise. Once you get it, and practice it a few times, you'll start to find a pattern. Once you're familiar with the pattern, you can do it in a few breaths.

This one's done lying down, on your back. Your arms are at your sides, your legs uncrossed. Take a few mindful breaths, then begin by directing your attention to the toes of your left foot. Continue conscious breathing and see if there are any sensations there. Imagine that your in-breaths are contacting this focal point of your body, and your out-breaths are exhaling any tensions. As tension and emotions are released, note them doing so. Note, too, how your sense of yourself changes with them.

After remaining with your awareness of your toes for one or two minutes, move on to the sole of your left foot. Stay with your breathing, and concentrate on your sole for a minute or two. Continue working your way up until you've scanned your left foot. Then scan your right foot the same way.

Hear and Now

"Your body can sink into the bed, mat, floor, or ground until your muscles stop making the slightest effort to hold you together. This is a profound letting go at the level of your muscles and the motor neurons which govern them. The mind quickly follows if you give it permission to stay open and wakeful. ... It's the whole body that breathes, the whole body that is alive. In bringing mindfulness to the body as a whole, you can reclaim your entire body as the focus of your being and your vitality, and remind yourself that 'you,' whoever you are, are not just a resident of your head."

—Jon Kabat-Zinn, *Wherever You Go, There You Are*

Following your feet, move up to your ankles, calves, knees, thighs, hips, and so on. Remain longer with any areas of tension or pain and sites of any medical conditions. Take your time when you scan your head. If you feel any tension in your jaw, note it, and let it release. The same is true for your chin, back of your neck, lips, tongue, palate, nostrils, cheeks, eyelids, eyes, eyebrows, forehead, temples, and entire scalp.

Finally, concentrate on the tip of your head, where your hair meets your scalp. As you do so, you might feel your entire skeleton. After a minute or two, move your attention beyond the tip of your head, to a point a few inches beyond your head. From that spot, let the focus of your awareness vanish into space.

Along the Path

Four key emotional reservoirs are hips, navel, chest, and throat. Aligning our lower back to make contact with the ground thrusts our hips out, sometimes releasing withheld anger. The hara center below the navel can have a warm, centering emotional influence. The center of our chest is our spiritual and emotional heart, reservoir of dark, tight sorrows and pains as well as warm, bright love. And, as messenger of our verbal feelings, the throat might feel like tears or song.

Do you feel different than when you'd started? You might have noticed particular spots are reservoirs of tension or emotion. Common speech reflects this awareness when we say someone's carrying the world on their shoulders, or saying life can be a pain in the neck, and so on.

Noting enables us to be aware of the grasping knots and tight ropes within our body that keep us from flowing freely. It can also help us examine what we're holding on to. Or think we're holding on to, since what's clutched on to often proves to be something not present in the here and now, buried in our body like heirlooms in attic trunks. Clinging; trishna. The scan is a good way to smooth out these knots.

It's perfectly rational to stop and meditate. Our words "reason" and "rational" (of a sound mind) come from ratio, relation; "meditation," similarly, comes from a root for measure. Both figures measure the universe in human scale, each differently. The person on the left moves outwards to encompass the circle (infinity, eternity); on the right, yielding to stillness, the person becomes a kind of circle.

This awareness is also very useful for keeping us from becoming overwhelmed or par-alyzed when in the thick of an emotional situation. First, we can defuse any sense of danger by noting it. Rather than saying to ourselves, "Oh no, end of the world, this is it," we note the conflict. "Feeling angry," "feeling defensive," or whatever. Then we note where the feeling "lives" in our body. Noting "constricted chest," or "light-headed," the sensation can dissipate.

Meditation's not about becoming an emotional zombie. Meditation's not a divorce from the world, but, rather, an opportunity to 1) root out unwanted feelings and bad habits, 2) water the seeds of good habits and beneficial feelings, and 3) establish and maintain the ability to have awareness of your choices rather than be paralyzed or overwhelmed. We'll conclude this chapter with emotions. Next, here's another bodily exercise, with profound implications.

Hear and Now

"When the surf echoes and crashes out to the horizon, its whorls repeat in similar ratios inside our flesh. ... We are extremely complicated, but our bloods and hormones are fundamentally seawater and volcanic ash, congealed and refined. Our skin shares its chemistry with the maple leaf and moth wing. The currents our bodies regulate share a molecular flow with raw sun. Nerves and flashes of lightning are related events woven into nature at different levels."

—Richard Grossinger, *Planet Medicine*

Where's Self?: It's Elementary

Meditation on the elements enables you to experience firsthand how what you're accustomed to calling "me" is conditional and limited, and to let you touch a more unlimited, unconditional reality of being. It's a guided meditation on the elements as they relate to your body.

Practicing basic meditation, consider your contact with the earth as you sit. Sink into that space. Feel that solid connection. As Native Americans say, "The earth is all we have." You might try and escape it but eventually you can never fall off the earth. So where does the earth end and you begin? Consider how you carry the earth, its minerals in your metabolism, its clay in your bones. Stay with that realization as you breathe a while more. Next consider water. We're 75 percent liquid. The salinity of our metabolism's precisely that of the sea, so you could say the very ocean runs through our veins and lymph. (No wonder we're affected by phases of the moon, just as the tides are.) Our liquidity is our major transportation system, making everything cohere.

After you further consider your blood, sweat, and tears (sounds like the name of a rock band!), urine, mucus, bile, and the fluid in your joints, connect it to rain and rivers, the ocean from which life emerges, and stay with that gooshy awareness. Next, our meditation turns to air. Consider how air covers the planet, filling all spaces, everywhere. As you breathe in, you don't have to will it; your lungs do it automatically, expanding and contracting with the universe. Feel that automatic rhythm of air. As you breathe in, you're inhaling the out-breath of trees; exhaling the in-breath of the grasses. No in or out, really—just one continuous motion of air. And just as the air you breathe isn't yours, so too your metabolism is fueled by fire. Along with chlorophyll you eat the sun, and keep warm by an internal campfire. Think of that fire within you as you consider your 98.6 degrees of warmth, keeping your metabolism homeostatic, and growing.

A vipassana instructor can take you further along on this tour, but meanwhile I hope I've sparked in you a bit of humble appreciation for the intertwining of your mortal frame and self with the identities of the immortal elements. From these things we come, and to them we shall return.

Along the Path

Who doesn't die? In India, the sight of death is commonplace. When Tibetans are dying, they're cared for by the whole community. China sets April 5 aside for visiting graves. In Korea, it's harder to avoid going to a funeral than a wedding. In Mexico, where the calendar has a colorful day for the dead, hearkening back to Aztec times, they say, "Isn't it a lovely day to die!?" The Sufis say, "Die before you die and you shall never die."

Here Today, Gone Tomorrow: Impermanence Meditation

Beginnings are easy, it's endings that are hard. Vipassana meditation shows us our clinging and craving, and the compassion of selflessness and the wisdom of insecurity. Remember the Second Noble Truth? The root of perpetual dissatisfaction is *clinging* to the notion of an abiding, separate self, craving for security, when in reality there isn't any. Remember the Buddha's final words: that which arises also passes away. So too for the ego: me, mine. Vipassana teaches us how to confront our impermanence in order to liberate ourselves.

The Buddha said, "Of all footprints in the jungle, that of the elephant is the greatest. Of all awarenesses, that of death is supreme." Buddhists have traditionally visited graveyards as a meditation (not necessarily the neatly trimmed parks of the West, but sometimes places where jackals and vultures vie for scraps). One section of the *Four Establishments of Mindfulness* takes the student on a guided meditation imagining his or her own death, becoming a corpse, bones whitening in the sun, turning to dust. In Tibet, a corpse is given a *sky burial*, facing the sky from under stones on the ground. Tibetans are famous for their *Book of the Dead* (more accurately translated as the *Book of Transformation*), a kind of travelogue. They are also known to fashion goblets out of human skulls, to remind them of the impermanence of life.

This might be a bit much for Americans, steeped in a culture of denial; as Woody Allen expresses it, "I'm not afraid of death. It's just that I don't want to be there when it happens." The American way of death is quite an industry, and often designed to cover up death. (For more on a constructive, mindful awareness of dying, see Chapter 19, "Happiness Is Not an Individual Matter: Engaging the World.")

Hear and Now

"Unless a corn of wheat fall onto the ground and die, it abideth alone: but if it die, it bringeth forth much fruit."

—Jesus

"The universe and its inhabitants are as ephemeral as the clouds in the sky; beings born and dying are like a spectacular dance or melodrama. The duration of our lives is like a flash of lightning or a firefly's flicker."

—Buddha

For us beginners, I recommend just letting life take us on a guided meditation in impermanence. Be mindful of *change* in your daily life through the change of the seasons and the changes in your life and those around you. When I see the first leaf of autumn let go of its tree and gently float down, it teaches me the meaning of trust. As simple as that. When I see the noble way my elderly neighbors carry themselves, I thank them for preparing the way for me.

Living in California, I witness mudslides, power outages, raging fire storms, and so many earthquakes that real estate agents joke about offering beachfront property in Arizona.

Medicine for a Healthy Heart: Friendliness (Metta)

How's your heart? When we say someone has a good heart, we don't just mean blood pressure. Qualities associated with good-heartedness are openness, empathy, generosity, lovingkindness, compassion, and even wisdom—ideals all Buddhists work toward. This next meditation is all about massaging the heart. If you find too much dullness in your world, or fear, or anger, this will be of particular interest.

Sublime States

There are four mental/emotional states which Buddhists aspire to, as a regular meditation. You could even call them energies which can be generated. In Sanskrit, they're called *Brahmaviharas,* which translates as divine abodes, immeasurable dwellings, sublime states. Living with them, in them, our hearts grow as immeasurable as life. It's interesting how Buddhist wisdom recognizes these states as interconnected with others. That is, each of the four sublime states have a "far enemy," the clear opposite of the quality, the flip side of the coin. And each has a "near enemy," somewhere in between the two.

The near enemy is like a deceptive substitute we settle for, instead of the real thing. The near enemy reinforces our sense of self and separation (sentimentality implies being attached, clinging; pity implies feeling superior, or fear) and so can eventually slide into the far enemy.

The Four Immeasurables (Brahmaviharas)

Virtue	Near Enemy	Far Enemy
Friendliness	Sentimentality/selfishness	Ill-will/hatred
Compassion	Pity/grief	Contempt/cruelty
Sympathetic joy	Boredom/cynicism	Envy/jealousy
Equanimity	Apathy/indifference	Resentment/greed/aversion

Metta is lovingkindness, or, if you will, friendliness. Compassion (Sanskrit, *karuna*), is the ability to feel with someone instead of for someone. It's more active than metta. Sympathetic joy (*mudita*) is the spontaneous response of gladness at the good fortune or success of others. (The gossip industry, hanging on the careers of stars, is mock mudita.) And equanimity (*upekkha*) is nonattachment, even-mindedness, based on the insight into the way things really are, and is considered the closest of the four to enlightenment. The synonym for equanimity in Hindi is *tatastha,* meaning one who sits on the bank of a river, watching the waters flow.

This Is

Metta (Pali; *maitri*, Sanskrit) is one of the four Brahmaviharas, literally meaning divine dwellings—"divine" because their boundlessness frees us from the illusion of a suffering, separate self, and "dwellings" because mindfulness of them can be practiced everywhere, at any time. Consider them like friends en route to nirvana. Metta's translated as friendliness, benevolence, kindness, lovingkindness, and unconditional love. The other three Brahmaviharas are compassion, sympathetic joy, and equanimity.

Things Go Betta with Metta

Your first task is to locate within yourself your own feelings of lovingkindness or just friendliness toward yourself. Stop and sit. Check in at Base Camp. Resting in tranquility, focus your mindfulness on your feelings about your personal health, happiness, and general well-being. Maybe you feel pretty good about yourself but feel vulnerable or even fragile about certain issues, such as illness, or lack of confidence, or insecurity.

Along the Path

Like counting breaths or mentally reciting gathas, or using mantras or beads, concentrating on each kind of metta—wellness, happiness, peace—serves as a focal point for tranquil basic meditation. At the same time, it invites insightful inquiry meditation: If you experience your feelings getting blocked or changing along the way, note the fact, ask why, note any response that comes up, all the while staying with your conscious breathing and concentration on metta. And notice changes in what you thought of as your self.

Next, see if you can fit all these feelings, positive and negative, into a feeling with which you're already familiar and which resonates with the notion of unconditional love, lovingkindness, kindness, or just friendliness and goodwill. Whatever you call it. The idea's not to try to reach for some new feeling off some imaginary shelf but rather to use your own experience. It's okay to draw from examples in other people, and even animals. Pets exhibit friendliness and unconditional love, too, as do little children and even plants. This feeling we're spotlighting is a natural force, within you and all around you. In Pali, this energy's called metta.

Metta opens your heart, to yourself, to those around you, even those you hate, and to the whole world. Begin by opening your heart toward yourself. If you can't be kind to yourself, who can you be kind to? So begin by thinking kindly of yourself. As you do so, say to yourself, "May I be well," and visualize yourself as being well. Send yourself a gift of metta. Then move on to wishing "May I be happy," and picture a happy you. Then, wishing "May I be peaceful," envision yourself at peace. It's as if you're harnessing this natural metta force, beaming it onto yourself, visualizing the result. Rather than beaming pure white light metta, you're varying the metta, as if using a different shade each time—wellness, happiness, peace. But it's all metta.

Hear and Now

"Just as a mother guards her child with her life, her only child, just so should you too cultivate boundless heart toward all beings. Let thoughts of lovingkindness for all the world radiate boundlessly, into the sky and into the earth, all around, unobstructed, free from any hatred or ill-will. Standing or walking, sitting or lying down, as long as one is awake, one should develop this mindfulness: this is called divine abiding here."

—The Buddha

After you've opened up your heart to 1) yourself, the meditation opens out to sending metta to:

2. Teachers

3. Parents

4. Relatives

5. Friends

6. Neutral people

7. Enemies

8. All beings

Leaves from the Bodhi Tree

Exiled peacemaker Thich Nhat Hanh is a veteran of America's war in Vietnam. But when he writes a letter to a politician with whom he disagrees, he doesn't harangue: He writes what he calls a love letter to them. Buddhists understand that anger begets more anger, and lovingkindness begets more lovingkindness. When asked if he hates the Chinese for their policies in Tibet, the Dalai Lama says that would be like hating a knife in someone's hand. It's just a blind tool. Rather, he has compassion for the karmic suffering they are bringing upon themselves.

If it's important, add a category, such as sangha or workmates. Similarly, you can re-phrase your aspects of metta, depending on what meets your needs and what you're most comfortable with. For example, some people use these four phrases: "May I be free of dangers; free of mental suffering; free of physical suffering; and be well and happy." (*Note:* Each time you send metta, you include the whole phrase "May my friends be free of dangers. May my friends be free of mental suffering. May my friends …" etc. I've shortened it here for reasons of space.)

The map of a whole meditation might go like this:

May I be well. May I be happy. May I be at peace.
May my teachers be well … happy … at peace.
May my parents be well … happy … at peace.
May my relatives be well … happy … at peace.
May my friends be well … happy … at peace.
May neutral people be well … happy … at peace.
May my enemies be well … happy … at peace.
May all beings be well … happy … at peace.

Tips for Practice

Having been blessed to be taught metta meditation by Sharon Salzberg, a living god-dess of the art, I can attest that a teacher can not only help you slide into the tran-quil stillness of basic meditation but also guide you through the various phases of metta. Practicing with a group of people, you feel metta in the air. And when you face difficulty, it helps to know you're not alone. Meanwhile, until you find the metta meditation group meeting in your neighborhood, here are a few tips:

➤ You're not showering your lovingkindness on the people in your mind's eye, or wringing their necks with it. Rather, with the same quick, light touch of noting, you gently tap them with the thought, then move on.

➤ Before sending metta to a new bunch of people, picture them very well in your mind's eye. When you pick "neutral people," think of people in your life for whom you have no particular emotions, no charge, one way or another. It's important to really make contact; otherwise, you might tend to rush to people with whom you're having difficult relations, enemies. Rushing in wouldn't be skillful; it would only reinforce the separateness you feel between you and the other person(s).

➤ One way to approach sending metta to your enemies is to see it as being the same as sending metta to your own inner enemies. That is, sending metta to yourself, you're embracing your problems and shadows as well as your accomplishments and lights.

➤ Metta isn't confined to a meditation cushion, but something to also be carried out in word and deed, as we write and speak, and in our daily actions. (Some American Buddhists, for example, sign their letters, "Much metta.")

Make friends with yourself. Expand your compassion for others. We're all in this sandbox for saints together. May YOU be well, happy, and at peace!

Hear and Now

"If we hold on to our humility, if we let go of our egos and stop clinging to whatever it is we're clinging to, we'll find the wonderful surprise that behind all that gunk is a natural kindness, a love for everyone and everything that we never thought we had. And if we let ourselves act from that place, we'll discover a kindness without limits and an unutterable peace."

—Geri Larkin

The Least You Need to Know

➤ Vipassana meditation (insight) combines stopping and seeing. It teaches us to observe our experience from a place of tranquility, enabling us to relate to life anew, with less clinging.

➤ Vipassana applies to body and speech as well as to mind; and our daily conduct as well as meditation sessions.

➤ There are hundreds of vipassana techniques. The most popular in the West are called insight meditations.

➤ Five key insight meditations are noting, the body scan, the four elements, impermanence, and metta.

➤ Insight meditation enables us to realize for ourselves impermanence, non-separateness, and liberation from suffering, using our own experience as an example, and so find greater harmony and peace in our daily lives.

Chapter 12

See? Words Cannot Express: Zen

In This Chapter

➤ One drop of zen meditation

➤ Lineage: Zen patriarchs

➤ For the sake of all: the bodhisattva vow

➤ A taste of zen

What can I tell you about Zen you don't already know? You *are* it. Zen isn't a way of life. It's life itself. We don't do Zen, Zen does us.

But, wait: all the books, all the tapes, all the catalogues about Zen—none until now have revealed the Ultimate Zen Truth, ever—which, in a *Complete Idiot's Guide* first, I'm going to tell you right here. And it is this:

(And you can quote me. Verbatim.)

Maybe you've glimpsed it already, in between paragraphs and at the ends of chapters, and now, there it is! The secret's out.

So now that I've told you what you already knew (no?), what else is there to say?

Hear and Now

"When Buddhism first came to China it was most natural for the Chinese to speak about it in terms of Taoist philosophy, because they both share a view of life as a flowing process in which the mind and consciousness of man is inextricably involved. It is not as if there is a fixed screen of consciousness over which our experience flows and leaves a record. It is that the field of consciousness itself is part of the flowing process, and therefore the mind of man is not a separate entity observing the process from outside, but is integrally in-volved with it. ... The practice of Zen is to experience the overall [flowing] pattern di-rectly, and to know one's self as the essence of the pattern."

—Alan Watts, *What Is Zen?*

Look, Where's Buddha?

Question: Where's Buddha? Zen answers, "Asking where Buddha is, is like hiding loot in your pocket and then declaring yourself innocent."

To repeat—*Question:* "Why be a Buddhist when you can be a buddha?" Now, you might consider yourself only a part-time buddha, and that's perfectly alright, too, holding down two jobs at once. Amazing. Or you might insist you're an unenlight-ened buddha, don't know, but seem as perfect at it as a full-fledged buddha. Amazing. What can I say?!

Now, if you're a buddha, then please read this chapter and check up on what people are saying about you these days. If you're not a buddha (yet), I hope you're still serene and calm amid all the trials and tribulations of not being a buddha (such as being a buddha and saying you're not). If so, your awakening mind is ever ready to spring into 100 percent total response when life's next emergency falls on your dear sweet head *(ker-plunk!)*. But if you're not serenely ready and readily serene, then this chapter will fill in the blank, hopefully, to fill you in on your buddhahood, Mr. or Miss or Mrs. Buddha.

The human is present within nature as part of an unbroken continuum. (See the fishing boats?) So, too, is the embededness of each of us within essential buddha nature. Mu Chi (1210–1280), Southern Sung Dynasty. Evening Glow on a Fishing Village (detail). Nezu Art Museum.

A Few Drops of Zen

Even before you begin any further, I'd like you to stop. (I know that might sound funny. But, hey, we're talking zen!)

Meditation on the Fly: Right Here, Right Now

I'd like to invite you to take a moment to awaken your mind. I'll explain how. Then you'll note your place, then close this book.

You'll notice your breathing, without pushing any air out or pulling any air in, without making any verbal note. Notice, then let your circle of attention widen outward, a larger circle of gazing at other objects around you, beyond your face, beyond your hands. Be aware of textures and colors and shapes, without necessarily considering what they represent. Widen your attention further, aware of all these things present together right here. Then keep your mind awake a little longer. See if you can turn down the dial on your mental radio, or unplug it. Suspend your conceptual and verbal activity, and let your mind quiet down. Just enjoy being where you are, surrounded by all that you've noticed.

Let your gaze flit where it will, unfocused, but not dwelling on any one thing. If you like, close your eyes. Let your mind flow, awake, without dwelling anywhere, without fastening it on anything in particular. No thoughts. Stay with that. Then, when you're ready, gently let go of your meditation. (But continue to enjoy your surroundings a bit more!)

Zen Meditation

Welcome to the zen zone. Here there's no intellectualization. No duality. No boundary. No separation. *Question:* How many Zen Buddhists does it take to screw in a light bulb? *Answer:* None. (A light bulb's empty of separate identity, as is everything, and everyone. No light bulb, no Buddhist, no separation. What's the difference between a Zen Buddhist and a light bulb? Tap them, they both sound hollow yet are full of light.) Hey, you gotta admit: When there's no problem, there's no solution.

This Is

Zen literally means meditation. Zen's a nonintellectual approach to Buddha's way. Clearing away concepts and seeing for yourself. All activities are embraced as meditation. *Za* means "sitting," so **zazen** means sitting meditation. A more precise definition of zazen would be **shikantaza** (*shikan*, nothing but … *ta*, precisely … *za*, sitting); just sitting and nothing else. One of the most durable forms of Buddhism in Asia, zen influence (lowercase) has extended to martial arts, gardening, haiku, motorcycle maintenance, you name it.

You might look at it this way: whereas various other paths focus on subject matter (content), such as impermanence or lovingkindness, or use a variety of tools—such as noting, or recitation, or mantras and visualizations and prostrations—Zen steps out off a thousand-foot pole with hands free. No content, no subject. No tools, no objects. (No hands.) Not even a "no" (itself a concept, a word, a sword of dualism, cutting everything in two, and setting up shop with price-stickers on everything, scales, and a cash register at the door). Zen enters the stream and is one with the water, going with the flow. Sure, counting breaths are okay for launching forth, to ease one's way in—but in Zen, even the counting, the "one," the "two," become meditation—as is letting go of counting. And just sitting. And getting up again.

Just Do It!

Sit just to sit, *shikantaza*. You don't assume meditation posture in order to attain enlightenment. Rather, the posture is the enlightenment. That is, you assume an enlightened posture in order to realize (and enjoy) that you're already enlightened. (So even if you're a part-time buddha, you can sit in the boss's chair right now—it's empty.)

The more I say, the more I might intellectualize it for you. Thus, I invited you to meditate, yourself, at the beginning of this chapter. Now what might make that impromptu meditation more zen might be improving your posture just a little, ("shoulders back, chin in, stretch the backbone") … letting your thoughts clear a little more … exploring opportunities to practice meditation throughout the day … encouraging you to realize your own mind as Buddha mind … identifying your practice with the universe all around.

To give you more of a feel for zen, we'll take a guided tour, looking at three Zen ancestors, Kasyapa, Bodhidharma, and Hui Neng, founders of the tradition. Plus, we'll introduce another important figure known as the bodhisattva. Then we'll take a look at Zen's famous way with words. And we'll wind up … continuing to begin.

Lineage: From the Buddha to You, with Love

In Chapter 1, "Why Is This Man Smiling?: The Buddha," we saw how the Buddha's life is his teachings, living the life he taught, and teaching the life he lived. In Chapter 2, "One Taste, Different Flavors: The Teachings Adapt to Different Lands," we saw how his teachings have continued on. Now, let's zero in a bit on the fascinating story of how Zen was born and grew. We'll begin by flashing back to the time of the Buddha.

The First Zen Patriarch: Kasyapa's Smile

The Buddha and disciples were on retreat, on Vulture Peak. Everybody gathered for a Dharma talk, at least a thousand people were there. The Buddha sat on the peak, in peace and at harmony with everybody and everything, and said nothing. Then— more silence. After three or four minutes, some recent disciples wondered to themselves if the Buddha was feeling well. Still more silence. Suddenly, he reached for a nearby flower and held it up, for all to see. Still not one word. Then a smile broke out on the lips of a disciple named Kasyapa. The Buddha looked at him, and could see that he got it. He smiled, too, and put the flower down. End of sermon.

Well, many there probably wondered what'd just happened. What did the Buddha teach and what did Kasyapa understand? The inescapable impermanence of reality? The flower's interdependence with the whole universe? Huh?! What!?

Well, it was a golden zen moment. As such, it bears four fierce characteristics that are almost the Pledge of Allegiance of Zen:

➤ Nonattachment to words

➤ Special one-on-one transmission, heart-to-heart

➤ Direct, immediate pointing at the mind

➤ Ever-presence of Buddha nature, our innate nature

201

The First Chinese Zen Patriarch: Bodhidharma

We flash ahead now to the phenomenal transmission of the Dharma from India to China. One of the first major carriers, of historical record, was a prince who went by the name of Bodhidharma. Because he was from India, he's often portrayed in Chinese, Korean, and Japanese paintings as looking quite foreign (to the painter), with formidable beard (rare for East Asians) and round, somewhat bulging eyes (also rare, where eyelids are narrower and often have an extra fold).

Now the emperor of China at the time had become very interested in Buddhism. When he heard that Bodhidharma had braved the three-year Spice Route to China, he invited him to his court. CNN wasn't there, but the meeting reportedly went like this …

> *Emperor Wu:* "I've had temples and monasteries built in my realm, commissioned translations of Buddhist works. Tell me, what virtues have I accumulated for myself thereby?"
>
> *Bodhidharma:* "None whatsoever."
>
> *Emperor Wu* [a little flustered]: "Well, then: please tell me, sir, what's the basis of holiness?"
>
> *Bodhidharma:* "There is no holiness, only emptiness."
>
> *Emperor Wu* [now quite perplexed]: "Then—then who'm I talking to right now?"
>
> *Bodhidharma:* "I don't know." [So saying, he stood up and walked out.]

Along the Path

Bodhidharma's famous "I don't know" to the Emperor is characteristic of Zen, which urges us to think no-thought. To not know. To have a don't-know mind. One word for it combines mind (*shin*) below the character for no-thingness (*mu*, which we saw in Chapter 8, "The Fine Print: Touching Deeper"). Mushin isn't mindless, heartless (you know, an idiot) but, rather, means getting out of one's own way. Having no conception, much less preconception. Not living in one's head. Experiencing life in full participation.

He crossed the Yangtze River (separating north and south China), on, of all things, a single blade of grass (what a guy) and settled in at a temple in a northern province called Shaolin (*shao* pronounced like *now*), where he sat facing a wall for nine years. No, he didn't stare at a wall out of frustration because he didn't speak Chinese! Hardly. He was practicing and teaching … Zen.

Bodhidharma is often depicted scowling, eyes glowering at the top of his balding head. Here's my favorite: six brush strokes, plus some extra brush-wipes for his mat. But if you think it could be just anyone seen from behind, look again. That fierce determination, that "no bull," commanding presence could only be … Daishin Gito, Wall-Gazing Daruma. *Ink on paper. 25 × 10¹/₄" New Orleans Museum of Art: Gift of an Anonymous Donor (79.220).*

One more Bodhidharma story: The legend was that Bodhidharma would only accept a student when the snows ran red. No takers, until one winter this guy named Hui K'o (Hwee Koh) cuts off his own arm and brings it to Bodhidharma as a token of his sincerity. (Don't ever think zen is trivial!)

Bodhidharma accepts Hui K'o as his student and says, "Okay, what do you want me teach you?" Hui K'o asks "Well, I have no peace of mind. How do I pacify my mind?" Bodhidharma looks at him and says, "Bring me your mind, and I'll pacify it." So Hui K'o bows, leaves, thinks it over, comes back, bows, and replies, "Where *is* my mind? I can't *find* my mind anywhere!" "There," Bodhidharma announces, "I've pacified your mind." In that instant, Hui K'o becomes enlightened.

Great story. Naturally, using the mind to find the mind is like trying to bite your teeth; forget about it.

The Illiterate Sixth Patriarch: Hui Neng

Now, Kasyapa and Bodhidharma were both noblemen from the Indian subcontinent. But the seminal patriarch of what would become the distinctly East Asian practice we know today as Zen was a man named Hui Neng (Hwee Nong). And the funny part of it is: He was illiterate! Who would've thunk it? (Maybe he was just faking it, playing dumb out of modesty. Who knows!)

Hui Neng gathered and sold firewood for a living. Delivering wood one day, he hears someone reciting the *Diamond Sutra*. It's news to him. Well, when he hears the phrase, "Awaken your mind without fixing it anywhere," *Shazam!* he becomes enlightened, right there on the spot. This is really curious: no counting breaths, no mantra, no noting of the watcher and the watched, no six years of training, no nothing! Blam, right out of the box, alikazam shazam, he produces awakened mind out of nowhere. He attains *kensho* (a.k.a. satori), oneness. Awakening to the immediacy of sunyata. His beginner's mind *is* infinite Buddha mind.

So what does he do? He hikes over a thousand miles to the Zen monastery, knocks on the door, and asks to join the sangha. The head of the monastery, its roshi—and current Zen Patriarch (Number Five, now)—opens the door, and greets Hui Neng with some derision: "Ha! An illiterate from south China!" Hui Neng replies, "Literate/illiterate, north/south, dualities don't concern the Buddha's way." "Smart guy," the roshi figures, so he admits Hui Neng into the sangha, and gives him menial duties, pounding rice in a shed way in back.

Meanwhile, the roshi was fixing to retire. The official rules were that the vacancy would be open for competition, by writing a gatha, to demonstrate intuitive understanding. Everyone knew that Shen Xiu (Shen Syew) was the shoo-in, so no one else tried. But Hui Neng asked someone to read to him the gatha Shen Xiu had posted on the wall, a quatrain about our body being the Bodhi Tree and the mind being a mirror we must constantly polish. *Ha!,* Hui Neng dictated his own gatha, rephrasing Shen Xiu's nice idea but without any duality whatsoever, and posted that: no tree, no mirror, only infinity, hence nowhere for dust to alight.

Leaves from the Bodhi Tree

Hui Neng was out for a walk when he came upon two monks quarrelling beneath a flag-pole.

"The flag is moving," one monk said.

"No, the wind is moving," argued the other.

So it went, as amongst two little kids, "flag," "wind," "flag," "wind," until Hui Neng stepped in.

"Your mind is moving," he said, and walked away, leaving them both stunned.

Well, that night, the old roshi appeared in Hui Neng's little monastic cell, and bowed to him. He said, "I know you wrote that second gatha and I can plainly see you clearly possess radiant Buddha mind and appoint you my Dharma heir. Now this is sure to cause a great ruckus when Shen Xiu finds out you're the Sixth Patriarch, and not he," the roshi says, handing Hui Neng his ceremonial Patriarch's bowl and robe, "so here—take these, go out the back gate before everyone wakes up, lay low for a while somewhere, and spread the Dharma a good ways away from here." He recites the *Diamond Sutra* to Hui Neng. Hui Neng understands it perfectly, departs and goes underground, living with hunters. Twenty years later, he starts his own monastery on the other side of the Yang-tze, near the big port city of Canton (Guangzhou)—but that's another story.

Illiterate or not, Hui Neng not only spread the Dharma, but consolidated the Zen Movement and shaped it into a resilient practice capable of weathering political upheavals and becoming a unifying force throughout East Asia. And, based on his own enlightenment, his teachings could be understood by an illiterate peasant. In fact, an ink brush portrait shows him wildly tearing up a bunch of sutras. (Show me your mind: Is it in a book?)

Now Why Not You?

Zen's gateless gate is wide-open. Come on in. Every session begins and ends with the same rituals. Even if you don't know the drill, it's easy to clue in. Everyone takes off their shoes before entering the meditation area, called a *zendo*. You sit a stretch. Then you walk; then sit some more. Next, often, someone shares their understanding, giving a little Dharma talk. Tea and cookies afterward, optional.

Along the Path

If you take refuge in a zen sangha, you're often given a woodblock **lineage tree.** (It's not a universal practice.) At the top of the scroll is a circle representing the Buddha. Below him, there's Kasyapa. Like a family tree, the genealogy branches out and down, until you get to your own roshi. Below your roshi, there's a circle, representing you. And, sometimes, in the margin, there's a red line, extending directly from the Buddha to you.

You can just show up, no introductions necessary, as often as you like. If you finally decide to seek refuge there, then you'll have a one-on-one interview with the roshi who'll ask you, "Why have you come to study?" Be honest. "I don't know," can be just as valid an answer as, "To attain enlightenment." You might find your roshi answering, "Me, too." But if your inmost urgency sounds like self-improvement, or some other way of getting off to a bad start, the roshi might go over your intentions with you (right view) and clarify the practice. After formal initiation into a sangha, you visit the roshi for periodic chats, called *dokusan,* or *sanzen* ("going to zen"). And you can attend meditation retreats, called *sesshin,* usually up to one week long.

Universal Participation: The Bodhisattva Vow

In Chapter 11, "Look Within and Know: Insight Meditation *(Vipassana),*" we looked at how to reach nirvana. But there's a choice of motive that historically distinguishes Mahayanans, including Zennists, from traditional Theravadan followers of vipassana (insight): Mahayanans take the *Bodhisattva Vow.* A bodhisattva seeks supreme enlightenment, an awakened heart (Sanskrit, *bodhi-citta*), nirvana, not for his or her self alone but for the welfare of all.

You might say this is the "greatness" of the Great Vehicle (Mahayana; vs. Hinayana, the narrow path): It's for all beings. A bodhisattva can forsake crossing over to nirvana, helping all other beings cross over first. Or a bodhisattva might attain nirvana, then come back (three times up the mountain, four times down) for the sake of others. And some transcendent bodhisattvas are enlightened beings who make their presence felt from within nirvana, embodying archetypal powers innate within all humans, and often referred to as deities.

This Is

A **bodhisattva** is one whose being or essence (*sattva*) is enlightened (*bodhi*) with the wisdom of direct perception of reality and the compassion such awareness engenders. He or she renounces all rewards for personal deeds, and works for the ultimate enlightenment of humanity, all beings, everything. An archetypal bodhisattva is Avalokiteshvara (*Kwan-yin* or *Guan Yin,* in Chinese, in feminine form; *Kwannon,* Japanese; and, in Tibetan, *Chenrezig,* as male, and *Tara,* as female), embodying compassion; another is Manjushri, embodying wisdom.

The Buddha took a bodhisattva vow when he answered Mara's question, "Who are you to say you're enlightened?" by touching the earth, invoking all beings. He then took a bodhisattva path when he left the Bodhi Tree and taught for the rest of his life. The profundity of a bodhisattva's affirmation of compassionate awareness, of love in action guided by wisdom, make its meanings illimitable. The bodhisattva path is open to everyone. For you, it will have a meaning all its own.

As a giant step, in your practice, you can take refuge in *The Bodhisattva Vow*. The Vow connects your practice with all bodhisattvas, like a lineage tree. On one level, that's all the ancestral bodhisattvas (including your grandparents, and parents, who cared for you above themselves). On another level, that's all the energies embodied by the bodhisattva archetypes or forces (often called deities). Two major archetypes are as follows:

➤ *Avalokiteshvara,* sometimes male, sometimes female, who listens to the sounds of this world and relieves its suffering; sometimes portrayed with 11 heads, a thousand faces, and a thousand arms with whatever's needed, right there on the spot.

➤ *Manjushri,* who looks deeply into the heart of things and people; usually depicted with a sword of wisdom and a book of wisdom.

In an informal pose of sheer grace and royal ease, the feminine bodhisattva Kuan Yin meditates with an awakened heart and a smile of pure compassion. The Water and Moon Guanyin Bodhisattva. *Eleventh to twelfth century, China. Polychromed wood. 95 × 65" (241.3 cm). The Nelson-Atkins Museum of Art, Kansas City, Missouri. (Purchase: Nelson Trust; 34–10.)*

(Photo: Robert Newcombe)

207

And the bodhisattva vow connects your practice with all living beings. Since all things possess Buddha nature, with *all beings*. A tree, a rock, a cloud are beings. Tibetan Buddhists see all beings as their mother. When I sat zazen this morning, I didn't do so alone. I did so with all beings, vowed for enlightenment, together. The first thing, the one thing needful. This is a shift from seeking to awaken the self as a solitary soul and, instead, taking one's place within a community of souls, finding meaning in connection.

Moreover, there's a seeming paradox to the vow. How can anyone honestly vow to help *all* beings? The sheer idea's overwhelming. Mind-boggling. But that's partly the point. The practice is just that all-encompassing; like swallowing the entire sea in one gulp. And yet a sparrow does precisely that when squawking the news of spring's arrival. Plants do just that, unfurling a flower to the universe. So why not us, too? As Michael Wenger, Dean of the Buddhist Studies Program at San Francisco Zen Center points out about the Vow, "You don't take it because it's doable. You take it to make it so."

Like I say, this vow is so profound it has innumerable interpretations. Here's one more: playing off the Calvinist doctrine underpinning American life, the Protestant work ethic, poet Albert Saijo likens the Bodhisattva Vow to the Buddhist work ethic. In a poem called *Bodhisattva Vows,* he compares the bodhisattva to someone who vows to be the last one off a sinking ship and then discovers it's something endless like being aboard the *Titanic* … getting passengers into lifeboats bound for nirvana … yet doing so with "spirit ever buoyant as we sink …"

Tracks Along an Untrod Trail

What's the particular taste of zen? Like the taste of clear mountain water, like the Dharma itself, it's no-taste, ever-present within everything; uncategorizable, yet …

➤ Nondual

➤ Everyday

➤ Complete

➤ Selfless

➤ Immediate

➤ Dedicated

➤ Authentic

➤ Spontaneous and humorous

➤ Active

Aware of the interpenetration of all things within each moment, a zen practitioner can be enlightened by anything. Enlightened by all things, one's being *with* things as they are also means being *one* with all things. So there's *no duality*.

Along the Path

"The mystery of life is not a problem to be solved, but a reality to be experienced."

—G. van der Leeuw

"Buddhism is to study the self. To study the self is to forget the self. To forget the self is to be enlightened by all things."

—Eihei Dogen (1200–1253), who brought Zen from China to Japan

If zen had a symbol it might be this. A circle ("enso," Japanese) universally implies completeness, all. A zen circle can also imply zero, sunyata, absolute, true reality, enlightenment, no beginning/ no end in all phenomena, no symbol, the spread of Dharma as a turning wheel, harmony, and womb.

(Calligraphy: Kazuaki Tanahashi)

Bowing, there's no separation between you, your act of bowing, and what you're bowing to. And every moment is *complete,* an adequate instance of Buddha nature, sufficient unto itself. In zen, there's no preconception about what the next moment might be like, because there *is* no other moment than now. Sitting, you're completely sitting, nothing else. Eating a grape, you're completely eating a grape, and nothing else. So there's no duality, and everything is complete, as it is.

And so it's always *immediate.* If a practitioner dons a robe, or bows, or quotes a sutra, it's not because of history but as an act of enlightened understanding in this very moment. There's nothing beyond or behind it. And it's fully authentic. The person is fully present in whatever he or she does. From the toes to the scalp. Intimate with life, their own life is genuine.

Hear and Now

"What we should do is not *future* ourselves so much. We should *now* ourselves more. 'Now thyself' is more important than '*Know* thyself.' Reason is what tells us to ignore the present and live in the future. So all we do is make plans. We think that somewhere there are going to be green pastures. It's crazy. Heaven is nothing but a grand, monumental instance of future. Listen, *now* is good. Now is wonderful."

—Mel Brooks

Being a lived activity, zen's in the *doing*. The Buddha said *try* this and *see*. Zen sitting isn't passive but a total commitment, body, spirit, and mind. It's as much an occasion for my complete immediate expression of my understanding of the Dharma, a total enactment of Buddha's way, as is tying my shoelaces (an interesting analogy since the Buddha wore sandals).

Zen isn't about waiting for nirvana to get it right. Every aspect of *everyday life* is an opportunity to practice zen. Work's thus a key element of zen practice, another opportunity to study yourself by forgetting yourself. Service, community action, is rewarding for just this reason.

Traditionally, the higher members of the Zen monastic order also perform everyday chores, like doing the dishes. A bookkeeper might be asked to work in the garden or something else they don't know, lest they identify too much with their number-crunching habit-self. And making everything part of practice cracks and wears down the tough shell of self. If zen practitioners often have short, military-style hair, it's because they're *selfless*, they don't have time to cultivate and keep up a hair-do. Zen isn't self-expression but expression of awakening mind, wherever that occurs.

So zen takes *dedication*, effort, like wearing shoes until the soles become thin. Shunryu Suzuki Roshi once told everyone present, "Each one of you is perfect the way you are. And you all could use a little bit of improvement." He stressed that when you engage in an activity, that you stand behind the activity, with the confidence that you are completely there, that you are the activity itself. Maintaining this attitude fulfills your experience and backs up your day-by-day *effort* just to sit.

And it's fearless. Samurai warriors of Japan were very impressed that a Zen monk could stand in front of a drawn sword (oh, how the samurai loved to test their new swords out) not flinching one iota.

Put all these together, and you're likely to bump into *spontaneous* happenings in zen, such as the improvised, quick circle. Quick thinking, such as averting a spill, or catching a ball, where's self? Zen *humor* is a popular manifestation of zen's love of spontaneity. Zen is like a joke: no one can explain a joke to you, you either get it or you don't. Zen hasn't cornered the market on wry, hard-boiled, crazy wisdom, but it sure has more than its fair share.

Leaves from the Bodhi Tree

Although zen can be brutally honest, it can also be goofy and funny—salty, blunt, and often wacky. During the late 1960s, for example, some filmmakers conducted in-depth interviews with spiritual teachers in the San Francisco Bay Area. ("In-depth reportage" always makes me think of underwater photography.) Anyway, Shunryu Suzuki Roshi's interview is the shortest of the lot. He stands venerable in his most formal, elegant monastic robes, head-shaven, wise-eyed, smiling imperturbably. Off-screen, the interviewer asks, "What is enlightenment?" In a twinkling of an eye, his hand flashes from its wide sleeve and flicks out ... a sparkling yo-yo!

Expressing the Inexpressible: *Mondo* and *Koans*

The last landmark along our tour of Zen is the *koan* (say *koe ahn*) and *mondo,* zen's hallmark contribution to the annals of crazy wisdom. If zen's typified by a minimum of techniques, we could say the two most important are just sitting (shikantaza), and koan/mondo. In the West, many zen sanghas practice both.

This Is True: I'm a Liar (Koans)

The above two statements are completely contradictory. Huh!?

Let's flash back to Hui Neng. Soon after Hui Neng had been appointed Sixth Patriarch and gone underground, an ex-soldier sniffed him out, ready to force him to return the robes and bowl. But once in Hui Neng's presence, he said, instead, "Master, teach me the Way beyond good and evil." Hui Neng replied, "Don't get hung up on good and evil. Instead, seek your original face, your face before your parents were born." Through this challenge the ex-soldier broke through the veils of rational thought, intuited his original nature, his Buddha nature, beyond labels of good and evil, and attained enlightenment.

211

This Is

The Japanese word **koan** means public notice or legal precedent. Just as a lawyer might refer to *Brown* v. *Board of Education* regarding evolution, so can each koan be referred to when illuminating a particular principle—such as Buddha holding a flower up and Kasyapa smiling, in reference to teaching without words. And like that story, a koan's meaning can never really be explained: It's not *about* anything but itself.

"Show me your original face, before your father and mother were born," is a primary koan. At first glance, it might seem like a riddle. But even a nonsensical riddle has a rational answer. Koans aren't rational. They use words to go beyond words … to short-circuit or bypass habitual thought patterns … habits hard-wired into both language and our brainpan … requiring something else, deeper within us, like intuition … a shock, almost, to enable us to perceive reality directly. When that happens, to respond fully, genuinely is the "answer." But it's not an answer in a book, as in a math problem, but rather an answer within the practitioner.

For example, a Zen monk once held up a bamboo stick before some other monks and said, "If you call this a stick, you fall into the trap of words, but if you don't call it a stick, you contradict facts. So what do you call it?" (*Answer:* A monk went up to him, took the stick, broke it over one knee, threw the pieces into the room, and sat down. And so it was resolved—at least, for that question at that time, in those circumstances, by that monk.)

"What!?" you might say. "What's the point?" Well, a koan's another way of asking "Who am I, really!?" Or "What is this?" These are actually generic koans you might try for yourself. Next time you settle into tranquility meditation, ask yourself "What is this?" Include "who" in your asking "what." As answers (this, that) and feelings (reverence, frustration) arise, don't become attached to any of them. Stay with the question, *"What … is … this?"* Stay with it through your day. That's your koan.

Along the Path

"What's true meditation? It's to make it all—coughing, swallowing, gestures, motion, stillness, words, action, good and evil, success and shame, win and lose, right and wrong—into one single koan."

—Zen master Hakuin (1686–1769)

"What is the sound of one hand?"

—A koan by Hakuin

212

You might start by considering a koan as another tool for focusing awareness. Unlike counting your breaths or fingering beads, koan contemplation addresses awareness itself ... zeroing in on logic, conceptualization, thought ... inviting *doubt* as part of the process ... like the inevitable dragon in your path ... so to get around it requires audacious fearlessness, one-pointed concentration. But even that's not enough. There it is—

—not just something for while you're perched on a cushion. You take your koan home with you. Wake up with it in the morning. Look at it in the mirror. Brush your teeth with it. Have breakfast with it. Bring it to work. Until you can't live with it—and can't live without it. And when your first koan finally yields its one true answer, congratulations: You're ready for all the others.

Leaves from the Bodhi Tree

Maybe koans seem remote or exotic. If so, consider the one-line zingers of Samuel Goldwyn and Yogi Berra. Samuel Goldwyn was the "G" in MGM, an irascible movie mogul who drove Hollywood people crazy by barking such unarguable, twisted statements at them as, "A verbal agreement isn't worth the paper it's printed on!" A koan might ask, "Show me that paper." (Would you shake hands with me on that one? It's a done deal! Now let's do lunch.) Yogi Berra, when not playing baseball with the New York Yankees, came up with such gems as, "When you come to a fork in the road, take it." "No one goes there anymore—it's too crowded." "It's déjà vu all over again." And, "It ain't over until it's over." Next time you're asked the time, remember how Berra replied: "You mean now?"

In Asia, over the centuries, about 400 Zen koans have been amassed and indexed out of about 1,700 in all. Each deals with particular phases of the Way. Primary ones, such as the sound of one hand, are designed to help tip the practitioner over his or her edge of fabricated self into immediate, boundless reality. Following this first breakthrough, there are more koans, either to gauge how far the first breakthrough went, or assist further breakthroughs. Additional koans can be grouped into categories:

➤ Initial insights into the true nature of things

➤ Differentiating real from unreal experiences

➤ Understanding the lives and teachings of Buddhist forerunners

➤ Resolving difficulties about any seeming dualisms between enlightenment and unenlightenment

➤ Realizing the innate unity of the transcendent, absolute dimension and the historical, relative dimension

If you take on koan practice, your teacher will work with you, asking you during dokusan, "How's your koan?" You can pick the koan you'd like to work on or be assigned one by your roshi. With koans, a roshi can guide a student through the zen landscape.

Who's on First?: Mondo

Another zen example of this testing of one another's attainment is question-and-answer style of dialogue called *mondo*. When Bodhidharma had that wild conversation with Emperor Wu, that was mondo. When Hui K'o asked him to pacify his mind, and he asked Hui K'o to bring him his mind: mondo. Hui Neng and the monks arguing about the flag and the wind: mondo yet again.

Watch what you say. Here's another example: One Zen monk said to the other, "Hey, that fish's flopped out of that net! How will it live?" The other monk answered, "When you've gotten out of the net, I'll tell you."

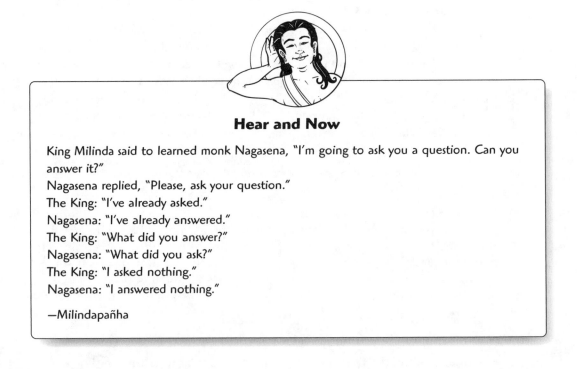

Hear and Now

King Milinda said to learned monk Nagasena, "I'm going to ask you a question. Can you answer it?"

Nagasena replied, "Please, ask your question."

The King: "I've already asked."

Nagasena: "I've already answered."

The King: "What did you answer?"

Nagasena: "What did you ask?"

The King: "I asked nothing."

Nagasena: "I answered nothing."

—Milindapañha

It takes two to tango like this: You can't surprise yourself! Some call this kind of exchange "dharma combat." It can be like two jazz soloists, exchanging riffs, or a vaudeville routine ("Who's on first?" "Who's on second—I don't know's on first."). You could say that a koan is a *special case* of mondo (remember, koan literally means "case"). The Buddha's holding up a flower was the koan and Kasyapa's smile made it a mondo.

Even if you don't take up formal koan practice, you can recognize koans and mondo in your daily life. Forks along your own path to take, straight ahead. The whole world's a koan, by including everything that is the case. It all applies. Like the Way, real koan practice becomes all your life long. Once you've exhausted all the koans your teacher gives you, life itself becomes the ultimate, inexhaustible source of koans. Right up to and including the moment called death. And there's nothing to do but just sit it out, roll with the punches, until—what is this?—the time comes.

The Least You Need to Know

➤ Zen characteristics are nondualism, completeness, immediacy, authenticity, activeness, everydayness, selflessness, dedication, and spontaneity (sometimes to the point of crazy wisdom).

➤ Like other branches of Mahayana, Zen subscribes to the bodhisattva vow. Sentient beings are numberless, the bodhisattva vows to awaken them all. Bodhisattvas include embodiments of archetypal energies, like compassion and wisdom, as well as living personages.

➤ Zen practice is typified by a minimum of means. Its primary techniques are just sitting, koans, and ...

Chapter 13

Paths of Devotion and Transformation: Pure Land and Vajrayana Buddhism

PURE LAND

VAJRAYANA

In This Chapter

➤ Pure Land Buddhism

➤ Tibetan (Vajrayana) Buddhism

➤ Gurus

➤ Shifts in emphasis

➤ Ritual and skillful means

➤ Tantra

Understanding Buddhism can be like mastering a multidimensional puzzle. As soon as you think you've gotten it, you glimpse a whole new dimension to it. But, isn't life like that sometimes? Closing one door opens another.

Till now, I've been progressively rounding out your understanding of Buddhism, each new chapter adding more pieces to the puzzle. Maybe you finally got it; well, now I'm about to lay two new cards onto our house of cards and see if it all still stands. Or will the cards all spiral upward like a mini-tornado or DNA-helix and vanish in a flash near the ceiling? We'll see.

First, I'll flesh out our picture of Pure Land, up until now gleaming in the background. It's short and sweet, and makes a very interesting companion to zen. Then I'll introduce you to Vajrayana. I can't think of a more multidimensional puzzle, in and of itself. Both have had about equal numbers of practitioners in the West and bear as many similarities as differences.

Say His Name and You'll Be Free

Pure Land is the most universal Buddhist practice of China and Japan and is commonly intermixed with Korean, Vietnamese, and other Buddhisms. I live in a suburb of San Francisco's historic Old Chinatown, and many of my neighbors practice Pure Land. Maybe you don't know it but you might have neighbors who practice Pure Land, too. You might even try it yourself.

This Is

Rebirth in the **Pure Land** is hosted by the compassionate *vow* of Amitabha (also known as Amida, Amita, and Amitayus), Buddha of Infinite Light and Life who presides over the Western Pure Land. Pure lands are outside the realms of desire (our impure world), form (realms of lesser deities), and formlessness (realms of higher deities), as well as samsara (never-ending wheel of deaths and rebirths), but some say they're present *within* samsara, that we're reborn into the purity of our own mind.

Amitabha is a supreme emblem of cosmic compassion, a bodhisattva who became a Buddha vowed to save all beings who called his name (Sanskrit, "Measureless Light"). In Chinese, the invocation of the name of Amitabha Buddha is Namo Ami-to-fo. In Japanese, Namu Amida Butsu. Vietnamese: Nammo Adida Phat. "Namo" is a form of homage, like saying "In the Name of the Father." Namo invokes the one upon which we rely, in whom we take refuge.

When we repeat Buddha's name, we're remembering him. Hearing just the name of Buddha is the same as hearing his voice. His name embodies his power, so invoking the name activates his powers.

Nothing could be simpler. Sincerely, single-mindedly, recite Amitabha Buddha's name, and, thanks to his compassionate vow to save all human beings who do so, you'll be reborn in his Pure Land called Sukhavati ("Blissful Realm"). No questions asked. It needn't imply anything otherworldly: You could be reborn into the pure land of your own mind, your very own innate Buddha nature. As J. C. Cleary comments in his book *Pure Land, Pure Mind,* "In reciting the buddha-name you use your own mind to be mindful of your own true self …"

Now pure lands aren't necessarily nirvana. Rather, they're an ideal place for its cultivation. The space for the chance of enlightenment to take place. (Our world's an "impure land," but Siddhartha's the Buddha who initiated its purification.) Some say pure lands are apart from this world, but to a pure mind any land becomes a pure land.

The three basic elements of Pure Land are *faith, vows,* and *practice.* Along with recitation, there are visualizations, contemplating characteristics of the Pure Land and Amitabha. There are both monastic and lay practices. Besides recitation, there are just two basic sutras: the *Amitabha Sutra* and the *Meditation Sutra.* And, oh!, by the way, some believe you might be reborn as a seed germinating within a lotus pod. But maybe that's better than wracking your brain with concepts like interbeing, impermanence, emptiness, and the like. Don't wait until you've cracked your koan or noted your ego dissolving: come as you are! That's it in a nutshell—or, more specifically, a lotus blossom.

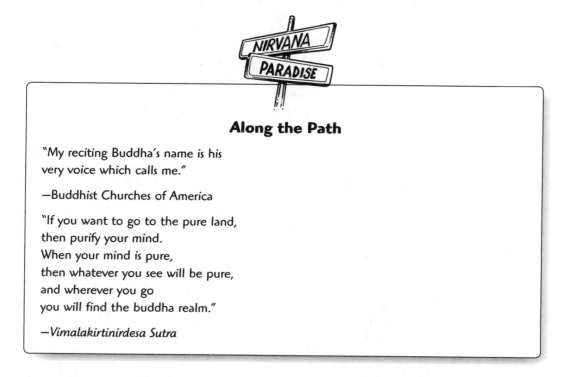

Along the Path

"My reciting Buddha's name is his very voice which calls me."

—Buddhist Churches of America

"If you want to go to the pure land,
then purify your mind.
When your mind is pure,
then whatever you see will be pure,
and wherever you go
you will find the buddha realm."

—*Vimalakirtinirdesa Sutra*

Pure Land actually began in India but didn't become a full-fledged school until it reached East Asia. (Chapter 2, "One Taste, Different Flavors: The Teachings Adapt to Different Lands," provides some background to the movement in Japan, 800 years ago. We've also noted that it's been practiced in America for over 100 years. Our bibliography online provides a few essential books for more information.)

Let's get a sense of Pure Land's range, and heart.

A Universal Method

Pure Land lives up to the name of its branch, Mahayana (Great Vehicle), in welcoming rich and poor, man and woman, old and young. Arguably, it's the widest path (since Amitabha has vowed to save everyone), so it's natural for it to reflect a range of beliefs and interpretation.

Pure Land Is Wide, with Varied Emphases

Some Adherents Emphasize	Some Adherents Emphasize
Pure Land as afterlife, only reachable after death.	Pure Land not apart from samsara; found in essential purity of mind.
Historical Amitabha, with arms to hold us, a voice to hear us.	Amitabha as formless power of universe to remove delusions of ego; Amitabha as "measureless."
"Other-power," outside assistance, granting favors.	"Self-reliance," use as manifestation of mind.
Some emphasize no self separate from the universe, "other power" vs. "self-reliance" being merely a skillful means to present teachings to people based on their capacity to understand them; unity of recitation and listening.	

It's easy to see how Pure Land became the most popular form of Buddhism in East Asia. Its faith is like an ocean, buoying up everybody. It can provide deathbed reassurance of a blessed afterlife, and be a general, moment-to-moment panacea, yet it doesn't distinguish between one or the other. You don't have to shop around for a teacher, roshi, or guru. You can go straight to Amitabha, who's vowed to save everyone, even the lowest of the low, and who accepts you just as you are. That simple.

Recitation can thus be seen as an alternative to rigorous practices such as noting or Zen, not to mention Vajrayana. Where other paths might seem like that of an ant climbing the alps, Pure Land might resemble sailing downstream in a boat (*with* the wind). Just sitting for an hour, much less a full week, while trying to make ends meet, can seem clear out of reach, whereas recitation's like mindfulness meditation: You can do it while washing the dishes or driving a car, as well as with a group.

Enlightenment is no longer a goal here, as the emphasis is being reborn in Amitabha's Pure Land (where one's resolution can be realized, enlightenment attained). The word "practice" hardly pertains, because that implies and reinforces a sense of a self that strives after something: When saying the name of Amitabha, it's done as a natural outgrowth of gratitude to him. Likewise, "meditation" neither applies nor doesn't apply. Shinran Shonen, founder of Jodo Shinshu (Buddhist Churches of America), states the transformation effected by this Buddha Prayer is "inconceivable, inexplicable, and indescribable."

Pure Land practice can also cross-fertilize another practice, such as Zen, for instance. Many traditions combine the two. The mutual practice of Pure Land with Zen provides a fail-safe, for example: If you don't crack the koan part, recitation will still earn you a seat in the Pure Land anyway.

Where Zen ropes off thought entirely—sometimes by using the koan as the poison of words to wipe out the poison of our egocentric, dualist verbal responses to the world, Pure Land uses the poison of conceptualization to fight conceptualization, thinking of Amitabha Buddha instead of inessential ego cravings, cleaning out mental earwax to listen to the universe.

Actually, if a scientist could freeze-frame a split-second of anybody's life, and sort out all the concepts flickering therein, they'd probably catalogue hundreds if not thousands, all mostly irrelevant fragments—"... a new car, blue, on sale now, yesterday ..." etc. How good to preempt, as it were, all those little ditherings with just the majestic, virtuous name of the Buddha instead! And since our minds can conceive of Buddha through a word, then our minds must indeed partake of the Buddha's mind. So when saying the name, the word, listen deeply, and hear its meaning resonate: Buddha.

Hear and Now

"On a single atom, there are as many Buddhas as there are atoms in the world, sitting in the midst of an ocean of his disciples. Likewise, the entire sphere is filled with an infinite cloud of Buddhas .... On each atom, there are as many pure lands as the number of atoms of the worlds. In each pure land, there are infinite Buddhas sitting in the midst of the disciples of the Buddhas. May I see them and perform enlightened activities with them."

—*Gandavyuha Sutra*

No Barriers

Recitation can dissolve the barrier between subject and object as effectively as noting or koan practice or just sitting. That is, the mind that's the *subject* reciting the name, and the awakening Buddha that's the *object* of invocation, are really one. Reciting the Buddha's name can thus be its own kind of koan. For example, notice the space in between its two syllables; the spacious, nameless boundlessness. (What is that!?)

You can also say "Namu Amida Butsu" or "Namo Amitabha Buddha" or just "Buddha" over and over—or thinking "budh" on your in-breath and "dha" on your out-breath—then ask yourself, "Who's reciting the Buddha's name?" You might find your own mind and the Buddha and all sentient beings are one. No separation.

And for those minds interested in advanced, further studies, Pure Land branches out into the interpenetrating universes intricately examined in the neighboring Hua Yen school, which takes Indra's web of infinite interconnection as its unofficial logo. The concluding chapter of the *Flower Garland Sutra* (a book unto itself, called the *Ganda-vyuha Sutra*), opens and closes with a Pure Land recitation, marking the beginning and end of the fantastic, epic journey of the child protagonist, Sudhana, who wanders all over the Indian subcontinent—as if the recitation framed it all, making the child's entire experience but one instant, and that but a bead of light on Indra's web, reflecting all the other beads and all their inter-reflections.

So if Pure Land might seem at first glance like a one-size-fits-all easy entry into Buddha's way, remember what jazz master Thelonius Monk once said: "Simple ain't easy." As we'll see next, that can go doubly for Vajrayana, also known as Tibetan Buddhism.

Since few of the practices that make Vajrayana unique can be taught without direct initiation from a teacher, our emphasis here will be an overview of its outlook, what kinds of things you need to *know* in order to practice, rather than instructions for actual practice, but with juicy bits of news you can use, as well.

Do You Believe in Magic?

You believe in magic, don't you? Have you ever walked in a forest or meadow and felt you were on sacred ground? Has a sunrise or sunset ever cast its spell on you? Did you ever have a special bond with a someone that seemed enchanted? And what about curious coincidences? Aren't they curious!?

Really, after all we've seen about karma and interbeing, untapped human potential and vastness without boundary, magic's only natural. It needn't be anything occult like brewing love potions. Magic can be just the recognition of how *super* everything in nature and human nature really is; super-natural, you might say. As we've seen in Pure Land, it needn't be otherworldly, but rather a realization of the unity of elements of human nature and cosmic nature. Besides pure lands, Vajrayana has doctrines about reincarnation, astral travel, and such-like, but we'll stick with magic as wonder. You can get your driver's license for the more esoteric things later on.

So: from a path likened to a log ever rolling down a mountain (Pure Land), we shift to a path likened to the summit of Mt. Everest. Indeed, just as Buddha's teachings metamorphosed after entry into China, so did they become something else again when they went forth from India's subtropical clime, crossing the Himalayas and ascending to the snowy roof of the world, Tibet—a civilization no less different from India than China.

Once you get used to the altitude, 12,000 feet above sea level, you'll be fine with Tibetan Buddhism, and its other Vajrayana cousins in Japan (called Shingon), Korea, and elsewhere. Long veiled by Western stereotypes of Shangri-la, Tibetans are very practical and down-to-earth, if I can generalize. They're also swashbuckling, and rightfully proud of their own Buddhist blend, rich with the world's greatest diversity of elements, blending rigorous scholarship with devoted daily practice, myriad rites, folk beliefs, and so on. Like the summit of Mt. Everest, there are differing approaches to choose from. There are four main schools, within which there's also a saying, "Each valley has a different teacher; each teacher, a different doctrine." Honestly, it's all Dharma.

Leaves from the Bodhi Tree

A visitor came upon a small crowd of Tibetan Buddhist monks. Their attention was riveted upon a single priest sitting on a platform. He joined them, watching this priest. When the ceremony of watching was over, he asked one of the monks what had happened. The monk told him that the priest had demonstrated the power of levitation. "But I didn't see him levitate," the visitor told the monk. "Oh," the monk said, smiling. "Then obviously you didn't receive initiation for the ceremony beforehand."

Vajra, *the Indestructible: Tantric Buddhism*

Before we learn about tantric teachings, let's first grasp the evolution and uniqueness of tantra itself. From there, we'll proceed to the importance of tantric teachers, and then a sense of what's being taught, and how.

The word vajra *(Sanskrit; dorje) means "diamond, adamantine." Used to indicate Vajrayana (yana, Sanskrit: "path" or "vehicle"), it means Diamond or Indestructible Path. Vajra also refers to a small ritual scepter, seen here, used in Vajrayana practice (and also, differently, meaning a thunderbolt, in Hindu practice).*

Let's begin with our frequently used image of a path as metaphor for a method of realizing spiritual growth. Vajrayana divides its path into progressive stages (called *lam-rim*). A teacher begins by leading a student leisurely but carefully through Theravada and Mahayana, until they're ready for initiation into additional teachings—intensive, accelerated training called *tantra*. They become proficient at the practice of visualization, mantra, prayer, and have prepared the psychic groundwork for then developing and harnessing spiritual energy. So what's this tantra?

Flashing back to the India of Buddha's time, let's recall the belief popular then that we're each manifestations of the eternal ocean, of which we're but waves, the cosmos playing hide-and-seek with itself. As you'll also recall, the common path for reuniting a seeker with this primal identity was extreme asceticism—renouncing all worldly manifestations, transcending its pleasures and pains.

But there was another path, lesser known, evolving in both Hinduism and Buddhism, side-by-side: tantra. In Chapter 2, we noted that tantra observes human emotions rather than suppressing or disassociating from them. It makes me think of the title of the book of poems Adrienne Rich, a great American poet, wrote when her husband committed suicide, *Diving into the Wreck*. I'm also reminded of the time a girl with whom I was quite enamored, Maggie, met me for dinner at the cafeteria of my college dorm, in my freshman year. I apologized for the fare, which seemed as bland and lifeless as a frozen dinner, but she replied, "It's all God food!"

In other words, since everything's interconnected, tantra sees everything as having buddha nature and thus suitable for practice. It's all *stuff* ... all sacred ... use it! Maybe you can detect the difference from Western alchemy, which strives to transform physical (or psychic) materials or lead into gold. Tantra says, "It's all gold!"

This Is

To prepare for tantric initiation, there's a system called **lamrim** ("stages of the path," Tibetan). Along the path are a progression of 21 meditation practices and topics (some familiar to the reader by now, but with unique emphases), including: the preciousness of human life, death and impermanence, taking refuge, karma, equanimity, remembering the kindness of others, the disadvantages of self-cherishing, advantages of cherishing others, exchanging self with *others (tonglen)*, developing great compassion (*bodhicitta*, the desire to attain full enlightenment for the sake of all beings), advanced tranquility meditation, and identifying with sunyata rather than ego.

We've defined tantra as "weaving" as well as "continuum," and "system." So Vajrayana further *continues* Theravadan and Mahayana practices with the *thread* of tantra running through it all. Recognizing the interdependent, interwoven nature of reality, it's evolved a science and art of *weaving* inner and outer truths, self and other. And its *system* of stages threads each practitioner through the Buddha's own evolution—from Hinayana self-disciplined awareness to Mahayana compassionate awareness, to totally enlightened awareness, all within one lifetime—in a process adapted to his or her individual temperament.

Of course, all paths lead to the same place: enlightenment. So no one is superior or inferior to any other. Vajrayana asks us to re-envision the process. Kyabje Kalu Rinpoche suggests we look at path in terms of *motivation*. Traditional Theravada (a.k.a. Hinayana) centers on the individual. And there's nothing wrong with that: if you're not for you, who will be? In Southern or Southeast Asia, you might retreat into the forest, or live in a cave, until you became enlightened, an arhat.

Then the question is, "If I'm only for me, what am I?" Not "How can *I* become enlightened?" but "How can I best fulfill my role in this life, and lives to come, until *this world's* finally enlightened?" In this Mahayanan version of the quest, a certain altruistic idealism is the motor. This isn't just for you, or about you, but for everybody, for all the needless suffering.

But tantra takes an accelerated route, which may not be for everyone. Lama Zopa asks us to imagine ourselves on the peak of a mountain, looking down at a pristine lake at the bottom called "enlightenment." (Westerners would probably have reversed the positions.) Where tantra diverges, he says, is how to reach the lake. Whereas all

Mahayanists take the bodhisattva vow to reach the lake, there are different ways of doing so. Some will pick their way carefully, so as not to slip and fall, because they're making their way for the sake of everyone. Tantra, on the other hand, dives right in, as it were. That is, the tantric way is to become a Buddha right now, in this life, for the sake of everyone. It depends on your personality type, which way you'll go. Tantra's not for everyone.

Along the Path

Vajrayana calls the texts "**tantras,**" rather than *sutras*, making it unique; yet both words have similar meanings (to sew or suture, and to weave). And our word *text*, from Latin, also means a weaving. Some mystics *read* the world as their text. Tantra interweaves an individual's personal life with the Buddha's way; it's a yoga, yoking together the sacred and the mundane, wisdom with compassion. Indeed, tantra practices "dak kang," pure perception or sacred outlook, seeing this world as an altar, every thing in this world as a Pure Land, and every being a bodhisattva or Buddha.

As we'll see again further on, tantra takes the end (the lake, in this case) as the means. And tantra is also known for incorporating both self and other, inner and outer truth, (aware they're not separate), dealing with them simultaneously, both at once. That is, it recognizes that the primal energies eternally shaping the cosmos also mould each individual, and so it yokes the two subtle energies together. Thus, each practitioner's treated as both a unique individual and as part of an infinitely interpenetrating matrix of all being.

As Tibetan Buddhism finds a following in the West, as Vipassana and Zen have, successive generations are exploring questions of transmission of tradition and cross-cultural fertilization. Tulku Thondup, an exile from Tibet, for example, has selected some nonesoteric (nonsecret) aspects of tantra not requiring initiation. So has Lama Surya Das (born Jeffrey Miller), who's not shy to joke about his Dharma name and title (saying he used to be known as Lama Seriousdass). Moreover, his business card has the image of a shiny toaster beside his Foundation for American Buddhism, as well as a Tibetan seal beside his teaching lineage (Dzogchen), and a bodhisattva beside the address of his home page.

Leaves from the Bodhi Tree

The lamrim stage of exchanging self for others (Tibetan, *tonglen*) exemplifies the enlightened goal of Vajrayana. It asks you to take in the sadness and pain of others and give them back your own happiness. Visualize someone's problem (anger, low self-esteem, greed, etc.) as a black smoke, and inhale it into your heart. Once it's settled into your heart, exhale the bliss of your pure heart visualized as a white light—upon them and the whole universe. Visualizations often picture inhalation as light and exhalation as the toxins, but the reversal here's instructive. Setting the pain of others before yours is a positive force, dissolving the personal ego, transforming yourself as you help others.

In a nutshell (or a lotus), you could sum up Vajrayana as Theravada and Mahayana with a tantric twist. To appreciate it better, let's look at it in terms of the following:

➤ The teacher (a.k.a. *lama, guru, rinpoche*)

➤ Emphasis on experience over emptiness

➤ Ritual

➤ Secrecy

And then we'll come to the summation of the road, the goal.

Careful! Don't Try This Stuff Alone: Finding a Lama

Honestly, I'm not kidding. Because tantra actively engages and transforms the student's deepest, darkest, most difficult personal emotional realms (as well as all the brightness and light), the student-teacher relationship is utterly crucial. Researching your teacher in advance of commitment is never more important than in Vajrayana. The very first stage of lamrim is learning why and how to rely on a spiritual guide, learning from someone already on the path.

For one example, when you get to the stage of identifying with the boundless transparency of being (a.k.a. sunyata), you're prone to a range of responses, such as weird dreams. Not that I mean to discourage you at all from the path, but a note of caution's appropriate.

This Is

A **lama** (Tibetan "none above" or "weighty") teaches, but also conducts rituals. Certain heads of monasteries, believed to be individuals intentionally reincarnated, are designated Tulku ("transformation body"). The honorific title Rinpoche (*rin-poh-shay*, "greatly precious") is akin to the Japanese *roshi*. And Geshe (pronounced *geshey*) is like Ph.D. Sometimes Tibetan or Mongolian Buddhism is mistakenly called Lamaism, somewhat akin to calling Catholicism "Popeism." And a llama's like a small, woolly camel, with two "l"s. (Sorry, there's no Illama.)

As we know, the Buddha faced this particular example when Mara the Tempter smirked, "And who are you to think you're the Enlightened One?" A certain, subtle, sacred pride is justifiable, but presumption and hubris can be dangerous. (The Buddha replied by saying nothing, touching the earth, deferring to the universe.)

The point is that 1) these challenges affect different people differently, and 2) you need your teacher's wisdom and compassion to personally make it through. In Vajrayana, your teacher (guru, rinpoche, lama, mentor, preceptor) becomes the living embodiment of the Buddha, taking *you* through the Buddha's own path.

The Hindu name for a spiritual guide or teacher is *guru*. This relationship's often sparked by an amazing sense of affinity ("when the student's ready, the teacher appears"). Beyond Vajrayana instruction, a guru often advises or guides in personal matters and family affairs. A guru can be more important than a parent, because while your parents raise you in one lifetime, your guru takes you through all your lives and brings you up in the most profound way.

But once a personal relationship's officially formed, a guru can demand unquestioning obedience. Even if a guru may be less strict, utmost devotion's necessary, since he or she represents your own Buddha mind and inner teacher, as well as the Buddha's teachings. The bottom line is this: A Vajrayana teacher's been there, done that, and, moreover, knows you, knows where you're at in what's new terrain to you, and knows how to get you through.

Our guidelines in Chapter 9, "Taking the Plunge: Beginning and Cultivating Your Practice," about picking a teacher apply here. Americans need to be extra careful about picking their Vajrayana teacher. For one thing, a practitioner in Tibet traditionally can take up to 12 years before deciding whether or not to commit to working with a particular teacher, whereas Americans might leap right in (as in impulse buying, point and click). Second, Americans need to understand the required discipline in advance. Sogyal Rinpoche once commented that Americans want to hear why they should do something before they do it, while Tibetans would do something first, and then their teacher would tell them why they did it.

Moving on toward the goal, let's take a little closer look at what the teachers teach.

Hear and Now

"Buddhists ... call the mentor 'spiritual teacher,' and 'spiritual friend,' as a close friend, not an absolute authority. This emphasizes how you have to free yourself, develop your own enlightenment. No one else can do it for you. But in Tantra the sort of transference relations to the teacher is very important. You spend twelve years to investigate such a central figure. You don't jump into receiving teachings from the first teacher. Not initiatory teaching."

—Robert Thurman

FORM Is Formless; Formlessness IS Form: Skillful Means

These two statements are reciprocal, identical. But my emphasis here's on the waves rather than the ocean; experience over emptiness; the phenomena, forms, techniques you use to get to the ground of being, timeless spirit, the infinite ultimate. From the standpoint of nirvana, they're interchangeable; from the point of view of someone trying to reach enlightenment, it's a question of which foot to put forward first. Zen begins by emphasizing the ocean; Pure Land begins with a formal technique, like a life raft; and Vajrayana begins with a fleet of forms of practice.

As we saw in Chapter 8, "The Fine Print: Touching Deeper," vajra and zen make an interesting contrast. A zendo is austere, very sparse. Monastic robes are gray or black. Nothing should distract the practitioner. In a Tibetan temple, no space seems unadorned. Robes are bright orange over maroon. Zen paintings emphasize blank canvas, spaciousness; in a Tibetan painting, a detail upon closer inspection seems to reveal pictures within pictures. Zen seeks to break through to enlightenment with a minimum of skillful means; Vajrayana employs myriad techniques, manifestations of formless, boundless, openness. We'll see an example in a moment.

To get another bead on the emphasis on technique and ritual, form over infinity, let's flash back to Buddhism's first teacher. The Buddha trod the Indian subcontinent for 45 years, teaching whoever was receptive (and crowds had to be turned away). We've seen how egalitarian this was, disregarding station in life or economic status. But we should also note how he adapted his teachings to each person. Looking at you and talking with you, as your mindfield intersected his, for instance, he could tell if you needed analogies and for-instances or analytical reasoning, if-this-then-that. And if it would take a miracle, accounts relate he'd do that, too.

Along the Path

Uppaya kausalya is Sanskrit for **skillful means,** device or method. It includes any number of excellent expedients to facilitate enlightenment, such as visualization, prostrations, bowing, miracle, mantra, koan, plain speech, the hit of a stick, insight, etc. They're traditionally compared to a raft, with nirvana as the other shore, to be set aside once nirvana's attained. On a more esoteric level, they not only express the view of benefit in seeking enlightenment but also enlightenment fulfilled in compassion toward others.

So different tools, or *skillful means,* emerged with different schools of Buddhism. Explaining this diversity, the Buddha notes that a cow and a cobra can drink the same water, but it turns into nourishing milk in one case and deadly poison in the other. So his medicine varies according to the malady. Buddha, the Great Physician, has 64,000 different treatments, one for each of the 64,000 afflictions of us mortal beings. Now, of all practices, Vajrayana seems to come closest to reproducing all 64,000.

One aspect to help us better appreciate this is ritual. So let's look at Vajrayana ritual, in particular, then in general.

Body, Speech, and Mind

Buddhist logic, in general, and Vajrayana practices, particularly, are fond of groupings and subgroups. That's partially an outgrowth of the rigorous logic in Buddhism, available once the "I" is no longer the subject of philosophy (and thus leading to an investigation of all and everything, rather than "I think, therefore I am"). For instance, a practice can have an *outer, inner,* and *secret* dimension. (Don't ask about the secret secret: that's Top Secret.)

Another subdivision breaks a practice into *body*, *speech*, and *mind* (and by so doing integrates all three)—for example, through prostration, mantra recitation, and mental visualization.

Hear and Now

"The fault that I always found in Western philosophic logic is that it doesn't have an ultimate courage in questioning whether the self exists. It starts with that assumption. Now if you take this logic to its absolute extreme fearlessly and question that, then you have a pure logic, and you can start building castles that have meaning on that basis, which is what the Tibetans have done. It's questioning the very basis of all reality, all existence, and the self itself. All phenomena."

—Richard Gere

Body

Prostrations are a common feature of Eastern practice. Muslims do it six times a day. Even if you don't feel any particular devotion, going through the motions might awaken the feelings within you. As in Mouth Yoga (lifting the corners of your mouth and smiling like a Buddha while you practice conscious breathing), or "just sitting" (to be a Buddha, sit like Buddha, sit as if you're Buddha), start with the result to work to the cause. As we've seen, this is an essential meaning of tantra, taking the end as the means.

Stand with your feet apart, the width of your hips or shoulders. Put your hands together as if in a gassho, but above your head. Then lower them to 1) the crown of your head, 2) your mouth or neck, and 3) the center of your chest (your spiritual heart). Then bow, bending your knees onto the earth, and slide your hands forward. Sliding your hands and arms along the earth above your head, your forehead also touching the earth, as well as your lower legs and feet. Smoothly reverse the process to a standing position. Congratulations! this counts as one full prostration.

A few things to keep in mind ...

➤ With practice, prostration can become all one, fluid motion.

➤ For all warm-blooded, bipedal mammals who sit in chairs, drive cars, and walk wearing shoes, I might remind you how wonderful it is to touch and become one with the earth, from time to time.

231

➤ Prostrations are practiced in many Buddhist schools. Typically, one makes three prostrations, to the Triple Gem, usually before an altar.

➤ In Vajrayana, prostrations are to be practiced 100,000 times, in sets of 108. In fact, many vajra rituals, preparatory to initiation, must be practiced 100,000 times before they're considered to fully take hold. Really train that mule!

➤ (*Question:* How many Vajrayanists does it take to screw in a light bulb? *Answer:* One, but they do it 100,000 times.)

Other bodily engagements found in Vajrayana include meditation on the six primary energy centers, called *chakras*, also found in yoga. Plus, *channels, winds,* and *tigles* are to be explored, bodily pathways and means of internal circulation of concentrations of subtle energy (also known as *chi* in chi kung and tai chi, the yogic practices of Taoism).

Along the Path

"Buddha's teaching is that I am my own master and everything depends on me."

—The Dalai Lama

"You live among illusions and in the world of apparitions. But there is a reality. You yourself are this reality, but you don't know this. If you awaken to this reality you will see that you are nothing and being nothing you are everything."

—Kalu Rinpoche

The importance of hand gestures (*mudras*) is also incorporated. Emulating a particular gesture of a buddha or bodhisattva deity further imparts their energy to us, physically (much in the same way that smiling evokes happiness). In general, tantra displays the greatest acceptance in Buddhism of the body and all its potentials and powers.

Speech

The bodily aspect is but one of three. An example of practice involving speech and mind is Pure Land visualization and recitation. Just add prayer beads to a recitation of Namu Amida Butsu, while visualizing a trait of Amitabha or the landscape of the Pure Land, and you're integrating body, speech, and mind.

In prostration, you might repeat a Refuge Vow (also speech) to the Triple Gem. Vajrayanists preface this vow with a refuge to the lama as a palpable, personal, living representative of the Buddha, the Dharma, and the Sangha.

The vajra path has a robust body of devotional literature to draw from, to engage speech in various meditations. For example, here's just a fragment of a devotion to gurus written in 1650 by the first Panchen Lama:

> We prostrate at your feet, O venerable Gurus.
> Sole source of benefit and bliss without exception.
> You eliminate the root of all faults and their instincts,
> And are a treasury of myriad jewel-like qualities.
> We prostrate to you, O benevolent Gurus.
> You are in reality all Buddhas,
> Teachers of all, including the gods;
> The source of eighty-four thousand pure Dharmas,
> You tower above the whole host of Aryas [noble ones].
> With faith, esteem and a sea of lyric praise,
> Manifesting with as many bodies as atoms of the world,
> We prostrate to you,
> Gurus of the three times and ten directions,
> To the Three Supreme Jewels, and to all worthy of homage.

Chapter 10, "Base Camp: Meditation Basics," introduced us to *mantras* as one tool for focusing awareness, and this chapter began with Pure Land's more intensive mantra. One etymology of the word *mantra* combines the Sanskrit root *man* ("to think") with the suffix *tra* ("tool"), to mean "a tool for thinking." It could also be read as *man*, from *manas* ("mind") and *tra* from *tranam* ("protect"), meaning "mind-protector."

Some mantras can be as short as one syllable. Some are believed to have intrinsic power, setting up a powerful vibrational field, such as "Om" (pronounced *Ohhhhwwwwmmmmmm*). Hindus consider *Om* the primeval sound of the universe itself; to Vajrayana Buddhists, *Om* manifests the Buddha's many bodies. The syllable *Ah* manifests the Buddha's speech, source of all sound. *Hung* manifests the mind of the Buddha. (It's often spelled Hum, but pronounced, to our ears, a tad like a funk singer going "hunh.") Reciting this mantra with one-pointed concentration bestows the blessings of the body, speech, and mind of all buddhas.

For instance, after settling into tranquility meditation for about five minutes, a practitioner might meditate on the mantra *Om Ah Hung*. Recite Om to yourself while breathing in. Then, holding the breath in the center of your chest (your spiritual heart), recite Ah. And on the out-breath, recite Hung.

When you engage in mantra practice, it extends outwards as well as inwards. In the sound of waterfalls, rivers, and waves, Buddha's speech becomes audible. In tantra, all sounds are gurus chanting Buddha's name, all sounds are Buddha's voice. And if you listen really well (as in the sound meditation along the path, in Chapter 9), you can hear that this chant is ceaseless.

This Is

Tibetans use a skillful means called a **mandala.** This circular form can represent our world of phenomena, as well as realms of consciousness and pure lands of bodhisattvas and deities. There's wisdom in their circularity; close your eyes, for instance, and ask yourself if your mind is square. Mandalas can be made up of heaps of rice or sand, or painted on scrolls (called tankas). They can be three-dimensional, metal or yarn sculpture, but often collapse within two dimensions of a three-dimensional representation of still higher dimensions, like beads on Indra's net. Practitioners might imagine themselves touring or circumambulating these pure lands. Or they might imagine themselves as their personal deity in the center or nucleus, and build up to more complex multi-dimensional pantheons.

Mind

As just a glimpse, I'll mention here that the written word for each syllable has its own visual symbolism. So you'd then visualize a diamond letter Om at the crown of your head, that your body might be merged with Buddha's enlightened body; a ruby-colored Ah at your throat, merging with his enlightened speech; and a sapphire Hunh at your heart (center of your chest), merging with his enlightened mind (heart). Additionally, you can meditate on Om as the Sangha, Ah as the Dharma, and Hunh as the Buddha. Thus the great Tibetan teacher Naropa said, "My mind is the perfect Buddha, my speech is the perfect teaching, my body is the perfect spiritual community."

Visualization's a mental process we do all the time. Think of the name of a movie star, and you're also visualizing them. Or think of your best friend out with someone else, and you're visualizing. And when you see someone you know on the street, and it turns out to be somebody else, that's also visualization.

In Vajrayana *deity visualization,* a practitioner doesn't just visualize. In so doing, he or she becomes one with the deity's energy. It's as if in Theravada practice I send metta (lovingkindness) from my cushion; in Mahayana, I join the bodhisattvas sending metta; and in Vajrayana, I become a bodhisattva sending metta. Now, some Vajrayana deities (or energy archetypes) are called "wrathful" and "semi-wrathful" deities, representing capability and power. They look fierce, but in visualizing and identifying with them, they're found to be exhilarating.

Plus, there are the pure land buddhaverses which each deity inhabits. These are mapped out within a circular diagram, called a *mandala,* ranging from very simple to mind-boggling.

234

A mandala. This man-dala is a compassionate deity with a thousand arms and eyes, flanked by 37 deities.

(Courtesy of Dr. Lokesh Chandra. From Tibetan Mandalas *[International Academy of Indian Culture])*

Integrating body-speech-mind is good, in and of itself. But we can also see how this has an extra tantric twist to it, working with what is, rather than trying to transcend it. That is, practicing a trio of skillful means can transform idle mind-wandering into constructive mind-wandering. For instance, if your mind wanders off while reciting a mantra, let it wander: it can alight onto visualization, and if it gets tired of that, you can do more prostrations—each shift of focus allowing the very tendency of the mind to wander to propel your practice.

Integration of body-speech-mind gives us a whiff of the variety of Vajrayana rituals, which are as extensive as they are powerful. Rather than sort through what can be "declassified" from secrecy and related in a short space, let's take a step back and look at ritual in general as a symbolic function.

The Rite Stuff

Ritual connects a person or group with knowledge, an idea, belief, or power. People of every nation might salute a flag with a pledge of allegiance and national anthem. People of every spiritual tradition give thanks for their food. When someone sneezes, in every culture there's usually a blessing or incantation. Of all Buddhist paths, Vajrayana's most actively engaged a wide variety of tightly integrated rituals.

A typical meditation ritual, such as one that involves visualization, prostration, and a mantra such as Om-Ah-Hunh, might start with a candle or some incense at one's altar, and bowing or prostrating, going for refuge. It would end with another bow, putting out the candle, and dedicating any merit possibly earned by the practice toward the benefit of all beings. Mantra practice could continue during daily activities, perhaps reinforced with prayer beads or even spinning a prayer wheel.

Along the Path

Buddhist ritual might seem idolatrous. Historically, icons were the source of a schism within orthodox Christianity, which had viewed devotional art as a manifestation of God. Earlier, Judaism prohibited worshiping images (which ban formed the basis for its traditional rejection of Buddhism). From a progressive viewpoint, however, altars and deities, mandalas and visualizations represent aspects of our own nature, with which we wish to be in tune. We don't have to even want to become an enlightened buddha, but just a more compassionate, aware human being.

We've already noted how the routine rituals of daily life can be considered sacred. That is, in sweeping the floor, a mindfulness practitioner sweeps the floor, and nothing else. We might note here the growing body of skillful verses, begun in Asia and continuing now in America, to help us slow down to enjoy each moment and so live our whole lives in heightened awareness. They provide a contrast for the way Vajrayana does so with a slightly different twist.

For example, filling a car at a gas station, one can be mindful of the moment by considering the ancient living beings which the gas distills and vow that it burn for the benefit of all present and future beings. Thich Nhat Hanh sees a stop sign as a reminder to stop and return to the present moment. Robert Aitken Roshi sees the occasion of kids fighting in the car as an opportunity "to show how the car doesn't move unless all of its parts are engaged."

Similarly, quoting the *Sutra of Great Approximation*, Bokar Rinpoche suggests that, when opening a door, we can wish, "May the door of profound reality open." Walking, we might wish, "May I progress on the path of Awakening." In a car, we might wish, "May I ride the horse of diligence." Upon arrival, we might wish, "May I arrive at the city of Nirvana." When I shave in the morning, I vow to cut the roots of ignorance. Encountering a flight of stairs (a challenge to mindful breathing), I acknowledge it as a path of liberation.

All could be said to be symbolic, though tantra often engages in a symbolism called "twilight language" (city of Nirvana, for example), poised between light and dark, revealing and concealing. (Another reason why a guru's important—for correct interpretation.) An insight into this dimension of Vajrayana is found in the roots of the word "symbol" itself: from Greek, symbolic literally means to pull or draw together, similar to yoga as yoking, or tantra as weaving, as opposed to diabolic, pulling apart. This "magic" isn't diabolical, as in Faust's pact with the Mephistopheles, but sympathetic (which means "fellow feeling"): It's just realizing kinship with the primordial innate wisdom within all things. Thus you could say it's an open secret.

Open Secrets

In Vajrayana, the mantra Ah can symbolize the entire *Heart Sutra* and the *Diamond Sutra*. But to understand and practice that requires *initiation* by a lama. It's thus called *secret*. This seems quite opposite from Pure Land, say, with no bar to entry. But even that open secret requires proper care.

Make no mistake, Vajrayana isn't a members-only secret society. Rather, it unlocks mysteries to those adequately trained. The secret isn't in the mantra, it's in your own response to their power.

The best way to explain this is by comparing it to a radio. I invariably wonder if I might really be tuning in to all the radio and TV waves that pass through space and thus bombard my head ("… and now *this!*"). Actually, I know they do, because I know that with a TV set I can tune in. But my brain doesn't necessarily unscramble the signals. And this is what secret teachings are like. Not having a set is equivalent to not having been initiated; something's there but it doesn't quite register.

Hear and Now

"Now I will tell you something about the Secret School. It's not that mantras are secret. The Secret School is the efficacious response which comes from *your* recitation of mantras; I can't know your response. I recite mantras and have my efficacious response, and you do not know of it. This is 'no mutual knowing.' The ability and power are unfathomable and unknown, and are therefore called the Secret School. It's not the mantras themselves, but the power of mantras that is secret. This is the meaning of the Secret School."

—Venerable Tripitaka Master Hsüan Hua

It's like Lao-tzu saying, "Those who know don't speak, and those who speak don't know," then going on to write 5,000 words. The words obviously aren't secret, but they only scratch the surface. And it's quite like the Buddha holding up a flower, and Kasyapa smiling. Except that transmission was mind-to-mind, and Vajrayana transmission, as we've seen, works on not just mind but mind, speech, and body.

To continue the analogy in zen, a curious occurrence concerning koan practice is relevant here. About a century ago, a book was published in Japan with a "cheat sheet" of answers to a couple hundred koans—answers that had been passed down teacher-to-teacher secretly for two centuries. Scandalous, but it was like trying to draw legs onto a snake. In zen, the koans are meant to be practiced, not read about. As Thich Nhat Hanh points out, koans aren't math problems: The right answers aren't in a book, but in the practitioner.

I can never know how you answer your koan, I can only know how I answered mine, just as I can't go to the bathroom for you. So that's secrecy and why, yet again, the teacher's so important here. A guru isn't giving you an abstract truth but something crafted for you personally. Secret transmission formally begins during a special ritual of initiation (also called an *empowerment*), following rigorous preparation yogas. At this time, you'll be given your own protector deity (*yidam*) to visualize, including the meaning of the deity's hand-gesture (mudra) and the deity's mantra. But transmission can also take place in ordinary conversation, or by a mere gesture. (*Thwap!*, do you believe me now?)

This Is

The Tibetan name for a personal deity is **yidam,** meaning "firm mind." A yidam corresponds to the psychological type of the practitioner, and is appropriately assigned by the guru. Common examples are Tibetan versions of Avalokiteshvara and Kwan-yin— Chenrezig and Tara, respectively.

The End of the Road

Having begun our discussion of Vajrayana in terms of a path, it's fitting that we return there. In simultaneous karma, we've seen how effect can produce cause. In Vajrayana, the goal can create the path. What might be one path's end result might be another's path's whole thing—the path itself.

When you're initiated (empowered) in tantra by your teacher, he or she will reveal for you a glimpse of the goal, so you have something to work for. And because you want to unite your path to the lama's path (which is the Buddha's path), the path of your lama becomes your goal. So finding your path becomes the path itself, and the goal becomes staying on the path. Scholar Bernard Guenther likens the process to a heat-seeking missile. Once it locks onto its target, they're one; although the fusion's off in the future, the contact begins here and now.

At the end of some Vajrayana paths is a practice known as mahamudra ("great seal"), outwardly seeming like basic tranquility meditation or zen "just sitting." Another formless meditation on pure awareness is called Dzogchen. They're arrived at following rigorous tantric training, and so they might be called tantric zen, with the emphasis on tantric. A zen saying applies:

> Before I studied the Way, mountains were mountains, and rivers were rivers. After I'd practiced the Way for a few years, suddenly mountains were no longer mountains, and rivers no longer rivers. But now that I've practiced the Way for many, many years, mountains are again mountains, and rivers are rivers.

In the end, it matters not if you find out that the secret was that there was no secret (I'm not telling: I don't know!). Be thankful you found out, once and for all—and send the rest of us a postcard, from the summit of Mt. Everest. (Postcards without correct ZIP code will be returned to sender.) And remember: three times up the mountain, four times down. Have a good journey!

The endless knot, a common symbol in Tibetan Buddhism, harmoniously weaves motion and rest, simplicity and profundity. Symbolic of interdependence, interpenetration, interbeing, it has no beginning, no middle, no end. Like the Buddha's knowledge, it's infinite.

239

The Least You Need to Know

➤ Pure Land and Tibetan Buddhism have about an equal number of followers in the West.

➤ Pure Land is the easiest Buddhism to access.

➤ Pure Land interpretation can range from traditional to progressive and from utter simplicity to mind-boggling complexity.

➤ Pure Land and Vajrayana emphasize experience over emptiness, but both are important.

➤ Vajrayana is Mahayana Buddhism with a tantric twist.

➤ Tantric practices are a late development within Buddhism. Laying great importance upon the teacher, and marked by rigor, ritual, and personal initiation, tantra engages human emotions as levers of transformation. Tantra takes the end as the means.

Part 4

The Pedal Hits the Metal: Buddhism Applied to the World at Large

Congratulations! Now you've seen how to steer, and you know the rules of the road. (Applying your foot to the gas pedal, the vehicle goes faster ... and your mind goes faster.) So where shall you go today? There's nowhere that Buddhism doesn't make major inroads.

Some Dharma teachers might decide which particular teachings are best for your personality type. Others leave it all up to you, which is what I'll do, too. Everything can be a teaching. Our own lives are a source of scripture. Here's a survey of the wide range of life events to which Buddhism applies. From food to work. The sciences to the arts. Take your pick. (Touch one deeply and you touch all the others.)

See how reality illuminates Buddhism in action for you ... how Buddhism illuminates reality ... and how the interaction illuminates your own path.

May these myriad occasions brighten your way like festive lights. And may your journey always be safe, pleasurable, and rewarding.

Chapter 14

Alone, Together: Buddhist Relationships

In This Chapter

➤ Siddhartha's family

➤ All equals: a cube of relationships

➤ Mr. and Mrs. Buddha

➤ Bringing up baby and rites of passage

➤ Buddhism as education and lifelong learning

➤ Living our dying

Steadfast in his solitary quest, at the end of his final night sitting beneath the bodhi tree, Siddhartha looked up and saw the morning star, and awakened fully. Seeing the morning star, the Buddha truly realized, "I and the universe are one." The self is interdependent with the universe; or, to put it another way, there is no self but in relation, interbeing.

Being one with life, realizing our interdependence, we attain *greater intimacy with life*. And so we ask ourselves, "Am I in right relation?" We're all in some kind of relation (if you don't think so, try missing a couple of payments on your credit card).

The Buddha says we're all equals. That doesn't mean everything's the same. Each relationship is precious. I'm sure you can relate to this.

But Would You Want Your Daughter Marrying Buddha?: Family Matters

Let's begin our survey of relationships by returning to the life of the Buddha. The sight of a monk was one of the four things that sparked Siddhartha's quest, but as the Buddha he transformed the spiritual path of his time from one of material renunciation to one that embraced relationships.

Bringing It All Back Home

In our opening chapter, Siddhartha left the palace vowing to return once he attained his quest. Well, he did return. Only, instead of heading straight for home, he went begging from door to door. When his father found out about this, he blew his stack, ashamed to have his own son, a prince, descended from a clan of warriors, begging for alms. He went out and confronted his son about this disgrace, but the Buddha's explanation of the way of life he'd found was so righteous and illuminating that the king began to wake up right there in the street. He ultimately died an enlightened man (and, it is said, the Buddha served as his pallbearer).

Along the Path

A basic outlook of Tibetan Buddhists is to consider all beings as their mother. Even if you don't believe in endless reincarnation, it's true we're all interrelated. Interbeing has no beginning or end. So imagine everyone once bore us in their womb, nourished us, helped us survive when we were defenseless. (Lama Sogyal Rinpoche has observed how Americans don't always experience the filial piety that Tibetans feel toward their parents, so he's suggested that Americans might consider all beings as their grandmother.)

Maybe you wouldn't want your daughter to marry this kind of guy. Certainly, this wasn't the happily-ever-after kind of ending most parents dream of for their children. Yet it is said, too, that his wife, Yasodhara, perhaps ready to bawl him out for hitting the road, knelt before him when they were reunited. She could see he'd become supremely enlightened, that he was now the Buddha. With compassionate divine love, he asked forgiveness for leaving her. If he hadn't been fair to her, he said, he'd been true to all sentient beings, and asked her to cross the sea of suffering with them.

So she, too, renounced a royal life to study the Dharma. And their seven-year-old son followed him as he left, asking for his inheritance, and became the Sangha's youngest monk. The Buddha's cousin Ananda also followed, becoming his closest attendant for the rest of his life.

Leaves from the Bodhi Tree

With a simple meditation, we can realize how our family ties reflect our interconnection, our lack of separate self. Sit and, when settled, put your hands out in front of you in a comfortable manner, palms down. Look at your hands. Notice the shape of your fingers and knuckles, the patterns of your veins and skin. See how you feel about your hand. Generate and send kindness to yourself, looking at your hand. Now see your mother in those shapes and textures, and see how you feel about her. Send her kindness. Now see your father in your hand, and see how you feel about him. Send him kindness. Turn your hands over, join palms, and thank them for this meditation. Gassho.

If Emily Post Met the Buddha: Ethical Codes

Hindus of the Buddha's time worshipped facing in different directions, honoring the sun and moon, mountains and rivers, and big trees. The Buddha adapted the practice to create a cube of six surfaces, for people to remember (be mindful of) life's important relationships:

➤ Father and mother, in the east

➤ Students and teachers, in the south

➤ Husband, wife, and children, in the west

➤ Friends and kin, in the north

➤ Colleagues, employees, and workers, below

➤ Spiritual teachers, monks, nuns, and saints, above

These relations form the network of human affairs. And these relationships, he explained, are of reciprocal power sharing, between equals. A mutual support system.

For example, consider relations between a temple and the community. The secular population provides economic support to the monastery, whose idea and ideals it spreads into society. Never isolated, the monastery, in turn, provides the local community with spiritual support as well as various services such as education, lodging, and medical care.

And it's important to recognize that the Buddha positions these relations as *between equals* ... since we're all human beings ... all sharing the same DNA. A radical concept even today, imagine how it must have seemed during the hierarchical societies of Brahmanic India ... or Confucian China?

Hear and Now

"Filiality makes the difference between people and animals, yet some animals seem to understand the filial piety. The lamb kneels to nurse. The crow returns to feed its parents."

—*The Flower Adornment Sutra*

"Brethren, I declare there are two persons one can never repay. What two? Mother and father."

—The Buddha

Relations East and West

As Buddhism spread East, it mixed with the thought of *Confucius,* a contemporary of Buddha living in China whose teachings would also spread throughout Asia. Just as Buddhism had deep similarities to Taoism, it harmonized with Confucianism, which helped lead to its widespread adoption. Like Buddhism, Confucianism can be seen as more of an educational system than a religion, although both have been revered as religions as well. In Confucius' essentially ethical system, relations are primary. Ranked in concentric rings, at its core are husband and wife, then parents and children, older and younger siblings, companions and friends, and, finally, political leaders and the public—each relationship mirroring the others (for example, the ruler on the throne being like the father in the house, and vice versa).

This Chinese word for piety is composed of the component for old and the component for son, both united in a continuum.

(Calligraphy: Chungliang Al Huang)

Here's a major difference between Eastern and Western traditions in general. In the East, the ideal is harmonizing with the group; in the West, on the other hand, individuality is the goal. So in the East, the family takes care of each other throughout their lives; in the West, we speak of our "nuclear family," a nest which we leave and come back to periodically.

In the West, we don't conceive of ourselves as oriented within a cube of social duties, nor within rings of concentric relationships. Here, we typically enjoy a diverse web of intertwined networks that might include affinity groups, sports, and clubs, as well as unions, political activities, religious associations, and so on. Yet they are all opportunities for us to see Buddhism in action and apply our Buddhist understanding. And at the core of our own experience is … family.

Marriage: How Would a Buddhist Wedding Cake Taste?

Lay practitioners are the majority here in the West, so family matters often become woven into sangha life, especially if a husband and wife are both on the path. When marriage and practice support each other, two can build together. If both spouses aren't Buddhist, the dance is just as interesting. ("Hi, honey, I'm home! I spent seven days sitting on a cushion looking into my mind!")

Marriage isn't a specifically Buddhist ritual. That is, although Buddhists can create rituals to perform a ceremony, weddings aren't part of the Buddhist canon, per se. Sorry, no Buddhist wedding cakes. Marriage is a secular matter, like a birthday or graduation, not a sacrament. Certainly, weddings are often performed by a lama or roshi, monk or nun, but not acting as divine intermediaries ("… by the power vested in me …"). In lieu of wedding vows, at a Buddhist ceremony a bride and groom affirm their refuge in the Three Jewels and the Precepts; additional vows might affirm the continuity of life and the importance of understanding and mutual respect.

Formally celebrating a relationship of two Buddhists, the emphasis isn't so much on how absolutely marvelous it is for two particular people to be coming together, but rather that they're both walking the same marvelous path together. Rather than vowing to honor and cherish each other, which they already do, they instead vow to honor and cherish their relationship (whether a marital or a nonmarital commitment), and their practice.

Leaves from the Bodhi Tree

Tibetan lore is full of stories in which women are as wise if not wiser than men. Saraha, for example, asked his wife to make him some radishes. He then meditated for 12 years nonstop. When he arose, he asked his wife, "Where are my radishes?" His wife replied, "You think I'd keep them?" He huffed and said he'd go off to the mountains to meditate. She responded: "A solitary body doesn't mean solitude. The best solitude is when the mind is far from names and concepts. You've been meditating for 12 years, yet you still haven't gotten rid of the idea of radishes. What good will it do to go to the mountains?" He realized she was right, and so abandoned names and concepts and ultimately attained enlightenment.

The equality of bride and groom permits either to divorce if need be and also remarry, all without stigma. (Stigma's worse than having a bad credit rating: Even with a bad credit rating you can still get credit cards. Stigmas can worsen and become stigmata.) They're not necessarily breaking any Buddhist vows, which they still hold sacred, still holding unconditional love for each other and staying on the path.

Happily Ever *After?* How About "Happily Ever *Here*"? (Buddhist Romance)

Now, Buddhism might seem bereft of lore about romantic love. The pages of Judaism, Christianity, and Islam are peopled with such legendary romantic figures as Abelard and Heloise, Solomon and Sheba, Majnun and Layla, Ali and Fatima, Muhammad and Khadijah, Rumi and Shams-i-Tabrizand (and, oh yes, Adam and Eve, if you call rib surgery and talking to snakes romantic). Tales of Buddhist true romance exist but remain to be collected.

But romantic love can really be another setup. Much of what's called romance is often an assortment of chocolate-flavored duhkha in a pretty, red, valentine-shaped box. (Not that I'm knocking chocolate, but it sure can be addictive.) How many people fling themselves on another person, only to stagger back, later, licking wounds from a wild but wobbly relationship that finally crashed and burned, yet still hoping to find "that certain someone" who'll relieve them of all this agony?

A misguided lover's stated goal may be *love, home, security,* and *family.* But wars, too, are often fought in the name of such admirable goals as peace. Buddhism teaches you to know and love yourself. To be at home in the present. To find security in that insecurity. And to identify yourself as part of a family that extends in all directions in time as well as space. So you could say Buddhism's good training ground for loving and being loved.

Hear and Now

"For one human being to love another: That is perhaps the most difficult task of all ... the work for which all other work is but preparation. It is a high inducement to the individual to ripen ... it is a great, exacting claim upon us, something that chooses us out and calls us to vast things ... the task of working on ourselves ..."

—Rainer Maria Rilke

Marriage or a committed relationship is an ultimate occasion for practice: the practice of love. Two people, interbeing. The intimacy of realizing we're all interconnected on Indra's net.

Buddhist practice accommodates the demand for "giving someone space." Space and silence are positive, not negative, and interconnect all things. When one feels overwhelmed, they need only tell their beloved they're going to visit the Breathing Room, or do walking meditation for 15 minutes.

Surveying a trying emotional landscape through mindful meditation won't necessarily result in any "solution," other than being able to come back and calmly and clearly say, "Here are the emotions that the situation arouses in me" (rather than trying to issue commands, "Don't do [such-and-such]!"). Knowing you're working towards a common *direction,* you can be *direct* with each other and state, "When you do *that,* it makes me feel like *this.*" (Anything else is extra.)

When talking with your beloved, see if you can keep each other in the present moment. When you see your beloved's mind wander, why not bring them back to the present by saying, "Is it just me or is it getting windier?" Or "Doesn't the air taste fresh?" This isn't necessarily to push away what may be bothering them, or refuse to talk about it yourself, but instead can invite them to join you at the healing base camp of the marvelous present moment, whence all roads depend.

Along the Path

"Love and compassion become the source of the greatest happiness because it's simply part of our nature to treasure them the most highly. The need for love is deeply human. Therein our interconnection is expressed."

—The Dalai Lama

"Nirvana or lasting enlightenment or true spiritual growth can be achieved only through persistent exercise of real love."

—M. Scott Peck, M.D.

Communication becomes practice by sharing a common language of deep listening and loving speech. Listen to what your beloved says and also to what your beloved is not saying. When you sense your beloved is hurt, why not say, "When you hurt, it hurts me, too." When you sense your beloved is happy, why not say, "Your joy makes me glad, too." (Wouldn't you like them to say this to you, in similar situations?)

It's a dance. If two beings come together, aware they're spiritually complete in themselves, then living together they'll find how their souls can be quite different yet learn to recognize themselves in each other. It's a dance of the cosmic principle of yin and yang, complementing and balancing each other, under a domestic roof ("not one, not two"). The relationship becomes a sangha. (Give it a name!) "Whenever two people gather in my name," the Buddha said, "I'll be there."

Leaves from the Bodhi Tree

The Buddha apparently never said anything about homosexuality. I happened to be present when a group of American gay Buddhists asked an authoritative Asian spiritual teacher what Buddhism says about homosexuality. I'd say it put the teacher immediately in the unenviable position of reflecting on his own celibacy and foreign cultural conditioning, in ways that he might never have publicly done before. I'm sure it will resolve well. Meanwhile, for gays or straights, the Third Precept is the judge. Being aware of the consequences of sensuality and sexuality. Not causing another or ourselves pain through breaking the bonds of trust.

Disrobing: Buddhism and Sex

We've discussed sexual ethics, the Third Precept, in Chapter 7, "The Art of Living: Cardinal Precepts." In a survey of Buddhist relations, we see further examples reinforcing how important it is to have such a basic ground rule to work from.

Life seems to offer up almost as many options for escaping the prison of a separate self ("the skin-encapsulated ego") as there are cell phones and dot-coms these days. Sex reigns as arguably Most Advertised (right up there with chocolate and cars). Of course, it's natural: Sex forms the blueprint for how we got here and perpetuate ourselves. That's a powerful energy to tap into.

Besides its *regenerative* aspects (producing children), it also *generates* pleasure, in and of itself. (The Buddha was hardly a virgin. He not only fathered a child, but had dallied daily with his harem of 500 concubines, before he became a renunciate.) And because that intense pleasure can transport one out of one's self, threatening at any time to topple the whole house of cards which sets up as a separate self, it can have its scary aspects. So the ego often pulls back and reasserts itself, resulting in sexual power politics of dominance and submission; at its worst, sexual abuse. Sexual abuse can cause wounds that might take a lifetime to heal, for an individual, and generations when occurring within a community of trust such as sangha.

This Is

The Western concept of **sexuality** might be summed up by Plato's analogy of a sphere that seeks wholeness after division. Sex here is the union of two incomplete halves. In Buddhist sexuality, two wholes can come together and experience something larger. Tibetan Buddhists say that orgasm is a glimpse of sunyata. Asian words for sexuality imply natural processes, such as "cloud-rain," evoking the union of heaven and earth.

Traditionally, a key difference between the lay sangha (householders) and monks and nuns (home-leavers) has been celibacy, but not *all* Buddhist monastics are celibate. Some Tibetan Buddhist lamas are celibate, for instance, while others aren't, depending on the individual and the school. Moreover, a few immigrant Buddhist teachers have thrown their vows of celibacy to the winds upon exposure to the relative sexual permissiveness of American society.

Extremism also manifests in some Westerners' yearning to shed their Puritan heritage by imagining Vajrayana as bursting with spiritually condoned eroticism. Well, this is to mistake the symbolic language of tantra for literal practice. In Vajrayana, an individual's visualization of deities paired with their consorts in sexual embrace (called *yab yum*) is a skillful means of identifying with and fusing the polar energies within the practitioner. The male deity represents compassion; the woman, wisdom. Such union is sometimes called "the jewel in the lotus," "the thunderbolt in the void." The allegorical sexual imagery is similar to *The Song of Solomon* and Christian mystics who seek union with Christ the Bridegroom.

Along the Path

A great scandal in modern Tibet occurred in the seventeenth century when it was discovered that the Sixth Dalai Lama had been sneaking out at night, drinking and having affairs. Here's one of his songs:

> By a few drops of water
> words of black ink can be effaced.
> But the heart's unwritten designs
> seem impossible to erase.

Suzuki Roshi once pointed out that the minute you say "sex," everything is sex. One Vipassana follower has noted how awareness of the impermanence of life has its own eroticism. Thai meditation master Ajahn Chah once confessed that when he'd walk in the forest in his early years as a monk, every sensation gave him an erection. And with Zen viewing everything as sacred, eccentric Zen master Ikkyu (1394–1481) wore his monastic robes to the brothel.

Whatever the school of Buddhism, the path inspires or requires a kind of nakedness to life, an openness to relations without costume or mask. And with commitment and trust, literal nakedness of two people, thus vulnerable, can be a sublime way of actualizing mindfulness, experiencing and expressing love, a sacred trust and beautiful fruition.

This exquisite, nearly life-size Mongolian Vajrayana bronze is a purely symbolic representation of the tantric union of polarities called yab yum (Tibetan, "father/mother"; Sanksrit, maithuna). Zanzabazar (1635–1723), Sitasamvara with His Consort (White Samvara; Mongolian, Caghan Demcig). Late seventeenth century. Gilt bronze. H: 21¹/₂ (54.5). Diam.: 13¹/₄ (33.8). Chojin-Lama Temple Museum.

Meet the Buddhas: Mama Buddha, Papa Buddha, and Baby Buddha

A baby's not automatically born Buddhist, per se, even if he or she looks like a little Buddha, smiling serenely within that juicy layer of baby fat. It's up to parents to train their children in the Dharma and to let them decide for themselves about taking refuge when they're ready; in the process, children have much they can teach their parents. Father, mother, and child all share Buddha nature. Each can remind the other of their true nature.

Mama Buddha and Papa Buddha

The rigors of parenting are comparable to monastic training, both with strict schedules; only parenting adds the test of a child's continuous stream of interruptions wearing down the ego. A child can also be a role model. You want to see an example of beginner's mind? Check out children. Little kids are capable of living so intensely in the present that just witnessing them as we go by is like hearing a bell of mindfulness, awakening us to the marvelous present moment. And watching your own bald little baby grow that first hair, cut teeth, and sprout up like a beanstalk, is quite a lesson in accepting impermanence.

Hear and Now

"Listen. Giving birth is like starting a fire: the father's the flint, the mother's the stone, and the child's the spark. Then, once the spark touches the wick of a lamp, it will continue to exist through the secondary support of the lamp's fuel. When that's exhausted, it flickers out. ... Since the parents too have no beginning, in the end they, too, will flicker out. Everything grows out of the void from which all forms derive. If you let go of the forms, then you reach what's called 'the original ground.' But since all sentient beings come from emptiness, even the term 'original ground' is only a temporary tag."

—Ikkyu (1394–1481)

Along the way, kids can be frustrating little Zen masters, testing their parents' ability to deal with fear, anger, and the whole soap opera of parenting (tune in tomorrow to *As the Dharma Wheel Turns*).

And when we're mindful of our feelings (as described in Chapter 11, "Look Within and Know: Insight Meditation *(Vipassana)*," we don't pass their charge along to our kids. When a child wants to do something outrageous, don't throw a fit ("I absolutely forbid you!"). Pay a visit to your breathing room, sit for 15 minutes, watch your breathing as you contact your feelings. Then you might return saying something like, "Well, I thought about it and it just doesn't feel right to me. I don't think I can handle your doing this. Please don't." Reacting with clarity and calm, rather than generating hysteria and trauma, is a good way of teaching by example ... which is Buddha's way.

What's Your "E.Q."?: Emotional Intelligence

One individual who grew up in a Buddhist household remembers that he never heard his father say, "Don't push your brother!" but rather, "Think about your state of mind when you push your brother." And that stuck with him, gently initiating him into mindfulness. This is an example of what's now being called *emotional intelligence,* which is basically being able to be aware of emotions rather than being run by them.

When Daniel Goleman wrote *Emotional Intelligence* in 1995, he could track down fewer than a half-dozen school programs in the nation that taught the ability to

254

manage feelings and relationships. At that time, a national survey of tens of thousands of American kids over a 15-year-period found a sharp, steady decline in the emotional capacities of successive generations of Americans. Five years later, there are hundreds of programs (sometimes called SEL, Social and Emotional Learning) in tens of thousands of schools.

New research has revealed that the centers of the brain regulating emotions continue to grow into adolescence, rather than stopping after the first years of life as previously thought. In fact, they're the last parts of the brain to fully mature. So, for example, 10-year-old girls who have had difficulty differentiating between feelings of anxiety, anger, boredom, and hunger will risk developing eating disorders when they're 12 and 13. Paying attention to self-awareness and social adaptation over the full course of a child's school years has proven to not only help emotional and social maturity but also help prevent eating disorders, depression, addiction, and violence.

Hear and Now

"When we teach our children, we focus on technical skills, on computers, on math, on content, on intellectualism, which are divorced from the human heart. In fact it is the paradox that our skill in working with emotion is a far greater determinant of our success, let alone our personal happiness. That of course is the paradox of modern education. We have focussed on the wrong things."

—Daniel Goleman

Learning to react to violence with nonviolence is always a major lesson, particularly apt as schools increasingly become tests of survival and street smarts as well as of history and math. Racism and violence aren't innate, they're learned behaviors. When a child's confronted by a bully, he or she can be taught not only to recognize his or her feelings in reaction, but also that the bully is really the one suffering. Mean people are actually sad because they want something they can't have. (The lesson's harder to teach when it's the child who can't get what they want.) Such a threatening situation can also teach reciprocity. A mean person is really being mean to himself. To harm him back would be harming one's self. (For more, see our section on psychology in Chapter 18, "The World Within and Without: Buddhism and the Sciences." All in all, I'd call a family versed in emotional intelligence very rich, indeed.

Along the Path

"Whenever you have a problem first remember the red light: stop, calm down, and think about it. Then remember the yellow light: think of a lot of different alternative things you can do and what their consequences are and then pick the best choice. Then advance to the green light: go ahead, try it out, and evaluate."

—Poster in classrooms in New Haven, Connecticut, teaching emotional intelligence

Dharma Family Treasures

Parents concerned about instilling family values in their children will find a treasury in the Dharma.

As we've just noted, teaching doesn't always have to be transmission through words. Teaching by example, a child learns to value what a parent values. A child familiar with mindful sitting, for example, can sit by a parent who's meditating in the family practice area, the Breathing Room, and practice being together. Dharma family practices include the following:

➤ Going on nature walks together

➤ Singing together

➤ Taking mindful meals together

➤ Talking with each other every day

➤ Celebrating Earth Day

➤ Celebrating Buddha's birthday

➤ Hugs

There's no set way for teaching Buddhism to kids. ("Paints mandalas within the lines; meditates well with others.") You might consider teaching kids yoga as early as possible, so that the lotus position isn't so much of a stretch. The Dharma will come as needed.

Being a mindful parent also means listening for when a child wants to be taught a particular Buddhist lesson, attuned to when they need to enter into the parents' practice and draw what they need for their particular level. Everyday life situations can be teaching opportunities. For instance, children can be taught to care for others by the example of how they play with their own possessions.

Formal teachings in a Dharma family treasury can include the Three Jewels, the Four Noble Truths, the Precepts, and, of course, the life of the Buddha. A number of Buddhist books for children are beginning to be published (perhaps in part because Western-boomer Buddhist publishers are becoming parents). Learning the precepts can be a core curriculum as a child becomes a young adult. Conscious conduct shows how kids can define for themselves their do's and don'ts, how that defines who they are, and how that can't ever be taken from them—a major step in the transition from child to adult, as we'll explore next.

This Is

A classic body of Buddhist literature for children is found in the 547 **Jataka tales** ("birth stories"), originally written in Pali. Some were adapted from folk tales of the Buddha's time. They all tell of the Buddha and his followers' past lives and so generally illustrate various workings of karma. They also have specific themes such as the spirit of forgiveness, the importance of correct faith, the value of charity, and so on.

Welcome to the Club: Rites of Passage

Every spiritual path has its *rites of passage*. In our culture, an adolescent boy or girl is welcomed into the community by such spiritual ceremonies as confirmation or bar/bas mitzvah. Buddhist culture also has its rites of passage, varying according to country.

In such Southeast Asian countries as Thailand and Myanmar, a young man becomes a Buddhist monk as a rite of passage. His hair is shaved, he dons a monk's robes, and he lives a monastic life for at least three months, usually after high school. And he may return to do this as a man, at any point in his life.

In Tibet, children are given a herd of yaks to tend, to acknowledge their growing independence. In the West, the Tibetan Buddhist Shambhala Center in Boulder has been maintaining a rite of passage program for the past twenty years. In preparation, children discipline themselves, studying such Buddhist arts as archery, flower arrangement, and poetry. During the rite of passage ceremony, the children and parents bow to each other, and exchange gifts representing childhood and maturity. They vow to be kind to themselves and to others. Other Western sanghas are adopting their own programs for young adults.

Children are our future, and, thus, they're our teachers as much as we are theirs. This reciprocity, which is the model for all Buddhist relationships, is a key attribute of Buddhist education, as we see next.

This Is

Our ancestors were very wise in creating **rites of passage,** initiating a new generation into the community and its customs. This is particularly true for the young men of the tribe. The adolescent male is full of testosterone, which can be very dangerous. Without such rites, young men might wreak violence on the community itself. The prevalence today of youth gangs can be seen as a case of misguided male rites of passage.

Learning to Learn: Buddhist Education

One of the various ways of addressing the Buddha is "Original Teacher." Now a teacher-student relationship's usually more informal than a parent-child or master-servant relationship, which are more typically the models for religious training and service. Buddha's egalitarianism was reflected in his pragmatic approach to education, as we've seen, saying, "See for yourself." You're the final, ultimate authority.

From the beginning, the first Buddhist teachers were also students, and the model was lifelong learning. Actually, the Buddha established the world's first continuing education program. During the three-month rainy season, Buddha's core followers would reconvene to share with each other what they had learned and receive further training.

Across Asia, Buddhism has traditionally furnished an educational space in society. In China, for example, there wasn't any national educational system, and Buddhist temples helped fill the bill. Buddhist temples had complete sets of books, not just Buddhist but also Taoist, Confucian, and ancient Chinese. As monks were familiar with all the works, the temples acted as more than libraries and translation centers, becoming full-fledged schools, scattered across the land. And for over a century in America, Buddhist centers have provided educational opportunities for Asian immigrants. Buddhist Churches of America, for instance, began Sunday schools in 1913, and by their first 25 years had taught 7,000 students through 56 temples.

We can see an example of egalitarian student-teacher relationships in the zen doctrine of "direct transmission of mind." As zen master Sokei-an (1882–1945) explains it, "At the moment the disciple's student reaches the same understanding as that of the master, a fusion of minds takes place, and the understanding of the disciple becomes one with that of the master, or, in traditional words, the master 'transmits' his mind to the disciple." For this to happen, teacher needs student as much as student needs teacher.

As with all relationships, all components have Buddha nature—the teacher, the student, and the teachings. That means if you've learned anything here, as I hope you have, what have I taught that you didn't already know, or that I didn't learn along with you? (Your diploma, however, won't arrive until its printer graduates kindergarten.) As we saw in Chapter 6, "Taking Steps: The Eightfold Path," wisdom isn't necessarily accumulation of bits of knowledge but can also be the shedding of the veils of ignorance that keep us from our innate knowing. Next, we come to the final veil.

Good Life: Good Death

Death. Our society as a whole doesn't do a great job of making it easy. We lack appropriate rites of passage. As Bo Lozoff, director of the Human Kindness Foundation, says, "Life is deep but the national lifestyle is not." We will examine the social dimensions of engaging with death in Chapter 19, "Happiness Is Not an Individual Matter: Engaging the World," but here we'll explore it as our own personal relationship.

The Ultimate Relationship

The Buddha said, "Just as the elephant's footprint is the biggest footprint on the jungle floor, death is the biggest teacher." Indeed, our relationship to death includes all other relationships. Consider, for example, how sex once again pokes its head at us when we consider death. You probably wouldn't think of death as part of "the facts of life" (although people whisper about death and shield children from it as if it *were* sex). The fact is if it weren't for sex, we might not ever face the mystery of death.

Consider, for a minute, that if we still reproduced by cell division, one cell dividing into two, two into four, and so on, instead of Harry meeting Sally and later bringing up baby Harry Jr., we'd have Billy becoming Bill *and* Lee. MaryLou will become Mary and Lou. And so on for everyone. (Imagine what weird family reunions all *that* would make.)

Now, if we looked at death as part of life's sexual embrace, we might not grieve so badly when one thing becomes another. A caterpillar becomes a butterfly. (Does the caterpillar die?) An infant becomes a teenager. (Does the infant die?) A breadwinner becomes a retiree. A strong parent becomes a frail being, lying in a bed, sipping nourishment through an I.V. tube. Who dies? It's the story of anyone.

Facing Our Own Death Fearlessly

Buddhism provides various skillful means for all life's relationships. As death is inherent in all our life transformations, all our relationships, we come now to the ultimate question: how can we face our lives if we don't face our deaths? The zen answer is, "Die before you die." Then, when your time comes, you'll be ready. (Nobody said it's easy.)

This Is

Our culture distances us from **death** through vocabulary. A funeral *home* (where no one lives) is now a chapel. An undertaker (formerly a *mortician*) is now a funeral director. He doesn't sell *coffins* but caskets. A corpse is viewed in a slumber room and isn't *embalmed* but prepared. Cremated ashes are remains. A *funeral* is a memorial service, attended by relatives and friends, not *mourners*. And *filling up a grave* with earth (not *dirt*) is now referred to as closing the interment space.

In the Japanese custom of the *death poem,* someone who's dying sums up their life in the briefest of sketches. The ultimate haiku. Here's the one Zen master Kozan wrote on the morning of his death, sitting up in bed:

> Empty-handed I entered the world
> Barefoot I leave it.
> My coming, my going—
> Two simple happenings
> That got entangled.

Even shorter, but no less sweet, is this one written by Senryu:

> Like a dew drop
> on a lotus leaf
> … I vanish.

Die before you die. Zen master Suzuki Shosan (1579–1655) made the word "death" his constant koan. One day, when the doctor said his pulse was poor, he was asked how he felt. He laughed and replied, "Shosan has attended to his own death more than thirty years ago!" Someone later asked him if he was afraid of death and he said, "Of course! Terrified! Why *else* do you think I made it my koan!?"

Here's an American example: When Henry David Thoreau was dying, a priest came to his bedside and asked him if he'd like to make peace with his God. Thoreau replied, "I wasn't aware that we'd ever quarreled!"

Ultimate nirvana awaits. Die before you die. Then, when your time comes, you can be present during your final moments, without suddenly (or slowly) going into a panic (such as, "Oh no! Did I leave the stove on!?"). Of course it takes practice. But if you get it right this time, this lifetime, then you can spend the rest of eternity doing absolutely *nothing* really well.

One of the West's first discoveries of Tibetan Buddhism was through the translation over 75 years ago of what was called *The Tibetan Book of the Dead,* a book about transformations whose literal title is *Liberation Through Hearing in the In-Between State.* In addition to its ceremonies for death and a kind of travelogue of realms where the soul journeys after death, it contains meditations that can be conducted within this life. Life is a continuous stream of moment-to-moment deaths and rebirths. We begin to see this when we notice various in-between states (*bardo,* Tibetan), such as noticing the moment in between breathing out and breathing in … in between falling asleep and waking up … in between thoughts … in between words.

Along the Path

"The prisoner condemned by a king merely to have a limb amputated as a punishment for a crime totally panics. His mouth goes dry, eyes bulge and he trembles with fear. How much more terrified is someone threatened with death?"

—Shantideva

"Then it is a fact, O Simmias, that true philosophers make death and dying their profession …"

—Socrates

In Theravada, there's an important sutra, *Four Establishments of Mindfulness,* with a guided meditation that takes you through your own death, as far as your own bones being bleached by the sun and turning to powder. Thinking about her own death, Buddhist teacher Geri Larkin decided she'd like all her friends to gather at her funeral to write poems about her, string them all together, and tie them up in a tree for the seasons to weather. How about you?

Take some time to visualize your own death. See what holds you back … what frightens you … what would make you most happy. Explore your feelings. Let the truth of death overcome your fear of death. Include your death in your life. Discuss your funeral with your loved ones, just as if you were talking about buying a house. Let the reminder of death motivate your efforts to live well each moment.

Hear and Now

"Not only is inattention to spirituality mourned on the deathbed, but the unlived life is as well: the trips never taken, the undeveloped talent, the heart closed to love. As some near-death testimonies indicate, the moment of judgment said to occur in the afterlife may have less to do with having done wrong than with having refused the gift of life."

—Pythia Peay, "A Good Death"

Like they say, life isn't a dress rehearsal. This is it. No curtain calls, no encores. No forwarding address. Live the words of the epitaph you'd like to leave behind as your exit line. Then the stone slab will be merely extra.

The Least You Need to Know

➤ Buddhism isn't an escape from relations. Buddha mapped out the range of human relations. His approach to all relations was for people to treat each other as equals.

➤ Marriage is not a Buddhist institution, per se. Nevertheless, Buddhism can provide a strong framework for marriage.

➤ Romance can be a slippery slope. Sincerity and truth are stronger bonds. When a couple shares a commitment to Buddhist practice and to each other, sex can be a natural, sublime expression of love.

➤ At its core, Buddhism is an educational system, and the first to promote life-long learning.

➤ Buddhism holds a wealth of teachings which children can tap into.

➤ The final relationship is confronting your own death, integral to living a meaningful life.

Chapter 15

No Work, No Eat: Work to Eat or Eat to Work?

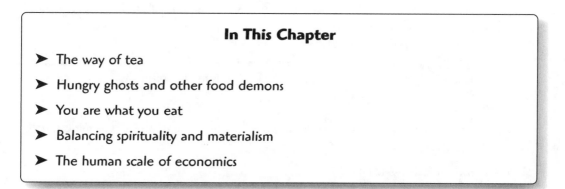

In This Chapter

➤ The way of tea

➤ Hungry ghosts and other food demons

➤ You are what you eat

➤ Balancing spirituality and materialism

➤ The human scale of economics

Somebody once scolded the ancient Greek philosopher Socrates for eating little, and he replied, "I only eat to live, whereas you live to eat." And it's interesting how working is related to this syndrome.

The crux of the matter is the interrelation of spirituality to materialism. Ultimately, there's no duality. But in most people's everyday workaday life there's a big split, with the emphasis on the material. ("Show me the money.") A Martian visitor might easily see how we're so into material things since so many of us eat french fries made out of cardboard and gummy bread you could use as an eraser. And so when it comes to work, is it any wonder that the fast-food business has become a big business model? McJobs: Now Hiring.

The Buddha can help us set our priorities by looking at our eating and work habits through the lens of mindfulness. Doing so can also shed further insight into the Buddha's way.

Take Tea and See: The Tea Ceremony

Let's start simple, with tea. The American Revolution had its roots in tea. It had been the national drink of England, featured in a ceremony known as "tea time." And here in the New World, colonial New York drank as much as all of England. Yet most Americans today think of tea as, at best, a side-order beverage, usually served up in the form of a bag on a string, faintly resembling a mouse with a tail. But—is it Buddhist?

Along the Path

"There are few hours in life more agreeable than the hour dedicated to the ceremony known as afternoon tea."

—Henry James

"If Christianity is wine and Islam coffee, Buddhism is most certainly tea."

—Alan Watts

"When tea is brewed with water drawn from unfathomable depths of the spirit, then we have truly realized the Way of Tea."

—Toyotomi Hideyoshi

Well, as we'll see, tea can be a model for the whole zen way of life. Imbibing tea has roots extending as far back as eighth-century China, when a Buddhist named Lu Yu spent five years compiling the first book about tea. He was a great press agent for his subject, laying out the whole ritual for appreciating tea, including no fewer than 24 different implements for preparation and serving. Actually, in true Taoist spirit, the rules are meant to be absorbed and then forgotten, untouched by any formality, simple, relaxed, and spontaneous.

When Japan learned the ceremony, two things happened. One, Japan liked following the rules. And two, the tea ceremony became closely allied with Zen, which likewise had its formal rules. But both sets of rule books were, as in square dancing, designed to make the spirit accessible to all.

Now, the Japanese Zen Buddhists became so fond of tea they began repeating the legend that during Bodhidharma's nine-year stint of zazen, facing a wall at Shaolin Monastery, he grew angry at his own dozing off. So he tore off his eyelids and threw them to the ground, where they took root and sprouted up as tea bushes. Hence the eyelid-shaped leaves with invigorating properties.

Hear and Now

"The philosophy of tea ... expresses conjointly with ethics and religion our whole point of view about man and nature. It is hygiene, for it enforces cleanliness; it is economics, for it shows comfort in simplicity rather than in the complex and costly; it is moral geometry, inasmuch as it defines our sense of proportion to the universe. It represents the true spirit of eastern democracy by making all its votaries aristocrats in taste."

—Kakuzo Okakura (1863–1919), *The Book of Tea*

Of all the arts of Japan, the tea ceremony is closest to being total, like theater or a High Mass, creating a pure land involving all the senses. Each element is worthy of study unto itself. Ideally, guests will first become acquainted at the host's exquisitely landscaped and groomed tea garden. The ceremony proper is traditionally held in a simple, 10-foot-square tea room. It resembles a zen monk's cell—a style which, in fact, highly influenced Japanese domestic architecture in general. The door's low, requiring a bow. The floor's made of textured straw matting (*tatami*); the small, irregularly shaped windows with paper panes admit a subdued light. At the entrance, in a small alcove, is the only decoration, a flower below a scroll of zen calligraphy. One stick of incense purifies the air. The only music is of a bamboo water pipe dripping outside and the water boiling inside on a charcoal burner.

The utensils and their arrangement catch the eye, and handling them pleases the touch. The cups aren't perfect porcelain but, rather, zen pottery—unglazed at the bottom, often with a drop of glaze running down the side as a zen "controlled accident." (For more on spontaneity in design, see Chapter 17, "New Ways of Seeing and Being: Buddhism and Fine Arts.") The fresh tea is a fine green powder, whipped into a "froth of liquid jade," as one Chinese writer put it. When ready, the color's to be admired, the fragrance savored. Then taste and aftertaste are appreciated, slightly bitter, walking the middle way between sweet and sour.

Top left: Garden of En-an teahouse. Design: Furuta Oribe, Yabunouchi school of tea, Kyoto (from Japanese Arts and the Tea Ceremony *by Tatsusaburo Hayashiya, Masao Naka-mura, and Seizo Hayashiya. Weatherhill, 1974). Top right: Tea ceremony room and paint-ing of cottage by mountain. Konchi-in Monastery of Nanzen-ji Temple, Kyoto. Bottom: Ido-type tea cup. Koho-an Monastery, Daitoku-ji Temple, Kyoto.*

Hear and Now

"It was at once as if nothing at all had happened and as if the roof had flown off the building. But in reality nothing had happened. A very old deaf Zen man with bushy eyebrows had drunk a cup of tea, as though with the complete wakefulness of a child and yet as though at the same time declaring with utter finality: 'this is not important!'"

—Thomas Merton, on having tea with zen scholar D. T. Suzuki

In America today, outposts for the tea ceremony dot the landscape, in Alabama and Georgia as well as New York and Los Angeles. But just knowing about it can be inspiring, too. That is, it's applicable to all the arts, as well as to the culinary arts, but also to your practice as a whole. As a complex, highly codified ritual, it takes a lifetime to master; but the spirit is something you can practice at home, with friends, at work, or anywhere.

Now, imagine if we ate our meals the way zen tea-people drink tea: in harmony and respect, with purity and tranquility. Plus a potent dash of joy.

Moral: How you eat is as important as what.

Do You Hunger and Thirst?: Food Issues

All living things hunger and thirst. Naturally, our appetite for edible food and for evanescent happiness are intertwined. We see their mutuality in the Chinese word for harmony, peace, showing a seed of grain next to an open mouth. The Catholic Eucharist unites the physical with the divine through the sacrament of consecrated bread and wine.

Yet in the West the twain don't always meet: "Give us this day our daily bread," we say, but also "Man does not live by bread alone." Even Siddhartha bought into this duality. (Even the Buddha had food issues.) Remember, he tried fasting his way to enlightenment, to examine and transcend the searing bonds of hunger hardwired into our physical makeup. Prior to that, he'd had his pick of the palace pantry. From out of these extremes, luxury and poverty, he taught a nondualistic alternative, the Middle Way. Furthermore, he showed (in the Second Holy Truth) that our discontent, our suffering, stems from unrealistic *cravings*, thirsting for what we can't have, for what only reinforces our addiction to illusions.

267

Leaves from the Bodhi Tree

Legend has it that a teamaster accidentally insulted a samurai, so the samurai challenged him to a duel at dawn. The teamaster begged the only swordmaster he knew to teach him swordsmanship, but it became clear the teaman wasn't going to learn the sword overnight. The swordsman consoled his desperate visitor by saying, "Approach the sword the way you do tea and you'll do fine." That morning, the teamaster appeared at the designated spot, and, with the one-pointed concentration of his tea ceremonies, hoisted a sword above his head. Suddenly, the samurai knelt and begged the teamaster to forgive him. "Had I known you were such a master of the sword," he pleaded, "I wouldn't have challenged you to a duel!"

Facing food and food issues means making peace with the present moment. Looking around, it's ironic to note that in a land with a relatively high standard of living, America also has such a high number of people with food issues, overweight, starving themselves, suffering from ulcers, or otherwise hung up about food. Who hasn't known someone like this if not experienced this themselves?

Along the Path

"The care and affection which once was bestowed on the human body now goes to the machines. The machines get the best food, the best attention. Machines are expensive; human lives are cheap."

—Henry Miller

"We live in an age when pizza gets to your home before the police."

—Jeff Arder

The American Diet

Fact: Americans now spend more on *fast food* than on movies, books, magazines, videos, and recorded music combined, making fast food a hundred-billion-dollar industry. Fact: Along with rising profits from fast food, there's been a rise in the national obesity rate.

Fact: We seem impotent to stem a rise in unhealthy substances mixing in with the food we eat and the water we drink, as well as the air we breathe. Pesticides have become a cornerstone of agribusiness. Fourteen million Americans, or more, now drink water containing carcinogenic herbicides. (Amazing to think how many people now drink bottled water.)

Leaves from the Bodhi Tree

In Tibetan Buddhist legend, eating disorders can lead to enlightenment. A master named Saraha chanced upon a glutton named Sarvabhaksa, writhing in pain because he couldn't find anything to eat. Saraha told him what a hungry ghost is, and the glutton asked how could he avoid such a fate. Saraha told him to visualize his belly as empty as the sky, all visible phenomena as his food and drink, and his appetite as a fire consuming it all. He did so until the light went out because he'd devoured the sun and the moon. Saraha then told him that everything he'd eaten was now nothing and to now meditate without food. Soon the sun and moon reappeared as he realized that appearance and emptiness are one.

Whether out of greed for profit, fear of the unknown, or ignorance on many levels, our nation's haunted by hungry ghosts (see the picture in Chapter 5, "The Handshake: Buddhism's Basic Beliefs"). Where's the Middle Way in middle America when it comes to food?

Eating Healthy

Fortunately, every yin element has its yang counterbalance. We spend $26 billion on fast food from vending machines but $33 billion on weight-loss programs, books, and tapes. Growing up in southern California, I remember roadside hotdog, hamburger, and taco stands that would be pioneer outposts of the fast-food industry; but, at the same time, this being Hollywood, eternally questing for the fountain of eternal youth, there were already one or two stores where you could buy mom-and-pop brand vitamins and herbal compounds, exotic juice drinks, proto-granola, gnarly fruit labeled "organic," and macrobiotics. (The book about the macrobiotic diet in those days used the word "zen" as a marketing ploy.)

Today this is all called "health food" (a redundancy no less funny than the oxymoron of labeling needless gunk added to packaged food as "natural"). As of this writing, organic food has become a six-billion-dollar industry. And, as we'll see further along in this chapter, zen has contributed to a national re-evaluation of our eating habits.

In a nutshell, we're becoming more aware, more awake, to food as part of our overall health.

This Is

Fast food (a.k.a. **junk food**) originated out of the shortages of World War II. Today's fast foods often contain such substances of dubious nutritional value as hydrogenated oils and fat, plus mysterious substances with scientific-sounding names like sodium propionate, carrageenan, carboxymethyl cellulose, dioctyl sodium sulfosuccinate, invertase, manitol, monoglycerides and diglycerides, monosodium glutamate, polysorbate 60, propyl gallate, propyulene glycol, sodium benzoate, sodium nitrite, sodium erthorbate, sorbital, sorbitan monostearate, and who knows what else.

You Are What You Eat

When I first heard this now-commonplace phrase, "you are what you eat," in the 1960s, it seemed as radical a concept as artist Allan Kaprow's "happenings" (spontaneous zen environmental performance art). (But then I was raised on frosted flakes and hamburgers.) It's a very succinct illustration of a Buddhist truth: life is interdependent, interpenetrating. Have you ever stopped to consider that every seven years your body completely regenerates all its cells (except bone)? So the "you" that you were seven years ago is no longer here except for your skeleton (and even the marrow is renewed). And from where do you derive this new you? From the food on your table …

… which is, in turn, part of the life of the soil, and the clouds, the sun, the lives of the farmers and the truckers and the grocers … and the lives of people with too little to eat … the 40,000 children who die daily for want of adequate food. It's all there to be experienced at your table, an intimacy with life we too often let slip through our fingers, reading or watching TV as we eat.

Any meal is, in and of itself, an invitation to see deeply into life and gain insight into our place in the universe. (*Wow!*) A childhood pal of mine is now a yoga instructor who's so busy she says the only time she has for meditation is when she sits down to eat. Fancy, a meal as meditation! Not just an affirmation of belief, that the material world is indeed no different than the divine, but to actually renew that faith, bite by bite. As the Bible says, "O taste and see!"

Along the Path

"Tell me what you eat and I will tell you what you are."

—Jean Anthelme Brillat-Savarin (1755–1826)

"... the smell and taste of things remain poised a long time, like souls, ready to remind us ..."

—Marcel Proust

"Dance the orange ...
... It has been deliciously converted into you."

—Rainer Maria Rilke

"Everything you see I owe to spaghetti."

—Sophia Loren

Here are four ways to enhance your mindful eating pleasure:

1. Give thanks.
2. Make meals a meditation.
3. Practice with family and sangha.
4. Increase your food awareness.

Thanksgiving's Every Day

The bottom line: Every spiritual practice on the face of this blue Earth blesses or gives *thanks* for food. And like saying Namu Amida Butsu, it can never be forced.

And food tastes better if you stop to thank it. Try it and see. I don't doubt that scientists will discover it's better for you, too. Cooks tell us that food tastes better when cooked with love. And that's true for how it's eaten. Food is love. You are *how* you eat.

A traditional Buddhist meditation of thanks before eating is the *Five Contemplations*. The general outline of it goes like this:

➤ **Regarding your food, consider all its ingredients and all the moves they took to come from farm to fork.** Consider the roundness of your plate as encircling the whole universe, and the food within it as its messenger. Be compassionate for the suffering *and* joy that brought it to your plate, the farmers', the truckers', the grocers', plus those who have not.

➤ **Regard your meal and vow to be worthy of it.** Being worthy of your food means eating it mindfully. Eating a carrot, eat a carrot; don't chew unresolved tensions or anticipated pleasures or anything else but the carrot buddha nourishing your own buddhahood in the present moment.

➤ **Look at how much food there is and vow not to be greedy (that old enemy greed).** Eat in moderation. Recognize there's a point beyond satisfaction where eating becomes greed. Also practice equanimity. Don't identify your personal likes and dislikes. This means that even if you're a vegetarian, you'll eat meat if it's offered.

➤ **Consider your food as good medicine.** Considering food as medicine means treating food as more than a comfort. Notice its *chi,* its life-force. Be mindful that food can help cause health or illness. Be mindful of what is and isn't healthy. (I think many people eat fries because they know they're not healthy.) And from considering food as a gift from the *whole universe,* to being a matter of *health,* it's only a hop to …

➤ **Vow to eat that you may realize the Way.** From considering food as a gift from the *whole universe,* to being a matter of *health,* it's only a hop to food as *holy.* See your meals as an essential part of your journey of awakening.

As the aroma of your meal wafts in your nostrils and you contemplate it in these five ways, try joining your palms, in gassho, bowing to the food and all it contains. Like you, food has buddha nature, too: asparagus buddhas, broccoli buddhas, carrot buddhas …

Actually, it's nice to dedicate a blessing, prayer, invocation, or gatha before *and* after a meal. In Judaism, for example, we give thanks for the food before us, and afterward we give thanks for the food within us. An appropriate Buddhist after-meal prayer can be the Bodhisattva Vow. Another might be to generate and send metta. Here's a fine model Donald Altman includes in his book *Art of the Inner Meal* which you can modify however feels right for you:

Hear and Now

A farmer hoes his rice
in the noonday glare;
I see his sweat dripping down
in big drops to the soil.
Ah! for the meal in your bowl,
don't you care
that each small grain
cost the farmer bitter toil?

— Li Shen (T'ang dynasty)

May all beings be free from pain, hunger, and suffering. May all beings live long and be healthy. May all beings receive physical nourishment, well-being, and spiritual awareness through food. May all beings experience lovingkindness and serve others with compassion.

This Is

Organic food is raised and processed without harmful chemicals such as pesticides, irradiation, or genetic engineering. (**Genetic engineering [GE]** modifies cell information, transferring genes of one organism into another. In 1999, 25 percent of American cropland was devoted to GE foods: 35 percent of corn and 55 percent of soybeans. 60 to 70 percent of supermarket foods contain GE food. Cattle are being treated with GE hormones. The Food and Drug Administration deems such food "substantially equivalent" to conventional food, so doesn't require mandatory labeling.)

Mindful Meals

As you now know, meditation doesn't begin or end on a cushion. Have you tried mindful noting during your daily life yet, as sketched in Chapter 11, "Look Within and Know: Insight Meditation *(Vipassana)*"? Eating is good occasion for it. Or should I say "the process of eating"? Each mouthful can be a self-contained world, akin to the birth, growth, and flare out of a galaxy. (Someone once asked Suzuki Roshi what nirvana was and he replied, "Following each thing through to the end.")

Consider just one bite. Imagine we're mindfully tuning in to bread, for example, noting: "eye looking at bread" ... "intention to eat bread" ... "hand breaking bread" ... "seeing texture and color and shape" ... "considering and visualizing ingredients and their origins" ... "smelling bread" ... "noticing salivation" ... "hand lifting bread to mouth" ... "opening the mouth" ... "lips taking bread" ... "lowering the arm" ... "tongue taking bread" ... "mouth feeling texture of bread" ... "front teeth chopping bread" ... "molars grinding bread" ... "flavor of bread" ... "bread softening with saliva" ... "bread releasing sweetness in mouth" ... "bread mostly liquid, with little crumbs" ... "bread all liquidy" ... "taste disappearing" ... "noticing impulse to swallow" ... ... And all the while—following breath(!). As with walking meditation, this might best be approached by beginners in slow motion.

Eating mindfully, let the flow of events come to an end. Then, do you lift your hand again, out of habit? Or do you *intend* to do each action before you do it? And do you follow through each mouthful swallowed, staying with the food and feeling it travelling down your throat? Supposedly, there aren't taste buds past your throat, but if I know my tummy, it has a range of signals it can send, like "warm," "sour," and even shadings like "pepperminty." After that, do you remain alert to feelings? Do food sensations spark desires? Do desires create intentions in your mind? Does your mind act on intentions by causing bodily movements? Check them out. Take note. Be mindful.

Leaves from the Bodhi Tree

Jack Kornfield teaches a meditation in which participants mindfully note the process of eating one raisin: It takes about 10 minutes. Likewise, Thich Nhat Hanh suggests an orange as meditation: being aware of each slice, rather than peeling while eating, and so on. And zen chef and author Edward Espe Brown has led a meditation on eating one potato chip, one orange slice, and one Hydrox cookie, each, "attentively in silence." His students have discovered that one potato chip wasn't satisfying (maybe why people crave more). Everyone loved the orange. And about half the participants couldn't even finish the Hydrox cookie! (See for yourself.)

By tuning in to the whole chain of mini-events, desire-as-craving-as-self becomes transparent, seen as a kind of fictional device ("Wow, am *I* hungry!"), telling a story not present in the immediate situation (such as food as reward, as failure, as security, as identity, as guilt, as blame, as shame, etc.). In truth, there's only a series of present-moment events, none with any intrinsic identity, and none like any other.

Just as breathing naturally slows under the lens of mindfulness, so, too, does hunger die down sooner when eating mindfully. We discover we can make do with less. We're no longer feeding abstract desires. We're directly experiencing through the evidence of our own senses the miraculous reality of food. And it's enough.

Leaves from the Bodhi Tree

The Buddha once told the parable of a man walking across a field who saw a big tiger. He ran, and the tiger chased him. He came to a cliff. He caught hold of the root of a wild vine and swung over the edge. The tiger sniffed at him from above. Trembling, the man looked down and saw another tiger, far below, waiting to eat him. Meanwhile, two mice, one black and one white, came and started to nibble at the vine that sustained him. Just then, the man saw a strawberry growing within reach. He plucked it. How sweet it tasted!

Lifting an Elbow Together

Eating mindfully *in company* magnifies the joy. But according to some reports, as much of a third of American families don't eat together. Here might be another root of our national eating disorders, as countries with more eating rituals have fewer disorders. And, difficult as it might seem at first, eating together in silence can be a way of sharing appreciation of being, and being together, in marvelous ways that words cannot express.

To keep you from wavering, here are five mindful tips:

➤ Don't read or watch TV while you eat. Just eat while you eat.

➤ Be mindful of your breathing and your body. Sit up straight, shoulders back, lower back curved, soles of your feet firmly upon the earth.

➤ Chew each mouthful through to the end, whether that means 30 times or a hundred. (Mixing food with saliva has a health benefit, as well: it can begin the digestive process in your mouth, taking a load off other digestive organs.)

➤ In the middle of your meal, stop. See if you're still mindful of your breathing, or whether you're escaping into the act of eating.

➤ What about the last spoonful? Enjoy it as fully as the entire meal. Or set it aside and contemplate practicing charity with those who have not. Or save it for compost, if you garden.

Even if it's your one meditation amid a busy schedule, betwixt life's bumpy roads, the oasis of a mindful meal can keep you on the path of peace.

Along the Path

"The ritual of coming to the dinner table was once the very basis of community."

—Alice Waters

"Let the progress of the meal be slow, for dinner is the last business of the day; and let the guests conduct themselves like travelers due to reach their destination together."

—Jean Anthelme Brillat-Savarin

Recipes for Peace: Increasing Food Awareness

Whether it's a matter of growing or just making your own food, or knowing more about nutrition, increasing your food awareness is another recipe for mindful meals. This means being conscious of good ingredients, fresh produce, and a balanced diet. For example, many Americans are addicted to either fat, salt, or sweets. If this is you, then please realize that it will take some time once you've weaned yourself off your habit before other foods begin to taste right.

Along the Path

"Bread makes itself, by your kindness, with your help, with imagination streaming through you, with dough under hand, you are breadmaking itself, which is why breadmaking is so fulfilling and rewarding."

—Edward Espe Brown, *The Tassajara Bread Book*

"Once you know how the dough becomes bread, you will understand enlightenment."

—Shunryu Suzuki Roshi

Maybe your extra dosage of fat, salt, or sweets come from prepared foods, which typically use these substances. (Do you read labels carefully?) There's nothing like being able to make your own food. (But ... is that Buddhist? Heck, yes.) Being self-reliant, seeing for yourself, getting to the source—these are all Buddhist virtues we tap into when we cook.

If you're worrying about pesticides in your foods or genetically modified crops, poverty, or the increasing lack of diversity of species (well, the list seems endless), I have a modest proposal: Bake bread.

Bread is one of the greatest inventions in the universe. Yet how many people have discovered this miracle? When's the last time you've walked into a room, not to mention your own home, and inhaled the sweet, earthy fragrance of freshly baked bread?

Take the most basic bread recipe from a basic cooking book. The ingredients are yeast, flour, something sweet to get the yeast going. You'll need a greased baking pan, and a flat space with enough elbow room for kneading. If you don't have a kitchen, your nearby church or YMCA has one and would welcome a freshly baked loaf. You don't have to complicate the plot by considering milling your own flour, or putting up preserves or making your own butter, to go with your bread—though those are options, too. But with just a humble loaf, you can practice mindful eating at its most sublime.

I won't push my recipe for brown rice on you. When I just say the word people shudder and run away, remembering the nuts and hard bread and wriggly green things of the 1960s. I'll admit, it's the first thing I learned to cook, but I also make polenta, couscous, millet, and barley. More importantly, I eat a balanced diet (such as *grains*, *greens*, and *beans*). So what I'm really recommending is that you invest some time into researching calories and a balanced diet. Include patience, joy, intimacy, and learning from mistakes. (Sit for 20 minutes, and enjoy.)

Hear and Now

"I take leftover whey out to the chickens who slurp it up contentedly. It's full of nutrients that flow into the eggs, the composted chicken and cow manure go into the garden to flow into the vegetables. ... Simple miracles. Satisfying work, like baking bread or building a shelf. Fresh, delicious food. Nutrient cycles close right at hand. Health for land and people. Sometimes I wonder with all our supposed progress, what we're rushing toward and what we're leaving behind."

—Donella Meadows, on home cheese-making on her farm

So take time to cook. And eat fresh. Patronize small farmers if you can. (When's the last time you actually visualized a farmer's sunburned face and hands as you ate the food he grew?) Farmers can tell you exactly what they're selling, and many have a variety not found in stores. When's the last time you tried a Jonathan Spy apple, a Blenham apricot, or a Chandler strawberry? It was getting kind of critical with apples not too long ago, with only one red and one green on the shelves. At one time, there were 500 different kinds of apples in America. (Fortunately, there are seed savers out there.)

Moreover, when you buy produce from a farmer's market, you're bypassing the whole process of shipping and freezing and storage that food goes through commercially. Buying direct, you're taking home a fully realized Buddha that needs nothing else but a little steaming or baking (don't overcook), plus hearty, mindful appreciation. If it's been in the refrigerator for two or three days, then you might need to fix it up a little, with recipes and whatnot.

Don't have a farmer's market near you? How about a community garden? Don't have a community garden? How about a backyard patch or unused empty lot?

Work well spent, not to mention the money you'll save—speaking of which …

Balancing Spirituality and Materiality: Awakened Work

Having been raised in a palace, the Buddha knew the value of money; having attained enlightenment in a forest, he also knew values apart from money. The Middle Way he found teaches us how to deal with the quest for the greatest good and the thirst for the greatest goods. Here are some key points culled from various interoffice memos and scrolls from the desk of … the Buddha.

Bringing the Buddha to Work

Just as we can make a space in our lives to have a mindful meal at home, so can we bring our practice to where we work. This means far more than an altar by your desk (optional). Stake out your turf. Find breathing room. Where can you go sit for ten minutes, undisturbed? Would walking meditation work better for you?

Practice isn't confined to your breaks. Giving each task your undivided, mindful attention, you'll find your energy's reinvigorated, not exhausted. One-pointed concentration gets more done in a day than if you begin by dividing tasks into those things you like and those you don't.

So much for things, but what about people? Be mindful when you feel yourself caught in an uncomfortable emotion. Stepping aside for a moment allows you the space to let go of the negative charge, and respond with clarity.

Leaves from the Bodhi Tree

In Vajrayana, every profession has its symbolic Buddhist interpretation. In Tibetan legend, a plain cobbler named Camaripta begged a Buddhist monk to teach him the way of the Buddha. The monk suggested he transform himself as he changed leather into a shoe: identifying his desires and conceptualizations (the roots of bondage) with the leather—placing it on the mould of friendliness and compassion (two immeasurables)—and piercing it with the awl of his guru's instructions (an instrument by which ordinary life is penetrated)—then, with the thread of equanimity, sewing together appearance and boundless reality with the needle of mindfulness—and, with the needle of compassion, clothing the beings of the world (in Buddha's body of the Dharma). Over time, the cobbler became a perfectly realized master of enlightenment.

It would be wonderful if your workmates were on the same path. You could all bow to a bell in the morning, share silent mindful meals or walking meditation breaks, and learn from disagreements to keep the sangha moving in the same direction. There's an emergency ward of a Northern California hospital where various members practice mindfulness; above the ER door handles are a note with one word: Breathe.

It's also wonderful just to keep up your own practice at work and watch the level of your work rise and maybe others' consciousness as well. The Four Noble Truths apply to everyone else as well as you. Any workplace is also a mindfulness classroom in awareness, wisdom, and compassion.

Chop Water, Carry Wood: Working to Live

A common misconception of the Buddhist is as a ne'er-do-well beggar in robes. Actually, I've worked in places where the people getting the handouts wore suits and ties while the rest of us worker bees had to buy our lunches. But, like they say, there's no free lunch.

It's true, the monastic tradition established by the Buddha has the core sangha live on the charitable generosity of the community. The bowl in the Buddha's lap is the begging bowl. In southeast Asia today, monks and nuns are still forbidden from working or even handling money. However, with its flair for creative innovation, Zen introduced the idea of monasteries being self-sufficient. T'ang dynasty Zen master Pai Chang Huai-hai, who established Zen monastic tradition, did heavy labor every day, even into old age. The monks, feeling sorry for him, tried hiding his tools. That day he refused to eat, saying, "I'm without virtue: why should others work for me?"

Hear and Now

"If you really think about what work is you see that everything is work—being alive and in a body is already work. Every day there is eating and shitting and cleaning up. There is brushing and bathing and flossing. Every day there is thinking and caring and creating. So there's no escape from work—its everywhere. For Zen students there's no work time and leisure time; there's just lifetime, daytime and nighttime. Work is something deep and dignified—it's what we are born to do and what we feel most fulfilled in doing."

—Norman Fischer

Liang K'ai (1140–1210). The Sixth Patriarch Cutting Bamboo (detail). Early Thirteenth Century. Hui Neng was a working man, even after he became the Sixth Patriarch. Indeed, he reached enlightenment while working. He's depicted here by a Chinese Zen monk whose strokes of ink are as vigorous, quick, and incisive as chopping bamboo.

(Tokyo National Museum)

Zen Enterprise

Striking examples of how Zen finds its way in America can be found in its enterprises. Two involve our old friend food. For example, the San Francisco Zen Center established a monastery on a mountain property that had been a hot springs resort. By renting out the guest houses in the summer, it supported itself. But so many guests wanted to take home a loaf of their home-baked bread that they also started a bakery in the city. That led, in 1970, to a book of recipes, *The Tassajara Bread Book*, a shot heard round the world, sparking a national revival of homemade bread, as well as locally produced organic cuisine. The Zen Center grew more businesses, organically, including a restaurant called Greens, which has survived 20 years in San Francisco's highly competitive gourmet arena, and produced two more best-selling, influential cookbooks.

Along the Path

"A day without work, a day without food."

—Pai Chang Huai-hai (720–814)

"If anyone will not work, neither let him eat."

—Thessalonians 3:10

"Before enlightenment you chop wood and carry water, after enlightenment you chop wood and carry water."

—Zen saying

Here's another example. On the East Coast, a Zen Buddhist meditation group led by a one-time aerospace engineer, Bernard Tetsugen Glassman, borrowed $300,000 in 1982 to open a small storefront bakery called Greyston. He was influenced by Tassajara's zen bakery but emphasized gourmet pastries, enabling the company to stay competitive but small. Today, they're building a socially responsible mini-conglomerate which they call a mandala (a circle, symbolic of the unity and interdependence of life), one that uniquely combines a for-profit business with nonprofit social services, interfaith programs, and alliances with the community. The bakery now generates more than $3.5 million in revenues and employs 55 people. They run an inn which provides housing and support for about 27 homeless families, job training and placement services, day care for up to 50 kids, and an HIV/AIDS support community.

Ed Espe Brown, former cook at Tassajara Monastery and co-founder of Greens restaurant; author of The Tassajara Bread Book *and* Tomato Blessings and Radish Teachings, *and co-author of* The Greens Cookbook. *His intensive work is like sublime play. As we can see, even the tools for making good food are music to his ears.*

(Photo: Butch Baluyut)

One more example. In 1985, a monk named Arnold Kotler at the San Francisco Zen Center started a publishing company, called Parallax Press, with loans from his family and friends. His first and primary author was the then-unknown Thich Nhat Hanh, who'd become his teacher. He edited the Venerable Nhat Hanh's talks into a book, *Being Peace*, which went on to sell several hundred thousand copies.

Hear and Now

"The Buddhist point of view takes the function of work to be at least threefold: to give a man a chance to utilize and develop his faculties; to enable him to overcome his ego-centeredness by joining with other people in a common task; and to bring forth the goods and services needed for a becoming existence."

—E. F. Schumacher, *Small Is Beautiful*

Moreover, the publishing house publishes what they practice. The staff practices mindfulness in the workplace, in the ways they talk to each other and deal with the world They offer incense every morning and recite a gatha together to start the day. When the phone rings, they hear that as a mindfulness bell, stop and breathe consciously three times before someone answers it. (In the interests of full disclosure, I should add they published a book of mine, an anthology called *What Book!?—Buddha Poems from Beat to Hiphop*, which couldn't have been done by most any other publisher in America. In 1999, the book was honored with the American Book Award, and it's now in its third printing, so I'd say it's a success.)

So if you follow your heart, and your zen ethics, the money will follow. There's nothing to making money, if that's all you want to make. Here's more on making peace ...

"Small Is Beautiful": Economics from the Heart

Small is beautiful. The phrase is now 30 years old. Actually, it was the title of a book by E. F. Schumacher, rallying for *human scale, sustainability, appropriate technologies* (skillful means applied to industry), and *decentralization.*

Sustainability can be defined by the Cherokee philosophy of judging the merits of an action in terms of its impact on seven generations. Today we might say long-term planning over short-term gain. As Gandhi said, "There is enough in this world for everyone's need, but not enough for everyone's greed." What are the limits of growth, what is enough? There's nothing Buddhist about passing the cost of unlimited expansion on to generations further along in the century.

Size matters. Success needn't mean the biggest market share. Taiwan, for example, is an economic success story built primarily of small businesses. We may not think about it, but half of America's businesses are small as well. Now, working from home is becoming more and more of an option, a workforce unit of one. The recognition here is that the larger the company, the more likely it is for everything it comes into contact with to be stained with exploitation and greed, its people less valuable than its products, and the bottom line outweighing the human factors.

Living lower on the food chain, as it were, realizes "the maximum of well-being with the minimum of consumption." Being aware of the necessities of life (food, shelter, clothing, and community) values creativity rather than number of products consumed. Creativity's one of our greatest wealths; it has no price tag.

Beyond the Ladder: Decentralization and Self-Organization

Traditional businesses are modeled on the hierarchical model of maximum power filtering down from a centralized point. A *decentralized* model is more like a network of units creating power bottom-up, a whole greater than the sum of its parts. The components add value to each other's services, and the fluidity keeps it all adaptive to change. Another thing about such decentralized systems is that they tend to be self-organizing. (We'll explore the scientific aspects in Chapter 18, "The World Within and Without: Buddhism and the Sciences.") This is also Buddhist not only in its respect for autonomy and realization of the value of interaction. Self-organizing businesses can remain small yet build quite large webs of interactions.

Case in point: VISA. Guess what: VISA has no central bank. Rather, VISA's owned by 22,000 member banks, who *compete* for 750 million customers, but *cooperate* honoring one another's $1.25 trillion in transactions, crossing countless borders and currencies. (Competition becomes "co-opetition," realizing we're all in this together.) Here's a viable Middle Way for working in between chaos and order. VISA founder Dee Hock calls it *chaordic.* Clearly it works, and in some ways better than organizations based on command and control.

Another fascinating example of a self-organizing business system comes from China, where Marxism's been colliding with free markets (and Buddhism's making a comeback). For major transactions, the current banking system is too clunky, taking as long as a month for a check to clear. So payments are often drawn from deposits in a credit card account. A credit card account verifies funds on hand immediately and transfers them immediately. So in China MasterCard's been transformed into a virtual, parallel banking system, and is worth about $73 billion. No plan, it just happened! Self-organization in action. Awakening of mind, all by itself.

What's to Lose? What's to Gain?

But what if it doesn't work? Ah, when the pursuit of money becomes a national religion, then the dreaded "F" word (failure) comes up, but in the hushed tones reserved for talking about freak lightning storms, plane crashes, and other unspeakable tragedies. Yet success and failure are dualistic criteria, external evaluations. Real values come from the heart, and inevitably prevail. But, like enlightenment, or gardening, fruition takes effort.

Case in point: Siddhartha walked away from ruling an entire empire. Offered a good position with the supreme yogis of his day, he said no because he still wasn't satisfied inside. Soon even his few forest companions walked away from him, because he seemed unable to meet the challenges. Was he a failure? His achievements influenced the entire world.

No one knows the Magic Recipe for Success. One thing is sure: defeat inevitably comes when we label choices in terms of success/failure, boring/exciting, work/play, me/them, and so on. Investing in a dualistic outlook is setting ourselves up for a fall. So when our workmates seem like enemies—then it's time for compassion in action, starting with ourselves. Here's how.

Is Compassion a Job Review Criterion?

Does your boss get your goat? Note your feelings, don't identify with them. Generate metta, lovingkindness, toward him or her. You might also practice *tonglen*.

Tonglen (Tibetan, literally "give and take"), seen briefly in Chapter 13, "Paths of Devotion and Transformation: Pure Land and Vajrayana Buddhism," can be a way of exchanging your energies with someone who seems to exert a negative presence in your path, and neutralizing the problem. As we've seen, tantra embraces and transforms life's trials and tribulations rather than trying to abolish them. The workplace can provide on-the-spot occasions for practice.

Let's say you're riding up the elevator at work and you're jammed in next to your department supervisor, who pushes all your buttons. Normally you might start to clench your muscles to repress your rage, or beat yourself up for feeling trapped in the same elevator with her: don't go there. Recognize the unexpected as a koan. Deal with the moment as a meditation.

Identify your stress and breathe it in. Whether it's a feeling of inadequacy, reducing you to something tiny as a mouse, or a fear of speaking out, like a mouse afraid of the cat, or an anger you think could flatten the entire city into a pancake, let it go. That stress, that pain, that anger or that fear, right now has the sound of her voice, the fragrance of her perfume. Now imagine that voice, that odor, and that presence is a cloud of hot, dark vapors. As you breathe this cloud in, let it make contact with your undifferentiated, timeless mind, your luminous, boundless heart, which isn't upset by anything, and exhale with relief, visualizing your out-breath as a fresh, bright, clear ray of light. Give your blessings to life.

Actually, you don't have to wait for an elevator to practice this; you can do it at home. Full tonglen takes a series of progressions not unlike metta meditation. Now, in an elevator, you might miss your stop if you begin with yourself and extend out to the supervisor, then other office workers, and from there to everyone in the building, all the citizens of your city, and all the sadness, pain, and negativity of the whole world. But, hey, once you've practiced tonglen, you'll be able to conduct an abbreviated run-through (sort of Tonglen-to-Go).

Your annoying, nagging, and seemingly uncontrollable quirks, stresses, and pains, and those of others around you, and all the world's nasty, vicious, unjustified suffering and anguish, transmuted into warm, compassionate, radiant white light, bliss energy, much metta, and good karma. What better way to start your day?

Whatever the ingredients of your practice, work is certainly a good kettle for keeping them brewing. Whatever your profession, you could think of it as being like the tea ceremony, with its utensils, its guests, and its essential ingredients. The whole universe is manifest in this moment now at your table. En-JOY!

Along the Path

"If you think you can't, why think?"

—Dee Hock

"Everything you need you already have. You are complete right now. You are a whole, total person, not an apprentice person on the way to some place else."

—Wayne Dyer

"Whatever you can do or dream you can begin it."

—Goethe

The Least You Need to Know

➤ The tea ceremony is more than a culinary art: It is a way of life, with lessons we all can enjoy.

➤ Giving thanks to food is a universal and primary spiritual practice. Enjoying a meal is an opportunity for active meditation, as is being food conscious, preparing your own food, and just washing the dishes.

➤ Work is a fact of life. As the Zen saying goes: "Before enlightenment you chop wood and carry water, after enlightenment you chop wood and carry water."

➤ Work is yet another opportunity to practice mindfulness. Mindfulness practices can be beneficial to your work.

➤ Be aware of people as well as products. In the human scale, size matters. Decentralization is another way to consider the work environment.

➤ Sometimes work can create situations calling for "on-the-spot" practice.

Chapter 16

Everybody's Doing It: Buddhism and Popular Culture

In This Chapter

➤ Buddha at the movies

➤ Buddhist soul music

➤ Flower power and garden gurus

➤ The inner game of martial arts and sports

What is art? What isn't! Everything we do (and don't do) has its art. Somewhere along the line, however, somebody sorted and divided everything into two heaps, "high" and "low" ("fine" and "popular"). It was a political thing, I guess, but hey, that's another story.

This boundary's unwritten, but as divisive as that between East and West. So, if you're studying Shakespeare, da Vinci, or Beethoven, there are walls of books for study. But arts of haiku and tanka, tangka and sumi-e, shakuhachi and the Tibetan Dance of the Skeleton Lords have been relatively unknown in the West. Interestingly, their ultimate purpose is to go beyond words, putting us in direct contact with reality, in the here and now. No need for walls of books. (What else can we say?!)

Call them skillful means. Vehicles of the Way. Opportunities for awakening mind and heart, and for expressing that awakening. In that sense, Buddhist arts are all popular arts: anyone can appreciate them. As in any art, appreciation is amplified by understanding the basic recipes, the formal game rules. But first, pick your art form. In Japanese, *"do"* means way, and it applies to *chado* (tea way), *chikudo* (bamboo way), *kado* (flower way), and *kyudo* (archery way). And so we hear now, too, about the Way of Pooh and the zen of changing diapers. Indeed, where's the museum of things that *aren't* art?! Where's the temple of things *not* to worship?! It's all meditation—which is an art.

Mind Mirror: Buddha at the Movies

The most popular and unique art form of the twentieth century was ... movies! Nothing goes around the world like a ticket to the movies. A truly universal language. But ... is it Buddhist?!

Now Playing: Film as Buddhist

Burmese meditation master Sayadaw U Pandita notes that when we watch a movie, the process can be like insight meditation. Each has four phases:

1. Appearance of object
2. Directing of attention
3. Close observation
4. Understanding

In insight meditation, 1) we focus attention on our belly, which leads to 2) appearance of rising and falling of the abdomen, followed by 3) distinguishing the process by noting, then 4) discovering special characteristics and how they actually behave.

Watching a movie, 1) we focus attention on the screen, which leads to 2) appearance of characters and scenes, followed by 3) making out what's happening by observing carefully, then 4) discovering the plot and appreciating the movie.

And film fiction is usually a neatly patterned karma tale. For an interesting meditation sometime, buy a ticket to a movie you otherwise don't care about and walk in on the middle (at a multiplex this is easy to do). Then stay for the beginning: You'll see how everything that happened in the second half was a result of the characters' actions in the first half. (You can also do this at home, fast-forwarding into the middle, starting from there, then returning to the beginning.)

Moviegoing's also a good example of the illusory nature of the unexamined life. We sit in a *theater* without thinking of the projection booth, where the images come from; instead, we take what we're seeing for reality. So it is with the projections of our own minds.

Next we add compassion and maybe even a little bodhisattva vow, hoping that it all turns out okay, and we identify with the characters. Without compassion, we'd be aware we're sitting in our chairs the entire time. But with compassion, we become one with other people. And this is part of the fun of watching movies: sitting there in our jeans and T-shirt, and at the same time being superstars, 33-feet tall, and shifting back and forth between the two. ("What a *kiss!* I'm going to get some popcorn, want some?")

This Is

In ancient Greece, the community went to the big local outdoor amphitheater to watch the rite of theater. Everyone, nobles and slaves together. The actors wore big masks called **persona,** with resonant little voice boxes inside to project their voice. Thus, when we say "So-and-So's a *real* person," we're saying we really like his or her mask. In a zen-based dance-theater called **Noh,** wooden masks even change expressions with different angles of light.

If we stop to think about this further, we see that when we're engrossed in a movie our ability to exchange our self with others' reveals the basic insubstantiality of the self with which we identify. This is how a great actor such as Laurence Olivier could say, late in life, acting didn't teach him to "get in touch with himself" but, rather, it taught him how he'd no idea who he was, really, having realized his heart's potential for being so many different people. Drama teaches that given the circumstances we could change who we thought we were in a second. There but for fortune go you or I.

We never think about these things at the movies. That's part of the open secret. We don't question it because, deep down, we're afraid that if we become conscious of the process we won't enjoy the magic anymore—as if the movie and life itself were something outside of ourselves, from which we might get permanently disconnected, like falling off the edge of the earth.

In this light, Buddhism is a radical form of independent cinema, if you will. Who needs a movie screen when you can settle in on your cushion, and look into your own mind screen?

Tibetan Buddhism, especially, emphasizes visualization mediations, empowering us to realize our unity with sacred energies by identifying with pictorial images of deities—and then recognizing their intrinsic emptiness. Who needs painting with light when we can recognize that we are bodies of light on the mandala of Indra's Net?! For example, here's a Tibetan body of light meditation, slightly shortened from Kathleen McDonald's *How to Meditate* (Wisdom Publications, 1984):

Sit comfortably, with your back straight, and breathe naturally. When your mind is calm and clear, visualize in the space above your head a sphere of white light, somewhat smaller than the size of your head, and pure, transparent, and formless. ... Contemplate that the sphere of light represents all universal goodness, love, and wisdom: the fulfillment of your own highest potential. Then visualize that it decreases in size until it is about one inch in diameter and descends through the top of your head to your heart-center. From there it begins to expand once more, slowly spreading to fill your entire body. As it does, all the solid parts of your body dissolve and become light—your organs, bones, blood vessels, tissue, and skin all become pure, formless white light.

... Think that all problems, negativities, and hindrances have completely vanished, and that you have reached a state of wholeness and perfection. Feel serene and joyful. If any thought of a distracting object should appear in your mind, let it also dissolve into white light. Meditate in this way for as long as you can.

Along the Path

"... the metaphor of movie for life is an interesting one. The frames go by so quickly that we retain the illusion of continuity and are distracted from the light that shines steadily through each frame."

—Robert Aitken Roshi

"... If you want to enjoy the movie, you should know that it is the combination of film and light and white screen, and that the most important thing is to have a plain, white screen."

—Shunryu Suzuki Roshi, *Our Everyday Life Is Like a Movie*

Cinema also provides a metaphor for reality's Eternal Now. I remember I once sat behind a five-year-old and an adult at a matinee, and every ten minutes or so the kid would ask the adult, "What's happening now?" and the adult would answer, "Now they're getting to know each other." Or "Now they're going to get married." Or "Now they're on their honeymoon." If you think about it, every moment in a movie is always about "now." Continuous present tense. And it can be elastic, instead of clock time: 10 minutes compressed into 3, or 3 stretched out into 10 (very reminiscent of quite a few sitting meditations I've had). Indeed, the more familiar we become with the eternal nowness of our lives, the more we see their elasticity.

Our minds are elastic in the same way. A good analogy is space. As with time, cinematic space is always breaking the ancient Aristotelian Unity of Time and Place (everything happening fixed in "real time") and opening out space like a jigsaw puzzle: one minute we're in her house, then his house, then outside, then inside a kitchen cabinet looking out, then outside looking in. So, as audiences, we're experiencing our own mind's vast space-without-particular-locality. (The person who keeps track of all this, the director, gets to play God: felt everywhere but nowhere to be seen. We can substitute "Buddha mind" for "God.")

Most of this holds for TV, too, which speaks the grammar of cinema only on a much tighter scale. So is *The Six O'Clock News* Buddhist? *Gone with the Wind? Blade Runner?*

Is Gone with the Wind *About Impermanence?*: Buddhist Films

Films intended to illustrate or convey Dharma are obviously Buddhist. My personal favorite Definitely Buddhist Film has a longish title, *Why Has Bodhidharma Left for the East?* a koan which is asking, in effect, "What, if anything, is the meaning of Zen?" For the first 10 minutes, we see a young man disengage himself from the suffering of city life and make his way to a remote Korean mountain monastery. Then the first words we finally hear are, "There is no beginning, no middle, no end." Loosely based on a famous series of 10 zen paintings called the oxherding pictures, it took the producer-writer-director-editor five years to put this intimate spiritual epic together, and it's deservedly made it to the top of many Top Ten lists since. The *2001* of zen films. G. G. says "Check it out."

In this moment from Why Has Bodhidharma Left for the East? *I wonder if sunyata, boundlessness, has cracked, revealing the fertile blackness within it, or are those people and trees standing against the sky?*

(Photo: Courtesy of Milestone Film & Video, New Jersey)

Leaves from the Bodhi Tree

More films of Buddhist interest include *Afterlife* (1998), *Caravan* (a.k.a. *Himalaya*) (1999), *Enlightenment Guaranteed* (2000), *Fearless* (1993), *Heaven and Earth* (1993), *Mandala* (1981), *The Razor's Edge* (1946 and 1984), *Storm over Asia* (1928), and *The Way of the Lotus* (1987).

There are also documentaries, such as *The Jew in the Lotus* (1996), *Jews and Buddhism: Belief Amended, Faith Revealed* (1999), *Genghis Blues* (1999), *The Saltmen of Tibet* (1998), *Regret to Inform* (2000), and Ellen Bruno's films about Tibetan, Burmese/Thai, and Cambodian women (*Satya*, *Sacrifice*, and *Samsara*).

In *The Burmese Harp* (1956), a Japanese soldier is injured in Burma at the end of World War II. As a Buddhist monk takes care of him, we see Theravadan practices in Burma, and he returns to his unit in Buddhist robes. Compassionate action is offered as a response to the struggle to find spiritual meaning in the destruction wrought by modern war. In the films of Yasujiro Ozu, however, the Buddhism's implied rather than explicit. A character doesn't experience a climax in their narrative so much as undergo a subtle change that enables them to appreciate the suchness of things.

Non-Buddhist films with Buddhist themes include *It's a Wonderful Life,* showing us how each person affects everyone else, and *Groundhog Day* (1993), in which a man relives the same day 10,000 times until he gets it right. And we mustn't forget *Rashomon* (1950), in which we see the same tale told from different points of view.

George Lucas refused to specify whether The Force referred to by Yoda in *Star Wars* stands for the Tao, the Holy Spirit, Buddha-mind, etc., or whether Luke Skywalker's journey represented the Buddha's. After all, the motto in Hollywood used to be, "If you want to send a message, use Western Union." Now there are more and more spiritually based films, often nondenominational though often seasoned with violence served piping hot.

Certainly recent films about Tibet, such as *Seven Years in Tibet* (1997), *Kundun* (1998), and *Windhorse* (1999), have come a long way from the Hollywood moonshine stereotypes of *Lost Horizon* (1937), whose inaccuracies must have involved enormous research. From Bhutan, *The Cup* (2000) was the first film made by a Tibetan lama. Bernardo Bertolucci's *Little Buddha* (1993) intercut the life of the Buddha with a contemporary boy who might be a reincarnated lama. A little more single-mindedly,

John Boorman's *Beyond Rangoon* (1995) tackles the Burmese democracy movement by showing it from the point of view of a vacationing American nurse (Patricia Arquette), who gradually transcends her narrow boundaries of self and pitches in.

For filmmakers, new technology is raising the bar to entry. It's relatively easy to shoot a video, edit it on a home computer, and put it up on a Web site. As the media octopus expands, I hope it's not idle speculation to anticipate the eventual reality of a Buddhist TV channel, as there is in Korea and Amsterdam. I want my B-TV!

Play It Again, Samadhi!—Musical Meditation

Music may be the oldest of human arts, requiring only a hand beating on a knee, or a solo voice. And it's perennially new, being created in the present moment; as jazzman Eric Dolphy once said, "When you hear music, it's gone, in the air, and you can never capture it again."

Music's a present-ation, making present. So it's Buddhist to the degree it attunes us to the freedom and fullness of the present moment, and its impermanence.

Broaden your horizons. If you've never listened to World Music (sitar, African drums, flamenco, etc.), now's your chance. New rhythms, harmonies, melodies, and scales seem strange at first, then eventually familiar as an old friend from far away. Follow how a single note can slide, wander, and go boing in elastic, mind-bending ways. Let your body and soul become one big ear. Be one with the musicians and the music, feeling each note resonate in your heart. And with your hands in meditation, you offer silent applause every moment.

Each land has its own musical flavor. I find Korean music invigorating, for example, once you get accustomed to its tendency to zigzag like a hummingbird or dragonfly. Vietnamese chanting, such as recorded by the monks and nuns of Plum Village, is, to me, one of the most soulful sounds on the planet. But the dharma has one taste. Let's spotlight some traditional and some newer Buddhist examples.

Giving Buddhism Its Chants

Singing in the shower isn't exactly essential but just fun to do. A little icing on the cake of life. But why do you suppose we sound so good in the shower? Because the tiles create a little extra reverb. And that reverb is what human self-awareness is, really. Icing on the cake. Other living things have awareness, but we humans are aware that we're aware. Wired with an extra layer of filigree. An addition of cortex to our brains. Maybe that, too, is another reason why we like singing in the shower! The self-awareness factor.

Mindfulness Exercise #93: Listening to any music, follow your breath, and note how the music moves it, taking us out of ourselves and bringing us back.

In and of itself, music is a mystery. Where did it come from? Who knows. We just do it anyway, humming a little tune just because we like to hum. Maybe we're serenading the microorganisms. Joining the *music of the spheres*. Vocalizing the deep rhythms of life that surges in each cell of our protoplasm and throughout the galaxies.

This Is

The idea of the **music of the spheres** (a perfectly harmonious music, thought by Pythagoras and other philosophers to be produced by the movement of celestial bodies) may not be so far–fetched, now that we know that matter is really energy. Tibetan Buddhism has an ancient notion of **bija mantra,** "seed sounds," with physical properties when pronounced. A guru gives a student a special bija mantra upon initiation, but Om is a universal one, for example.

In this light, the Buddhist skillful means we've already mentioned that reverberate with the music of the spheres are deity invocation, recitation, and mantra practice. Whether it's the *Heart Sutra,* or the name of Amitabha Buddha or of the *Lotus Sutra,* chanting in community makes it even more powerful.

If you haven't heard Tibetan chanting before, check out the CD by the Gyuto Monks to get a sample of this unusually deep-toned vibrational resonance. The monks chant two octaves below C, a feat unrivalled in Western music. Such tones of low vibration travel farther and through more obstacles than high-frequency sound. Asian and African elephants communicate long-distance using this "silent thunder." Whales can communicate this way from Newfoundland to Puerto Rico (what might they be saying?). Actually, the monks chant so that you can hear the overtones in just one note—they're actually singing a chord! Sanskrit scholar and poet Andrew Schelling has described it as "craggy guttural prayer, like the sound of stones crumbling down a mountain precipice ... comforting to hear as your own mother's voice, but above that, almost on wings, a distinctly audible angel's tone, sublime as its originating note is terrifying."

Now, a common mantra exercise you can practice to center yourself is breathing in, and on the out-breath chanting "Aum." Feel its one syllable form three waves: ahhhh, as your breath releases, ooooouhh expressing your calm and peace, and sealing it off with your lips, mmmmmmm. Then do it again, slower, longer, calmer, and lower; then one more time. Over time, see if you can let the chant come from way back down deep in your throat and resonate in your belly. Close your eyes. Follow it with your mind.

Hear and Now

"Music is part of life, not separate from it, and life itself is musical, with its rhythms, variations on themes, episodes, fugues, counterpoints, cadences, silences, and tonalities. When we listen to music, we are contemplating the very structures and colours that make up our own lives."

—Thomas Moore

"After silence, that which comes nearest to expressing the inexpressible is Music."

—Aldous Huxley

Blowing Zen

The oldest wind instrument on the planet may be the Australian didjeridu, a long wooden trumpet whose continuous tradition dates back at least 30,000 years. Tibet has a similar-length horn made of copper, 10 feet long, said to represent the strength of the earth. It's often played with shorter horns representing the delicacy of the heavens, bringing these two forces into balance in the mind of the listener.

If the long horn's unique to Tibetan Buddhism, so is the Japanese flute called the *shakuhachi* truly zen. Made from the root of thick timber-strength bamboo, its sound is made by blowing perpendicularly across the end, rather than directly down into the flute. Just as it takes time to learn how to sit zen, or serve tea, or make one line with a bamboo brush, so with blowing one note on the shakuhachi: The hard-earned result, in both cases, can express the player's distinct signature. The sound is hauntingly like a voice and all its moods but, as with a rock garden, abstracted somehow.

Listening to shakuhachi, I wonder where else have I heard the sound of thunder echoing within precipitous peaks, the cry of distant deer, and the voices of cranes as the young ones leave the nest? The music is also reminiscent of haiku and zen brush scrolls, as well as Debussy's impressionism (evoking fireworks, goldfish, dancing snowflakes, gardens in the rain, and so on).

Rhythm isn't foot-stompingly obvious, but there's always a pulse or heart rhythm. There's a melodic line, but sometimes the notes seem placed at random, like an act of nature. Each note's variable, the listener's mind slows down to pay due attention to each one, and, like good jazz, you're continually surprised to find where it's going next. Just like life.

This Is

A Japanese word for "true feelings" or "real intentions" has two components, hon ne: "root"/"sound," inner voice. The Japanese word for meditative music, honkyoku, can mean the original tuning for a particular instrument, but can also be read as "sounds from the origin."

The word for the Japanese zen flute, shakuhachi, means 54.5 centimeters, referring to its length. The Japanese word for playing shakuhachi, suizen, means "blowing zen" (just as zazen means sitting zen). No duality: Sitting is zen, blowing is zen; it's all meditation.

Country 'n' Eastern, and Other Soundtracks

If you have the opportunity, go hear a live concert of shakuhachi or Tibetan chant, that's how such acoustic music's intended to be experienced. Meanwhile, everything's becoming available electronically, and the selection can be dizzying.

One of my favorite genres is country 'n' eastern, which is country 'n' western plus Eastern influences. Jimmy Dale Gilmore and Joe Ely are two good examples. My flat-footed favorite is Butch Hancock, composer of such mindful ditties as "My Mind's Got a Mind of Its Own" and "Just a Wave, Not the Ocean."

For your Buddhist listening pleasure, I heartily recommend two more composer-musicians who've both done double duty with soundtracks: Kitaro and Philip Glass. Shelved under "New Age" somewhere in between Enya and Yanni (say those two names together fast, three times), Japanese composer-musician Kitaro ("Man of Many Joys") interweaves traditional Eastern instruments with electronic synthesizers to make ever-unfolding, soundscapes to heartily, mindfully hum along to. I recommend *Mandala,* for starters.

On first listen, Philip Glass's music might sound like something's stuck. Actually, he weaves wonderful soundscapes out of very small, rhythmic, repeated haiku-like fragments. He has a huge body of work, but start anywhere: string quartets, violin concerto and symphonies, operas, and film scores. Listening to Glass is meditation.

So, to sum up: Sing in the shower. Join a choir or a recitation sangha. Serenade the spheres. Listen, and you shall hear. Stay tuned!

Along the Path

Contemporary lyrics with Buddhist meanings, intended or otherwise: the Beastie Boys' "Bodhisattva Vow" and "The Update," Steely Dan's "Bodhisattva" and "Roll Back the Meaning," Donovan's "The Way" and "The Evernow" (from *Sutras*), George and Ira Gershwin's "I've Got Plenty of Nothing," Joni Mitchell's "Both Sides Now," Malvina Reynolds's, "Where Have All the Flowers Gone?" John Lennon's "Imagine," Lennon and McCartney's "Give Peace a Chance," Natalie Merchant's "All I Want," Alanis Morisette's "All I Really Want," REM's "Everybody Hurts," Patti Smith and Tom Shanrahan's "1959," and Van Morrison's "Hymns to the Silence."

A Gift from a Flower to a Garden

In the neighborhood in Los Angeles where I grew up, there was a Japanese movie theater where I spent some time. One thing that impressed me, in my many armchair travels to the countryside of Japan via film, was the way windows worked over there, as if most of an entire wall slid open. This way, the garden isn't only an extension of the house: The house is also a gift from the garden. I'd grown up also seeing Modernist buildings merging inside and outside, such as those designed by Frank Lloyd Wright, who took cues from the East, where garden and grounds are an integral part of the design.

Indeed, as I think back, I'm struck by how many of my first impressions of life came from nature. There was a garden out back where my sister and I would commune with nature, and I wrote my first haiku about a neighbor's garden. It's never too late to have a happy childhood: Just take up gardening or flower arranging!

Along the Path

"The garden is a metaphor for life, and gardening is a symbol of the spiritual path."

—Larry Dossey

"This garden is no metaphor—more a task that swallows you into itself, earth using, as always, everything it can."

—Jane Hirshfield

"Forget not that the earth delights to feel your bare feet and the winds long to play with your hair."

—Kahlil Gibran

Flower Power: By the Flowers, of the Flowers, and for the Flowers

I learned some very powerful Dharma once on a Buddhist retreat at a place called The Land of the Medicine Buddha, nestled in a forest of old-growth redwoods along the California coast. After a mindful walk through this living cathedral, led by zen gardener and Dharma teacher Wendy Johnson, we returned to our zendo and she passed around a large bowl of the topsoil we'd just trod. Talk about reverence for life! Here we were passing around billions of microorganisms, each one of us inhaling them like some rare perfume. Of such roots are we made, yet how often do we have the occasion to gaze in their mirror?

Hear and Now

"We are intertwined. Some bacteria sip nitrogen from the living air and fix it on the roots of host plants in plump pink purses of protein, while other bacteria consolidate sulfur from stone and render it available to our classic roses. And all the while, throughout solid ground where well-intentioned gardeners prune and pontificate on the surface, mycelial threads of a vast fungal network spread and radiate out in widening circles, attaching to plant roots for nourishment while fending off disease in the garden."

—Wendy Johnson

You might not realize you're always interacting with the web of life. For example, there's the invisible carpet of microscopic beings along floors. Underneath chairs. A film of invisible life in every nook and cranny. (Imagine how we might look to them!) What better way to affirm and enjoy our kinship with all life, than by cultivating a pretty plant or two? Just tending a houseplant draws us into the cyclically unfolding dharma of the seasons, the sources of life, the planet.

Whether or not you raise them yourself, one place for contemplating plants is in your breathing room and at your altar. If you have a backyard, enjoy the blessings of sun and wind and water. If you have a front yard, share your gardening with others. And if you want to take this work into the world, become involved with the community garden movement. An empty lot can make many rows of fresh edibles, flavorful herbs, and bright flowers.

Let a little Earth into your life. Plant a seed and tend its holy mystery. Something comes up and flourishes. It's nice. Tend to this new life as if its weeds and its sheen were your own life. When your garden flowers, your work is being applauded by charming flower faces, simple buddhas happy to be alive.

Saying It with Flowers

A Japanese floral arrangement might seem thin or skimpy compared to the more abundant still-life style preferred in the West. But with an unprejudiced eye, Japanese flower arrangements look more as if they were still growing, like an extension of a garden. Like shakuhachi music, and much of zen aesthetics, the style is somewhat abstract, to convey the essence of things. Rather than have the audience become attached to words, images, and symbolism, the idea is to provide a skillful means for each person to recognize their own essential Buddha nature through direct communion.

Ikenobo traditional shoka-style ikebanna.

One of the early Japanese masters of the art of floral arrangement describes the process: "Flowers should be placed in the container as one throws pebbles into a garden pool. It is done quietly and deliberately, and then left alone. To make changes is the sign of a novice."

You can also find Confucian symbolism and practically everything else in flower arranging, but the Buddhism was there right from the start. Prince Umayada was largely responsible for bringing Buddhism to Japan, and he sent envoys to China to seek cultural and spiritual guidance. One of these envoys, named Ono-no Imoko, eventually retired, living as a hermit by a lake. As a priest, one of his devotions

299

remained to arrange flowers for altars, and soon priests of newly built temples came to him for instruction. Thus was born the first known school of flower arrangement, which was called *ike-no-bo,* meaning "hermit by the lake."

Soon, flower arrangement became a big thing, with nobles and monks competing in annual contests. Ikenobo gave birth to Japanese flower arranging, *ikebanna,* which today is full of philosophy and symbolism, extensive vocabulary, and dozens of rules. Yet even I practice ikebanna, using only a few rules and concepts. When I see these flowers bearing their message from the whole universe as I pass by them, I sometimes forget who put them there. Instead, I stop and admire them and wonder how am I any different.

Ooh, Ooh, Ooh! What Just Five Rocks Can Do

At first, Buddhist gardens in China and Japan were colorful, expansive replicas of pure lands, with lakes and rocks, grass and bright flowers. But eventually the economy grew flat. Monks turned to *dry* gardens, using only sand and stones. Now, sand as ground cover goes all the way back to the beginning of Japanese history, but separate gardens made of sand began around the eleventh century and came into their own around the sixteenth. They became a common feature at the growing numbers of Buddhist temples and homes of the elite. Made of granite gravel or sand, they're called *karé-san-sui,* meaning "dry mountain water," which is a kind of koan.

Actually, karé-san-sui were often used to imitate classical Chinese ink-brush landscapes. Flat-topped rocks imitated brush-stroke mountains, and raked gravel or sand imitated waterfalls, rivers, and ocean. But the Sphinx of rock garden art is at Ryoanji (Peaceful Dragon) Temple. Fifteen stones are arranged there in five groups across a horizontal bed of gravel about the size of a tennis court, raked horizontally and in concentric circles around the stones. (An interesting phenomenon of the rock garden at Ryoanji is that you can never see all 15 rocks at once. You can only see, at most, 14 at any one time. Turn slightly to take in the fifteenth, and one other rock drops out of sight.)

The stones resemble mountain peaks jutting through clouds, or islands in the sea, but the overall impression is like the play of volume and mass in abstract art, or shakuhachi music with its almost random-seeming arrangement of notes that are yet perfect, just so.

The austerity of form and color is like the brush landscapes discussed in Chapter 17, "New Ways of Seeing and Being: Buddhism and Fine Arts," and is reflective of zen culture in general. Like a haiku, a

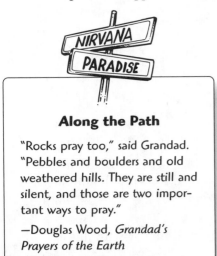

Along the Path

"Rocks pray too," said Grandad. "Pebbles and boulders and old weathered hills. They are still and silent, and those are two important ways to pray."

—Douglas Wood, *Grandad's Prayers of the Earth*

"Compress thirty thousand leagues into a single foot."

—Hannyabo Tessen, chief priest of Ryoan-ji Temple

miniaturization of the real world, a small pure land of mountains and rivers, islands in the sea (like Japan is). Also like haiku, there's a twin obedience to strict rules and utterly natural spontaneity. The result is an indescribable feeling of spaciousness and presence.

Physical Culture Is Culture

Culture isn't just high-brow stuff. Physical culture is also a culture—of growing popularity as attested to by all the joggers and baseball caps and 24-hour workout palaces dotting the landscape. So let's huddle! Buddhism has key moves here, too, in martial arts and sports.

KWAAAAATZ!: Martial Arts Are an Art

Martial arts date back to pre-civilization. ("Hey, Joe, where ya going with that rock in your hand?!") Many a Buddhist country, such as Tibet, for example, has contributed its fair share to the art. But Shaolin Temple, in China, is a good candidate for Mother of All Martial Arts. When not doing zazen before a wall, Bodhidharma would get up and work out. When he found out the Temple's monks were falling asleep during meditation, or were too restless to concentrate, he diagnosed they were out of shape, and devised exercises for them, which became the basis of *kung fu*. Here we have a Buddhist yoga, if you will. As with Zen in China, it mingled with Taoism, whose own yogas are known as *chi kung* and *tai chi*. Shaolin Grandmaster Wong Kiew Kit finds Shaolin kung fu contains all the techniques of the world's martial arts: karate punches, *tae kwon do* kicks, judo throws, *aikido* locks, wrestling holds, Western boxing's jabs and hooks, Siamese boxing's elbow and knee strikes, and Malay *silate's* twists and turns. So you could say the sun of Shaolin shines on all martial arts.

This Is

Kung fu ("skill from effort") is a generic catch-all for the numerous forms of Chinese martial arts, with hundreds of styles and sub-styles. Some are soft, redirecting an opponent's momentum and energy; some are hard, meeting force with force. Some work internally on *chi* ("life force"), such as chi kung (a.k.a. qi gong, "energy work") and **tai chi,** with its slow, flowing movements; others are external and work on muscular energy.

Now, the martial, war-like aspects are an interesting story. Their original purpose was not only to help the monks meditate by getting them in shape but also to teach them to overcome that renowned enemy fear. And since bandits periodically tried to raid the temple, monks were designated to defend the grounds. Some were then enlisted into service by the emperor and saved the throne from usurpers, so such Buddhist temples eventually multiplied across the land, with official patronage.

Leaves from the Bodhi Tree

A zen master was out for a walk with one of his students. Suddenly, both saw a fox chasing a rabbit nearby. "According to tradition," the master said, "the rabbit will get away from the fox."

"I don't think so," said the student. "You can see the fox is faster."

"But the rabbit will escape," the master persisted.

"How can you be so certain?" asked the student.

The master replied, "Because the fox is running for his dinner while the rabbit is running for his life."

Way of the Warrior: The Zen Sword

The link between Zen and the samurai, of the twelfth century, which we saw in Chapter 12, "See? Words Cannot Express: Zen," continued in Japan as the military aristocracy remained in power for nearly seven centuries (until 1867). Thus monks' temples were on the finest plots of land, and advised by the finest teachers imported from China. And martial arts flourished alongside.

Like Zen monks, samurai shaved their heads, donned Zen robes, and learned Zen discipline: one-pointed concentration, following the breath, quieting the mind, dissolving the ego. When a samurai holds a sword, it becomes part of his purified heart, his *mushin* (no-mind). Without fixing it anywhere, his attentive mind flows everywhere—for any move that comes to his mind, his opponent will make a countermove, and so he'd lose the higher ground of original nature. He doesn't think, feel, or react. And when he holds his outsized bow and pulls back an arrow, he becomes the bull's eye. The koan's answered ... with a *thwack!*

This Is

Japanese **martial arts** are practiced at a dojo (dojang, Korean; kwoon, Chinese), meaning "place of the Way." The teacher's called the sensei (Japanese); sen means "before," sei "born"; one who was born before you. Aikido (Japanese, "way of harmonious energy") aims at controlling an opponent's momentum through locking and throwing. Judo, involving throwing and grappling, is like Western wrestling. Karate emphasizes the fist-blows; a Korean variant, tae kwon do emphasizes foot-blows. A recent body-movement art derived from martial arts is shintaido, where every technique is meaningful both for combat ("control life") and for health ("develop life").

So when Kublai Khan sends two envoys to Japanese soil, dictating terms of surrender, *Kwaaatz!*, they're beheaded on the spot. Soon thereafter (1281), these zen warriors defeat the Khan's attack by sea, one of the largest naval forces in history, about 100,000 men. Thus, Zen's survival ensured that it would embue Japanese culture.

Hear and Now

"The mind must always be flowing. If it stops anywhere, the flow is interrupted and this is injurious to the well-being of the mind. In the case of the swordsman, it means death. When the swordsman stands against his opponent, he is not to think of the opponent, nor of himself, nor of his enemy's sword movements. He just stands there with his sword which, forgetful of all technique, is ready only to follow the dictates of the unconscious."

—Takuan Soho (1573–1645)

Martial arts began achieving critical visibility in the West in the 1960s as Westerners learned its techniques. Phrases like "Look within" crept into the vocabulary thanks to a TV series called *Kung Fu* (created by Bruce Lee but starring David Carradine). By 2001, the Taoist martial arts parable *Crouching Tiger, Hidden Dragon* won 4 out of the 10 Academy Awards for which it was nominated. Eastern martial arts continues to enjoy a growing following in the West—including sports stars.

But doesn't all this contradict the idea of Buddhism as peace, tranquility, serenity? Not necessarily. No duality: True peace doesn't blow away at the first gust of unfavorable wind. Peace implies fearlessness, be it of the samurai, the Tibetan warrior, or the Korean monk who leads a battle to defend his nation.

Aikido, for example, is the "art of peace." The aim is to align one's self with the life force of the universe, and to disarm an opponent. No paradox. Similarly, the samurai code says the sword that kills also gives life. That is, the samurai uses his sword when forced into it by another warrior who insists on causing harm to others and so kills himself by placing himself in the samurai's path. The samurai ideal dwelt without duality, no distinction between self or other, killing or giving life.

How all this played out historically and politically is another story. But we should also note that the Buddhist warrior also includes the concept of the one who breaks the cycle of illusion by turning the other cheek, as Christ said; the Buddha said, "hatred is not ended by hatred." Such fearlessness may require the most courage of all.

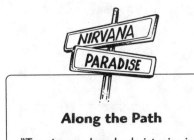

Along the Path

"To win one hundred victories in one hundred battles is not the highest skill. To subdue the enemy without fighting is the highest skill."

—General Sun Tzu (circa 500 B.C.E.), *The Art of War*

"One who injures living beings is not noble. One becomes noble through nonviolence to all beings."

—The Buddha, *The Dhammapada*

Maximum Performance: BE the Ball!

Buddhism is a natural in any sports arena. Buddhism is a training that unites body and mind. In sports, as in daily life, this means a Buddhist can remain alert in calm, and calm amid high-stakes danger. For example, did you ever throw something into a wastebasket, without thinking, and have it sink right in, but then miss it a second time, because you thought about it too much? Buddhism helps maintain that initial, intuitive excellence all the time.

Golf legend Tiger Woods has explained his success in terms of his upbringing. Thanking his parents, he's acknowledged his Thai Buddhist mother for teaching him to understand the power of the mind. When Tiger Woods tees off, he isn't thinking about how he's going to look on TV, or will he miss the ball and slice the turf, or any of that. His goal *is* winning but, like enlightenment, if you strive for it, you lose it. So he's bringing all his training in one-pointed concentration to the moment in front of his nose. On the course, following his victory at the 2001 Masters tournament, he declared he was never thinking about its landmark significance (a winning streak including the four most prestigious tournaments of the era all in a row). "I was so attuned to each and every shot," he said, "that I focused so hard on just that one golf shot. I finally realized I had no more to play. That was it. I was done. It was such a weird feeling. Then I started thinking, I had just won the Masters. Then I started losing it a little bit."

This Is

Sports buffs often talk about players entering **the zone,** a mystical state of consciousness that seems neither physical nor mental ... effortless amid tense exertion ... as if playing in slow motion ... perceptually sharp, keenly alert, with heightened concentration ... almost as if being psychic. Such profound experiences, often commonplace to athletes, bear comparison to daydreaming, communion with nature, and spiritual contemplation.

Mindfulness applies no less to team sports, where any player at any time might suddenly see a fleeting opportunity that could spell the one-point difference between being good and winning. The poster child for spirituality and team sports to date has been Phil Jackson, coach of the Los Angeles Lakers, and one of sports' all-time greatest coaches, the first to lead his team to 70 wins in one season (not too shabby). Raised in a Christian fundamentalist family and holding a degree in divinity, he's played mindfulness trainer to a pack of multimillion-dollar superstar egos who've dominated the game, such as Michael Jordan, Shaquille O'Neill, Scotty Pippen, and Dennis Rodman. He emphasizes teamwork (a new definition of sangha?). Like a good chef, he doesn't reveal his secret recipe, but, along with Sioux lore, yoga, and love of God, you can see the Buddhism in his approach to basketball.

Jackson believes the basis of teamwork is selflessness and interconnectedness, and it shows on the court. In the crunch of competition, a Laker can keep his cool and awaken to what's called for in each moment. Because of Jackson's trademark triangle defensive strategy, his players keep flowing. Win or lose, up or down, they cleave to the Middle Way, and grow as a team. The selflessness of the players enables their best to make a direct link to the audience's best. It's a joy to watch, even when the ball wobbles out of the rim instead of in. Draft Phil Jackson for President!

Hear and Now

"Basketball is a complex dance that requires shifting from one objective to another at lightning speeds. ... The secret is not thinking. *That doesn't mean being stupid,* it means quieting the endless jabbering of thoughts so that your body can do instinctively what it's been trained to do without the mind getting in the way." [emphasis added]

—Phil Jackson

Now, if you don't relate to competitive sports, consider swimming or Frisbee. The bottom line was laid out by Bodhidharma, back at Shaolin. Be it race-walking or sit-ups, tai chi or tae kwon do, keep in shape! Notice how meditation improves your physical abilities, and how physical culture improves your meditation. It's a slam-dunk double-bogey rare-orchid wisdom-eye homerun!

The Least You Need to Know

➤ Everything is an art and an occasion for expressing an awakened mind and heart.

➤ Film has analogies to Buddhist concepts, through such physical components as its projection and blank screen, and through its aesthetic aspects, such as its eternal present tense and its essentially illusory nature. There are also films with particular Buddhist themes.

➤ Traditional schools of Buddhism have particular brands of music associated with meditation, such as shakuhachi and chanting. Examples of Buddhist influence can now be heard in rock music, country, and soundtracks.

➤ Gardening is a Buddhist activity. In fact, the first flower–arranging school was Buddhist.

➤ A variety of martial arts can all be traced to Buddhist origins.

➤ Athletes and sports stars are finding Buddhism can add a winning ingredient to their training.

Chapter 17

New Ways of Seeing and Being: Buddhism and Fine Arts

In This Chapter

➤ What is sacred art?

➤ How to haiku

➤ Writing mindfully

➤ Zen painting

➤ Life as art

I've mentioned in Chapter 3, "What Might an American Buddha Look Like?" that, just as the revival of Greek and Latin in Italy in the fourteenth to sixteenth century contributed to one of Civilization's Greatest Hits, called the Renaissance ("new birth"), so, too, might the West's relatively recent study of Sanskrit and Chinese be molding the Renaissance II. Thus, some call this the Pacific Century.

To better appreciate this rebirth, we turn from food and work, movies and sports, to pictures and words; the realm often called *culture*. I know, that word *culture* can sometimes conjure up all sorts of dreary nonsense. Don't worry about it. Buddha's Museum of Art and the Great Buddhist Novel are all open for interpretation, 24/7 (24 hours a day, 7 days a week). Buddhist culture's way cool. Check it out!

But ... Is It Buddhist?

The boundary between high and low culture can be arbitrary and illusory. For years, people threw away woodcuts by the great Buddhist master Hokusai because they were made in mass production and sold for a pittance, and so often winding up as lining to packing boxes. Similarly, there's a seeming boundary around art and around spirituality that's no less discouraging: as if beauty and awareness were somehow slightly above reach, not available here and now, every day.

And there's less of a border between spirituality and art as some might believe. Art sharpens our perception of reality. The appreciation of beauty takes us out of our sense of a bounded, limited self and so furthers our spiritual development. And art stimulates the imagination, which is certainly an important spiritual dimension, too often overlooked.

Now all this is in keeping with the Dharma. But Dharma often suffuses culture like intangible fragrance or fog, rather than anything solid like the columns erected by King Ashoka. As philosopher Friederich Nietzsche said, "Soundlessly, on doves' feet, they make their way amongst us—the ideas that change the face of the earth." This can lead to some interesting detective work.

Let's say we're walking through a museum of art, and our guide points out how a landscape painting has a low horizon line, emphasizing more sky, to give a feeling of spaciousness. Some of us beginning Buddhists might say to ourselves, "Aha! Sky represents emptiness, sunyata." But does this mean the painter was Buddhist? If not, can the picture still be Buddhist, anyway?

Along the Path

"Zen students understand that the conclusion of Zen is daily life; but there is one more stage—that is Art."

—Sokei-an (a.k.a. Sasaki Soshin, 1892–1945)

"Beauty—be not caused—It is—
Chase it, and it ceases—
Chase it not, and it abides—"

—Emily Dickinson

Now, here's another puzzling example. Consider such contemporary artists as Richard Long and Hamish Fulton whose art consists of taking walks, communing with nature. As documentation, museums show photos of things done along their journeys. Are they Buddhist pilgrimages? Moreover—is it art?! In this chapter, we'll answer all that, and more.

First things first. Sleuthing the spiritual in art, let's take it as a fact that art's a formal expression of a feeling or idea. The skillful communication of a perception or understanding. Art museums are considered judges of these things, but usually art has sacred origins as well. When our ancestors lived in caves and painted animals on the walls, they were expressing their relationship to the universe. Yet today the art by indigenous peoples isn't deemed proper for some museums of fine art (*humph!*). Why not?! Their work reminds us of our kinship with the universe; a highly skillful communication of a vital understanding.

For the answer, why not flash forward to Western civilization. By the twelfth century, the anonymity of artists ends with the Renaissance. Enter the individual and self-expression. The greatest experiment in individuality would be America, founded upon Puritanism and Calvinism, which rejected pictures from the church, and spread that austerity to the rest of everyday life. Then the Technological Revolution came and dealt devotional art another body blow. The telegraph, for example, was dedicated to messages of commercial or military matters rather than anything like devotional poetry, which dwindled away like a faded blossom. Dit-dot-dot-dash ...

Catching up with the present, we find now a renewed interest in 1) devotional poetry and art, and in 2) spirituality embracing some relatively uncommon teachings. Renaissance II seems to be drawing us away from self-expression and back to spirituality. Now, to mindfully appreciate contemporary art that is spiritual, we might recognize three categories suggested by Asian art scholar Ananda K. Coomaraswamy:

1. Phenomenal (objective/outside world)
2. Mental/Imaginative (subjective/inner world)
3. Consciousness (mind/spirit)

The first is like the painting of grapes so lifelike a bird might peck at it. So a photograph of a garish green Buddha at the thirteenth hole at some miniature golf course might fall under this category, too; not necessarily spiritual.

Then there are the dream-like paintings of things rarely actually seen. A personal interpretation of hills. A sunset with two banks of clouds forming red lips. A fur-lined teacup. They demand a little more from us. But sometimes a bigger reach can be demanded of us from something seemingly obvious, like the birds of Morris Graves.

Morris Graves, Bird and Snail *(sumi-e, 1950);* Bird and Avocado *(pastel, 1979). Private collections. The painter uses a bird to speak for himself, and so for us. In the top figure, the bird's attention is riveted on the snail shell. (Anybody home inside?) In the bottom figure, seeker and sought close together, and of similar substance as well as size. Neither drawn from life nor symbolic, there's nothing beyond the bird, beyond the snail, beyond the avocado. Just this, endless life, thus, just so.*

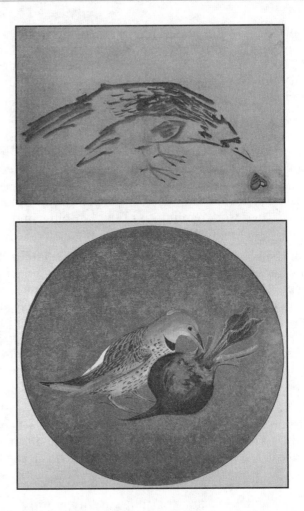

So we come to the spiritual in art drawing from either the phenomenal or imaginative world, or both, with new perspectives: mindful of the origin, workings, and ultimate experience of our consciousness. It shares our quest for the meaning of life and supports us in our journey. Such art calls us to personally seek its resonance within ourselves.

This is quite different than a tour shuffling through a museum with a guide spelling everything out. This kind of art requires our own spiritual participation to fulfill its meaning, as co-creators. So there are as many different versions of such art as it has viewers. But it's timeless in the same way that a sight is impermanent but seeing is timeless. Or in the way we each respond to something timeless like the Sphinx, differently.

So that's the general story about this mystery of the spiritual in art. Here follow some more specific clues, both in words and in pictures. Keep an eye out for them as you journey on the path.

Words for the Wordless: Buddhist Literature

Words and the Wordless aren't mutually exclusive. Yes, Buddhism dissolves the dualism born of language, but it doesn't set up another dualism in its place, of silence vs. speech. Words have their place, as skillful means, such as a mantra or a koan. And "Please pass the chopsticks."

Words process our internal information on many levels, sometimes letting us see and know things we ordinarily wouldn't have, otherwise. So mindful writing and skillful speech play many roles along the Way. For example, it's traditional in Japanese Zen to express one's personal stage of awareness or enlightenment with a poem, one's own or another's. Once a student answers a koan, for instance, the teacher then follows up by asking, "Now what's a verse that expresses that?" And the student draws from a commonplace book of "zen verses," an album of classical poetry and folk proverbs, on hand in the monastery library, picking phrase or verse fragment to commemorating his stage of awareness. After all, the student could have gotten lucky in his koan answer, so the poem acts like a quality control inspection. And words help make that stage become real, and form a landmark.

Words don't have to express or cause enlightenment but can also serve as *pure lands*, ideal situations where the reader can go to cultivate understanding and awareness and advance closer to enlightenment. In a way, that's what an artist does, setting up a frame and arranging within in it selected elements, creating for an opportunity for a special experience.

Along the Path

"Spring river flowing flat into the sea; bright moon rising with the tide."

"Trees show the shape of the wind;
waves blur the shape of the moon."

"Seamless chaos!"

"Chill waters await spring;
ice dwindles away.
Dawn mountains face clear sky;
their snowy peaks are soaring."

—*Zen Verses*

Some Picks for a Buddhist Reading Group

Shakespeare is full of Buddhism. ("A rose by any other name would smell as sweet." and "So shalt thou feed on Death, that feeds on men, / and Death once dead, there's no more dying then.") Wordsworth can be supremely zen. ("To sit without emotion, hope or aim, / In the loved presence of my cottage-fire, / And listen to the flapping of the flame, / Or kettle whispering its faint undersong.") But I'm just cribbing from a sturdy Buddhist literary guide by R. H. Blyth (1898–1964), called *Zen in English Literature and Oriental Classics,* which even ferrets out the zen of *Don Quixote.*

Along the Path

American poets with affinities for Buddhism include Antler, Anita Barrows, Jim Cohn, Diane di Prima, Patricia Donegan, Norman Fischer, Allen Ginsberg, Susan Griffin, Sam Hamill, Jane Hirshfield, Garrett Hongo, Lawson Fusao Inada, Robert Kelly, Jack Kerouac, Joanne Kyger, Alan Chong Lau, Russell Leong, Peter Levitt, Jackson Mac Low, Michael McClure, Stephen Mitchell, Kenneth Rexroth, Al Robles, Albert Saijo, Steve Sanfield, Leslie Scalapino, Andrew Schelling, Gary Snyder, Charles Stein, Robert Sund, Arthur Sze, John Tarrant, Amy Uyematsu, Anne Waldman, Lew Welch, and Philip Whalen.

Contemporary authors influenced by Buddhism include Gretel Erlich, Thaisa Frank, Susan Griffin, Jim Harrison, Charles Johnson, Joanna Macy, and Peter Mathiessen, whose novels, essays, and nature writing resonate with Dharma.

But the genre that's literature's purest pure land is poetry—where words can be looked at as if under a microscope, that is, without the distracting interferences of getting a heroine, say, from Scene B to Scene C. The Chinese word for *poetry* literally means "temple of words." It's largely been on wings of poetry that Buddhism has glided into Western literature. For now, let's zero in on the poetic genre that has introduced zen to millions of Westerners.

One-Breath Meditation: Haiku

If you don't know what haiku are yet, ask kids. Just as recycling came to national consciousness through kids (taught it at school and then bringing it back home), so, too, have haiku found fertile soil in kids, who naturally live close to the subtle, vivid, wild mind of haiku. It's no wonder millions of kids are being taught haiku in school.

This Is

The most popular traditional Japanese poetic form is tanka, five lines (5-7-5-7-7 syllables, respectively). It also formed the basis for group composition of long sequences of linked verse (renga). The opening of a renga, the first three-liner (5-7-5 syllables), later took on a literary life of its own and became known as **haiku.** A haiku is a breezy, delicate, miniature impressionist sketch in words. (*Example:* "Islands ... shattered bits in the summer sea." —Basho)

Kids are invariably flashing on life around them like fireflies. Haiku is an expression of such life-flashes. Awareness buzzings. Light and airy, they're miniature impressionist sketches in words—half on the page and leaving the other half for the reader to fill in. Here are a few:

➤ Plum blossoms here, there—it's good to go north, good to go south.

➤ In the dark forest, a berry drops. ... Splash!

➤ The old dog looks dazzled by the song of the earthworms.

➤ Seconds before the next sneeze; waiting. What a funny face!

(And the authors, respectively, are Buson, Basho, Issa, and Anonymous.)

They're printed here as one-liners, though they're often done in three lines, like this one by James W. Hackett:

A bitter morning:
sparrows sitting together
without any necks.

Haiku originated in Japan, where there are precise rules for them, which the West has been trying to adapt (not unlike our relationship with zen, really). Sometimes this can be like holding a plant next to a rock and just hoping it will transplant, until enough suitable conditions are present, as now they seem to be.

The biggest misconception persists that a haiku is anything written in three lines of five syllables, seven syllables, and five syllables, respectively. That's okay for getting started, like training wheels, but not always necessary. Many practitioners prefer three lines of two beats, three, and two, respectively. What's important is paring the words down to the bone. And that resonates with counting breaths in Buddhist meditation, 1 2 3 4, returning to the simplest things, again and again.

Here are five general haiku basics. 1) Like photographs, or mini home videos, they're about real, present-moment things. 2) They often give a sense of time (winter, noon, graduation day) and place (backyard, garage, secret waterfall). "Snowy hill," for example, indicates both time and place. 3) They usually don't refer to the speaker (third-person narration). Buddhist art isn't self-expression, much less exhibitionism. 4) Subjects are drawn from nature, or human nature.

And 5) They often present two related images, leaving the connection to be made by the reader, as in this one, by Bashô: *A flash of lightning … and the jagged screech of a heron, flying through the dark*—here evoking the unity of heavens flashing and a bird's voice in the night. Like a bell, it seems to call us to stop and return to our true home in the present moment.

Similarly, a haiku often has a little space in the middle where it breathes (like in the middle of the line, "To be or not to be, that is the question"), such as in *"alone even when I cough."* (After "not to be" and after "alone.")

How does all that translate into Buddhism? That incompleteness of form is an expression of sunyata, whereby nothing's separate. By omitting "I" from their vocabulary, they demand an active awareness of nonself. They treat reality as is, in its utter suchness, not to mention oneness, impermanence, interbeing, compassion, and karma. They're precise instances of bearing witness to nature. And their being in the present moment is what Buddhism's all about!

They're short, but not small: simple hymns to the bigness of being. *Ants float down a river on a twig, singing and dancing.* (That's by Issa.)

Haiku are one-breath meditation; just that long. As simple (and profound and everyday) as that. You'll find more guidelines a little further along, called "How to Haiku." As you immerse yourself in haiku, you'll discover they aren't something you just read. Once bitten by the haiku bug, you'll probably want to try your hand at writing them, too. But as with any culture, they're a whole way of life, of seeing and being and finding meaning. But … is it Buddhist? Well, not all haiku are zen, but all zen is haiku. Just so.

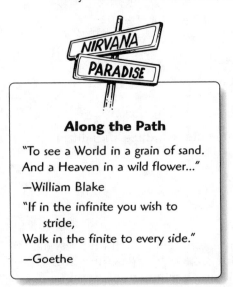

Along the Path

"To see a World in a grain of sand.
And a Heaven in a wild flower…"

—William Blake

"If in the infinite you wish to stride,
Walk in the finite to every side."

—Goethe

Leaves from the Bodhi Tree

Haiku master Matsuo Bashô and his pal Kikaku were walking through the fields one day. Looking at the darting dragonflies, Kikaku made up a haiku that went: "Red dragonfly. Break off wings and legs. You have a chili pepper."

But, "No," Bashô said, "that's not haiku," and made up the following: "A chili pepper. Add wings and legs. You have a dragonfly."

Moral: Haiku never takes life away from life. Haiku always adds life to life.

How to Haiku

One of the charms of haiku is that you don't have to even think about being a "writer." That is, the evolution of haiku in the West has somehow largely escaped all the starchy professionalism and sticky labels of Poetry and Authorship. So: Amateurs welcome! Haiku *are* beginner's mind.

You can't go after haiku with an elephant gun or a butterfly net, anymore than you can *try* to become enlightened. Haiku require just three tools: 1) mindfulness, 2) a notepad, and 3) a pencil, with eraser because you might get a haiku right on the first try, but you should get used to editing also being part of the process.

Haiku can be about a flash of lightning if that's something you experience where you live. That is, they're about your own ordinary life. This is an important point in Zen: Enlightenment isn't some pie in the sky. Everyday mind is Buddha mind. Chopping wood and cooking rice.

Haiku are a skillful means for enriching and developing your Buddhist practice; opportunities to read the world as a text illustrating Buddhist truths about your own life, and spontaneous bells of mindfulness returning you to the wonderful present moment.

Three final tips. 1) *Pay attention.* Notice what you notice. 2) *Bear witness.* Don't dramatize or judge. Take your subject's point of view. 3) *Keep it simple.* Be concrete, vivid.

Just so you know that haiku don't have to be masterpieces, like the ones already quoted, here are two of my typically so-so haiku, both written during my lunch break walk today:

from out of nowhere …
one vine of ivy, creeping
into hollow tree trunk

life in the city …
taking a walk just to see
if the car's still there

(You're welcome to use the opener of either if you want a little nudge to get you started.)

A Day of Mindfulness Writing in Community

In the early 1960s, when I was in college, creative writing seemed as rarified an option as marine biology. Today, spirituality and writing are more widely available as majors as well as classes. A writer can pick up such books as Natalie Goldberg's *Writing Down the Bones* and Deena Metzger's *Writing for Your Life* for spiritual as well as creative enrichment, as well as major in poetics at a Buddhist college such as Naropa Institute.

While the supportiveness and interchange of a creative writing class or writing group can make it a writing sangha, it's not necessarily a Buddhist sangha. So I'd like to introduce to you the idea of writing *mindfully* in community. I don't know where else it's practiced, but I'll tell you how I've learned it, as invented by Maxine Hong Kingston. As she recently described it, it's something like zen calligraphy with an emphasis on story.

Set aside a day, just as for a day of mindfulness. You can meet with other writers you know, or members of your church or synagogue interested in writing and meditation, or people sharing a common experience, such as veterans of wars, as I've done, not necessarily with prior writing experience, but all interested in using the combined practice of writing and mindfulness to transform life into art.

Hear and Now

"Look at people! Remember your high school teacher told you to make eye contact? It means you're being sensitive to other people. It's caring about how words go out and back. Not watching is protecting yourself from intimacy, and criticism.

"Reading aloud is a good editing process. You'll feel if it's not comfortable in your mouth, or if rhythms are off. You'll hear it."

—Maxine Hong Kingston, leading a mindfulness writing sangha

The best seating arrangement's a circle. A candle in the center of the group is nice. A small altar, with a Buddha and some flowers, is also a good option. Designate a leader and a bell-minder: the leader introduces and facilitates the various sections, and the bell-minder sounds a bell to mark them. A sample schedule might run like this:

10 to 11 A.M.	Bowing in and meditation
11 A.M. to 1 P.M.	Writing in community
1 to 2 P.M.	Mindful lunch
2 to 3:30 P.M.	Reading and listening
3:30 to 4 P.M.	Walking meditation
4 to 5 P.M.	Responses

Bow in. The leader introduces the day to the members. Some newcomers might want to meditate but not write. Please invite them to consider joining in for everything. It's important to stress that the circle of sangha supports everyone. Everyone's here for each other. One member of the writing sangha with which I've been involved compared it to the pattern on a windshield hit by a stray baseball: Every single crack is an important part of the pattern.

Meditation can be conducted as in zazen, an hour of meditation, following the breath, watching the mind, being present to the moment. Then the circle breaks apart for writing. For members without any prior writing projects already begun, suggest making a list of important life experiences and choosing one incident to write about. Stress the basic guidelines of vividness and simplicity. Explain how bearing witness through words on paper means being honest to a life-experience, truthful as well as sincere.

In our sangha, we practice silent meals, eating mindfully. Then the circle reforms and each person reads what they've written (with a bell in between each of our readings). This, too, is a mindful practice, of loving speech and deep listening. The leader might explain how it continues the dialogue of bearing witness (self no different than other, other no different than self). The bodhisattva Avalokiteshvara can be invoked, who *hears* the suffering of the world.

Map out in advance where to take a half-hour walking meditation together, both in terms of the terrain as well as timing the distance to cover. Then the final time's devoted to each member expressing what particularly moved them in each other's work. Each respondent begins by a gassho to the sangha. Criticism's phrased in terms of positive feedback. What did each member remember and like best? The bell-minder sounds the mindfulness bell following each response. The leader might make the final response. And you meet next month, or next season, and do it again.

Writing mindfully enables the work to be transformative, spiritual, offering insight into the meaning of this raindrop ephemeral crazy dance called life. Writing's typically a solitary art, or at least up until now. But the bodhisattva vow includes all beings. Writing in community weaves a writer deeper into the interconnected circle of life.

Leaves from the Bodhi Tree

"Write about something you really loved, a time when you felt whole and complete in an activity all for itself. It could be something as simple as learning to make a grilled cheese sandwich, or a time your uncle taught you to tie your shoelaces into a bow. Something you concentrated on as a kid because the ability to concentrate is where the bliss and love come from. Be specific but don't forget to throw in a detail about a cloud out the window as you bent to tie the shoe or the chandelier above your head as you leaned down. This is good practice. While you concentrate and narrow in, you are also aware of the whole world."

—Natalie Goldberg, *Wild Mind*

The Eye in the Heart of the Heart

"Show me your mind," Bodhidharma asked Hui Ko (and us). And, aha!, we realize we can't. It's colorless, imageless, boundless, without fixed location. So how can anyone *show* buddha mind to anyone else? And yet Buddhism reveals a canon of visual art equal to Rembrandt and da Vinci, as mind opening as it is eye-opening.

Drawing the Buddha Is Drawing One's Teacher Is Drawing One's Self

When Buddhists express their devotion and enlightenment through pictures, it shines through the national cultural aesthetics of each school and each country. For example, Buddhist art goes back nearly three millennia, but Tibetan or Mongolian paintings, masks, and bronzes, for example, are only recently being seen in the West. The bronzes are sublimely refined and uncannily lifelike, (the ones shown in Chapter 14, "Alone, Together: Buddhist Relations: Engaging the World," and Chapter 19, "Happiness Is Not an Individual Matter," are life-size). The masks are incredibly vigorous. And the paintings (*tangka*) are exquisitely graceful and vibrant. If you compare the image of the Russian Christ and the Tibetan Buddha shown side by side in Chapter 4, "Different Travel Agents, Same Destination?: Interfaith," you'll feel their beauty and harmony resonate within you. Such a fusion of analytical perception with elegance of movement, such freedom found within strict traditional guidelines, hearkens back to pre-Renaissance arts in the West, when cathedrals were created as completely anonymous works of devotion.

There's a curious side to some Tibetan art. Museums of fine art are now commissioning Tibetan monks to construct such painstakingly meticulous mandalas as the *Wheel of Time (Kalachakra)*, out of colored sand, on their premises. It's a bit ironic to the nature of museums as repositories of permanence, everything with its neat descriptive tag, that, in the end, the monks ceremoniously scatter their masterpieces to the elements, in affirmation of the impermanence and interpenetration of all things. They do something similar with their renowned, intricately detailed, multicolored sculptures carved out of … butter!

The Way of the Brush: Zen Eye-Openers

A number of illustrations in this book were done with brush and ink, on a porous surface such as rice paper. Consider the tool. Meals are different if you eat with chopsticks. You could play Bach on a shakuhachi, but it would sound different. So, too, does the nature of the brush shape Asian art. When you see art students in a museum, copying a work in their sketchbook, they use pencil or pen but seldom brush. That is, they're copying lines and forms, but, as zen brush master Kazuaki Tanahashi puts it, "When you copy an Oriental piece of art, you attempt to copy the process—the posture, the way of holding the brush, the order of strokes, the way of putting pressure on paper, the brush moving in air, the breathing, feeling, and thinking."

Using a zen brush, as in Zen and zen culture in general, training and craft are essential, yet heart and spontaneity are also paramount. (Think "Tiger Woods, teeing off" or a batter facing the pitch.) At the slightest hesitation the ink will blot and spread on the extremely fibrous paper. The painter must have absorbed the rules so that technique becomes unconscious. Skillfully trained, the zen artist must become one with her or his subject matter (be it bamboo, a watermelon, or a mountain), its essence poised on the tip of the brush. (Hesitate here and the ink dries up.) Then with blank mind, facing a blank page, the painter takes the leap and *Aha!* a single word, a single image, a single circle can be an unpremeditated discovery.

Consider, for example, the calligraphy for the Chinese word for mindfulness, in Chapter 11, "Look Within and Know: Insight Meditation *(Vipassana)*." The artist presents the essence of the word. And while he doesn't call attention to himself, the work doesn't need a signature: it is his signature. (True self seen through selflessness.)

Now, in the East a word can be a picture (such as the Chinese word for heart, shown in Chapter 6, "Taking Steps: The Eightfold Path"), rather than letters representing abstract sounds. So reading involves seeing, a more direct way of making meaning. And so a brush is used for writing and for painting, both. Thus all the Chinese and Japanese words shown in calligraphy in this book are works of art. And in such portraits as of Bodhidharma (Chapter 12, "See? Words Cannot Express: Zen") and Hui

Neng (Chapter 15, "No Work, No Eat: Work to Eat or Eat to Work?") we can admire the calligraphy of some abstract word or hieroglyph making up the person.

Untitled one-stroke painting by Kazuaki Tanahashi, from a series of 60. Following a 15-year hiatus from making art, a friend gave him some handmade cotton paper. "One day," he recalls, *"without any definite intention, I drew a straight horizontal line across the center of a piece of paper. At the moment the brush would have moved to another stroke, something stopped me from adding anything. I had a feeling that what I wanted to express was all there—in the single line and in the space above and below. So I put down the brush. … As a calligrapher, I seemed to be stuck at stroke one."*

(From the book Brush Mind, *Kazuaki Tanahashi [Parallax Press, 1990])*

Zen calligraphy then is a dance between dwelling in transparent boundlessness (sun-yata) while dealing with form. That is, zen painting's like a game of giving the limitless openness a chance to take a dip in the waves of form. But just as the painter doesn't call attention to his or her self, the subject isn't smack dab in the middle, either. (Think of Hamlet's line, "By indirection find direction out.") To depict a mountain, the painter might just show someone looking off into the fog. We're shown relations as well as things. In the painting a little further on, the sixth persimmon that's not in a row, for example, calls attention to the poses of the other five. Or think of Bodhi-dharma: he's seen from behind. He's also the same as the wall he faces, utter blank canvas. In fact, no floor or ceiling. (Same for the persimmons: no horizon.) Which brings us to space.

Because a finger pointing at the moon is not the moon (a picture or word is not the actual thing being represented), the zen painter often uses space to call forth awakened mind or sunyata (the undifferentiated, fertile void). (How do you show someone the light of the full moon, or the enlightened mind, the awakened heart?) So what the West calls negative space, in the East becomes positive. Look again at the landscape in Chapter 12. On first glance, you might think zen paintings look unfinished, but their flowing rivers and clouds of utterly blank canvas are intentional. We can sense twilight mists in the unpainted spaces, as boats and birds find their homes for the night.

Hear and Now

"In the Oriental calligraphic tradition, you are not supposed to touch up or white out a trace of your brush. Every brush stroke must be decisive; there is no going back. It's just like life.

"If each moment is our entire life, how dare we kill time? If each stroke is our entire breath, how dare we correct it?"

—Kazuaki Tanahashi, *Brush Mind*

As Lao-tzu said, a potter can't make a bowl from clay without empty space. (Thus, you must have space inside yourself, in order for things to take place.) Like haiku, and Zen itself, the space as well as the thing being pointed at must be intuited within your own heart. (This effect is much like radio drama, which relied on the listener's imagination to fill in details. A young kid once told Norman Corwin, a writer of radio drama, that he preferred radio to movies. "The pictures," he said, "are better.")

Bearing witness to essence is a dialogue. Artist and subject, but also viewer and subject, and artist and viewer. Gazing at zen art can be an act of meditation, like looking in a mirror, or looking within. Let your gaze unfold the way you'd listen to music. Imagine the landscape of the fishing village becoming an internal portrait, a mental soundscape. Awakening your mind without fixing it anywhere, the artist will guide your awareness to the infinite and eternal in the immediate present, the picture right before your eyes. Here the painter's essence and the natural object (and the viewer) become one.

Curiously, portrait can become landscape, and vice versa. Bodhidharma can resemble a mountain, monumental, a force of nature, appropriate to his towering status in Zen history. And an imaginary terrain, such as a river flowing through glowing hills, can depict an interior landscape, as well, of the soul. Landscape becomes human in-scape, rendering the visible world without as interchangeable with our invisible landscape within, its lofty peaks and deep valleys, twists and turns. So a seemingly plain picture of swimming fish, or persimmons, can be taken on different levels, literal, figurative, and ultimate.

(Now, does this hold true, too, for brushing your teeth?!)

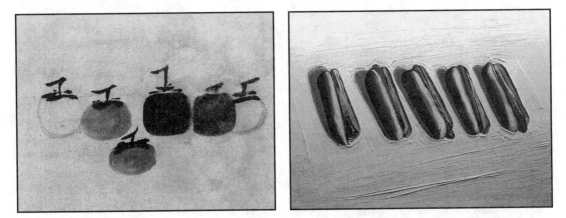

*Two studies in suchness. Is-ness. On the left, a classic Chinese zen ink brush painting of persimmons. Each with its own distinct, unique shape, texture, and sheen. Each a buddha … placed just so. As fresh today as when painted. On the right, five hot dogs by a contemporary American painter. Each hot dog sits in its bun with its own personality. Each perfect thus. Mu Ch'i, *Six Persimmons (1269). Ink on paper. 14 × 15. Daitokuji, Kyoto. Wayne Thiebaud, *Five Hot Dogs *(1961) Oil on canvas. 18 × 24. Private collection.*

Art as Life: Life Is Art

We've been investigating art, traditionally defined, but when you meditate you discover the source of all art within yourself. Thou Art That. So art's neither worthless nor expendable: its presence in the landscape is a great encourager, teacher, and sacred space. Yet we shouldn't become attached to it. In the final analysis, what *isn't* art? This is also a good lesson, with important medicine.

Perhaps the two most influential artists of the twentieth century were Pablo Picasso and Marcel Duchamp. Picasso, as we know, put two dots along the side of a nose, so the portrait faces front and sideways at the same time. In so doing, he takes the flat two-dimensional canvas and reproduces not only three dimensions but the fourth, time. Duchamp, on the other hand, went beyond paint entirely and concentrated on the retina, and the mind behind it. He once took an ordinary bicycle wheel, mounted it very nicely, and exhibited it as art. And why not?!

To return to the question with which we began: if I come in the front door, go out the back door, and take a pilgrimage through nature, is it art? Well, as Duchamp once said, "The only thing that is not art is inattention." And so we see next how Buddhism, the art of attention, erases the boundary between life and art.

Hear and Now

"From the age of five I've had a mania for sketching the forms of things. From about the age of 50 I produced a number of designs, yet of all I drew prior to the age of 70 there is truly nothing of any great note. At the age of 73 I finally apprehended something of the true quality of birds, animals, insects, fishes, and of the vital nature of grasses and trees. Therefore, at 80 I shall have made some progress, at 90 I shall have penetrated even further the deeper meaning of things, at 100 I shall have become truly marvelous, and at 110, each dot, each line I make shall surely possess a life of its own. I only beg that gentlemen of sufficiently long life take care to note the truth of my words."

—Hokusai (1760–1849), at age 75

The Sounds of Silence: Music Without Horizon

Smack-dab in the middle of the twentieth century, an American composer named John Cage asked us all to consider life as art when he premiered his concert piece entitled *4'33"*, (pronounced *4 minutes, 33 seconds*). The pianist performing the work, David Tudor, sat down at the piano and played not one single note for precisely 4 minutes, 33 seconds. (Maybe you've heard this somewhere before?)

Actually, it's in three movements. And it can be played by any number and combination of instruments. Anyway, at its premiere, at the Maverick Concert Hall in Woodstock, New York, the back of the hall was open to the surrounding forest. During the first movement, you could hear the wind sighing through the trees. Light rain pattered on the roof during the second movement. And during the final movement, the audience whispered amongst itself, in counterpoint to the sound of other people exiting.

Mind you, it's not some mere bagatelle just anyone can perform. I've seen an art student perform it very timidly, and it didn't quite work. But another time I saw a pianist in a tux perform it quite well, and still remember the high sound of a bus turning a corner as a girl's wooden heels tapped out a faint metronome on the street, outside, as a few people inside rustled in their seats like autumn leaves, and a generator hummed. The generator was the keeper: Who would have thought such an ugly-seeming sound could be art!? What tensions lurk in its electronic hum! It took shedding my prejudices to hear it, as it is. And so I began to listen to my hearing itself, tuning into the sheer act of attention.

Leaves from the Bodhi Tree

In 1946, John Cage learned Indian musical counterpoint from Gita Sarabhai who told him that in her country the purpose of music is to quiet the mind. He later attended D. T. Suzuki's lectures on Buddhism at Columbia University, for two years. The year before Cage composed 4'33" he visited Harvard's totally soundproof chamber and was surprised to discover it wasn't silent: he heard his nervous system (high sound) and his blood circulating (low). And so he realized the difference between silence and sound is awareness, or *intention,* and spent the rest of his life creating music without personal intention, in order to stimulate awareness.

In other words, for four minutes and thirty-three seconds, the composer puts a frame around life and says to us, "Here! *This* is art." Here's the spontaneity of haiku and zen painting, Buddhist interpenetration and impermanence, conveyed through yet another disciplined skillful means—awakening us to mindfulness of the present moment ... without limit.

Hear and Now

"I have a commonplace book for facts, and another for poetry, but I find it difficult always to preserve the vague distinction which I had in mind, for the most interesting and beautiful facts are so much the more poetry and that is their success. ... I see that if my facts were sufficiently vital and significant—perhaps transmuted into the substance of the human mind—I should need but one book of poetry to contain them all."

—H. D. Thoreau, *Diary,* February 18, 1852

Cage came to see music "not as communication from the artist to an audience, but rather as an activity of sounds in which the artist found a way to let the sounds be themselves." This could then, "Open the minds of the people who made them, or listened to them, to other possibilities than they had previously considered. ... To widen their experience; particularly to undermine the making of value judgments." In this way, he aligned the purpose of his art with meditation's goal of changing habitual mindsets. Ripples from that stone he threw in the pond are still reverberating on our shore today. (Listen: that soundscape of silence and noises never stops!)

This is like the unintentionalness of haiku. That is, you don't go out of your house declaring, "Today, I'm going to write a haiku about dogs." That creates an unnecessary gap between writer and dogs, thought and reality, as two separate things. Haiku *happen,* like the sound of a berry falling in a stream, or the sound of the refrigerator, or the sight of the morning star.

And it's about time. Think of all the tragic lives spent chasing after some lofty ideal called Art, up on some pedestal in an airless museum. From the moment David Tudor first opened a piano to play *4'33"* and didn't press a single key, artists no longer had to create timeless objects of art: what a relief! Critics, grasping for labels, called this new approach "formless," because it didn't obey classical patterns. But such art can be shapely because mind is shapely.

Hear and Now

"My favorite piece of music is the one we all hear if we are quiet.

"Theater [the use of all one's senses] takes place all the time wherever one is and art simply facilitates persuading one this is the case.

"We open our eyes and ears seeing life each day excellent as it is. This realization no longer needs art."

—John Cage

Leaves from the Bodhi Tree

In 1961, visitors to an art gallery were led by Yoko Ono to each piece of hers on exhibition there. For each work, she'd give them instructions. For *Smoke Painting,* for instance, the viewer was asked to burn the canvas with a cigarette and watch the smoke; the piece was finished when the canvas had turned to ashes. Many of her art works are printed instructions, marking some of the earliest examples of Conceptual Art. Consisting of words alone, the art is constructed in the reader's head, or mind, such as her *Lighting Piece, 1955: Light a match and watch till it goes out.* (The match is never the same twice. And who watches?)

Printer Larry Hamlin with John Cage in the Crown Point studio, 1986. John Cage, Eninka 26, *1986. One in a series of 50 smoked paper monotypes with branding printed on gampi paper chine collé. Published by Crown Point Press. "Eninka" is Japanese for "circle, stamp, fire." These etchings were created by setting fire to newspapers, putting the fire out by running the press across them, laying a piece of special Japanese paper on top, and running that through the press. Then the paper was branded with an iron ring. Utterly nonrepresentational, the work has a perfect naturalness of form as of a pavement being painted by raindrops. Yet it was created under very controlled conditions: the number of newspapers, the duration of the fire, the placement of the ring, the strength of its mark (its temperature) were all predetermined by tossing coins—"imitating nature in her manner of operation," as Cage would put it. The circle echoes the zen enso (see Chapter 12).*

(Photographs: Kathan Brown and Colin McRae)

Erasing Borders

And the beat goes on. There are still plenty of dividing lines holding us back from awakening our hearts, opening our minds, to the infinitely present moment. For example, consider the Art-vs.-Life boundary between fiction and nonfiction. As if journalists or essayists don't select and organize facts to tell a story in a certain slant or spin. As if novelists don't model background, characters, and plot from research into real life, if not veiled personal memoir. So when Maxine Hong Kingston, say, places an imaginary tale side-by-side with factual events, in *The Fifth Book of Peace*, it rubs away at that arbitrary, illusory border between fiction and nonfiction, life and art, self and other. Just as the peace that is her subject is made up of nonpeace elements, so, too, is her book made up of the actual world, with all its imperfections, and the imaginary world, with its limitless potentials, so both can feed into each other. Wise, compassionate peace knows no borders.

And this new kind of life art often bears a wry, wacky zen humor. In a 1966 piece called *Postman's Choice,* for instance, artist Ben Vautier dropped a postcard in a mailbox. On one side, it was addressed to a friend, and to another friend on the other side, with stamps on both sides. The postman (life) thus became part of art. This was part of a movement called Fluxus (great name), with ideas often evoking koans, and whose antics often resembled "zen vaudeville." Korean artist Nam June Paik, for example, proposed having an adult seated in lotus posture on a baby carriage, pushed by another adult or several children through a shopping mall or some calm street. He called his instructions *Zen for Street.*

Around this time, Allan Kaprow founded a kind of spontaneous zen environmental performance art called a *happening.* The word crept its way into common vocabulary, but does anyone remember his wondrous explanation at the time? "Not satisfied with the suggestion through paint of our other senses, we shall utilize the specific substances of sight, sound, movement, people, odors, touch. Objects of every sort are materials for the new art: paint, chairs, food, electric and neon lights, smoke, water, old socks, a dog, movies, a thousand other things which will be discovered ..."

Amen. Sometimes we need artists to point out things Buddhist teachers only imply, such as the importance of *imagination,* and the *continual* nature of our practice and its limitless *applicability.* In the end, we might say that all the sutras and gathas are poetry and Buddhism itself is an art. An art of awakening into freedom.

The Least You Need to Know

➤ Buddhism returns us to long traditions of Western sacred art that diminished following the Renaissance.

➤ There are numerous examples of literature expressing Buddhism. If "poetry says it best," then haiku may be Buddhism's ideal Buddhist literature.

➤ Haiku are as much a way of life as an art. There's no bar to entry. Anyone can see, write, and appreciate haiku.

➤ When Buddhists express their devotion and enlightenment through pictures, it shines through the national cultural aesthetics of each school. Appreciation of this devotion and enlightenment can be an act of meditation.

➤ Contemporary artists in the West are becoming influenced by Buddhism. One way Buddhist liberation is manifesting itself is in the blurring of the boundary between life and art.

Chapter 18

The World Within and Without: Buddhism and the Sciences

In This Chapter

➤ New science shaking up old worldviews

➤ Fuzziness, chaos, and complexity

➤ Holistic: healing body, spirit, and mind

➤ Mind/body and mind/mind interrelations

➤ Buddhist psychology

Art is one our highest human expressions, right alongside science. Traditionally, art and science are set in opposition to each other. Art: intuitive, personal, particular. Science: analytical, objective, general. But that's dualistic thinking, keeping us from seeing how much the two have to say to each other. Buddhism is proving to be a perfect place for the two to have dialogue.

Buddhism's an art, to be discovered, practiced, and expressed by each person differently. So, too, is it a science. You could say the Buddha conducted an experiment he invites others to test (it's unbiased) with the evidence of their own senses (it's empirical) and prove for themselves (it's replicable). So the essence of the scientific method is also Buddhist attitude. And the neat thing is that you don't need an atom-smasher or cloud chamber: You can use yourself as the subject of your investigation. Your meditation is your laboratory. Instead of test tubes, arc lamps, and filter paper, you can utilize a bell, incense, and flowers. Here are some of my own lab notes, from the science of happiness.

The World Around Us: The New Physics and Ancient Buddhist Thought

Science is experiencing a revolution. Up until 1900, science thought it had explained 99 percent of the universe. But it's that darned last 1 percent that's opened up a can of worms for scientists. As microscopes zero in with greater and greater detail, more and more things are popping up on the invisible atomic and subatomic levels that contradict everything known up until now. And telescopes reaching farther and farther out are finding not only enigmatic black holes but also impenetrable "dark matter" suggesting that the visible world analyzed so far may comprise only 10 percent of the real universe.

To appreciate this better, we might break down the entire universe into three categories of interrelationships:

1. Matter and matter
2. Mind and matter
3. Mind and mind

Up until recently, science limited itself to studying matter. Buddhism, on the other hand, has been studying all three categories, and for over two millennia. If you think back over what you've learned about Buddhism thus far, you'll appreciate how complex but comprehensive it is. Now you can sense how up-to-date it is, as science "discovers" what Buddhists have been saying all along.

This Is

A paradigm is a framework of ideas and tools that make up a worldview, a mindset, an exemplar of reality. If some reality isn't included in your paradigm, you won't see it until you shift your paradigm. If you've only walked and then learn to ride a bike, you'll see the world in a new way. A **paradigm shift** takes time to be realized and to resolve itself in society as a whole, affecting many walks of life as it does so.

Holism: Keep Your Eye on the Doughnut AND the Hole

To begin, let me explain what I mean by scientific revolution underway. ("Scientists in sandals are seizing control of the laboratory in the name of the people! Free cyclotrons for everyone!") It would be more accurate to call it a *paradigm shift,* a change in viewpoint—in this case, from a *mechanistic* point of view that breaks everything down into parts and analyzes each separately, to a *holistic* view that looks at how parts interrelate to form wholes. As it does so, it seems to move toward the Buddha's paradigm of life. As we've seen, Buddhism doesn't treat the universe as isolated, separate things but, rather, as events forming a web of karma, a multidimensional interdependent network. Interbeing.

Along the Path

"We are now in the middle of a scientific revolution, one in which the very position and meaning of the scientific approach are undergoing reappraisal—a period not unlike the birth of the scientific approach in ancient Greece or of its renaissance in the time of Galileo."

—Ilya Prigogine

"We used to think that if we knew one, we knew two, because one and one are two. We are finding that we must learn a great deal more about 'and.'"

—Sir Arthur Eddington

It's important to realize how deeply our assumptions condition our notions of reality. Was it coincidence that when science saw the universe as concentric spheres revolving around the earth, the model for society was a similar hierarchy, revolving around a king and his medieval court? Similarly, as Newton described atoms with fixed properties, Western democracy was describing citizens as autonomous entities with inalienable rights.

Today, science has smashed the atom and the nuclear family is breaking down, and there's no map anywhere for how components cohere. People often find it hard to take the world seriously. The mechanistic worldview has broken reality down into so many bits that our world is fragmented, like shattered pottery, or a TV with 50,000 channels. But the mechanistic paradigm, it is a-changing.

We can only glimpse this transformation, as it's so big and we're intrinsically caught up within it, like fish in water. Before we see how it's affecting healing, prayer, and psychology, let's stay a little longer with how science itself is changing its fundamental premises. This is important because, up until now, science was our gold standard of truth. The very definition of objectivity. But now, current evidence is forcing scientists to reject their own notions of objectivity.

In the dawn of the twentieth century, science came up against the limitations of its very vocabulary to describe what it saw when it advanced as far as the atomic and subatomic levels. For example, one test proved that light was composed of waves, and not particles, while another test proved that light was particles, not waves. Physicists had to make up the word "complementarity" to discuss its being waves *and* particles (rather than call them "wavicles"; I guess they'd never heard of a koan ... much less that floor wax that's also a dessert topping).

Now, what's really interesting is that scientists were only recently discovering what the East had been saying about reality for thousands of years. For instance, complementarity. So when Einstein proposed that matter is energy, and energy is matter, he was echoing an ancient premise of both Taoism and Buddhism, expressed in the yin-yang symbol as well as the saying, "Form is emptiness, and emptiness is form." (Einstein knew of and admired Buddhism—particularly, as he put it, its "covering both the material and spiritual, ... natural and spiritual, as a meaningful unity"—but he was the first to do the math.)

Hear and Now

"If we ask ... whether the position of the electron remains the same, we must say "no"; if we ask whether the electron's position changes with time, we must say "no"; if we ask whether the electron is at rest we must say "no"; if we ask whether it is in motion, we must say "no." The Buddha has given such answers when interrogated as to the conditions of a man's self after his death; but they are not familiar answers for the tradition of seventeenth- and eighteenth-century science."

—J. Robert Oppenheimer

Using their minds as a laboratory (and with all the time in the world), early Buddhists made maps of the universe that scientists are now studying. Here's another example: The early Buddhists unequivocally stated the universe is made not only of particles but also subatomic particles; they required only observation of their own mind to make this discovery. ("I." Am. A. Series. Of. Events. Divisible. Into. Sub-events. And. Sub-sub-e-vents. E. Z.!) And their sense of the actual proportions of sub-atomic levels are proving to coincide with science's measurements. Uncanny!

A little after Einstein, a physicist named Werner Heisenberg discovered you can't measure both location and direction of a subatomic particle simultaneously, because the measuring tool enters into the equation. Buddhists might call this fact co-dependent origination, mutual arising; interbeing. ("This is because that is." The electron's there because I'm over here.) It became known as the Uncertainty Principle, which more generally meant observation affects function.

Newer breakthroughs in physics further reconfirm ancient Buddhist truths. For example, a hologram can create a 3-D mirage in mid-air. A sculpture made of light. If you haven't seen one, they're really neat. Now, the really interesting thing is that if only half of the negative were used, you'd still see the full image, only a little dimmer. Using just a tiny corner, you'd still have the entire object, only dimmer still.

That is, the entirety of information about the whole is present everywhere through-out all parts of the holographic negative, the way a bead on Indra's net of beads reflects all the other beads. One instant or thing contains all others. (Something as small as a hair tip contains millions of Buddha realms, each containing bazillions of subatomic Buddha realms, each a perfect pure land.)

Fantastic. Yet the Buddha said:

> As a net is made up of a series of ties, so everything in this world is connected by a series of ties. If anyone thinks that the mesh of a net is an independent, isolated thing, he is mistaken. It is called a net because it is made up of a series of interconnected meshes, and each mesh has its place and responsibility in relation to other meshes.

The Flower Garland School, and its influence in Vajrayana, Pure Land, and Zen, have been saying all along that we're all bodies of light interpenetrating each other in one vast radiant 10-dimensional mandala of light. (A still unproven but interesting avenue of note, too, is Superstring Theory, which holds that this is but 1 of 10 parallel universes. Stay tuned.) Okay, so what does all this have to do with you and me?

Well, as paradigms shift they affect everything from art to "ego" to economics. And one thing that affects them all is that materialism isn't everything. Why? Up until now science has been like a tree whose trunk is the study of physics ("This is a rock, you got a problem with that?"). Now the study of matter alone is no longer enough. Now scientists are waking up to relationships. Between mind and matter, and mind and mind, as well as matter and matter. And interrelationships. Patterns.

Hear and Now

"One finds in the realm of experience, essentially the same type of structure that one finds in the realm of elementary particle physics, namely a web structure, the smallest elements of which always reach out to other things and find their meaning and ground of being in these other things. Since this same type of structure is suitable both in the realm of mind and in the realm of matter, one is led to adopt it as the basis of an over-all world view."

—Henry Peirce Stapp

Fuzzy Wuzzy Was a Bear: Chaos and Complexity

Twentieth-century discoveries came to the limits of the logic of looking at the world in terms of Aristotle's patterns of "either/or" (something's *either* this *or* that, but not both). Besides complementarity, a new branch of science called *Fuzzy Logic* has been studying such so-called gray areas.

Electricity's *either* on *or* off. (Hence the Digital Revolution: all ones and zeros.) But a sunset can be pink-orange or orange-pink. Now that's fuzzy. ("When is a door not a door? When it's ajar.")

Japan was about five years ahead of the West in exploring and applying fuzzy logic, maybe because Eastern language patterns are familiar with this way of seeing and dealing with the world. Certainly, the Buddhist ground of Japanese culture didn't hurt. Fuzzy logic's now programmed into certain makes of camcorders, cars, and nuclear power plants. And scientists are discovering that gray areas occur anywhere, from 0 to 100 percent. Indeed, there's a whole science now, called *chaos theory* that studies the orderly patterns of what previously seemed merely grainy, in between, pimply, pocky, seaweedy, wiggly, wispy, and wrinkled. (Sounds like they're studying my uncle Melvin!)

Out of chaos theory also comes complexity theory, and they're both very relevant to Buddhism. And vice versa.

Chaos: There's a Method in the Madness

The boundary between yin and yang isn't straight but curvy. Now, as scientists study such nonlinear patterns, they're finding out some remarkable things. For example, the formula for plotting the seemingly random pattern of the outline of clouds matches the formula for plotting the seemingly random pattern of coastlines. So are they random, after all?

Chaos theory says, no, randomness has patterns, too. This is interesting from a Buddhist perspective. The fact that what was once thought to be goo can really be quite orderly, is like the "controlled accident" of zen—the way gardens always have an odd number of stones or trees, because asymmetry looks more natural ... or the way an artist can splash some ink with a flick of the wrist and it looks like a mountain cliff. And it's a good parable of yin-yang: conversely, too high a degree of structure can ultimately look like goo; a warning to all control freaks.

Another interesting aspect of the underlying orderliness of seemingly chaotic shapes is what's called their *self-similarity*. For instance, the jagged edge of just a chunk of cloud will be similar to that of the entire cloud. That is, the shape of the whole is similar to itself at varying levels of scale. Fantastic. And this is true for the outline of a cauliflower as well as a cloud. Mountains as well as coastlines. Lightning and ferns. This reflects the coherence of the Buddhist principles of the infinite interpenetration of worlds within worlds, and the integrity of identity.

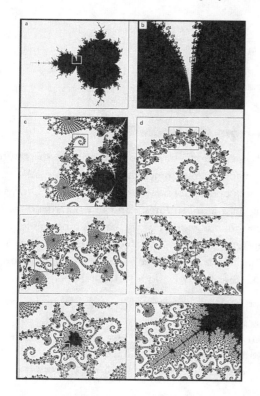

Starting with the basic fractal pattern in the upper left, we enlarge a tiny sector of it and find an entirely new expression of its underlying pattern. Isolating a fragment of that, we can probe further, and so on, seemingly to infinity. From The Science of Fractal Images, *Heinz-Otto Peitgen and Dietmar Saupe, editors (Springer-Verlag, 1988).*

The accompanying figure illustrates the order inherent in a seemingly random or chaotic pattern, through a shape called a *fractal*. Fractals illustrate the unreliability of rigid, hard-and-fast, straight-line boundaries, particularly dualities. Fractals are like a scientific map of the flow of the Middle Way. Now this middle way between order and chaos is called *complexity*. And it's here where you're most likely to find viable patterns for life.

Complexity: It's Basically Simple

Based on chaos study, *complexity theory* looks at living systems and their evolution, over time, through interaction of simple component elements. The word here is *interaction*. Reaction only goes from A to B, while interaction represents ongoing communication between A and B (perhaps also with the environment C, plus other factors D, E, and F).

Just as science finds chaos isn't at all random, it's finding complexity is composed of really simple things, but *organized* in ways that create the diversity necessary to adapt to unpredictability and change. Self-organization is such a model, as we've seen in two examples, in Chapter 15, "No Work, No Eat: Work to Eat or Eat to Work?" with VISA's chaordic integrity and China's parallel banking network. Yet another example is Buddhism: created from the interaction of simple components, dynamically evolving as a self-organizing complex system.

Leaves from the Bodhi Tree

When scientists make a map, they normally don't take into account how the territory has changed during the time they were mapping. But things change, and even infinitesimal change can have unpredictable consequences. Consider the Butterfly Effect, in which a single butterfly flapping its tiny wings in a Brazilian forest can cause a tornado in Texas. This is possible because the essentially chaotic motion of the earth's atmosphere amplifies small disturbances into broader long-term behavior. Actually, since the theory was proposed by a meteorologist named Karl Lorenz in 1962, we've been discovering how the depletion of rain forests in places like Brazil actually do affect the global weather.

In Chapter 2, "One Taste, Different Flavors: The Teachings Adapt to Different Lands," for example, we've seen how Buddhism maintains its integral core while evolving through interaction with various cultures. In Chapter 14, "Alone, Together: Buddhist

Relationships," we've seen the Buddhist organizational principle of interaction amongst equals—with you at the center of the universe … interlinked with all of creation … everything equally at the center of the universe … moving toward unlimited freedom. And this has enabled Buddhism to be as complex as you'd want, yet based on just a few fundamental premises, such as the Three Jewels and the Four Noble Truths.

The Buddha said all it took was just two people gathering in his name for there to be sangha. A fair amount of competition and cross-fertilization exists between schools.

And perhaps now you might better appreciate how you've learned a complex system of interrelated simple facts—such as the Middle Way, the Three Jewels and the Four Noble Truths—that grow with your own understanding. Though these facts are simple, we've seen their interaction create a complex, comprehensive system capable of adapting to change, like life itself.

Indeed, the ultimate example of a complex system is life. Some carbon comes in contact with a few more simple, basic ingredients, and, *Shazam!* it's alive: watch it evolve! We've noted that besides consciousness (which is nice), we have the power of self-aware observation. Remember: "Mindfulness is the opposable thumb of consciousness." And, presumably, we keep growing and evolving.

Having grown past primal survival, flight-or-fright, what's next? One way to get a glimpse is to further delve into our changing paradigm for the universe, which, as we've noted, is moving from the purely material into the less neatly divisible aspects of life itself … such as health.

Hear and Now

"Nothing novel can come from systems with high degrees of order and stability, such as crystals. On the other hand, completely chaotic systems, such as turbulent fluids or heated gasses, are too formless. Truly complex things—amoeba, bond traders, and the like—appear at the border between rigid order and randomness."

—John Horgan, *From Complexity to Perplexity*

Infinite Healing: Healing the Whole Person

Sickness was one of the four things that obsessed Prince Siddhartha. And so he became a healer of humanity. Having seen how his teachings are like good medicine, now we can appreciate how his prescription differs from what our general physician might prescribe. In a word, it's *holistic*.

Buddhism and Holistic Health

Traditional medicine favors a mechanistic model. Its logic is compartmentalized; linear cause and effect. You have a headache? Take an aspirin. (Of course, if you keep doing this over time, you'll need to take three aspirin instead of one or two, then extra-strength, and so on. But worry about that later.) When you get worse, see a specialist for each problem.

This Is

Like the array of Buddhist schools housed within Buddhism, **holistic medicine** can be an umbrella term encompassing a spectrum of practices, including acupuncture, ayurveda, herbs, homeopathy, nutrition specialties, etc. These practices have long traditions, yet holistic health was termed alternative medicine by Congress. (A recent study found that Americans visit nonphysicians for health care more than physicians.) A term gaining popularity is complementary medicine, since various practices can complement each other; antibiotics plus a basic herbal extract, for example, plus maybe visualization meditation.

A holistic approach would begin by looking at underlying factors that cause headaches, such as posture, diet, stress, escape valves from stress such as alcohol, and so on. It focuses on *process* rather than outcome; interrelations. As we've noted, the word *heal* comes from the same root as *whole* (here, looking at the whole person), as well as *holy*. So for bad posture it would be appropriate to examine spiritual and emotional attitudes. Thus Dr. Dean Ornish, for example, has reversed incidents of heart disease with a regimen focusing on consciousness and behavior as well as diet.

For our purposes, one of the holiest of holistic doctors was the Buddha. In his day, medical knowledge was called *ayurveda*, meaning "life knowledge" (a very viable system still practiced today). As a prince, he'd studied medicine but chose not to be a specialist. Instead, he became a general practitioner, in the widest sense, for all humanity. In some representations, the Buddha's bowl is not for alms, but contains medicine.

Buddhist teachings often call suffering an illness, the Buddha a doctor, and his teachings good medicine. Considering the Four Noble Truths in this light, the Buddha first identifies the symptom (Duhkha), second diagnoses the cause (craving, attachment), third makes a prognosis (an end to the illness exists, called nirvana), and, fourth, writes out a prescription (the Eightfold Path). Elsewhere, in diagnosing causes of unhappiness more specifically, the Buddha labeled them the Three Poisons: greed, hatred, and delusion. (The three antidotes might be equanimity, compassion, and wisdom.) Holistic, the Buddha addresses the whole person, body, mind, and spirit.

It's interesting to note that in Greece, at around the same time as the Buddha taught, a man named Hippocrates (from whom we get modern medicine's Hippocratic Oath) seemed in tune with the Buddha when he trusted the body's innate powers of self-healing and defined health as a harmonious interaction of factors. The Buddha's radical step was to invite fellow seekers to investigate such findings themselves, using themselves as subjects. Of course people are different, so different paths emerged.

This Is

In the commentaries on sutras made by the Buddha and others, known as **abhidharma** ("ultimate doctrine"), there exists an extensive, systematic, and intricate literature of psychology, human personality, and mental health, including healthy and unhealthy mental factors, descriptions of personality types, and prescriptions for each. A science of introspection, it takes as its basic unit a single moment within the stream of consciousness. It thus starts with mind, proceeds with mind as its focal point of reference, and culminates in liberating mind.

Different Strokes

Each practice has different emphases. Theravada literature recounts how the Buddha cured himself of severe illness during his final retreat. "With patience and without distress," it is said, he was mindfully aware of his painful physical sensations, and then they no longer occurred. That is, he noted the momentary nature of the painful sensations, breaking them down into segments, and they went away.

Mahasi Sayadaw has recorded cases of mindfulness leading to disintegration of tumors as well as elimination of arthritis and asthma. The primary sutra for practice here would be *The Four Establishments of Mindfulness*. At the University of Massachusetts Medical Center, a major American hospital, such teachings are simply called stress reduction. (I wonder if insurance companies would still pay for these practices if they knew they came from sutras and were called "Vipassana," "Buddhist" or even "meditation." But the proof is in the pudding.) The Stress Reduction Clinic, established by Dr. Jon Kabat-Zinn, accepts patient referrals for all kinds of symptoms, many of which don't have easily identifiable sources, such as cancer and heart disease, with remarkable results.

Thanks to such trailblazing work, the use of mindfulness meditation to help patients suffering from chronic pain (pain which doesn't go away) and stress-related medical disorders is becoming more widely accepted. Less stress *is* best.

Along the Path

"In due time the basic Zen exercise leads to certain mental accomplishments, resulting in powers of healing that are not directed toward any specific medical condition but all the more freely and deeply pervade the meditator's entire constitution."

—Heinrich Dumoulin

"... Zen liberates all the energies properly and naturally stored in each of us ... to save us from going crazy or being crippled ... giving free play to all the creative and benevolent impulses inherently lying in our hearts."

—Erich Fromm

From a Mahayana perspective, the bodhisattva vow defines our own healing in terms of the healing of others. Like our happiness, our health isn't necessarily a personal matter. Here's one gatha for this you might try sometime: *Breathing in, I heal myself; breathing out, I heal others.*

A zen approach identifies with neither illness nor health but the boundlessness and interpenetration of both. Zen patriarch Yun-men said, "Medicine and sickness mutually correspond. The whole universe is medicine. What is the self?" As Buddhist author Rick Fields said during his noble confrontation with cancer, "I don't have a life-threatening illness, I have a disease-threatening life." Visualizing a disease as being part of sunyata doesn't set up within the body the barbed wire of self vs. other. Sometimes attacking a disease too violently causes only more damage.

East Asian Buddhist doctors are likely to be influenced by Chinese five-element theory. Tibetan Buddhist doctors are influenced by Hindu Ayurvedic medical theories. Tibetan Buddhism itself has a large repertoire of healing techniques, including guided meditations and visualizations. Dr. Herbert Benson, of Harvard Medical School, has documented how a Vajrayana meditation technique called *tumo* enables Tibetans to generate warmth in zero-degree weather, at will. Tibetans also teach *lucid dreaming*, consciously interacting with dream material during sleep (as well as treating waking life as a dream). Which brings us to the power of the mind.

No Matter, Never Mind: Mind/Body Connections

The University of Massachusetts Stress Reduction Clinic has found their high records of success includes positive changes in not only behavior normally believed unchangeable, but also positive physical changes. This brings up the whole mind-body topic. You can't change one without transforming the other.

This Is

Immunology is one of physiology's newest chapters. Fifty years ago, it was established as the study of the immune system (spleen, bone marrow, lymph nodes, white blood cells, T-cells, etc.). But now it's discovering that the immune system, the endocrine system (glands and hormones), and the nervous system behave more like a network than isolated systems, as they intercommunicate and interact. Thus a new science of **neuroimmunology** has been born. Your health is bound up with your sense of who you are, mind and body influencing each other.

Who are we, really? From the way I was taught science as a child, I remember imagining that my skull contained a small executive office with a big desk, equipped with a video screen and speakers, where the mind sat, the real me, monitoring my body's activities. Aside from the video and speakers, this was pretty much the model in vogue for about five centuries, ever since a French philosopher named René Descartes said "I think, therefore I am." But is our gray matter really the throne of our mind?

A current theory is that mind simply represents the process of knowing, cognition, and thus isn't necessarily confined to the brain. Consider the buddha flower by my window, exchanging ions with the atmosphere: It knows when it's dark and light, knows when I add soil fertilizer to its water, and has a preference for Mozart and Bach. It *minds* when I don't feed it.

Wherever the mind actually is, science is discovering it may not be in just one place. For example, mind-body connections are being studied in the new field of *neuroimmunology.* Here it's being discovered how emotions create chemicals (such as peptides) which affect health and, conversely, how health creates emotions, each creating feedback loops between identity and well-being or disease. Indeed, our immune network is being thought of as a parallel neurology, "a chemical brain," so to speak. This backs up the "relaxation response" discovered by Dr. Herbert Benson in the 1970s, showing how meditation creates less stress, which in turn can be beneficial to people with such stress-related disorders as cancer, high blood pressure, heart disease, infertility, and premenstrual syndrome.

And it backs up a realization that's common in meditation: "Hey, I'm not in my head! Yet I'm still alive!!" (Until this point, some people might have a hard time with their breathing and attention; feeling, for example, like an oboist whose head's about to burst.) This outlook reminds us not only of the Chinese word for mind being the heart, body and mind as one. Moreover, it underlines the Buddha's advice not to grasp after a thing called self, nor any independent world outside such self that would thus come along with it. (A package deal.)

So the mechanistic model, with its image of a foreman with his gloved hands on the levers of some central control panel (and don't ask what that little red button does), is giving way to a more holistic model, with an image more like a network of networks, all internetworked, operating autonomously through the checks and balances of feedback loops. (This is what the word "internet" means, of course: the internetworked network of networks. Thus, it's no surprise that humans should have invented it sooner or later.)

In the network model, there's no center, top, nor bottom. When one node of the network attains a greater degree of knowing, the other nodes bootstrap up, sharing that new complexity. And the network can survive failure of separate nodes because energy or information can reroute along the many alternative paths. Thus, in network terms, any node is defined by its relation to all the others, its interactions. This is of consonant the Buddha's program asking us to be mindful of our lives, our selves, as a successive series of events, we find these events interacting with other events in an endless and impermanent flow, and discover no separate identity to any of them, or ourselves, other than their unique moment within a lattice or flow of interpenetrating happenings.

The mechanistic model of science dissects life into parts and particles, substances and molecules. The holistic model of science observes life in terms of patterns, relationships, systems, forming wholes.

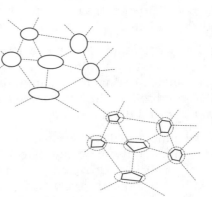

And if our mind's not in our brain, but is rather part of our whole bodily network of awareness—maybe we're not confined to our body at all. Let's go there …

Along the Path

"There is no matter as such! All matter originates and exists only by virtue of a force. We must assume behind this force the existence of a conscious and intelligent Mind. This Mind is the matrix of all matter."

—Max Planck, Nobel Prize–winning father of quantum theory

"The universe is made of stories,
not of atoms."

—Muriel Rukeyser

Imagine: Mind/Mind Connections

Recent scientific developments seem to be closely attuned to Indra's Net of interbeing. Physicist David Bohm (1917–1992) called it *implicate order*. His colleague A. J. Bell discovered an example of it when 1 he separated two electrons across enormous distances and changed one. *Bingo!,* the other one changed instantly, and with no time for a signal to pass between them—unless the signal traveled faster than the speed of light, which would disobey a basic law of physics. A current scientific word coined to categorize such events is *nonlocal*, because they operate outside the normal bounds of space and even time.

Dr. Karl Pribram, for example, believes that memory is nonlocal. It doesn't seem to live in any one lobe or part of the brain (selective brain damage doesn't erase specific memories), but is rather distributed throughout the network of our nerve cells much in the same way an image is equally dispersed throughout a hologram. Indeed, the universe is looking more and more like one big hologram, or Indra's Net, or a tenth-dimensional mandala of light.

"Awakening your mind without fixing it anywhere" means the mind is nonlocal. ("Show me your mind.") Some other neat nonlocal phenomena include animals finding their way across incredible obstacles and distances, twins developing similar idiosyncrasies even when raised separately, visualizing far-away objects ("remote viewing"), and … prayer.

Leaves from the Bodhi Tree

A Prayer for Prayer

May we let prayer be.

May we allow it to follow the infinite patterns of the human heart.
May we learn to practise the most difficult art, the art of noninterference.
May we be guided by prayer instead of attempting to guide prayer.
May we allow prayer to be what it needs to be, to be what it is.

May we let prayer be.

—Larry Dossey, M.D.

In 1988, for instance, doctors conducted a scientific experiment ("a controlled, prospective, matched double-blind study") in which a group of people prayed for a group of cardiac patients. To make it scientific, they included a second group of cardiac patients not being prayed for. Neither group knew which was the object of prayer. Well, the group being prayed for responded as if they'd been given a miracle drug. And only they did so, not the others. By now, there have been at least 150 such tests, all positive.

Of course, rabbis, priests, imams, and flocks of the faithful have known all along that prayer works. Only now it's scientifically proven. ("Nine out of ten doctors agree …") So when Buddhists generate metta, now you know we're really generating metta!

When you're sick, pray. For yourself and others. And when you're not sick, pray. For yourself and others. If you don't do metta meditation, but just sit zazen, dedicate a session to the health of yourself and others. A sangha can dedicate a morning's zazen to someone. Prayer works. Mind is boundless.

Along the Path

Emotional intelligence is the capacity for self-awareness of our feelings and those of others and the ability to deal with them. As defined by Daniel Goleman, this has five major domains:

➤ Self-awareness, or mindfulness, of emotions

➤ Dealing with emotions (managing anger, handling anxiety, soothing yourself, resisting impulse, etc.)

➤ Ability to motivate yourself, to persist and stay hopeful in the face of obstacles and setbacks

➤ Empathy, being sensitive to what someone else's emotions are

➤ Art of the relationships, emotionally satisfying interaction with other people

Listening to the Heart of the Heart: Buddhist Psychology

Just as the Buddha influences the holistic health movement, so, too, does he make a good partner with psychology. Indeed, in introducing a middle way between either total renunciation or immersion, the Buddha's unique transformation of the spiritual path of his time explores engagement with the world through a scientific process of examination we'd now call psychological.

Just as meditation brings us back to awareness of our body, so, too, does it recognize that our feelings have a mind of their own. Don't be ruled by the primitive fight-or-flight wiring of our brains that allows our emotions to override our thoughts. Be aware of your feelings, the Buddha said, honor and befriend them.

What If Freud Met Buddha?

In childhood, we weren't necessarily aware of our feelings, lacking training in emotional intelligence. And so our emotional experiences of childhood laid down patterns of behavior that today we might wish to change. Thus, many people often turn to psychology for a remedy. Historically, this rising popular interest in psychology and therapy led to much of the West's initial discovery of Buddhism. Psychology and Buddhism certainly influence and complement each other. It's worth comparing and contrasting the two.

Both psychology and Buddhism are arts of being in the moment. Of being in touch with one's own experience, with life as lived now, and realizing one's fullest potential for active awareness and a rewarding, meaningful, happy life.

This Is

Psychology literally means care of the soul. In Freudian terms, "self" is a constellation of id (instincts), ego (reality principle), and superego (conscience and self ideal). Health is a harmonious balance of the three. Depression is an uncontrollable mood or habitual emotional state of anxiety or melancholy, not necessarily based on immediate reality. This is an example of neurosis, which can progress to psychosis and then to psychopathology, if symptoms withdraw further away from immediate reality.

Both are healing arts. Both seek to liberate the practitioner from needless baggage keeping him or her from being open and available to life's potentials. Baggage here might be thought of as a thick shell once needed for self-preservation but since outgrown, such as a swaggering manner that paid off in the sandbox but doesn't cut it anymore in the world of grown ups—or a thick scar over a wound now long gone, such as a childhood trauma.

Both practices aspire to the clarity of recognizing thoughts and emotions without identifying with them. Psychoanalysis locates the clingings or cravings of the Second Noble Truth in attachments rooted in the past. Just as the Buddhist learns being *in* the world not *of* the world, the practitioner of psychology recognizes ego (visible personality) without identifying with it, seeing how to *have* an ego without *being* one, molding it for maximum benefit and happiness in this world.

Both practices require enormous patience. Attitude is important toward practice in general: not striving for enlightenment, although enlightenment is the goal. So the practitioner has to learn how not to force a result or become disappointed at seeming lack of progress. In meditation as in therapy, some days there's little to note, or little to tell a therapist or a teacher, and still one shows up anyway. Other days, there's a rush of things to deal with.

Psychology has been called "the talking cure," but it's also the listening cure, a situation in which two people agree to meet and listen. In this, it has similarities to meditation's open awareness, deep listening, and bearing witness. And there's Buddhist resonance in Freud's instructions for therapists (a model for patients, as well) to hold "evenly suspended attention." (Sounds like Hui Neng's "Awaken the mind, without fixing it anywhere.") Suspend judgment, he says, and give "impartial attention to everything there is to observe. The doctor should simply listen, and not bother about whether he is keeping anything in mind."

A relationship with the therapist can become very intense, and a successful practitioner will understand that any surprising uprush of difficult, violent, or overwhelming emotions aren't being thrust at him or her by the therapist but are rather manifesting from his or her own mind, having been repressed for too long. In this, it's very similar to the trust, intimacy, and identification that can be crucial in Vajrayana practice with a lama or guru, and to a degree with a roshi when studying koans.

Now, one difference between analysis and meditation is that a psychoanalytic plan of treatment is like a division of labor between analyst and analysand (client), until the client can do it independently. That is, during a 50-minute session, the client is asked to free associate, describing the flow of sensations, memories, thoughts, aversions, and desires passing through awareness, and the psychologist monitors and provides appropriate labeling, similar to insight meditation. (Perhaps this is one reason that vipassana and insight meditation are so popular amongst people active in one way or another in therapy.)

Along the Path

Imagine unwanted thoughts are weeds. The zen gardener doesn't tear them up, with a violence which might sow seeds of new unwanted thoughts, but cuts off conditions that nourish them, and as they die lets them become mulch to fertilize the soil for healthy seeds. (The Buddhist concept equivalent to the unconscious, the soil where seeds are nourished, is called "store consciousness," *alaya vijnana*, where karma accumulates.) This is "bowing to habit energy."

A psychologist is an external "watcher," whereas vipassana is an internal one. But awakening an internal watcher to act as one's inner therapist—asking you "Are you aware of that?" and "What do you think of that?"—won't necessarily guarantee mental health. A practitioner can still curl up inside a comfort zone that denies seeing situations and possibilities that are present; hence the need for sangha and a teacher.

While psychology sorts through and prioritizes emotions as happy vs. sad, good vs. bad, vipassana simply notes them. Buddha throws out both "happy" and "sad," saying they're all bound to duhkha, all setups for further stress and anxiety, dissatisfaction and pain. In addition to asking psychology's question, "How can the script be changed?," Buddha asks "Are scripts necessary? How can consciousness itself be transformed?"

Hear and Now

"It will take quite a long time before you find your calm, serene mind in your practice. Many sensations come, many thoughts or images arise, but they are just waves of your own mind. Nothing comes from outside your mind. Usually we think of our mind as receiving impressions and experiences from outside, but that is not a true understanding of our mind. The true understanding is that the mind includes everything; when you think something comes from outside it means only that something appears in your mind."

—Shunryu Suzuki

As Ram Dass has put it, "Western psychotherapy rearranges the furniture in the room. Eastern techniques help you get out of the room." From this perspective, most contemporary psychologists seek to adjust the self to better adapt to the world, whereas the Buddhist says there is no self, no difference between self and world, no dualism ("me," in here; the world, "out there"—stimuli, out there, sensations, in here). "Show me your mind," as Bodhidharma replied to the question, "How can I quiet my mind?" It's all Buddha mind.

This has lead some to say that Buddhism goes further; that psychology is good for dealing with the nature and meaning of emotions and Buddhism with the nature and meaning of life. Yet traditionally psychology embraces life in its fullest, as well.

Whatever Works

The practice of mindfulness certainly can help the practice of psychology awaken a person to an outmoded script for living. And mindfulness practice can help someone break out of being stuck at that point of awareness, in some vicious cycle such as understanding a habit but repeating it anyway, and using the guilt at so doing to reinforce the whole problematic habit. That is, a traumatic episode of the past no longer has control when it's recognized that the self of that situation (the person abused or denied or withheld) no longer exists in the present moment. As Buddhist psychoanalyst Dr. Mark Epstein puts it, "There is no true self waiting in the wings to be released."

If an overly strong self is a problem to be avoided, a strong self is needed to overcome the problem. No paradox here. It's like the seeming contradiction of Right Attitude, seeking enlightenment without forcing it. Buddhism's answer is, partly, the sixth tenet of the Eightfold Noble Path, Right Effort. It means not giving up because progress seems slow. The Path requires active energy or effort to abandon unwholesome thoughts, prevent them from arising, and develop wholesome thoughts.

Along the Path

"The more a human being feels himself a self, tries to intensify this self and reach a never attainable perfection, the more drastically he steps out of the center of being, which is no longer now his own center, and the further he removes himself from it."

—Eugen Herrigel

"Selflessness is not a case of something that existed in the past becoming nonexistent. Rather this sort of 'self' is something that never did exist. What is needed is to identify as nonexistent something that always was nonexistent."

—The Dalai Lama

Here we can underscore a common misunderstanding about Buddhism. Recognizing self as a convenient fiction, a mask hung around boundless awareness, an adaptive strategy, doesn't mean that enlightened people don't look both ways before crossing a street. Freud's "ego," the reality principle, still applies. Buddhists still remember their zip codes.

So, on a psychological level, being Buddhist isn't a license to become passive, or walk away from feelings; not at all. On the contrary, it's freedom from identification and attachment to the "frozen block of the emotions and thought," as Zen teacher Charlotte Joko Beck describes a neurotic ego. Conversely, becoming attached to meditation can be another form of narcissism.

Taking responsibility for your actions, thoughts, and emotions simply means the total *ability* to respond, without necessarily *reacting* or acting out. Buddhism and psychology are both responsible paths. Practiced in tandem, from time to time, they can check the possibility of either path being a dead-end. Meanwhile, ... the dialogue between Buddhism and contemporary science is creating a radiant laboratory of sacred knowledge ... illuminating life within and without."

The Least You Need to Know

➤ The Buddha's mode of thought applied the scientific method. But whereas Western science has centered itself on studying the interrelationships of matter and matter, Buddhists have studied the interrelationships of matter and matter, mind and matter, and mind and mind.

➤ New scientific findings confirm things Buddhists have known for millennia, casting them in a new light. As science changes its model, or paradigm, it comes closer to embracing Buddhism as a model.

➤ Some new branches of science that harmonize with and illuminate Buddhism are fuzzy logic, chaos, and complexity; holistic health; and psychology.

➤ Buddha's application of the scientific attitude was unique for using the human mind as both subject and laboratory. This can be seen to be a psychological process of analysis. Freud and the Buddha have thus shaken hands and begun to work together for mutual benefit.

➤ Sometimes the benefits of Buddhist techniques such as mindfulness meditation can become more easily and widely accepted when given a more generally descriptive name, such as "stress reduction" and "emotional intelligence."

Chapter 19

Happiness Is Not an Individual Matter: Engaging the World

In This Chapter

➤ By the bedside of the dying

➤ In between the bars of prisons

➤ Care of the earth

➤ Awakening feminine energy

➤ Erasing racism

➤ Engaging the world

By now, I hope I've dispelled any myths of Buddhism as bloodless, emotionless, detached, otherworldly navel-gazing. Renouncing greed, fear, and illusion, the Buddhist doesn't walk away from the world of human relationships but, rather, joins a community of good friends heading in a common direction in the world. Lay person or monastic, the Buddhist lives *in* this world without being attached *to* it.

The Buddhist approach to change in the world is interesting. When there's trouble on the road, angrily honking the horn only compounds the difficulty. When witnessing the same trouble from a place of peace, then we can be of service.

The doorway to enlightenment is in this very world. In this chapter, we explore right relationship that lead to, if not open that door. It's possible to be happy within the fortress walls of a palace. But, sooner or later, signs of life slip through. Then it might come time to seek for a deeper happiness. It's time to move beyond a relationship of "me," "it," to one of "me" and "you," and "ours." As Thich Nhat Hanh says, "Happiness is not an individual matter."

One Big Circle of Giving

We've looked at close, intimate relations in Chapter 14, "Alone, Together: Buddhist Relationships." We turn now to our intimacy with the larger tapestry of life. Engaging the whole world. This tapestry's not a big fabric rectangle, though: It's a big living circle.

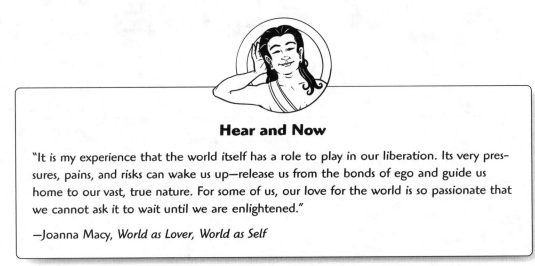

Hear and Now

"It is my experience that the world itself has a role to play in our liberation. Its very pressures, pains, and risks can wake us up—release us from the bonds of ego and guide us home to our vast, true nature. For some of us, our love for the world is so passionate that we cannot ask it to wait until we are enlightened."

—Joanna Macy, *World as Lover, World as Self*

We often begin our path by trying to get free from others, only to find out our freedom isn't independent of everybody else. Whatever our faith, religious paths all point to leading a life bigger than ourselves alone. This fulfillment can come from family, or from work, or community service, working for the environment, or involvement in the arts.

When I can, I work as a volunteer at a nearby needy nonprofit whose cause I relate to. Small organizations that live low on the food chain can use all the help they can get, and miracle workers in adversity's doorway deserve support. From a certain light, volunteering could be seen as selfish, because it can be a great boost for the person giving. It all depends. Ram Dass sees service as a circle: helping people as he works on himself, and working on himself to help people. Perfecting that circle can be quite a pleasant game.

The helping hand and the begging hand are indistinguishable in the act of charity. Charity in its original meaning, from Greek, is a word for love. It's like the tea ceremony, for instance, where guests and the host are clearly distinguishable but also indistinguishable: Are we the guests of the tea? of the flower arrangement? of the universe? *Final answer:* We're united by the love of the simple pleasure of tea.

For example, consider the homeless. Rather than being given money, I've found it can be real important for a homeless person to have someone stop and talk nonjudgmentally with them, to bear witness, to awaken to the Buddha nature within all the grime. There but for fortune go you or I. As one homeless guy once said as I was walking away after giving him a quarter and talking with him: "Hey, thanks! The money's nice, but thanks for stopping—I was beginning to think I was on Mars!" And how could I think *him*—for giving me an opportunity to practice compassion?!

The bodhisattva vow, taking refuge with all beings, affirming our interconnectedness, is a kind of a yoga. In the great Hindu epic, *The Bhagavad Gita (The Celestial Song),* Krishna calls this *karma yoga,* a path to liberation practiced by using consciously disinterested but considered, intentional action for the benefit of others. There are as many paths to this yoga as veins and arteries massaging your heart. Practice just one avenue deeply and you're practicing all the others.

Two kinds of fellow human beings with whom to practice karma yoga are the dying and the imprisoned.

Living Each Other's Dying: Service in Hospices

Yogi Berra once quipped that he went to everyone's funerals so he'd be sure they'd all come to his. Of course, it's not being dead but the dying that's difficult. And so it's no surprise to see Buddha at the bedsides of the dying. A Buddhist was once voluntarily taking care of a dying man. One day, the dying man finally asked the Buddhist why he was always so cheerful at his duties, unpaid, and all for a perfect stranger. Without hesitation, the Buddhist smiled and replied, "I'm treating you the way I expect to be treated when my turn comes."

The Golden Rule applies to our ultimate, final moments; yet, as we've seen in Chapter 14, our society looks the other way. We don't witness the burning of corpses on public pyres, as has been the custom in India since before the time of the Buddha. We don't drink from a bowl made from a human skull, as was the custom in Tibet. Only once or twice a year might we even visit a graveyard. But what is becoming more commonplace in our society is the possibility of making a commitment of time volunteering at a *hospice.* The first hospice service began in the United States over 30 years ago, and there are now 3,000 such agencies in operation. The Zen

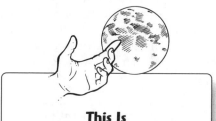

This Is

Palliative care brings relief to symptoms and pain for the terminally ill without hope of cure. A **hospice** provides interdisciplinary comfort and support outside of a hospital setting for the terminally ill and their relatives. It allows patient and family to focus on emotional and spiritual aspects of care, so that medical concerns don't dominate the entire focus of dying.

Hospice in San Francisco echoes another ancient tradition by calling its function as serving as "midwives to the dying."

The Buddha is depicted as lying down during his paranirvana (literally, "final" or "total extinction"). Even then he continued to teach. And it looks like it would be a real pleasure to sit by his bedside. Paranirvana Buddha. Glazed ceramic. $54^{1}/_{2}$" × $43^{1}/_{4}$" × $1^{1}/_{2}$".

(Photo: Loraine Capparell)

But isn't it depressing? Well, a friend of mine who volunteers at the Zen Hospice tells me that every time he leaves he feels so appreciative of life in general ... mindful of each step he can make, responding to suffering ... aware how each time is different, keeping a not-knowing mind. For example, no one knows how long any guest will stay at the hospice. When doctors give up on a person's mortality, there's no telling how long he or she has, or, more important, how they might respond to love. In one instance, a hospice worker fell in love with a person she was caring for, and he moved in with her. Ten years later, they're still married. Amazing things can happen.

A hospice can be a place of great creativity. Awakening of mind can occur anytime, such as while counseling a client and family, often overwhelmed with the initial news of the medical diagnosis. Or while lending a listening ear to someone who needs to be heard. Or offering new options to someone during a spiritual crisis. In one hospice, a young volunteer asked each guest, "If you weren't here, where would you like to go?" Then, he'd visit that place—the local piano bar, say, if that's what the person said. He'd bring a small video recorder, and he'd say to the people there, "You know one of your regulars is staying at the hospice and she wishes she could be here at this piano bar right now. Is there anything you'd like to say to her?" Then, back at the hospice, being shown the video, the guest would often talk about his or her whole life, and its whole meaning would unfold.

You don't have to be Buddhist to volunteer at a Buddhist hospice. Death doesn't screen its participants. Like any hospice, a Buddhist hospice will have the same obligations as anyone to the constellation of concerned parties and related institutions. But it does embody a unique, 2,500-year-old tradition of conscious care, fusing spiritual insight and practical social action, compassion, and service. And so, it's a wonderful way to engage your Buddhist practice in the world around you.

This Is

Funded by the public, America's **prisons** are now the fastest-growing segment of the U.S. economy. During the past 25 years, the national budget for building and operating prisons has gone from $500 million to $31 billion per year. The number of penal institutions has quadrupled. The prisoner population has risen from 187,000 to 1.4 million, the largest in the world. One out of every 50 children in America now has a parent in prison.

Be Free Where You Are: Service in Prisons

Bearing witness to the execution of a prisoner at San Quentin, Zen priest Norman Fischer reports feeling the utter incomprehensibility of the situation. Here he was, he recalls, a living being, joined with a hundred other living beings, holding hands, come together to witness life slip out of another human being, by order of a decree in a book, through the injection of a lethal substance.

The death penalty having become a lightning rod for interfaith concern, he went on to note that many Christians were there, passionately seeing the victim as like Christ, the warden as Pontius Pilate, and so forth. But he could see no Bad Guy or Good Guy in the situation. Only the utter futility of punishing violence by violence. In so doing, he recognized that violence is internalized throughout society, conditioned into all our hearts, his included.

How can we ignore the existence of human life, and its potential for awakening, even if it's walled off from our everyday life? Had Siddhartha seen a prisoner on one of his outings from the palace, that, too, might well have had an effect equal to the old man, the sick, the dead, and the monk.

The French say, "The sun shines on the whole world"; so prisons as well as monasteries and palaces have their high walls, but also the same sunshine as above you or me. Like a monastery, the prison affords plenty of time for practice. Suffering, and the cycle of violence, can be ended anywhere. Buddhist teacher Sakya Jetsun Chime Luding reminds us, "The Buddha himself said that the place of practice is your own mind. It's not a physical place."

Hear and Now

"*We must do the work that will change the way we think. ... Buddhist practice is not just something to study, it is a way of living, a way to be safe and to lead a better life. It is a way of taking responsibility for our actions. And for those of us who will be getting out someday, it will help us stay out.*"

—Jarvis Masters, Death Row, San Quentin

It's estimated that 70 percent of current prisoners are serving time for nonviolent crimes, but can they remain nonviolent upon their release from hell on earth? That is to say, prisons are not only lonely and spiritually barren, but can also be abusive and traumatic ... a training ground for crime ... perpetuating the cycle of violence. Besides death penalty activism, Buddhist engagement within prisons includes teaching meditation, correspondence with prisoners, volunteer chaplaincy, and ex-convict employment.

Under surveillance of a guard from the women's jail, Gregory Carter, James Crowley, and Carlton Allen (left to right) begin a 10-day Vipassana session, up to 12 hours a day, at San Francisco County Jail No. 7. Giving up most of the daily privileges that typically define identity and dignity for prisoners, they cannot wait until they get on the outside in order to water seeds of positive outlook, action, and understanding on the inside.

(Photo: Anthony Pidgeon)

As viable forms of self-rehabilitation, Vipassana, Zen, Pure Land, and Vajrayana are now being taught in various prisons. In the 1970s, for example, Burmese Vipassana master S. N. Goenka taught prisoners in Tihar Jail, India's largest prison and one of the most dangerous in the world; today, there's a Vipassana center within Tihar. Similar programs have begun in Seattle and San Francisco. For men and women accustomed to failure, just completing the rigorous training is a victory. While mindfulness can't transform a criminal overnight, it can furnish a crucial turning point with tools for understanding and transforming karma, detoxifying, and leading a more peaceful, rewarding life upon release.

Of course, when the prisoners' crimes have victims, they are part of the story as well, but they seldom knock on monastery doors. Geoffrey Shugen Arnold, of Zen Mountain Monastery in the Catskills, teaches in the prisons and is quite aware of this. His final answer: "Nothing you do can be singularly about yourself, and once you see it that way, everything changes."

Have You Hugged a Tree Today?

If you saw me on my walks in San Francisco you might notice I stop to hug a tree at random at least once a day. Nothing sentimental. Hugger and huggee mindfully become one. Mutually embraced by the All. After all, just as we're related to the animals, so, too, are we related to the plants, whose minerals still flow in our own veins. A tree hug can also be a reminder how to grow tall and still sway. (Have you hugged a tree today?)

This Is

Buddhist environmental attitudes often fall under the relatively new science called **deep ecology.** Ecology (literally, "care for our house") studies relations between beings and their environment. Superficial ecology takes an anthropomorphic view, with humanity separate from nature; deep ecology sees humanity as inseparably embedded within nature, part of a continuum of interbeing. Buddhist ecology has been called Dharma Gaia. Gaia (say "gaya") is the scientific theory (named after the Greek goddess of the earth) that the earth's a living organism, a sentient being, a self-regulating entity.

Do Buddhists have some particular thing about trees? Well, the Buddha became enlightened sitting by a tree. Indeed, of all its many applications in the world, Buddhism is closest, at heart, to *ecology*. Ecology here means more than recycling paper and cans. Understanding Buddhism, we can speak of *deep ecology*. That is, some people see nature as a warehouse of goods. Others see nature as a big park to play in or cool one's

Along the Path

"The entire range of living matter on Earth, from whales to viruses, and from oaks to algae, could be regarded as constituting a single living entity, capable of manipulating the Earth's atmosphere to suit its overall needs and endowed with faculties and powers far beyond those of its constituent parts."

—James Lovelock, on the Gaia hypothesis

heels. Buddhists see that we ourselves are an integral and inseparable part of the park, that we and the park are part of a continuum of life, the workshop of nature, the web of living being.

Deep ecology is a key player in the paradigm shift, introduced in Chapter 18, "The World Within and Without: Buddhism and the Sciences." After several centuries of a mechanistic mindset, breaking everything down into its parts and analyzing each part, we're moving into a frame of mind that sees how molecules and nebula form coherent patterns and become living systems, intertwined.

Now, the Buddhist approach to ecology doesn't turn a blind eye to the presence greed within the total picture. This compassionate understanding is realist, as Buddhism typically is. So, too, is the recognition of each tree as a complete being with a right to life, even if it can't cast a ballot. Taking refuge with all beings, the Buddhist vows to protect and preserve life in all forms. And so Buddhism is quite likely to embrace ecological issues from a deeper awareness than commonly considered.

When eco-catastrophe threatens our earth, our water, our air, stemming the tide isn't necessarily an altruistic duty. That implies sacrificing Self, for the "higher" interests of Other. The Buddha says that separate self is an illusion. As activist Joanna Macy has put it, "It would not occur to me to plead with you, 'Oh, don't saw off your leg. That would be an act of violence.' It wouldn't occur to me because your leg is part of your body. Well, so are the trees in the Amazon rain basin. They are our external lungs. And we are beginning to realize that the world is our body."

To give you a sense of what's currently at stake, the World Conservation Union maintains a Red List, the fruit of 20 years' work, itemizing species under the threat of extinction. In 1998, the list included:

➤ One out of every eight plant species

➤ One in ten of all birds

➤ One in four of all mammals

More recently, in 2001, journalist Bill Moyers cited an international survey, the Millennium Ecosystem Assessment, which found half the world's wetlands have gone in one century, half the world's forests chopped down, and 70 percent of the world's major marine fisheries depleted. This is our own body.

Staggering statistics just keep on coming. At some point, the sane thing is to not dwell on the negative but to take charge of the positive, through outlook and action. This can be great fun and quite awakening, as well as a survival stance. For the city dweller, it might not seem apparent, but meditation on the four elements within our own bodies, on the pull of nature within an urban environment, on the communion we make with our food, all awaken this deep ecological heart. The migration of commuters is as sure as the flight of geese. And sometimes the wind rushes down the high-rise–lined streets of downtown like a hawk.

Nature informs our thoughts and actions. The spiritual and the natural are indivisible. As Buddhists have been saying for thousands of years, Buddha's body can be seen in the colors of the mountains; in the sound of water, we can hear Buddha's voice. (See?! Hear?!)

So, my fellow mammal—have you hugged your tree today?

Have you hugged a tree today? Julia "Butterfly" Hill hugs a 200-foot-tall 1,000-year-old redwood named Luna that, along with its family of nearby old-growth trees, had been designated for the axe by the owner of the land. This photo was taken during her two-year sojourn in a treehouse set up on a canopy of Luna's arms. She said, "Here I can be the voice and face of this tree, and for the whole forest that can't speak for itself." (Trees can't vote.) She continues her activism deeply rooted in love and respect for all life and the interconnectedness of all things.

(Photo: Shaun Walker, OtterMedia.com)

Along the Path

Here's a campfire game that Buddhist poet-ecologist Gary Snyder sometimes invites visitors to play with him when they visit his home in the wilderness of the Sierra Nevada mountains (with wood stoves for heat and photovoltaic cells for electricity). Describe the location of your house without referring to anything manmade. *Think:* Basin, range, watershed, flows, drainages. *Hint:* Where does your water come from? Where does it go when you're through with it? Are you in the sun or the shady slope? What grows around you? What doesn't?

Whatever Happened to Buddha's Mother?: Equality for Women

Reverence for feminine energy is found in every spiritual path. Before the Crusades, there were sects that worshipped Mary more than Christ. Jewish spirituality speaks of the feminine energy of God, Shekinah. Now we'll see how Buddhism relates to the feminine, and feminism.

Zanzabazar (1635–1723). Sitatara (White Tara; Mongolian, Caghan Dara Eke). Late seventeenth–early eighteenth century. Gilt bronze. Height: 27¹/₈" (68.9 cm) Diam.: 17⁵/₈" (44.8 cm).

(Museum of Fine Arts)

360

A Question of Balance

Wisdom and compassion know no gender. Nor do charity and peace. But when male-female interrelations get out of balance, the underside needs emphasis. Harmony is a basic law of nature.

Along the Path

Molly Dwyers has catalogued male-female imbalances in terms of culture over nature, mind over body (or matter), life over death, the transcendent over the imminent, independence over dependence or interdependence, activity over passivity, order over chaos, objectivity over subjectivity, control over surrender, conscious design over spontaneous arising, clarity over mystery, reason over imagination, doing over being, competition over cooperation, work over play, private enterprise over public service, the professional over the amateur, the creative over the receptive, quantification over qualification, and the conscious over the unconscious, to name a few.

The feminine has tilted the scales of Buddhism more than once. We've seen, for example, how the bodhisattva of compassion, Avalokiteshvara, manifested as a woman, Kwan Yin, in ancient China, and thence Tara in Mongolia and Tibet. Another example was the influence of Chabai, the wife of Kublai Khan, who helped the spread of Buddhism in Mongolia and herself influenced Mongol rule; when Kublai conquered southern China, she was instrumental in preventing revenge.

Buddhism in general offers generous helpings of what we typically define as feminine traits: for example, emphasis on the intuitive over the mental, feelings over intellect, and acceptance over denial. We should also add understanding. When we see a feminine bodhisattva, sometimes we notice she has an eye in the palm of each hand, and even on the soles of her feet. The eye means that her actions, represented by her hands and feet, are informed by the wisdom of understanding, the insight born of mindfulness. As Thich Nhat Hanh says, "Unless our love is made of understanding, it is not true love."

The imbalance of masculine/feminine energy in our lives is reflected across the board of contemporary social relation and felt in the world at large. It's no surprise, for example, to see deep ecology's paradigm shift addressing feminine energy. The exploitation of nature is typically a male-dominating-female paradigm, with nature playing the female. Likewise, that biased mindset's also visible in the military (kind of a guy thing) and the workplace (the hierarchy of power). Restoring the balance is an activity that, by definition, needs participation by men just as much as women. Nothing happens in a vacuum. Western Buddhists are learning this, as they strip away the accessories of self and awaken to their true nature.

At some deep level, the entire gamut of our conceptual dualities (self and other, good and bad, etc.) could be traced to our division into male and female. Having over-emphasized the masculine, it's merely nature's law of harmonious balance that leads us now to seek to restore the feminine energies of our lives, whether we be men or women. This, too, is part of the Middle Way.

History? ... or Her Story?

Perhaps it's no coincidence that mass acceptance of Buddhism in the West coincided with a major movement of feminism. Historically, the Buddha was the first major religious leader to honor women. The Buddha not only held women equal in marriage relations, he declared women could become enlightened (a far cry from the patriarchal set-up that sees everything, including women, as vehicles for guys' enlightenment). His stepmother who'd raised him became the Sangha's first ordained nun (*bhikkhuni*). In the Sangha, women held the same roles as men. He also broke with the notion that male sons were superior.

But, alas, old habits die hard. That is, how else are we to reconcile these clearly feminist stances of the Buddha with the prejudice against women running through ancient texts like a dark, muddy river? By Buddha's time, humanity's ancient matriarchal traditions were already being overshadowed by male dominance, the patriarchy which has been the general norm right on up to today. My answer is that some misogynist monks recorded their own disparaging remarks about women and ascribed them to the Buddha. Studying the records, we see, too, that the illustrious history of women teachers, nuns, and saints was glossed over. (Who's writing history around here? Is that why they call it "his story"?)

"Old habits die hard," they say. Our society doesn't practice the religious animal sacrifice that the Buddha railed against, but the sexism of his times has persisted, certainly in Asia. For example, the custom in ancient India called for a widow to immolate herself on her husband's pyre. The British outlawed the practice in 1829, although it continues. Widows in India today are still largely powerless.

As Buddhism adapts to different cultures, it's only natural for Western women to demand that Buddhism furnish the awareness and understanding of the feminine they've come to expect from their society. And it's natural, too, that Western women will take up the cause of sisterhood across boundaries, whether the cause be restoration of the tradition of nuns in southeast Asia or the plight of Tibetan nuns ... the healing of the trauma of war widows ... women's role in rebuilding war-shattered nations ... the wholesale slavery of young girls recruited or kidnapped into the labyrinthine Asian sex industry.

The most famous historical example in our times of a Buddhist woman resisting submission to the patriarchal elements in her society is Nobel Peace Prize laureate Daw Aung San Suu Kyi (pronounced *Dah Ohng Sahn Sue Chee*). In 1990, the political party she leads won the overwhelming majority vote, but the military wouldn't relinquish power over the throne. Despite threats to her life, she's chosen to remain inside her country, speaking out according to her conscience, rather than live in exile.

Hear and Now

"Political prisoners have known the most sublime moments of perfect communion with their highest ideals during periods when they were incarcerated in isolation, cut off from contact with all that was familiar and dear to them. From where do those resources spring, if not from an innate strength at our core, a spiritual strength that transcends material bounds? ... Nobody can take away from us the essential and ultimate freedom of choosing our priorities in life."

—Aung San Suu Kyi

Now, some critics of her Western supporters say, "Why pay so much attention to someone so far away?" Of course no one is an island. But another answer is that many Western Buddhists are aware of the debt they owe to the East, and the many ways they can be of service over there. So, to answer the question with a question, can you drink from the well without putting back? And this brings us to another topic of engaged Buddhism.

Along with the old, worn paradigm of woman-as-exotic-Other, another imbalanced energy now turning to Buddhism for healing is race.

Making the Invisible Visible: Healing Wounds of Racism

To answer what it means to be human (which is the meaning of our lives), we're challenged by the question of how far might we widen the horizons of how we define "family." Is the Family of Man too far-fetched an idea? Buddhism defines family as all beings, respecting *all* life forms. Other dominant creeds might not always be as tolerant. Buddhism might thus provide a fit meeting ground for carrying on the work of healing wounds of racism.

That movement is astir in American sanghas and it bodes well. As a recent Buddhist study group that met at Spirit Rock Meditation Center expressed it, the work is "making the invisible visible." It won't happen overnight. Just as domestic abuse leaves deep emotional scars, the legacy of slavery, social abuse, and racism are ingrained deep within our institutions, our families, and our self-regard. And yet it's quite possible that here, too, Buddhism can help us find our way through.

Hear and Now

"Buddhism ... places the greatest value on man, who alone of all beings can achieve the supreme state of Buddhahood. Each man has in him the potential to realize the truth through his own will and endeavor and to help others to realize it. Human life therefore is infinitely precious. 'Easier is it for a needle dropped from the abode of Brahma to meet a needle stuck in the earth than to be born as a human being.'"

—Aung San Suu Kyi

Race matters. Of course, when you wake up in the morning, you probably aren't aware of how old you are, what race you are, or what's your zip code. These are issues in the relative, samsaric, dualist realm, as when confronted by someone who labels you "Other," especially when it's pejorative.

Interbeing reminds us that nobody's purely just one race, be it black Irish, Italian Irish (Friuli), Irish Mexican (like Anthony Quinn), German-Hopi, or Afro-Cuban. Filipinos are Asian-Hispanic. So most everyone's a walking column of interraciality.

But the essence of race, and racism, is a central but rarely discussed fact of our national experience. In contemporary race riots, the American Dream of a melting pot has met a meltdown. Instead, we might be coming instead to a more realistic model, such as a salad bar in which there's a wide variety, each capable of maintaining individual identity in conjunction with others. This American experience can also be an international exemplar for ethnic conflict resolution. But ... is this Buddhist?

The Buddha taught regardless of race as well as class. Enlightenment knows no color lines. Buddhism nourishes self-esteem, dignity, and freedom from the bondage of fear, that powerful poison. The Buddhist goal of spiritual liberation coincides with a parallel goal of liberation from social and economic oppression. Freedom.

For people of European descent, Buddhism furnishes the tools for awakening to the roots of racism, within and without, and its twisted effects. It would be mistaken to expect persons of color to patiently explain to the white-skinned majority what's at stake or what's expected. At a recent retreat for Buddhists of color, a recurrent refrain was, "I'm tired of having to explain." This is, rightfully, a white person's homework rather than putting an individual in the continued uncomfortable position of having to speak on behalf of a whole race. People would rather not keep repeating the story that's become the nightmare from which they'd rather wake up.

Of people of color, the heritage of Asian Americans is most closely allied with Buddhism and deserves particular attention. As mentioned in Chapter 4, "Different Travel Agents, Same Destination?: Interfaith," Asian immigrants have contributed enormously to the evolution of Buddhism in the West for over a century, and continue to do so. The responsibility of the white-skinned Buddhists is to take opportunities to learn more about their Asian, and Asian American, brethren. This isn't necessarily confined to visiting Asian American sanghas. For instance, it's important to recognize that Koreans aren't Japanese. Cambodians aren't Chinese. And Asian Americans are Americans. Indeed, many of my Chinese neighbors have been in San Francisco and America for many more generations than the Gachs.

Underlining the fact that paying attention to such issues as racism, classism, and sexism isn't primarily about helping others (missionary work), but ourselves, Buddhist activist Rosa Zubizarreta concludes a poem thus:

> As long as we ourselves
> are not able to feel completely close
> to all other human beings,
>
> it is we ourselves
> who are living
> in illusion.

Along the Path

"As we are liberated from our own fear, our presence automatically liberates others."

—Nelson Mandela

"Our deepest fear is not that we are inadequate. Our deepest fear is that we are powerful beyond measure. It is our light, not our darkness, that most frightens us."

—Marianne Williams

Making Peace

Some critics remark that Buddhism has been around for over two millennia, yet the world doesn't seem to be any better off. Well, Buddhism's only been addressing the state of the world relatively recently. Its failure to keep its monasteries integrated with the rest of society aided its undoing in India. Traditionally, Buddhism has been largely monastic throughout the East. But now with its absorption into Western society, in primarily nonmonastic circles, Buddhism is facing the challenges of the modern West.

Leaves from the Bodhi Tree

During the war in Vietnam (called the Vietnam War by the Americans, but the American War by the Vietnamese), it was a test of faith to remain peaceful and happy during the traditional Buddhist tea ceremony while jet bombers strafed from the skies. It became evident to Thich Nhat Hanh and others that practice couldn't be confined inside monastery walls. If a child whose parents had been killed needed help, a helping hand needed to be outstretched. And monks and nuns put bodies into body bags while maintaining mindful awareness of their breath and feelings. These occasions for the compassionate practice of nonself weren't even matters of choice: They presented themselves to choiceless awareness.

Engaged Buddhism

A renewed Buddhism that addresses the modern world is generally called *engaged Buddhism.* It was coined by peace worker Thich Nhat Hanh. Its elder statesmen and women also include Dr. B. R. Ambedkar, of India; Thai reformer Buddhadasa Bhikkhu and his mentor Sulak Sivaraksa; A. T. Ariyaratne and the Saravodaya Movement in Sri Lanka (Ceylon); the Dalai Lama; Daw Aung San Suu Kyi, of Burma (Myanmar). They, in turn, walk in the footsteps of Mahatma Gandhi and other cousins from other faiths, such as Joan Baez, César Chávez, Ram Dass, Dr. Martin Luther King Jr., Joanna Macy, Dr. José Ramos-Horta, Brother David Steindl-Rast, and Bishop Desmond Tutu, to spotlight a few prominent names. The issues we've been discussing in this chapter are all branches of engaged Buddhism.

Engaged Buddhism takes the First Precept, nonharming, as a watchword. Respond to violence with nonviolence, with peace. Recognizing we're all one, there's no higher moral ground for the Buddhist. So, on the one hand, I'm called to action by the needless suffering of which I can't help but be aware if I'm open to the interdependence of all things. On the other hand, while wishing to help, by bringing reconciliation and peace to a violent, criminal, or harmful situation, I can't act against the welfare of anyone—even those who've caused others pain. There is no enemy. Good Guy vs. Bad Guy doesn't apply. The awakened human heart can see all "sides" are acting out of their own wish for happiness. And I am as much responsible for racism, ecological degradation, and mindless violence as anyone else.

Along the Path

"No man is an island, entire of itself ... / Any man's death diminishes me, because I am involved in mankind; / And therefore, never send to know for whom the bell tolls; / It tolls for thee."

—John Donne

"All the happiness there is in this world comes from thinking about others, and all the suffering comes from preoccupation with yourself."

—Shantideva

Knowing a Better Way to Catch a Snake

Buddhism rephrases basic premises of Western social engagement, of activism. Gandhi, for example, knew it was not enough for his message to reach the Indian people. He had also to change the minds of the British. His nonviolence effected a change in the *ends* by *changing the means*. This is an engaged Buddhist perspective, as well. Remember: "There is no path to peace; peace is the path."

Naturally, this approach might initially seem difficult to grasp. For instance, Americans are used to quantitative, if not All-or-Nothing, results. So it's helpful to recall here the model of complexity: Small changes can result in large results within a network (the Butterfly Effect). And, as we've seen in Chapter 18, change in one subatomic particle affects another nonlocally (faster than the speed of light). Expressing all this from a more general perspective, it's a paradigm shift.

Along the Path

"Never doubt that a small group of thoughtful, committed citizens can change the world. Indeed, it is the only thing that ever has."

—Margaret Mead

"We are caught in a network of mutuality, tied in a single garment of destiny. Whatever affects one directly, affects us all indirectly."

—Martin Luther King Jr.

"I still believe that people are good at heart."

—Anne Frank

Whether addressing sexism, racism, ecocide, or mindless violence, change of consciousness is needed as much as action. My consciousness affects yours, and yours affects the people you come into contact with, and so on. Eventually a critical mass is reached where the message gets out there. When all parties recognize they're equally responsible, and wish to change, then they can begin the process of peaceful reconciliation. (The Truth and Reconciliation Committee in South Africa is a fairly recent example, designed to make reparations for violence and human rights abuses under apartheid *committed by all sides.* It's interesting, too, that some South Africans have unofficially sounded out Buddhist approaches for their difficult task.)

Hear and Now

"When Prince Siddhartha saw an old man, a sick man, a corpse, and a wandering monk, he was moved to seek salvation, and eventually he became the Buddha, the Awakened One. The death and destruction throughout the world today compel us to think and act together to overcome all suffering and bring about the awakening of humankind.

"To alleviate suffering, we must always go back to our own spiritual depths—to retreat, meditation, and prayer. It is nearly impossible to sustain the work otherwise. It is easy to hate our enemies—the industrialists who exploit us and pollute our atmosphere. But we must come to see that there is no 'other.' We are all one human family. It is greed, hatred, and delusion that we need to overcome."

—Sulak Sivaraksa

So Buddhists don't necessarily write angry letters to Powers That Be but rather address them with love letters. (Do unto others ....) The Buddhist doesn't angrily shout slogans, but rather stands with others bearing witness. Being peace. And the Buddhist recognizes that the whole world won't change overnight: Peace is formed of non-peace elements. After all, there wouldn't be Buddhism if there weren't human beings.

By the way, here we can sense the deeper meaning of the word "idiot." The word "idiot" goes way back to ancient Greece and means private. Someone cut off from the world. So don't be an idiot.

Look around you. What's happening? What would be good to help, and how can you help? Whatever falls across your path is an opportunity to practice. When you practice fully, you'll be practicing with all the others on this path, who, in turn, are practicing for the sake of all beings. One big circle.

The Least You Need to Know

➤ In our relations, our engagement with the world at large can be a vital area of practice. As Buddhism addresses the conditions of the modern world, such practice is called "engaged Buddhism."

➤ Community service of growing Buddhist participation is the hospice movement and prisoner education.

➤ The Buddhist perspective toward conservation, environmentalism, and ecology is a profound consciousness of and reverence for the interpenetration of all life and place.

➤ Reawakening the feminine in our lives concerns us all, men and women. Issues of racism need to be understood, within ourselves and those around us.

➤ Engaged Buddhism is nonviolent, changing the means to change the ends. It's also nondualist, not dividing the world into enemies and friends. We're all responsible for the state of the world.

Times and Places to Celebrate

In This Chapter

➤ Buddha's birthday and other festivities

➤ Making travel meaningful

➤ Buddhist pilgrimage destinations around the world

As a grand finale to our survey of the myriad applications of the Buddha's way, we'll consider time and space. Buddha's way: Wherever you go, there you are. Cause for celebration ... and so we'll look at key traditional times and places for doing so.

To Every Thing, There Is a Season: Buddhist Events

Question: Without looking at your watch, right now, what time is it? (Answer: It's now.) It takes getting used to the fact that time is eternally present. The Chinese have an adage expressing it quite well: "Life unfolds on a great sheet called Time, and once finished it is gone forever." That's not to say it's monotonous. Not at all, and that's the beauty part. For instance, if you try varying your daily practice period you'll see how times of day just feel different: You can feel how 5 in the morning starts the day, whereas 5 in the evening bridges day and night. The spring equinox likewise feels different than the autumn equinox.

This Is

What's often called **Chinese New Year** is actually Eastern lunar new year. Each year is named for one of twelve animals. Why? One legend tells us that the first sentient beings to pay their respects to the Buddha were animals. First a little rat skittered out to the Bodhi Tree to behold the Fully Awakened One, then a friendly water buffalo, next a tiger, and so forth. To repay the honor, each has a year named after them.

So, though it's all now, Buddhists mark red letter days on their calendar, just like everyone else. An orthodox Buddhist calendar notes birth dates of all the bodhisattvas, months for studying certain sutras, and so on. But the high points commemorate days in the life of the Buddha.

As we saw in Chapter 1, "Why Is This Man Smiling?: The Buddha," it's said that the Buddha was born, enlightened, and died on a full moon of the sixth lunar month (sometimes April, sometimes May). A very convenient way to remember and celebrate. Called *Vesak,* it's a national holiday in many Eastern nations. (Just think, if the Buddha hadn't lived, you might be reading *The Complete Idiot's Guide to Understanding the Still-Unsolved Mystery of Life* instead.) Vesak is a time for celebration for the whole family, honoring all things new, children as well as the new year.

Other festive days are *Asalha* (full moon of the eighth lunar month), the day the Buddha gave his first sermon (so sometimes called Dharma Day), and *Magha* (the full moon of the third lunar month), the day 1,250 ordained monks assembled without prior call to pay respects to the Buddha (sometimes called Sangha Day). *Paranirvana* (full moon of April or May), when the Buddha died, is a day to consider one's own death and the recently deceased. You can find out the date of each festival from a sangha or a Buddhist calendar.

The events marked on a Western calendar have Buddhist significance, as well. On Presidents' Day, for instance, we can consider our national karma and be thankful to live in a country that honors freedom and the pursuit of happiness. Veterans' Day can be a time

Hear and Now

In spring, hundreds of flowers;
in autumn, a harvest moon.
In summer, a refreshing breeze;
in winter, snow accompanies you.
If useless things
don't hang in your mind,
any season's
a good season to you.

—Mumon Ekai (1183–1260)

for making peace out of nonpeace elements, as well as honoring those who made the ultimate sacrifice for our country. New Year's is a day to celebrate beginnings, and beginner's mind. April Fool's can be a day to celebrate no-mind. Each day has significance.

Days with no events attached are open for suggestion. For example, in several American cities, in early June, *Tricycle: The Buddhist Review* sponsors Change Your Mind Day. Change your mind from whatever state it's in to enlightenment. Free introductions to meditation techniques are offered by a range of teachers, interspersed with poetry and music. It was founded to demystify meditation and follows in the tradition of the Buddha's own method of teaching: outdoors, for free, in a public space.

Along the Path

Calendars vary from country to country. Thai years are calculated from the death of the Buddha, believed to be 543 years before the birth of Christ. Thus 2000 is 2539 B.E. (Buddhist Era) in Thailand. Yet it's 4333 in Korea, 4698 in China, etc. Similarly, Buddha's birthday might be celebrated in April in some countries, but in May in others.

Any day at all can be set aside as a retreat. In Chapter 17, "New Ways of Seeing and Being: Buddhism and Fine Arts," we saw a sample schedule for a day of mindful writing. A Saturday or Sunday are obvious choices. A retreat for meditation alone is called a *sesshin* in zen, lasting from a day to a week. Thich Nhat Hanh calls it a Day of Mindfulness. From the time you wake up to the time you go to sleep, go light, go slow, and follow your breathing, being mindful of whatever you're doing. Use words sparingly. Practice sitting and walking meditation at various times in the day. Like the Sabbath, one day inspires our practice throughout the week. All the time.

Destinations for Journeys Inward: Pilgrimages

In a sense, we're all pilgrims through this life, as a writer named Geoffrey Chaucer pointed out seven centuries ago. The banker, the baker, the lawyer, the tailor, and the wife. All of us. Life's a parade, if not a pilgrimage, and to make a conscious pilgrimage can be one of life's most profound spiritual affirmations, be it to Jerusalem, or Canterbury. Or Chartres, Lourdes, Turin, or Santiago de Compostela. (The latter pilgrimage has been made by such luminaries as Dante, St. Francis of Assisi, Charlemagne and, more recently, Shirley MacLaine.) Now, Westerners are discovering the footsteps of the Buddha, as well.

Today, a pilgrimage can furnish rationale and meaningful destinations for an overdue get-away. By connecting timeless stories to real places, the abstract becomes real. For the tourist as for the pilgrim, each moment is new. The pilgrim needn't set out to find the choicest oasis, but rather holy land beneath each footstep. The vacationer comes back with a little change and souvenirs; the pilgrim returns a changed person.

Historically, the Buddha made pilgrimage an essential core of the Way. Buddhists followed truth, wherever the Path might lead, a pilgrimage without fixed destination, meeting other buddhas rich and poor, religious and secular, men and women, children and spirits, humans and animals, outcasts and exalted figures. Through such very wanderings did Buddhism spread, take hold, and become a great civilization.

Hear and Now

"Passage—immediate passage! the blood burns in my veins! / Away, O soul! hoist instantly the anchor! / Cut the hawsers—haul out— shake out every sail! / Have we not stood here like trees in the ground long enough? / ... Have we not darken'd and dazed ourselves with books long enough?"

—Walt Whitman

One of the many names for Buddhist monks is "homeless," those who've renounced the life of householders, or laity. Travelling, you recognize this essential nature of the contemplative life: Every moment, wherever you go, your only home is the here and now. This recognition can come in very handy as you encounter some of the vagaries of travel in Asia. It's easy, for example, to let your patience get frazzled because things don't always turn out as planned. But in Asia, nails that stick out get pounded down. Collectivity often rules, not individuality. Waiting in lines can be a way of life and pretty demanding in the middle of a heat wave. Actually, boredom's an essential Buddhist meditation, like the drip of water relentlessly wearing down stone. As Kazuaki Tanahashi puts it so well, "enjoy waiting instead of waiting to enjoy."

This Is

Thoreau derives the word *saunter* (to leisurely stroll) from Old French, Saint Terre, holy land, making a saunterer a holy-lander. A vagary is a wandering thought (sharing the same root as "vagrant" and "vagabond"). The word **pilgrim** is often associated with the Puritans who voyaged to New England; the root means "away from home" or "across land." A layperson who's taken vows without being formally ordained a monk can be called anagarika, homeless wanderer, monastic life being a condition of homelessness.

And hard-scrabble, close-to-the-bone poverty and pain can be a culture shock. Remember, this is the same culture shock the Buddha first experienced when he left his palace walls. As much as the sights of the Bodhi Tree and Deer Park, these in-your-face encounters with duhkha are powerful reminders to practice every moment, each footstep. Also, you'll see the East revealing how material underdevelopment isn't the same as cultural or spiritual underdevelopment.

So by the simple act of mentally saying that you're on a pilgrimage, that your every encounter will be part of your Buddhist practice, you'll be more likely to have a rich, rewarding experience. (It works when you step through any door, as well.) It's both a splendid way to appreciate the everyday life of the East and its marvels, and a way to access deep truths about ourselves. As we follow his path, with each step and breath the Buddha comes alive.

Along the Path

"I only went out for a walk and finally concluded to stay out till sundown, for, going out, I found, was really going in."

—John Muir

"... Passage indeed, O soul, to primal thought!
Not lands and seas alone—thy own clear freshness,
The young maturity of brood and bloom;
To realms of budding bibles. ..."

—Walt Whitman

Standing on the Rock Where the Buddha Stood: The Indian Subcontinent

The Buddha was born in *Lumbini* (now Nepal, where Vajrayana is the dominant form of Buddhism today). He attained enlightenment in *Bodh Gaya* (in India). He gave his first sermons at Deer Park in *Sarnath*, taught for 25 years in the city of *Shravastri*, and died and was cremated in *Kushingar*. He also taught at Vulture Peak, in *Rajgir* (also known as Rajgriya).

Most commonly visited, perhaps, is Bodh Gaya. As one pilgrim has put it, "If the Buddha was born in Lumbini, Buddhism was born in Bodh Gaya." At first glance, it might strike you as a Buddhist annex to Disneyland: branch temples and Buddhists from all over the world catching your attention. But intense practice is very much alive here (as are some scorching desert winds). A descendent of the Bodhi Tree stretches its limbs before the soaring Mahabodhi Temple, a nine-story, 180-foot second-century edifice adorned with buddhas and bodhisattvas. These sacred spots are the focus and backdrop for a medley of pilgrims from all over the world, themselves no less interesting. And amid the rickshaws and contemporary markets, life goes on as it did in the time of the Buddha.

This Is

In India, as far back as 2000 B.C.E., when an important person died, a tooth or relic was enshrined in a burial mound called a **stupa.** Buddha commended the practice, and when he died eight separate stupas were built for his remains. The architectural form of a Buddhist stupa stands for not only the Buddha but also his enlightenment. The **pagoda** is the East Asian cousin of the stupa. Its positioning is also significant; in a cave, for example, it's symbolic of revelation.

Leaves from the Bodhi Tree

A Jewish mother traveled to Nepal to seek an audience with a guru. When she arrived at the monastery, she was told that she could have an audience with him but visitors could only utter five words to him. So she passed through the outer doors and entered the inner sanctum. She approached the guru, putting down her bags, and said, "So Sheldon, come home already!"

Sarnath's very beautiful. Excavation having been completed long ago, the site's been turned into a park that makes a big contrast with downtown Varanasi. The grounds are green, still cultivated as during the time of the Buddha. But only the foundations of the ancient monasteries remain. A fifth-century stupa, called Chaukhandi, marks the spot where the Buddha first met the five ascetics. Past an archeological museum, another stupa, called Dhamekh, marks where the Buddha gave his first teaching. Nearby is Mulagandhakuti Temple, built by the Mahabodhi Society in 1931.

In central India stands the Sanchi Stupa, dating from the time of King Ashoka, third century B.C.E., who consolidated Buddha's remains from other stupas. It's said to be the oldest stone structure in India. Two more prime sites for Buddhist pilgrims are *Vaishali*, a site where the Buddha liked to teach, and *Nalanda*, site of the first Buddhist university and Amaravati Stupa. Additional destinations for Buddhist pilgrimage are Ajanta and Ellora, Nagarjunakonda and Amaravati,

Tawang, Rumtek and Pemagyantse, the Orissa sites, Tabo, Vulture Peak near Rajagriha, and Leh. And most anywhere you go, English is spoken.

Sikkim, Ladakh, and Bhutan

For the intrepid trekker, Sikkim, Ladakh, and Bhutan are rugged outposts of Tibetan Buddhism. Ladakh is possibly the most remote part of India, and the high altitude makes it snowy for six months out of the year. Yet they've been practicing Buddhism there since three centuries before Christ. Trekkers return reporting they've met the most emotionally healthy people they've ever met, attuned with their surroundings and the greater scheme of things.

Bhutan may be the last bastion of vibrant Himalayan Buddhism in an independent nation (the movie *The Cup* was filmed here). The size of Switzerland, the whole country was like one big medieval monastic domain until the 1960s when they developed towns and roads. Here you can sense Buddhism as more than a source for meditation, but rather an entire way of life. And you can also see a nation dramatically poised between the Old and the New.

In the southern Himalayan region of India, the Dalai Lama lives in exile in Dharmsala, site of pilgrimage for Tibetan Buddhists from around the world. Don't expect to find a replica of Lhasa's Potala Palace here, but rather ditches and tents. It's a good place to learn about Tibetan Buddhism, but be prepared to brush aside Hindu skeptics milling around.

Hear and Now

"Why do people talk about the 'solidity,' the 'still majesty' of mountains? Nothing is more theatrical, more unstable. Each shift of light changes them. You look up; they seem immeasurably distant, about to vanish over the horizon. You look up again; the light has brought them so close you think you could breathe on them."

—Andrew Harvey, *A Journey in Ladakh*

Northeast Asia

These days, the frontiers of travel are unlimited. In 1997, a group called Hell's Buddhas made a pilgrimage across India … by motorcycle. These days, you can find retirees from North Carolina travelling in a mobile home across the Silk Route, being passed by college students on spring break, on motorcycles.

A pivotal pit stop along the Silk Route is Dunhuang County. An oasis in the Gobi Desert, it's at the west end of Hexi Corridor in Gansu Province. At the foot of Sound Sand Mountain are the Mogao Grottoes, which at one time had a thousand distinct caves, built by Buddhist monks. In their day, they provided not only shelter but also medical care and other travel amenities. Today, about half the caves are in good condition, containing over 2,000 painted clay statues and 45,000 square meters of frescoes.

Leaves from the Bodhi Tree

In 629 C.E., Buddhist monk Hsuan Tsang (Shwohn Tsong) set out from the capital of China to southern India, via foot, horseback, elephant, and camel, in search of original Buddhist texts. Seventeen years and 5,000 miles later, as he was about to return to China, he noticed that the scrolls he'd been given were blank, and was told that the blank scrolls are the true teaching but if he liked he could have some texts with writing on them. This journey formed the basis for the classic Chinese travel epic *Journey to the West* (a.k.a. *Monkey*); more recently, *New York Times* journalist Richard Bernstein retraced Hsuan Tsang's route (in only four months), as recorded in his book *Ultimate Journey*.

Besides Russia and Mongolia, which have their choice Buddhist sites as well, here are some further spots to visit, plus some travel tips.

The Flower Kingdom: China

A common translation for "tourist" in Chinese is "foreign guest." So return the respect and you'll have a great time. You don't have to gassho, although it's universally recognized. In China, as in Japan and Korea, a bow from the shoulders or waist is a local version of paying respect to another.

There are tour groups and even Buddhist ones now, but if you're travelling alone, a good way I've found to enlist the aid of ordinary people in the street is to smile at strangers and ask, "Practice English?" You're likely to find young people happy to try out their English in a real-life situation, with a native speaker.

Another ice-breaker I've found for getting around is to buy the most detailed map of the city you can find, in the native language, and have the area where you're staying circled. Before you go out, have someone in your hotel circle the places you want to visit. That way you can always hail a cab, whip out the map, and point to where you want to go.

Touring a monastery or temple, you might ask if you could meet the abbot (in which case an interpreter might be mobilized). Since most tourists just gawk and move on, interest from Westerners can be a welcome rarity. Also take into account that Buddhism is just officially reviving in China, though many people have kept it alive in their homes, in back rooms of barber shops, and so on.

While historic monasteries are being restored, there are unofficial temples and sanghas, as well. How secret are the unofficial ones? Well, a Catholic friend of mine was winding up his first visit to an official church, when the priest asked him if he'd like to visit an unofficial church.

Along the Path

Many Asian countries have come to the table of modernity through socialist revolutions of various kinds. Marxism and Buddhism are as similar as they are different. Both are critiques of everyday reality, for the betterment of humanity, one based on material conditions, the other on the nonmaterial. Marxism subscribes to a theory called dialectical materialism, for example, to account for interconnectedness, much as interbeing (a.k.a. co-dependent arising) does in Buddhism. Marx condemned religion as "an opiate of the people," yet Marxists are often "true believers," like monks and priests of a new religion.

As a port city, Shanghai has a cosmopolitan history. If Beijing's the nation's capital, comparable to the District of Columbia, Shanghai's like New York City. Besides visiting the incredible row of new skyscrapers along the waterfront at night and its gorgeous museum of art, visit the Jade Buddha Temple, and see where that takes you.

The further south you go along the coast, Western influences are evident, owing to thriving international trade. Hui Neng was enlightened on the streets of Guangzhou (*gwang-joe*, formerly called Canton) and ordained at Guangxiao Temple. From there, you can visit Nan Hua, the temple he later founded, in Shao Guan; if not on a tour, take a train to Ma Ba Mountain and walk four miles from there. The restoration of the monastery and the monastic order was the formidable work of renowned monk Empty Cloud, who lived to be 120 (1840–1959)!

Other interesting sites are the Dong Shan Monastery, where the "just sitting" school of Zen (Soto) began; Dong Lin Temple, focal point for Pure Land practice in China; and Moshu Temple, rebuilt around 1990, using the original foundation, now accommodating 500. The latter is the home of many celebrated koans by Joshu, who once told a seeker who'd asked what was zen, "The cypress tree in the courtyard." Those cypresses are still there.

Leaves from the Bodhi Tree

Philosopher-critic Lin Yutang recounts the story of some Chinese ladies who invited an American to join them going to a hill in Hangzhou (*hong joe*), China. It was a misty morning. You could hear the soft beat of drops of moisture on the leaves of grass. The American lady was discouraged by the fog but her friends insisted. After a while they saw an ugly rock enveloped by clouds in the distance, called the Inverted Lotus. The American wanted to go down but her friends insisted there was a wonderful sight on top. At the summit was an expanse of mist and fog, the outline of distant hills barely visible on the horizon. "But there's nothing to see here," the American protested. "That's exactly the point," her Chinese friends replied. "We come up to see nothing."

There are also many monasteries and temples in Hong Kong. (Not so long ago, the island was a British colony, which means English may be spoken here.) One of the biggest attractions is on Lantau Island, with the world's largest outdoor bronze Buddha.

Leaves from the Bodhi Tree

"I can't tear myself away from Tibet," wrote Alexandra David-Neal (1868–1969). Following World War One, she was one of the first Westerners to travel extensively in Tibet and learn its religious practices. When it was off-limits to foreigners, she disguised herself as a lama and travelled with her adopted Sikkimese son. Soon after, Ernst Lothar Hoffmann, now known as Lama Govinda, likewise went and studied the Dharma. He wrote, "The longer I stayed on in this magic world into which I had dropped ... the more I felt that a hitherto unknown form of reality was revealed to me ...."

Across the Straits: Taiwan

Buddhism's always been very active here, perhaps because of the influence of the Japanese who colonized it for 50 years (1895–1945). The leading Buddhist center is in Shitoushan (Lion's Head Mountain). While visiting temples amid splendid scenery, you can stay in a monastery, though wake-up's at dawn. One of the largest temple and monastery complexes is Fo Guang Shan (Mountain of Buddha's Light), founded by Master Hsing Yun. Its 400 monks and nuns work as counselors in factories, jails, and homes, teach all levels of school, and maintain an orphanage. Indeed, you'll find Taiwan Buddhists are very humanitarian, with the world's largest population of nuns.

The Kingdom of Snow: Tibet

To the Tibetan Buddhist, pilgrimage can be performed mentally, visualizing one's own spine as Mount Meru, and the surrounding subcontinents as one's four limbs. But the outer journey remains, as well. Westerners are beginning to discover for themselves the magic and majesty of Tibet, the way they've become familiar with India, Japan, and China.

The principal holy site of Tibet is the city of Lhasa. Its principal temple, the Jokhang, was built in the seventh century, and the city evolved around it as the center of a new Buddhist kingdom. Today, there's a Holiday Inn, with all the amenities. More intrepid pilgrims may want to book with a tour of outlying regions, such as the sacred mountains and rivers.

Lands of the Elders: Southeast Asia

From Mahayana and Vajrayana, we turn next to the lands of Theravada. Here we find monarchy, monastery, and the masses still interlaced through Buddhism, or, as they call it here, Buddhadhamma ... the Way of the Buddha.

Thailand

Thailand affords a chance to see both ancient and contemporary Buddhism, in both city and forest. The city of Chiang Mai, for instance, has a Hyatt, different streets devoted to crafts of nearby hill tribes, and fourteenth- and fifteenth-century temples (called *wats*). Also in the north of Thailand are the ruins of the original capital, Sukhothai, alongside a contemporary city. Also of interest is Wat Pah Baan

Hear and Now

"If you do not find a prudent companion, a wise associate leading a good life, then travel alone, like a king abandoning a domain he has conquered, like an elephant roaming the forest. It is better to walk alone; there is no companionship with a fool. Walk alone, like an elephant in the forest, with few desires, doing no evil."

—*The Dhammapada*

Taad, the monastery of the Venerable Ajahn Maha Boowa, six hours from Bangkok, in northeast Thailand, and Nanasampanno, in Udorn Thani.

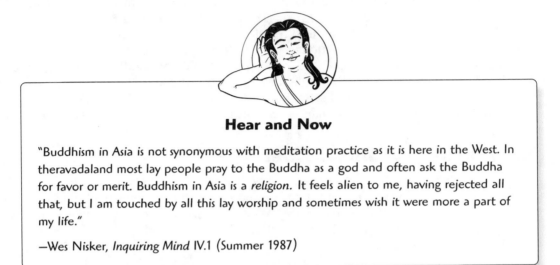

Hear and Now

"Buddhism in Asia is not synonymous with meditation practice as it is here in the West. In theravadaland most lay people pray to the Buddha as a god and often ask the Buddha for favor or merit. Buddhism in Asia is a *religion*. It feels alien to me, having rejected all that, but I am touched by all this lay worship and sometimes wish it were more a part of my life."

—Wes Nisker, *Inquiring Mind* IV.1 (Summer 1987)

The Thais tend to mix Buddhism with Hindu ceremony and native spirit propitiation. Buddhism's quite evidently a common social bond, interwoven into contemporary urban life. Don't be surprised if your taxi driver might be cruising at 50 m.p.h. when suddenly he'll take both hands off the wheel and bow to a roadside Buddhist deity; fortunately, it's a patron of transportation, so there are never any accidents. Everyone understands.

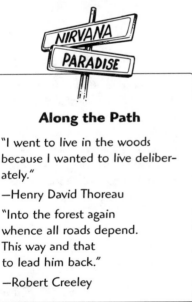

Along the Path

"I went to live in the woods because I wanted to live deliberately."

—Henry David Thoreau

"Into the forest again whence all roads depend. This way and that to lead him back."

—Robert Creeley

Thailand also has a tradition of forest Buddhism. (Do I need to sell you on the beauties of Thailand's tropical forests? If the government continues selling them off as timber to the highest bidder, they may be gone.) The primary forest temple in the tradition of modern teacher Ajahn Chah is Wat Pah Pong, in a beautiful forest on the outskirts of Ubon, about 20 minutes from Nanachat. Any taxi driver will know the way. Pah Pong is head temple for about 200 other forest monasteries across Thailand and the world. One gets the feel of a large, thriving monastery of practicing monks, perhaps akin to the Buddha's own favorite monastery, Jetavana, where he spent many a rainy season.

About 20 minutes from Nanachat is Wat Pah Nanachat, a full-scale traditional forest monastery that accepts "day" pilgrims. The abbot receives guests every day from 9 to 11 A.M. There's also an afternoon tea at 4:30 P.M. Overnight guests require writing in advance to receive written confirmation from the guest monk. To stay longer and practice there, prior experience in formal meditation retreat is necessary, and they request that retreatants stay at least one month. Late October to early February, the cool season, is typically popular.

The Gulf of Thailand, to the south, has some fantastically beautiful beach paradises, such as Koh Samui. On the nearby island of Koh Phra-Ngan is Wat Kow Tham, accessible by ferry from Samui or Surat Thani, with 10-day vipassana and metta retreats.

Sri Lanka (Ceylon)

You could spend two weeks on this tropical island before you begin to exhaust its scenic and historic sites. Every full moon is a Buddhist holiday (*Poya*). Besides its cosmopolitan pleasures, it hosts Asia's oldest landscaped gardens surrounding the holy mountain monument of Sigiriya. Up in the hills, the city of Kandy is one of the most beautiful in the world. The best time to visit is in July and August, during the weeklong celebration of Buddha's tooth, with drummers, dancers, a hundred or so elephants, and so on. Kandy is also host to many monasteries and temples.

Owing to politics, you'll want to stay away from the north, but that shouldn't stop you from visiting the paradise of the south. Similarly, in Myanmar (Burma), you'll be discouraged from visiting outback. If you're politically-minded, our online bibliography has some references. And always check State Department advisories before visiting anywhere.

Myanmar (Burma)

The balancing boulder of Kyaiktiyopaya resembles, in a way, modern Myanmar, a modern nation-state doing a balancing act out of diverse communities and allegiances. Pagodas are more common than cars.

A primary site for Buddhist tourists is Yangoon (Rangoon) with its hundreds of pagodas. If you wish to actually meditate while here, I recommend Mahasi Meditation Center. Tourists are discouraged from visiting outback.

Vietnam

With relations normalized, Westerners are discovering the beauties of Vietnam. In central Vietnam, a boat trip up the River of Perfume is a pleasant journey taking in many temples, highlighted by Linh Mu Pagoda. In Saigon, the temple in Chinatown is a colorful if crowded experience. From here, you might take the boat and train to Chua Huong to visit the older Huong temple, in the north. In Dalat are relatively newer and very peaceful Chinese and Vietnamese temples.

Hanoi has many easily accessible temples. Fragrant Mountain Pagoda, in a province neighboring Hanoi, is a soulful spot in beautiful, exotic surroundings. This is the legendary home of Quan Am, the Vietnamese equivalent of Kwan Yin. Roads are bad and mercenaries along the way can make this an arduous trek, but it's worth the effort.

Tu Hieu pagoda, outside Hue (say *hway*), is a wonderfully tranquil spot in a small pine forest. A number of monks there speak English and might offer to put you up. As Thich Nhat Hanh is associated with both temples, bringing along one his books would make a good calling card.

Further East

Why do we revere the East? Because the sun rises on it first! Here are two more big Buddhist watering holes, further east.

Korea

Korea is under-recognized by Westerners, and yet its people are cordial and fun and the sites are gorgeous and sometimes profound. (So maybe it's good it isn't overrun with tourists?) Diamond Mountains, to the north, have only recently been made accessible to tourists. Buddhist monasteries and rock carvings can be seen in a setting of stunning waterfalls and mineral springs, including a 50-foot tenth-century Bodhisattva.

Besides Diamond Mountains, I recommend Kyongju, in the south, accessible from the airport in seaside Pusan. This was the capital of Korea during the Silla Dynasty, when the kings adopted Buddhism as the state religion. Also during this period, Korea became a unified nation. The Kyongju Museum (with acoustiguides in English) will help give you a feel for the amplitude and refinement of this civilization.

Actually, Kyongju itself is an open museum, named one of the world's ten historic sites by UNESCO. Two prime Buddhist spots are Pulguk-sa Temple and Sokkoram Grotto. Pulguk-sa is a beautiful example of Korean architecture, located in mountain scenery that's gorgeous all year round.

Pulguk-sa monastery.

(Photo: Courtesy of the Korean Cultural Center, Los Angeles)

Atop Mt. T'omsan, facing the sea, is Sokkuram, where the Buddha sits inside a domed, circular room within the mountain. One of the world's simplest but most beautiful examples of Buddhist art, this monumental Buddha hardly smiles but gazes with the benevolent wisdom of enlightenment.

Hear and Now

"From the seventh through the eleventh centuries, there is virtually no surviving work of painting and sculpture in Japan that is not Buddhist in inspiration, for Buddhism there en-joyed a prestige higher than in any other land of Asia, except Tibet. To this day, the strong imprint of the faith may be sensed in the character of the people, in their thought processes, ethical standards, and artistic values."

—John M. Rosenfield and Shujiro Shimada, *Traditions of Japanese Art*

Land of the Rising Sun: Japan

The two major Buddhist centers in Japan are the cities of Nara and Kyoto; if you have more time, Esai and Kamakura. Beside the deer in Nara, you can't miss the giant Amitabha Buddha statue (Daibutsu) in Todai-ji Temple, pictured on the cover of this book. (His big finger's four and a half feet long.) Formerly the capital in the eighth century, Nara's adorned with gardens and parks as well as Buddhist shrines and pagodas.

Kyoto has 2,000 temples and shrines, most dating from the Heian period (794–1192), many featuring famous gardens such as Ryoanji and Tenryuji. (*Tip:* Visit Ryoanji first thing in the morning when they open, and you'll miss the crush of the invariable crowds, then visit another garden after.) The gardens of the Gold and Silver Pavilions are also world famous, both being villas built by shoguns around the fifteenth century.

West as Well as East

Have you noticed? If you go far enough east, you wind up in the West. Don't exclude the West from your pilgrimage itinerary. Here's where the Lotus is blossoming its first new bud in a thousand years.

Europe

In Europe, Buddhism's largely practiced in churches, with the Benedictine Order an unofficial leader in interfaith dialogue between Christians and Buddhists throughout the West. Richard Baker Roshi has established a zen center called Johanneshof in Germany's Black Forest. The Theravadan forest tradition is also alive and well in the forests of Europe, as well as Asia. In West Sussex, England, an entire forest of 108 acres is devoted to Thai Buddhism. (The land was donated by a jogger who stopped at the sight of a Britisher in robes walking on his alms round. Thus has Buddhism spread.)

Along the Path

"The impulse to ramble is as old as humankind. ... For most human beings, for tens of thousands of years, home was quite literally "on the hoof." The hunter, the nomad, the rambler, and finally the pilgrim."

—Andrew Schelling

"We travel, initially, to lose ourselves; and we travel, next, to find ourselves. ... Travel, for many of us, is a quest for not just the unknown but unknowing ..."

—Pico Iyer

France has Vajrayanan, Zen, and Theravadan centers. Near Limoges, for example, is a college called Dhammaville. France having had a historic presence in Vietnam, it's no wonder there are vibrant Vietnamese Buddhist communities here. Thich Huyen-Vi maintains a Zen/Pure Land temple in Joinville-le-pont.

Near Bordeaux in southern France is Plum Village, a Buddhist monastery and a practice center for laypeople, founded in 1982 by Thich Nhat Hanh. The annual summer and winter retreats are open to all. Visitors have the opportunity to practice by sitting, walking, and working in mindfulness, as well as listening to Dharma talks. Once a week is Lazy Day, which allows for exploration of the beautiful countryside. The sangha recently also established Green Mountain Dharma Center in Woodstock, Vermont, and Deer Park Monastery near San Diego, California, where visitors can also enjoy a Day of Mindfulness. Which brings us to America, already.

Big Sky: North America

The wide skies of North America make an appropriate backdrop for transplantings of Buddha's big sky mind. As discussed in Chapter 3, "What Might an American Buddha Look Like?" America is arguably Buddhism's most dynamic home today. Though a recent phenomenon in this relatively young country, it already has historical roots worthy of pilgrimage.

For example, at any given time, Naropa University, in Boulder, Colorado, hosts a lecture series or conference with America's foremost scholars, holy people, healers, and artists of all kinds. Further up on 350 secluded acres in northern Colorado, there's the Rocky Mountain Dharma Center, a Tibetan contemplative center established by Naropa's founder, Chögyam Trungpa Rinpoche, commemorated by a very fine stupa.

The Washington, D.C., Buddhist Vihara, founded in 1965, is America's first Theravadan monastery. Leading meditations for the community at large and being in D.C., that's doubly good karma. Further east, the Insight Meditation Society opened its doors in 1975, on 80 wooded acres in quiet central Massachusetts (Barre, pronounced *Barry*), offering Vipassana classes and retreats. In 1988, a west coast offshoot in Woodacre, Northern California was established on 488 acres, called Spirit Rock, after a boulder that greets visitors as they enter.

We spotlighted the Greyston community of New York in Chapter 15, "No Eat, No Work: Work to Eat or Eat to Work?" Other power centers in New York include the Temple of Enlightenment in the Bronx, headquarters of the Buddhist Association of the United States (BAUS), with Chuang Yen monastery in upstate New York; the Karma Triyana Darmachakra (KTD), seat of Gyalwa Karmapa, head of the Kagyu sect of Vajrayana.

I must confess that as a native Californian, I take a Pacific Rim view of things. For instance, the first Buddhist stupa in America arrived on the roof of the San Francisco branch of the Buddhist Churches of America in 1938, which remains a striking part of the skyline. (They also have the best Buddhist bookstore in town.)

A 30-minute walk away, the doors of the San Francisco Zen Center (SFZC) are always open, except during sesshin (retreat). The first formal zendo in America, it's housed in a former Jewish girls' residency designed by Julia Morgan (who also designed Hearst's San Simeon castle). In 1969, SFZC established Tassajara Zen Mountain Center, America's first Zen monastery. It's a five-hour drive from San Francisco, high in the Ventana National Forest, near Carmel–Big Sur, overlooking the Pacific. Its hot springs were used by the local Indians, and it's been a popular resort since the 1860s. Tassajara's open to the public May to September for rest and relaxation (and that great bread), with Zen training and meditation available. And, nestled along Mt. Tamalpais along the Pacific, in Marin County, SFCZ's 70-acre Green Gulch Farm is well worth an afternoon.

The courtyard of the San Fransisco Zen Center, founded by Shunryu Suzuki Roshi in 1959. At the former hot springs resort of Tassajara, Suzuki Roshi founded America's first Zen monastery. Here is the path to the baths.

(Photos: Barbara Wenger and Dan Howe)

Also in San Francisco is Gold Mountain Monastery, established in 1968 by Venerable Tripitaka Master Hsüan Hua (*shwahn hwa*) (1918–1995) as part of Dharma Realm Buddhist Association. Master Hua was a Zen master from northeast China who taught the full spectrum of Chinese Buddhism to European Americans as well as Asians and Asian Americans, with an emphasis on monastic practice. Recitation is in Chinese, but books have phonetic translation, and people will be glad to help you along. Up north, DRBA has a complex in Talmadge, California (based in a former insane asylum which closed due to drought), called the City of Ten Thousand Buddhas, which now includes Dharma Realm University, Buddhist Text Translation Society, an elementary school, and an educational bureau, as well as a monastery and a nunnery.

Another major center of Chinese Buddhism is in Los Angeles County, 30 miles east of Monterey Park, where the Hsi Lai Temple (pronounced *see lye*) sits atop 20 acres on a hill in Hacienda Heights, the largest in the West. It's a branch of Fo Guang Shan, Taiwan. The best time for a first-time visit is lunch; vegetarian, of course.

In northern California, the Nyingma Institute, founded in 1974 in Berkeley, California, by Tarthang Tulku, is creating an incredible retreat center called Odiyan, which welcomes workers as well as pilgrims. Up near Mt. Shasta, way up in Northern California, Shasta Abbey has been maintaining a Zen monastery for over 30 years. Further north, in Canada, there are plenty of Buddhist temples, some particularly scenic or remote. There's Gampo Abbey, for instance, on the northwestern coast of verdant Cape Breton Island, a Tibetan-style monastery, complete with a traditional three-year retreat, whose primary teacher is an American woman named Pema Chödron. (Also, in Nova Scotia is the rural contemplative center Dorje Denma Ling, on 300 scenic acres.)

In British Columbia, some familiar sites are Amazenji Zen Training Temple for Women, Birken Buddhist Society, Kalu Rinpoche's small but beautiful retreat center on Salt Spring Island, Siddhartha's Intent International, and a number of Pure Land temples established in the interior following the second World War. In Manitoba, there's Dakshong Gonpa; in northern Ontario, Arrow River; in eastern Ontario, Dharma Centre of Canada; and in Quebec, Maple Buddhist Society.

For more information and resources, please visit us online: awakening.to … (*Gassho.*)

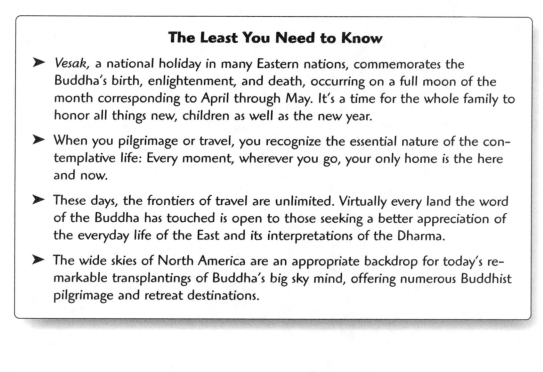

The Least You Need to Know

➤ *Vesak*, a national holiday in many Eastern nations, commemorates the Buddha's birth, enlightenment, and death, occurring on a full moon of the month corresponding to April through May. It's a time for the whole family to honor all things new, children as well as the new year.

➤ When you pilgrimage or travel, you recognize the essential nature of the contemplative life: Every moment, wherever you go, your only home is the here and now.

➤ These days, the frontiers of travel are unlimited. Virtually every land the word of the Buddha has touched is open to those seeking a better appreciation of the everyday life of the East and its interpretations of the Dharma.

➤ The wide skies of North America are an appropriate backdrop for today's remarkable transplantings of Buddha's big sky mind, offering numerous Buddhist pilgrimage and retreat destinations.

The Vocabulary of Silence: A Glossary

ahimsa   To do no harm. Reverence for life.

arhat   "One worthy; worthy one." The ideal of arhatship means having nothing more to learn, free of cravings and desires, having attained *nirvana*.

Atman   Hindu concept of a highest self, inherently one with the transpersonal, Eternal Self ("*Brahman*"). To Buddha the ultimate reality is "no self" ("*an-atman,*" "*an*" in Sanskrit being like our prefix "un-" or "non").

bardo   The state in between death and rebirth.

bhikku   Buddhist monk; literally means "beggar," as monks beg their meals from the lay community each day.

bhikkhunis   Buddhist nuns.

Bodhi tree   The historical tree (fig, of the Indian *banyan* variety) under whose leaves the Buddha sat and attained enlightenment.

bodhicitta   Awakened mind/heart. The compassionate desire to attain full enlightenment for the sake of helping all beings.

bodhisattva   A person who is ready for or who has even attained enlightenment but has vowed to help all beings become enlightened.

body scan   A tour of your bodily sensations, head to toe; takes 45 minutes at first, but can eventually be conducted in a few minutes; commonly practiced in *Vipassana* meditation.

Brahmaviharas   "Divine dwellings." Four boundless, sublime states that can be practiced anywhere: lovingkindness (*metta*), compassion, sympathetic joy, and equanimity.

Buddha   From the Sanskrit root *budh*, "to wake." The Fully Awakened One. Awake and capable of awakening others.

buddha nature   The capability of realizing buddhahood. Original nature, true nature, dharma nature. *See also* emptiness; nirvana.

Buddhism   A way of life in accord with the teachings of the Buddha; often called

Buddha Dharma in the East.

Buddhist   A person who studies, teaches, and lives the basic principles of the Buddha's teachings.

Chaos Theory   Study of the order underlying the seemingly disordered.

compassion   Universal sympathy. The sincere wish to end the needless suffering of all beings, born out of recognition of the oneness of all things. Commonly expressed by *bodhisattvas*. Often paired with *wisdom*.

Complexity Theory   Study of the creation and maintenance of complex systems out of simple parts.

concentration   Buddhism has many words analogous to concentration (much as Eskimos have many words for snow, because they pay so much attention to it). *Samatha*, stopping, or stillness, is an important basis for concentration. Used in conjunction with mindfulness and effort as part of the Eightfold Path, concentration is called *samadhi*, which is often translated as one-pointed concentration. However, in one-pointedness there's no duality between a mind and an object. This nondualistic state is the basis for meditation (or *dhyani*), which can further lead to what's often called self-realization (*kensho, satori*), except there, too, there's no duality of self and other.

Confucianists   Followers of the doctrines of Confucius (551–479 B.C.E.), China's "philosopher king"; in some countries his philosophy became imperial ideology.

Dalai Lama   Dalai means "ocean," as in ocean of wisdom. The Dalai Lama is both a religious and a national ruler. Tibet was ruled by Dalai Lamas since the seventeenth century, until the sixteenth Dalai Lama fled into exile in Dharmsala, India, in 1959.

deep ecology   Ecology (literally, "care for our house") studies relations between beings and their environment. Deep ecology sees humanity as inseparably embedded within nature, part of a continuum of interbeing.

Dharma   The Buddha's teachings and the things to which they pertain (everything). Also means law, path, righteousness, phenomena, and reality, depending on the context.

dualism   Division of the world into oppositions, based on verbalization, conceptualization.

duhkha   Dissatisfaction, stress, suffering, anguish, pain, caused by craving or attachment to what is without a stable, separate identity.

emptiness (Sanskrit: *sunyata*)   The state of being empty of any separate, lasting existence; without boundary, fertile void, openness, transparency. *See also* suchness.

esoteric   Intended only for those sufficiently spiritually developed and properly initiated to grasp the true meaning.

Flower Garland School (*Hua Yen*, China; *Kegon*, Japan)   Branch of Mahayana emphasizing the infinite interconnectedness of all being.

fractal   Having to do with the shapes, dimensions, and geometry of irregular patterns and qualities.

fuzzy logic   Study of the gray areas in situations.

Gaia Hypothesis   The scientific theory, named after the Greek goddess of the earth, that our planet's a living organism, a sentient being, a self-regulating entity.

gassho   Palms of hands joined together and held near the breast in greeting, gratitude, request, often accompanied by a bow. (*Namaskar/namastey,* Hindu; *añjali,* Sanskrit, *wai,* Thai.)

gatha   A short poem or meditation.

haiku   A short impressionist sketch in words.

hara   A point (*chakra*) about the size of a quarter or a dime, three or four finger-widths below your navel, considered your true center—physically in posture, and spiritually as central repository of life-force (*prana, chi*). (*Dan tien,* Chinese.)

holistic   Pertaining to a whole, such as a whole system; taking into account inter-relations of parts.

hospice   A setting providing comfort and support for the terminally ill outside of a hospital.

insight   Seeing deeply; penetrating into the true nature of things; gaining understanding and wisdom. *See also* Vipassana.

interbeing   The interconnectedness of all things; interdependence, interpenetration.

karma   Universal law of cause and effect, with moral implications; not limited by time or space, it encompasses reincarnation, rebirth, or, less figuratively, continual perpetuation, and the means of liberation from such repetition.

karma yoga   A path to liberation using action for the benefit of others.

koan   A Zen meditation demanding the resolution of a phrase or story that transcends rational intellect and common logic; one of a tradition of teaching tools. Different koans are used as tools pertaining to particular stages along the path.

lamrim   Stages of the path in Tibetan Buddhism, leading to initiation into *esoteric tantra.*

Mahayana   Blanket term for Buddhist schools flourishing in North Asia, such as Flower Garland, Nicheren, Pure Land, Vajrayana, and Zen.

mandala   Two- or three-dimensional circular diagram of cosmic forces, used for meditation; often depicts deities and their abodes.

mantra   Meditation practice using sound or syllables or words.

meditation   One of three components of the Buddhist way, along with wisdom and morality. More than a relaxed state, it's an activity of nondualist, self-reflexive aware-ness, with various degrees of formal training available from a *teacher,* depending on the school. Meditation isn't confined to sitting on a cushion, but is also practiced walking, working, and so on.

metta   Lovingkindness, friendliness, goodwill.

Middle Way   Harmoniously navigating between extremes, not choosing opposing positions. The Madhyamika School of Buddhism recognizes relative truth and ab-solute truth, the latter being *emptiness.*

mindfulness   Self-awareness, sober attention; being aware of things as they are, in and of themselves, and nothing else.

mondo   (Japanese) Zen question and answer, like koan practice, only an immediate answer is required.

mu   (Japanese) Nothing, not, nothingness, un.

mudra   Postures and gestures often associated with a particular Buddha or an inner state of being. In Vajrayana, they assist in visualization of a Buddha or deity.

mushin   ("No mind.") Innocence, nondualist awareness, no-thought.

nembutsu   Recitation of the name of Amitabha Buddha (*Namo Amida Butsu,* Japanese; *Namo Amitofu,* Chinese), in Pure Land Buddhism.

nirvana   Liberation; union with ultimate reality; state of perfection.

nonself   (Sanskrit "an-atman") Absence of a permanent, unchanging self. *See* atman.

noting   The mindful process of self-observation often used in *insight meditation;* ob-serving whatever's passing through your body, feelings, thoughts, and consciousness, making a short mental note of it, and moving on.

paradigm   An example or model, representing the prevailing mind-set.

paranirvana   The state achieved by one who has completed the incarnation in which she or he has achieved nirvana and will not be reborn on earth; dissolution of mundane conditions upon death.

precepts   Guidelines for conduct and discipline.

pure land   Paradise.

Pure Land Buddhist school (also known as Amidism)   Emphasizes faith in and de-votion to Amida Buddha's compassion. Meditation is focused primarily on recitation of the name of Amitabha Buddha.

refuge   Taking refuge means appreciating, trusting, and relying on something.

samsara   The world of endless cycles of rebirth into the same illusions, such as the illusion that true happiness consists in satisfying our ego.

samurai   The military elite who seized power from imperial aristocracy in feudal Japan, Kamakura era (1185–1333). As soldiers of fortune, the samurai appreciated the fearlessness, irreverence, intuition, spontaneity, and strict discipline of Zen.

Sangha   "Assembly, crowd, host." Generally, the Buddhist community; more specifically, the Buddhist monastic order, the oldest monastic order in the world.

Sanskrit   An ancient language of India, now used only for sacred or scholarly purposes.

satori   The experience of awakening or enlightenment. (Usually satori is reserved for the Buddha, and personal satori is called *kensho*.)

sesshin   "Touching mind; unifying mind; joining of mind to mind." A Zen retreat lasting from one to seven days.

shikantaza   Zen practice of sitting just to sit; choiceless awareness.

skillful means   Teachings, techniques, methods designed to further spiritual practice.

store consciousness (*alaya vijnana*)   The Buddhist concept, akin to the unconscious, of the realm where karma accumulates, the soil where seeds of future energies and essences manifested in phenomena are nourished.

stupa   A burial mound. The architectural form of a Buddhist stupa stands for not only the Buddha but also his enlightenment. ("Pagoda," China; "chorten," Tibet.)

suchness   The positive manifestation of emptiness. The immutable nature of things beyond all categories or concepts; their Buddha nature, in which there is no boundary between perceiver and perceived.

sutra   Dialogues or discourses of the Buddha.

tantra   Originally a school of Hindu yoga which combined with Buddhism and native Tibetan beliefs. A distinguishing element of *Vajrayana Buddhism,* it's often characterized by its harnessing and transforming natural energies rather than suppressing them; and also taking the end as the means. The word can also refer to tantric teaching texts, which are called tantras instead of *sutras*.

Tao   "The Way." The way of the universe and the way humanity would live in harmony with it. Its primary literature was written by Lao-tzu, a contemporary of Confucius. Shares affinities with *Zen*.

Theravada   Blanket term for Buddhist schools flourishing in South and Southeast Asia, the most popular one today being Vipassana. (Sometimes called Hinayana, which carries a disparaging connotation of "lesser, inferior.")

Three Jewels   The Buddha, the Dharma, the Sangha.

tonglen   A meditation of exchanging self for others.

Tripitaka   The Buddhist canon, recorded in *Pali,* including sutras, rules for discipline and conduct, and special teachings.

Vajrayana   The Buddhist school predominating in Tibet, Mongolia, Ladakh, but also diffusing into China, Korea, and Japan. It embraces Theravadan and Mahayanan beliefs and adds beliefs and practices, often with much symbolism and ritual, such as mantra, mudra, and visualization. Its uniqueness also includes teachings of *tantra,* a school that harnesses and transforms natural energies rather than suppresses them. A form of *esoteric* Buddhism.

Vipassana   Mindfulness meditation practiced in Theravadan school. Often taught as *insight* meditation in the West. Insight into the impermanence and lack of abiding separate identity of all things, leading to understanding of the true nature of reality.

visualization   Picturing an image in the mind's eye. In Buddhist practice, uniting with the energy symbolized by a particular visualization, then realizing its essential *emptiness.*

wisdom   Often another term for enlightenment, wisdom can refer to insight into the true nature of reality, which is *emptiness.* Whereas the West often typifies wisdom as the result of an accumulation of knowledge, in the East it's often the result of the shedding of veils of ignorance. As in the Western sense of good judgment, it's largely intuitive. In terms of spiritual development, often paired with *compassion.*

yoga   Literally "to yoke," or unite, such as yoking the mundane and the divine, ntegrating teachings and practice, learning and experience, and so on. (Note: The word "religion," similarly means to bind.) Specifically refers to particular Brahmanic (Hindu) practices in India, but can apply to any spiritual path. The practitioner is called a yogi.

zazen   Total concentration of body and mind in an upright, cross-legged sitting posture; seated meditation.

Zen   A school of Buddhism emphasizing directly seeing into the nature of mind. The word derives from the Sanskrit for "meditation," *Dhyana; Chan* in China, where it mingled with Taoism; *Son* in Korea, and *Thien* in Vietnam. With its directness, innovation, spontaneity, and dry wit, it's proven one of the most resilient schools of Buddhism and has inspired numerous cultural applications.

Index

Y–Z

IDIOTSGUIDES.COM

Introducing a new and different Web site

Millions of people love to learn through *The Complete Idiot's Guide®* books. Discover the same pleasure online in **idiotsguides.com**–part of The Learning Network.

Idiotsguides.com is a new and different Web site, where you can:

- ⚛ Explore and download more than 150 fascinating and useful mini-guides—FREE! Print out or send to a friend.

- 🌐 Share your own knowledge and experience as a mini-guide contributor.

- 💬 Join discussions with authors and exchange ideas with other lifelong learners.

- 🏛 Read sample chapters from a vast library of *Complete Idiot's Guide®* books.

- ✗ Find out how to become an author.

- ✂ Check out upcoming book promotions and author signings.

- 🏠 Purchase books through your favorite online retailer.

Learning for Fun. Learning for Life.

IDIOTSGUIDES.COM • LEARNINGNETWORK.COM